CONVERSION: OLD WORLDS AND NEW

STUDIES IN COMPARATIVE HISTORY

ESSAYS FROM THE

SHELBY CULLOM DAVIS CENTER

FOR HISTORICAL STUDIES

Animals in Human Histories: The Mirror of Nature and Culture
Edited by Mary J. Henninger-Voss

The Animal/Human Boundary: Historical Perspectives
Edited by Angela N. H. Creager and William Chester Jordan

Conversion: Old Worlds and New
Edited by Kenneth Mills and Anthony Grafton

A Publication of the
Shelby Cullom Davis Center for Historical Studies
Princeton University

Directors
Lawrence Stone (1974–1988)
Natalie Zemon Davis (1988–1994)
William Chester Jordan (1994–1999)
Anthony T. Grafton (1999–)

CONVERSION
Old Worlds and New

EDITED BY

KENNETH MILLS

AND

ANTHONY GRAFTON

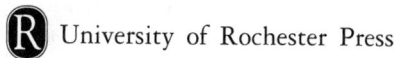 University of Rochester Press

University of Rochester Press
668 Mt. Hope Avenue
Rochester, New York, 14620, USA
Boydell & Brewer, Ltd.
P.O. Box 9, Woodbridge, Suffolk IIP12 3DF, UK
www.urpress.com
ISSN 1539-4905

Library of Congress Cataloging-in-Publication Data

Conversion : old worlds and new / edited by Kenneth Mills and Anthony Grafton
p. cm. — (Studies in comparative history, ISSN 1539-4905)
Includes bibliographical references and index.
ISBN 1-58046-123-9 (alk. paper)
1. Conversion—Christianity—History. I. Mills, Kenneth, 1964–
II. Grafton, Anthony. III. Series.

BV4916.3 .C66 2003

248.2'4'09—dc21   2003002358

British Library Cataloguing-in-Publication Data

A catalogue record for this book is available from the British Library

This publication is printed on acid-free paper
Printed in the United States of America
Designed and typeset by Straight Creek Bookmakers

CONTENTS

v

ACKNOWLEDGMENTS

This book is the fruit of two years' concentration upon the subject of conversion. As such, it represents more than the eleven essays that appear here. Thus, the editors wish first to thank the presenters of all the papers given over these two years, as well as the commentators on these papers and the many other participants who contributed to discussions. We also thank Kari Hoover for her help in the Davis Center office and Timothy Madigan and Molly Cort at the University of Rochester Press for their assistance and good cheer. And we are grateful to David Prout for his meticulous preparation of the index, as well as to Gavin Lewis, whose editorial care and creativity are evident on every page.

INTRODUCTION

KENNETH MILLS AND ANTHONY GRAFTON

This book is one of two collections of essays that focus upon conversion to, within, and around forms of Western Christianity. While the other volume treats religious conversion in late antique and early medieval Europe, one of this theme's most established playing fields, the essays here study conversion over a broader temporal and geographical expanse, considering cases from the thirteenth through the twentieth centuries and from settings across the world.[1] The contributions have been chosen for the rich connections they suggest with one another, and with the hope that their broad mixture of examples and approaches will spur new thinking about conversion and its related themes of cultural and religious transmission, diffusion, interaction, and change.

We have organized the essays in a chronological fashion, but readers will not find this the only, or even the most fruitful, way to consider them. Indeed, as a few examples will show, ideas in later chapters develop suggestions begun in earlier ones, and vice versa. Comparisons, too, will emerge all along. The exercise of setting vastly different comparative units alongside one another brings considerable advantages at this stage in the investigation of religious conversion; we hope through this book not only to encourage a deepening of specialist knowledge about particular times and places, but also to spark new thinking about religious conversion across disciplines and various subfields of history.

Religious conversion has been associated with an unyielding form of conquest—with the takeover of human identity, imagination, and consciousness. Where church and mission historians of an earlier generation often sided with what they saw as a totalizing enterprise of conversion, most scholars now resist such understandings. As Gauri Viswanathan stresses in discussing nationalist attitudes towards the perceived propagation of Christianity in modern India, conversion can easily appear as an exploitation of the poor. In India, as far beyond, religious conversion is historically attached to the catalog of uncompromising demands made by the powerful upon the vulnerable. It is often studied through sources that insist on the separation of an imposing "us" from a "them" whose inferiority is undoubted, and whose destiny lies in their subordination and radical rupture from older understandings.

For these and doubtless other reasons, students of contact and interaction between and among religious communities in history now often quietly avoid religious conversion or else append it to a brace of more fathomable (and historiographically fashionable) alternatives. The preferred alternatives decorate the subtitles of recent books and draw in audiences at scholarly meetings: cultural interaction, cultural transmission, diffusion, religious change, selective appropriation or borrowing, interactive emergence.[2] The motivations behind the shift are mostly laudable and might be summarized as twofold. First, there is a scholarly repudiation of any approach that would treat representatives of a world religion, and expansionary Western Christianity in particular, as the only truly active participants, while a vast array of impacted non-Christian, suspect-Christian, or otherwise subaltern actors are relegated to solely reactive or passive roles.[3] Second, and just as fundamentally, there is a shared assumption that complete religious conversion—prescribed change or pure transmission, if you prefer—was and is impossible to achieve. The analytical space allowed by what might be called an old world of inquiries into religious conversion has been found antiquated, dissatisfying, and constraining.

This collection of essays offers a response to the current state of affairs, by giving leading scholars from a variety of historical subfields the opportunity to address the challenge of religious conversion and to take it where they will. In traversing both old and new worlds of inquiry within and around the theme of religious conversion, they identify promises and pitfalls, and offer exciting ways forward. A few of their broadest suggestions introduce the reader to the book and begin the process of relating its particular pieces to one another as well as to wider bodies of work.

The contributors to this volume demonstrate the power and meaning that familiar narratives of conversion and exemplary individuals' lives commanded in many different times and places. This appeal could cut across otherwise divided communities, and it could see a reconfiguration of Christian forms according to local needs. Thus Brad Gregory shows how St. Paul's words on the testing of man that would be allowed by God were quoted as readily by the Catholic Thomas More in his hour of need as by his sixteenth-century contemporaries the Anabaptist Jacob Hutter and the Reformed Protestant Pierre Brully. And the example and vernacular writings of the Italian woolworker's daughter Catherine of Siena inspired all manner

of people towards religious lives. From pious members of the laity dissatisfied with the state of the church in the late medieval Low Countries and
England studied by John Van Engen to the aspirant Iroquois Christian
women in seventeenth-century New France, the subject of Allan Greer's
essay, Catherine was a powerful religious model, and one that constituted
ecclesiastical authorities found persistently difficult to control.

The reader will also find in this book new ways of imagining and discussing the changes sparked and encouraged by such messages, narratives, and
examples. When people were baptized, when confessions were heard, and
when doctrine was preached and taught, intended messages often failed to
be transmitted or were transformed before and after receipt. Yet if mistrans-
lations abound, they are not interpreted here as the simple results of one or
another person's failure to communicate. Misunderstanding, whether inad-
vertent or not quite, proves to be the flash and fuel to invention and, as
such, is critical to an appreciation of the roles of translators, interpreters,
and the legions of women and men who were the hearers and reimaginers
of Christian messages within broader processes of change. Broader and loos-
er kinds of communication among individuals and groups are favored in
these essays, and the cadre of those who might be called the agents of
religious and cultural transformation is much expanded. A number of these
protagonists are the cultural (and sometimes racial) byproducts of interaction, and they live within a web of hybridic social and spiritual relationships.

When cultural contact takes place, certain groups can often muster more
military, economic or political power than others. But the powerful have no
monopoly on dynamic energy. Change is found everywhere and does not
settle at some rhetorically convenient endpoint, but tends, rather, to be
plotted along gradual and incomplete gradients. Thus Allan Greer finds in
seventeenth-century New France neither a triumph of one culture over
another nor a convergence of cultures or religions which might neatly be
labeled syncretism or assimilation. The emergence of Catholic Christian
elements as parts of an Iroquois identity in colonial Kahnawake does not
spell the end to vital Iroquois traditions, any more than it means a capitu-
lation of Jesuit missionaries to the impossibility of their pastoral task.

Peter Gose, who explores Andean Christian religious change in sixteenth-
and seventeenth-century Peru, and R. Po-chia Hsia, who studies Catholic
enterprise and indigenous response in contemporaneous China, are more
sanguine than Greer about the blending of originally Christian and non-
Christian ideas, symbols, commandments, and representations in their respective settings. While aspects of both Andean and Chinese traditions
remained apart from Western Christianity, Gose and Hsia emphasize exam-

ples of cross-appropriation, and the emergence of new fields of religious and cultural meaning, fields which appear to have differed greatly from individual to individual. European purveyors of Christianity as well as native Andean and Chinese Christians sought and found opportunities for explanatory and practical continuity in an early period of their encounters. These opportunities were seized and effectively exploited by so diverse a set of actors as to dissolve forever any dichotomous image of a simple face-off between the explanatory needs and intercultural creativity of European Christians on the one hand and those of native converts on the other. Even when political and spiritual attitudes hardened in the post-Tridentine atmosphere of the late sixteenth and seventeenth centuries and what Gose calls the "dichotomies of conversion" were asserted (in Peru and China, as elsewhere), it proved impossible to erase the intricate and multiauthored tracks of religious and cultural conversion begun in earlier times. Thus religious conversion of the complete, unilaterally, and strictly defined variety—the "fulfillment," in Greer's words, "of that perennial missionary fantasy, a sudden and fundamental transformation of individuals and societies"—appears to have been as rare in colonial Peru and contemporary China as it was in New France.

A number of the contributors to this volume concur, abandoning any quest for complete religious conversion in favor of inherently incomplete processes of religious conversion with moments, parts, and phases. In her examination of the construction and spread of shrines dedicated to the relic of the Precious Blood of Christ in thirteenth-century England and France, Valerie Flint focuses upon an instance of religious compromise on the part of prominent churchmen which recalls Gose's and Hsia's delineations of a period, some three centuries later, when conversion became effectively pursued through native forms in the Andes and in China. Flint argues that an increased employment of the charged imagery surrounding the Blood and Passion of Christ by these churchmen, and members of the Cistercian religious order in particular, amounted to "motions of appeasement" carefully chosen for their resonance among certain suspect or deficient members of the laity, especially ordinary laywomen but also marginalized practitioners of unacceptable forms of magic.

Ines Županov, in her exploration of sixteenth-century Jesuit missionary endeavor in Portuguese Asia, points out a similar phase of calculated compromise. She characterizes the effort of Jesuits and their native interpreters to translate an array of key Christian texts and pastoral complements into the Tamil language, and the conscious move away from preaching, instruction, and administering sacraments in the European vernacular language (in this case Portuguese) as the beginning of a "second conversion." Not only does the Tamil language embark on "a new life of its own" among readers and hearers, but the Christian faith itself effectively passes into native hands. Increasingly, Indian converts organize lay groups, contribute money, pay key salaries, and take responsibility for the financing of charitable projects. Županov's suggestions bring to mind many other contexts in which the Jesuits, among other churchmen, embarked upon similar "linguistic offensives" in order to reach prospective converts and neophytes more effectively.

The rise of piously proprietorial activity among new Christians in Portuguese Asia marks an advancing second phase of self-conversion that begs comparison with other transitions explored in this book, not least Carol Summers' conclusions about what lay behind the rise of Wesleyan Methodist Christianity in southern Rhodesia in the first half of the twentieth century. For Summers, Africans' eventual embrace of this brand of evangelical Christianity was inextricably linked to money and to the growing need for it felt by the poor in societies increasingly enveloped by Western capitalism. She shows how a missionary insistence upon cash payments for tickets of membership, fund-raising concerts, and fees for schools accompanied more standard conversion efforts. Increasing involvement in these financial transactions and schemes soon linked Africans to the institutional church in ways that exhortations and teachings alone could only begin to do, and this greater stake in church affairs would see them emerge not only as this faith's most devoted spiritual participants but also as the managers of its critical resources.

What Peter Gose calls "submerged realities" seem to be everywhere, and at various times, from Deventer to Goa, from Austria to southern Africa. Local Christianities emerged as features of the landscape where conversions were attempted. The birth, historical justifications, and survival of these local religions indicate how much could change, how change need not signify only loss or failure or impoverishment, and how time and circumstances soon rendered the easy divisions—Christian from non-Christian, missionary from heathen, evangelizer from evangelized, donor from recipient culture—distinctly unhelpful to a student of these historical phenomena.

In a determined twist on the imperative of recovering the voices and agency of hitherto largely neglected peoples affected by enterprises of Christian conversion, many of the contributors to this book demonstrate how reliant such a recovery is upon due and simultaneous attention to the missionaries, preachers, and religious chroniclers on whom we necessarily rely for key sources. Even the parochial religious judgments and general high-handedness of the late sixteenth-century priest Bartolomé Alvarez, whom the reader meets in Gose's essay on Peru, or the early eighteenth-century Jesuit father Joseph-François Lafitau in Allan Greer's piece about New France, have to be set alongside both men's prevailing curiosity about indigenous societies around them and their passion for thick and often surprising descriptions. Both authors beg for careful reading and not for rejection.

Some contributors make the case against the obstinately dichotomous frames of traditional historiography even more sharply. In many historical contexts, dichotomous thinking, wedded as it so often was (and is) to assumed hierarchies of human inequality, informed the political and religious approaches of the representatives of official Christianity and civility towards originally non-Christian peoples. David Murray takes value-laden concepts such as fetishism, idolatry, and animism as his points of entry in an investigation of how and why ideas about primitive religion developed as they did in colonial British America. His study of a process by which Euroamerican thinkers increasingly came to attach Romantic notions of pantheism and natural religion to indigenous peoples, while a supposedly lower mixture of materiality and magic was reserved for African Americans, suggests the power of these perceptions about the mental and spiritual capacities of subjected peoples. Murray's instructive focus upon the trajectories of a "differential racism," and what amounted to a measure of intellectual redemption for one group and a crude dismissal for another, complements one of the lines of thought in Peter Gose's essay. Attempts by dominant thinkers and governing officials to reorient the lives of their often multiethnic populations of subjects were bound up in the reigning (and frequently dichotomized) suppositions about races of people and these races' spiritual and civil prospects.

Thinking in terms of faiths, races, religions, and cultures locked in religious and cultural combat creates other obstacles to a better understanding of religious conversion, too. It can cause us to miss internal processes, and what many people in the past would themselves have understood as conversion—namely the significant transformations which were fervently sought and sometimes achieved by individuals and groups *within* or just apart from dominant social and religious communities rather than in the borderlands *between* cultures. The classic works in the field by Arthur Darby Nock and Karl Morrison had as one of their foci this internal understanding of conversion,[4] and John Van Engen turns our attention once again in this direction. Van Engen studies a spiritual crisis developing within the late fourteenth- and fifteenth-century societies of the Low Countries and England, places in which most people took a basic adherence to Christianity for granted. He argues that while the appearance of new monastic orders and exemplary mendicant friars had, in the course of the twelfth and thirteenth centuries,

offered significant outlets for Christians who quested after closer relationships with God and ways of life more in keeping with the primitive church,
many of these outlets no longer seemed sufficient by the mid-fourteenth
century. Van Engen explores the conversions of individuals who, in a context of heightened spiritual yearning and dissent, sought to move from
ordinary to more intense kinds of religious life. He finds a rejection of their
society's approved options for such an intensification of religious life, especially the profession of vows in one of the established religious orders.

Van Engen's characterization of fifteenth-century conversions by the Devout in the Low Countries and by Lollards in England as "a reversal from
customary practices and powers," and as a daily and continuous battle by
individuals who aimed to turn away from "things visible and material,"
finds exciting resonance in other work in this volume.

As a number of the essays remind us, gender often plays a central role in
the drama of conversion, and many of the "internal" converts were women.[5]
Their roles differed as radically as the historical experience of a medieval
Catholic mystic such as Catherine of Siena did from that of a female martyr
in sixteenth-century Europe, or from the experiences of native women newly converted to Christianity in Latin America or India. A significant challenge is put to historical scholars to take account not only of how women
became a powerful "figuring ground" for male religious imaginations,[6] but
especially of the creative energies women showed, even in faiths and teachings in which they could not assume priestly or exalted status.

And the exploration of internal forms of dissonance as powerful kinds of
conversion does not stop there. Ines Županov finds within various of the
missionary schools of sixteenth-century Portuguese Asia places that invited
"cultural nomadism, 'refugee' movements, . . . social dissent, and political
extremism," and where even religious conversion might be "improvised." In
the southern Indian context, Županov explores a rejection of colonial policy
and rule in the many translations of Scripture and other Christian works
into Tamil crafted by Jesuit linguists and their omnipresent native assis-
tants and interpreters from the 1560s through the 1580s. What Francis
Xavier began through his cultivation of "syncretic languages" amounted in
time, she contends, to a Jesuit "linguistic offensive," a gradual assault which
was directed not so much against non-Christian rivals as against the Portuguese language and ultimately the aims and effectiveness of Portuguese
Christian control.

Almost three centuries later, in the community of Lac qui Parle in the
North American borderlands of western Minnesota during the 1830s and
1840s, so Andrew Isenberg argues, the autonomous world briefly inhabited
by some four hundred Dakota people and a handful of evangelical Protes-

tant missionary families was more than merely a place of forced acculturation in Euroamerican ways. Isenberg shows how Lac qui Parle was simultaneously a new beginning, a refuge where Euroamerican ways might in fact
be rejected by missionary and missionized alike. As in Master Geert Grote's
Devout home in late fourteenth-century Deventer, so too in certain Jesuit
mission stations among the Parava Christians in sixteenth-century India
and among the nineteenth-century Dakotas in precariously Protestant
Lac qui Parle: the brave act of seeking purer, more essential Christianities involves proselytizers as much as proselytized and centers upon a
decisive turning away, a conversion, from dominant Christian rules and
societies.

The surviving letters and other writings from captivity of three men who
were executed for their divergent Christian beliefs in the age of the European Reformations encourage us to stretch our treatment of the theme of
religious conversion further. In the spirit of Van Engen's suggestion that
conversion is sometimes most fruitfully understood in negative terms, as a
"reversal" or rejection of customary practices, Brad Gregory embarks on a
cross-confessional comparison of the lives and deaths of the martyr-victims
Jacob Hutter, Thomas More, and Pierre Brully in the 1530s and 1540s.
Again, we are ushered within an overarching Western Christendom, albeit
one fractured under the strain of dissenting political and reformist agendas.
Gregory contends that what is most remarkable about religious conversion
in the contexts of these three individuals is the strength of their resistance
to it. They faced fear and believed in the "eternal ramifications" of their
actions and that their subsequently steadfast resistance to conversion, in the
case of More, and "reconversion" in the cases of Hutter and Brully, would
gain them God's favor and heaven. All three persevere to the death by
writing, liberally applying the lessons and consolations of Scripture to their
own dismal circumstances, and by communicating with other "beleaguered
believers" in their respective communities of faith. There is resonance, here,
with Viswanathan's exploration of the threat which the idea of conversions
to Christianity can pose to some Hindu religious organizations in modern
India. Never mind the fact that broad calls for new education programs
seem unlikely to usher in the end of Hinduism, it is the perception of a
threat and of the need for a vigilant resistance to Christian conversion that
counts and requires thinking about. If other contributions to this book
explore the myriad processes of change that occurred (and need to be contained) within and around the fulsome theme of religious conversion, the
essays by Gregory and Viswanathan remind us of conversion's power even
when it does not happen at all.

NOTES

1. The Davis Center's two-year theme was entitled "Conversion: Sacred and Profane." The other collection is Kenneth Mills and Anthony Grafton, eds., *Conversion in Late Antiquity and the Early Middle Ages: Seeing and Believing* (Rochester, N.Y., 2003). Late antiquity and medieval Europe have drawn the bulk of scholarly attention. Recent collections include James Muldoon, ed., *Varieties of Religious Conversion in the Middle Ages* (Gainesville, Fla., 1997), and Guyda Armstrong and Ian Wood, eds., *Christianizing Peoples and Converting Individuals* (Turnhout, 2000). An exceptional volume, both for its range of contributions and for its interdisciplinary nature, is Robert W. Hefner, ed., *Conversion to Christianity: Historical and Anthropological Perspectives on a Great Transformation* (Berkeley, Calif., 1993).

2. This change in emphasis can be perceived in many contexts. In the study of the medieval Spanish kingdoms see, for instance, Mark D. Meyerson and Edward D. English, eds., *Christians, Muslims, and Jews in Medieval and Early Modern Spain: Interaction and Cultural Change* (Notre Dame, Ind., 2000); and on China following contact with Catholic Christianity, Nicolas Standaert S.J., "Christianity in Late Ming and Early Qing China as a Case of Cultural Transmission," in *China and Christianity: Burdened Past, Hopeful Future,* ed. Stephen Uhalley Jr. and Xiaoxin Wu (Armonk, N.Y., 2001).

3. Transformations that were once presented as imagined, compelled, or at least paternally guided by missionaries, colonial officials, or other agents of centralized power or orthodoxy are now increasingly found to be subject to the needs and decisions of affected populations, who consequently determine the pace and extent of any religious and cultural change. See for example the bewildering number of alternative processes set out in Steven Kaplan, ed., *Indigenous Responses to Western Christianity* (New York and London, 1995).

4. Arthur Darby Nock, *Conversion: The Old and the New in Religion from Alexander the Great to Augustine of Hippo* (London, 1933); Karl F. Morrison, *Understanding Conversion* (Charlottesville, Va., 1992).

5. This point was strengthened during a day-long workshop on "Gender and Conversion" convened by Davis fellow Julia M. H. Smith in Princeton in May, 2000.

6. The phrase and notion of women as a " figuring ground" are Kathryn Burns's.

CONVERSION: OLD WORLDS AND NEW

I

CONVERSION AND COMPROMISE IN THIRTEENTH-CENTURY ENGLAND

VALERIE I. J. FLINT

Under the year 1247, the St. Albans chronicler Matthew Paris tells the story of the reception into England of a phial of the Precious Blood shed by Christ on the cross.[1] King Henry III of England had, he says, received the phial directly from the patriarch of Jerusalem and the masters of the Temple and Hospital. They, in their turn, had decided to send it to Henry to keep it safe from the Saracens. King Henry received the ancient crystal vessel containing the Blood, had it stored in the Church of the Holy Sepulchre in London,[2] and summoned the prelates and nobles of England to attend the Feast of the Translation of King Edward the Confessor (13 October). This was, we might note, also the anniversary of the eve of the Battle of Hastings. The prelates and nobles appeared, Henry fasted on St. Edward's Eve, and then carried the vessel and the Blood (with banners and crosses and lighted candles) from St. Paul's Cathedral to Westminster Abbey on the feast day, walking the distance of about two miles barefoot and in the dress of a poor man, and looking outwardly, therefore, just like the pilgrim the Confessor himself had once, famously, helped. The king placed the vessel close to the shrine of the Confessor in the abbey; a shrine, and indeed abbey, he was shortly enormously to embellish.

The bishop of Norwich, Walter of Suffield, said Mass, and then took the opportunity to expand upon the reasons why the patriarch of Jerusalem had sent the Precious Blood to England. England, he said, was chosen on account of the holiness of England's king and the safe government he provided (both somewhat risible propositions in 1247, and the second especially so). The bishop then announced an indulgence of six years and one hundred and sixteen days for those who came to pay reverence to the Blood whilst it lay within the abbey. The feast of the Precious Blood was to be celebrated annually thenceforward. When the bishop stopped speaking, the king conferred knighthood upon his half-brothers and a number of other young aspirants.

The relic of the Precious Blood, placed next to the shrine of the Confessor, was meant, then, to afford a great boon to King Henry III, to those who remembered the Conquest with pride, to those who cared for the military protection of the Holy Land for Christians, and to those who visited the relic. The Blood was much venerated in succeeding years at Westminster and, in 1248, Henry III attached a fifteen-day fair to the celebrations, ordering the cancellation of all competing fairs (to the annoyance of several of his bishops who had their own fairs to defend). The new fair posed an especially direct challenge to that which normally accompanied the feast of the translation of St. Etheldreda of Ely (17 October). Henry had the grant of his fair witnessed by the greater magnates, prelates, abbots and priors of the kingdom. By the mid-thirteenth century, therefore, the king of England, his major churchmen (some perhaps under a measure of constraint), prominent members of the royal family, and the flower of the military aristocracy had pledged their public support for the veneration of the Precious Blood.

There had been a little grumbling at the outset. How was it (it was asked) that when Christ's body was resurrected he had managed to leave his blood behind? This question was answered in short order by Bishop Robert Grosseteste of Lincoln.[3] Joseph of Arimathea had been able to collect Christ's body from the cross (because he was rich and powerful, qualities Matthew Paris clearly admired). He had then washed it, and had squeezed the blood and sweat he had collected in the washcloth, and that still flowing from the wounds, into the crystal vessel.

Within a larger European context, King Henry can be shown to have been quick on the draw. The associated devotion to the Body of Christ had been instituted only a year before, in 1246 at Liège. St. Juliana of Liège had had a vision about this devotion, and declared it a great lack in the church's cult; and the feast of the Body and Blood of Christ (as it came to be known) was widely supported by the communities of religious women with which she was associated, especially the canonesses regular of Mont Cornillon (her own house in Liège) and the Beguines. The feast was publicly legalized for the whole church by Pope Urban IV in 1264,[4] and Thomas Aquinas himself is popularly supposed to have written the office for it.[5] Henry was also, however, advancing upon dangerous ground, for the cult was greatly (and immediately) opposed. Juliana was described by hostile critics as a dangerous dreamer (*somniatrix*), and these same critics maintained that such a feast was in any case superfluous, given the daily Eucharist and the remembrance of its foundation each Maundy Thursday.[6] Thus, Urban IV's decree was not widely published until 1317. It is hard at first to understand quite why St. Juliana's initiative met with such hostility, although I hope some reasons may emerge a little later. Meanwhile we may note that at the height of the hostility, and until her death, Juliana was protected by the Cistercian Order.[7] The Cistercians in fact adopted the Feast of the Body and Blood of Christ in 1277, in the face of the indifference of Rome.[8] We may note also that the Cistercian Order of the thirteenth century seems to have been generally sympathetic to many of the spiritual aspirations and achievements of women, even though (because?) they had reservations about the incorporation of nuns into their order.[9]

The devotion in England to the Precious Blood remained important and popular and, in the year 1268, it was reinforced. Henry III's brother Richard of Almayne, earl of Cornwall and king of the Romans, together with Edmund, his son, brought back in that year a further authenticated phial of the Precious Blood. Richard and Edmund brought this phial from the Continent, where it had been in the possession of William II, count of Holland, Zeeland, and Friesland, and credibly therefore at St. Juliana's Liège.[10] A portion of its contents was given to the Cistercian abbey of Hayles, Richard's own foundation. Earl Richard of Cornwall's eldest son Henry had been born at Richard's manor at Hayles and baptized there in 1235,[11] and Earl Richard promptly built the abbey at Hayles in thanksgiving for this birth, and peopled it with monks from King John's Cistercian foundation at Beaulieu. The Blood was placed behind the high altar in the east end of the church, which was rebuilt for the purpose.

The foundation at Hayles was, from its beginning, another major royal repository of financial, spiritual, and, perhaps above all, emotional energy,[12] and the special nature of this second gift of the Precious Blood made Hayles another central object of pilgrimage, this time patronized, remarkably, by the Cistercians—ordinarily no friends to pilgrims in their churches. On Holy Rood Day 1270, Earl Edmund of Cornwall himself carried the relic and placed it in its shrine, and it was cared for thereafter by a special custodian, and displayed at appointed times to pilgrims, who paid for the sight of it.[13] As early as 1275 the Cistercians of Hayles acquired permission from their general chapter to hold an exceptional annual ceremony in honor of the Precious Blood.[14] Edmund's mother, Sanchia, was buried at Hayles, as was her elder son Henry of Almayne (after his murder at Viterbo in 1271). In this care for births, family memory, and burials, in the circumstances of Hayles's foundation, and in the trouble taken to publicize the relic, we may perhaps begin to see a further association between the Precious Blood, the English court, the Cistercian order, and the religious interests of women.

Devotion to blood-relics and to relics of the Precious Blood itself has a long history,[15] and this English interest is certainly not without precedent. Relic cults were, we now know, far more the products of contemporary and local circumstances than we used to imagine, however, and this particular one does have certain distinctive features about it which deserve our attention. The English devotion was, for instance, profoundly royal, aristocratic, and more than a little popular with Cistercians and with the holy women they protected. It was also sudden. Why was the feast of the Precious Blood made suddenly so prominent in mid-thirteenth-century England, and by these sections of English society in particular? And why, above all, have I chosen this particular event as a means of furthering our discussions upon conversion? There are three reasons. The first is a purely academic one. Current explanations of the intense thirteenth-century interest shown in Passion relics are, in my view, incomplete; always a red rag to an historian. We might, then, look to try and extend these explanations. Secondly, I have a bee in my bonnet about this particular cult, and the Davis Seminars have always been an excellent place for the nurturing or (more often) dismembering of bonnet-bees. The third reason is concerned directly with our theme. I have come to believe that current explanations of the phenomenon are incomplete precisely because they take no account of conversion; conversion itself, that is, and also those conditions which fall short of it and those which actively obstruct its full achievement.

I was fortunate enough to attend the very first paper given on the theme of conversion at the Davis Center: "Conversion and Christianization in Late Antiquity: The Case of Augustine." by Peter Brown. In this seminal paper, Brown drew our attention to several ways of looking at the problem of Christian conversion (albeit to disagree with the crude application of many of them to the period within which he works). He spoke of the differences, proposed largely by A. D. Nock, between what might be called "Christianization" (a process of incorporation directed, often bullyingly, by the state, and thus frequently resented); "adhesio," (a devotion to certain elements of religion as useful, but requiring no deep inner change, and so stopping short of conversion); and true conversion itself. True conversion, on this definition, demands a total and committed change of life on the part of the convert, and commands and sustains an energy quite lacking in the other states.

I return to these distinctions here because they remain useful (indeed, they were useful in the thirteenth century),[16] but I do so principally because they help us greatly with the Precious Blood. I should like to direct our attention, through this devotion as it emerged in thirteenth-century England, to a particular aspect of conversion; the problem of the true conversion of persons apparently "Christianized" but in reality doing little more than "adhere" to the church at best. Second-stage conversion of this kind is, I think, a more complex matter than that usually undertaken by missionaries or conquerors. It requires, I would aver, both the acceptance by active Christians that all is not wholly well within the church, and some effort to attend to those failings which offend the hoped-for true converts and reduce them to mere adherents: some compromise, in short.

I hope to show here that this mid-thirteenth-century interest in the cult of the Precious Blood was, at least in part, a bid for the true conversion of persons only nominally attached to Christianity; this in the face of a style of "Christianization" which was failing and a style of "adhesion" which was now insufficient for the hierarchy's needs, as the Cistercians, above all, knew. The supporters of the cult aimed, then, at "change by conversion" within an apparently cohesive society. I shall contend, furthermore, that this bid was directed at two sections of the medieval "Christian" community in particular; women, especially married women with husbands and children, and men and women who felt themselves ill served by certain of the contemporary Christian intercessory structures. Whether the bid worked we cannot yet know; but I very much doubt it, for reasons which I hope might become clear as we proceed.

CURRENT EXPLANATIONS

I have said that current explanations of the mid-thirteenth-century concern for the Precious Blood are incomplete. I do not mean to suggest in any way that they are wrong; merely that they do not go quite far enough, and (more seriously) that in going any distance at all they distract from other possible ones. There are three reasons generally given for the English enthusiasm. The first of these is competition between the kings of England and France for Passion relics. King Louis IX of France had, between 1238 and 1241, acquired a whole load of such relics from Byzantium, and immediately began to build the Sainte-Chapelle in his own capital, Paris, to contain them. It behooved his rival King Henry III, therefore, to try and equal these efforts in London. The larger reason behind the acquisition of Passion relics is thought generally to lie in the need to restore the flagging fervor for the crusading movement (Jerusalem had fallen once again in 1244). And the still larger (third) cause of this excitement was that devotion to the Virgin Mary and the wounds of Christ which had so flourished in the thirteenth century, under the special encouragement, we may remark, of the Cistercian Order.

Each of these explanations has much to be recommend it. There was undoubtedly a touch of patriotic pride and xenophobia involved in the English excitement. Even Bishop Robert Grosseteste fell prey to this, for he

expatiated at some length upon how much better was Henry's relic of the
Precious Blood than those the king of France had so recently (and expen-
sively) acquired.[17] The correspondence in time, too, between the enthusiasms in France and England, is very close. King Louis gained legal title to
the Passion relics in June 1247, a mere four months before King Henry put
on his great show,[18] and Louis had the Sainte-Chapelle dedicated in 1248,
just as King Henry III was ordering his fair. We may also add another
element to this story of competition, one which is generally passed over.
Earlier in 1247, King Louis had secured a considerable propaganda coup at
King Henry's expense, for on 7 June 1247 he had presided over the translation of the relics of St. Edmund Rich of Canterbury to the Cistercian
abbey of Pontigny.[19] St. Edmund, archbishop of Canterbury 1234–40, had
quarreled mightily with King Henry, had stayed at Pontigny during the
resulting exile, and had been accorded a papal bull of canonization in January 1247. All of this was humiliating to Henry III, and, to say the least,
unhelpful to his relations with the Cistercians; so much so indeed that
Henry's brother, Earl Richard of Cornwall, made a pilgrimage of expiation
to Pontigny just as the Precious Blood was being carried through the streets
of London.[20]

Competition makes quite a lot of sense, then, and so does the second
explanation, the need to revive interest in the Crusade. Records of Christ's
bloodstained sufferings at Jerusalem were certainly a superb means of fortifying that fervor which originally drove the movement, and which was
faltering after the fall of Jerusalem. Louis IX departed on Crusade immediately after the dedication of the Sainte-Chapelle,[21] again much to the
discomfiture of King Henry, who put on a show of going in 1250. England
was in fact overwhelmed by pleas for help in the Crusade, and the six
months to October 1247 saw a barrage of papal collectors of subsidies.[22] In
the 1250s both the abbot of Westminster and Bishop Walter of Suffield
were prominent preachers and collectors. Edmund of Cornwall's placing of
the Blood in the shrine at Hayles is his last recorded act before he himself
left on Crusade in 1270.

Devotion to Passion relics and to the Crusade did indeed go together,
therefore, and were highly relevant to the anxieties of Henry III and his
court. Henry III's sudden reverence for the Precious Blood could certainly
be seen as an attempt to repair his tarnished image as a crusader. And lastly,
we know well that devotion to the Virgin Mary and the suffering she
endured at the sight of Christ's five wounds abounded in thirteenth-century
England.[23] Louis IX rested the upper section of the Sainte-Chapelle, containing the Passion relics, upon a lower chapel dedicated to the Virgin
Mary. The story of the motherhood of the Virgin Mary, and of her share in

Christ's bloodshed, is obviously inseparable from the story of the Passion and Redemption, an inseparability which achieved the status of a commonplace in the Middle Ages. It is conveyed in a host of sources, of which we may perhaps take Peter Damian's (d. 1072) statement of it as a type example: "That body of Christ to which the Blessed Virgin gave birth, which she nourished at her breast, which she clothed in swaddling clothes and nurtured with a mother's care, is that which we now receive from the sacred altar and whose blood we drink in the sacrament of our redemption."[24] It is inseparable too from certain crusading enthusiasms. Such outpourings lacked refinement, of course, and failed to satisfy university theologians; but they made fine material for sermons and pastoral teaching and, as such, reached a wide audience. We can always call quite securely, therefore, upon this aspect of the Virgin's role if we want a quick explanation for the interest in Christ's blood.

Competition, Crusade, an efflorescence of devotion to the sorrows of the Virgin, and perhaps a wish to please the powerful Cistercian order offer much, then, in explanation of English enthusiasm for the Body and Blood of Christ; but still they leave certain questions unanswered. Why were religious women such as St. Juliana so very interested in the Precious Blood? Why did the Cistercians themselves take to it so readily as actively to invite pilgrims to a normally secluded abbey, and to the east end of the abbey at that? Why exactly were there tensions about the cult? And, perhaps most significantly of all, is it just to ascribe the apparently similar aims of the two kings solely to competition? Is it not at least possible instead that they were moving along parallel tracks? Both Henry and Louis were undoubtedly concerned about the Crusade and the need to find greater support for the movement, but what exactly was the nature of their concern, and from whom precisely were they hoping to obtain this support? We may turn now to try investigate some of these questions.

LATE MEDIEVAL CHRISTIANITY AND THE POSITION OF WOMEN

After even the smallest dose of the misogynistic sermons of the late medieval preacher,[25] one may be forgiven for asking a simple basic question—how was it that late medieval women remained Christian at all? They could apparently do nothing right within the Christian dispensation—or nothing right that they might enjoy. Their vulnerability to criticism began, of course, with the start of creation; with Eve's transgression in Genesis 3:1–13. St. Paul added the authority of the New Testament to this tradition, notably in

I Tim. 2:14.[26] Its effects were most enthusiastically registered in medieval England. Noah's Flood itself, for instance, was held to have been caused by "the pride and the disguysinge that was amonge women."[27]

Once the authority of Paul was acknowledged, justifications for the subjection of women poured into medieval Christian teaching. All interest in clothing, fashion, talk, was accordingly outlawed (I Tim. 2:9–13); we need hardly speak of sex. Childbearing, in proper holiness, may possibly rescue woman (I Tim. 2:15), but even her capacity to give birth is explained away as essentially an Old Testament virtue. Those proper to the New Testament are virginity or widowhood. Marriage comes at best a poor third to these, and appears mainly to be justified as a means of keeping persons from sin, in accordance with I Corinthians 7:9. We may perhaps encapsulate many medieval English attitudes in this quotation from the thirteenth-century English *Speculum Laicorum*; "Woman . . . is the confusion of Man, an insatiable beast, a continuous anxiety, an incessant warfare, a daily ruin, a house of tempest, a hindrance to devotion. Man must flee the society of woman for three reasons; firstly because she will ensnare him, secondly because she will corrupt him, thirdly because she will rob him of his potency and his possessions."[28] In somewhat more sober language, this Pauline view of woman's essential corruptibility and so necessary subjection to superior Christian man passed into canon law. Gratian took his dictum "vir est caput mulieris" (man is the director of woman) straight from 1 Corinthians 3, "Omnis viri caput, Christus est; caput autem mulieris, vir," but pressed it even more enthusiastically, and further, than did St. Paul. Women are servants of men and may not teach, bear witness in court, swear oaths, or render justice.[29] In the late thirteenth century Archbishop Pecham of Canterbury called upon the Pauline castigation of women teachers as a means of slapping down the supporters of Hildegard of Bingen. As a mendicant friar Pecham disliked her views, of course, but he reached for the gender of the one expressing them as his first line of defense.[30]

There is some hope for woman; but the sole source of it is Mary. Mary redeemed the sin of Eve and may therefore redeem Eve's successors.[31] This hope, however, is not, to my knowledge, as greatly stressed as Mary's sacrifices are. The burden, particularly of the medieval preaching I have examined, bears upon the duty sinful woman has to obey her lords, human and divine, and to await the Judgment Day. Many thirteenth-century *exempla* collections for sermons are designed to reinforce these views.[32] Much depends, of course, on the audiences to which these sermons are addressed—sermons "ad conjugatas," for example, may be a little less harsh than sermons "ad conjugatos."[33]—but the strain of antifeminism is very prominent in them. We may perhaps take the sermons of two especially active thirteenth-century preachers as typical of what women might generally expect to hear about themselves: those of the great Augustinian crusading preacher Jacques de Vitry (d. 1240) and those of the Franciscan Saint Bonaventure (d. 1274). The former is wholly relentless in his criticism of women: "In paradise God and Adam had between them only one woman; but she did not rest until she had done the one thing for which her husband would be turned out of paradise and Christ hanged."[34] In Jacques's third "Sermon to the Married" (written perhaps shortly before his death), women bear almost all the blame for the breakdown of marriage; through their extravagance, untrustworthiness, poor control of their children, and general tendency to steal things.[35] Adulteresses are worse than adulterers because they are guilty both of deceit and theft, in that they give to another that which belongs to their husbands.[36] Jacques has also some peculiarly unpleasant stories to tell about the miseries inflicted by wives upon their husbands (I have found few with the opposite message).[37] In one he relates, with apparent approval, how a wronged husband asked for a cutting of a tree upon which two wives had hanged themselves, so that he might treasure the stock; in another, how a man originally wishful of having two wives came to offer the one he had to a known criminal, in the hope that the latter might be as severely punished as he, the husband, had been.[38] In one quite extraordinary *exemplum* Jacques relates how the Virgin Mary refuses to help a wronged wife against her husband's mistress because of the latter's devotion to herself. In the end, the mistress has a change of heart, so all is well[39]—but no thanks to the rights of the wife, or even (or so it seems) to the Virgin's persuasion. Jacques de Vitry may have been especially savage about women; but then, as Augustinian canon, preacher of the Crusade, bishop of Acre,[40] and eventually cardinal bishop of Tusculum, he was also especially influential.

St. Bonaventure was no better. In one of his sermons he quotes, with evident satisfaction, that same passage from the *Speculum Laicorum* I quoted above,[41] and adds a further piece: "What is woman but an enemy of love, an inescapable punishment, an unavoidable evil, a temptation built into nature, a disaster made of desire, a danger to every household."[42] He too blames Eve,[43] and attributes to St. Francis the view that converse with women is a waste of time, save for (brief) periods of instruction and the hearing of confession.[44] No matter that there was nothing in the Gospels or in the teaching of Christ to justify such views; that Christian teaching on redemption, sanctity, and the human being in general all speak of equality,[45] vocal sections of the medieval Christian establishment believed in the inequality of the sexes, and did their level best to enforce it.

Much of this has long been known.[46] There has been little effort made (as far as I know), however, to explore its actual effect upon women themselves, and still less to inquire into how this effect might be countered. The above onslaught may qualify perhaps as attempted "Christianization," but it is hardly an incentive even to "adhesion," let alone to true conversion. Is it possible, then, that reluctant adhesion might, at best, describe the attitude to Christianity of the generality of thirteenth-century women; that they were nominally Christian only because they had no other option; and that resistance to the dictates of Christianity was more characteristic of them than we have been encouraged to believe? We know that women of all classes, Englishwomen among them, took willingly to movements deemed heretical and that they were especially enthusiastic Lollards and Cathars.[47] Might disaffection of this order have been widespread? And if so, might anxiety about women's true conversion have been more widely spread among the late medieval Christian authorities than we have so far realized?

I believe so; and there is in fact evidence to support this picture of women's resistance. Jacques de Vitry himself provides some of it. Women, he says, constantly rebel against the strictures he utters, even to the extent of happily becoming the concubines of priests. He expresses amazement that the ground does not swallow them up, but, sadly, it seems not to do so.[48] It is indeed possible to argue that the very volume of such sermonizing is itself proof that the women so addressed were generally impervious to its messages; rather as a great volume of legislation may sometimes be evidence that the law was *not* being obeyed. The accusations of frivolity against women may attest to their laughing away such demands, and those of untrustworthiness to their simply ignoring them. That anger, described by Alfonso X (half-brother of Henry III's daughter-in-law, Eleanor of Castile) as "the one thing which most quickly leads women to sin" may have been a sign of their frustration.[49] We may perhaps argue in addition that the thirteenth-century efflorescence of the writing by men of the *Lives* of women saints provides similar upside-down evidence. The *Lives* of such virtuous women as could be found were written up most strenuously in that century,[50] yet, the more certain female Christian virtues were stressed, perhaps the more we might deduce that they were rare.

Occasionally, moreover, revealing cracks appear in the facades even of the most carefully constructed accounts of female holiness. They may be found in the thirteenth-century lives of a small group of northern European holy women to whom I mean to turn more fully below. It is admitted by their biographers, for instance, that Lutgard of Aywières (d. 1246) only became a nun because her dowry was lost through imprudent investment, and that Elizabeth of Thuringia entered religion because, as a widow, she was too poor to support herself, yet resolutely refused to remarry.[51] A number of much-lauded pious women in fact initially undertook their lives of religion principally as a means of escaping marriage or a difficult husband.[52] Ivetta of Huy (d. 1228) was forced into an unhappy marriage against her will. She made it clear why she objected. She feared the loss of her freedom, the dangers of childbirth, the pains of bringing up children, the untrustworthiness of men, and the constant care a household demanded.[53] Her father made her marry nonetheless, and, on the death of her first husband, attempted to make her marry again. Each of the proposed marriages was presumably acceptable under Christian auspices. It has, in other words, to be admitted even by the writers of their lives that the apparently advanced Christianity of the most lauded of Christian women developed often as a result of their social vulnerability in the face of crippling "Christian" demands. As an expression of true conversion, then, even such lives ring hollow.

It is hard to come to firm conclusions about how strong the resistance of the generality of women was except through condemnations and such upside-down evidence as male accounts of the clearly exceptional experience of holy women, for they had little direct voice themselves. There is one testing point we may use, however, and which has not, to my knowledge, been used before—the Crusades.

WOMEN AND THE CRUSADES

Matthew Paris tells a striking story about a woman's attitude to the Crusade in England. The story comes from a period very close to that which saw the establishment of the devotion to the Precious Blood. It recounts the vision of the countess of Salisbury. Under the year 1250 Matthew tells how, when the Countess Ella was told of the death of her crusading son, William Longespée II, at the disastrous battle of Mansurah, she did not moan and cry with "verba lugubris querimoniae." She was, on the contrary, delighted, for she had had a vision earlier in the year that her son would win a martyr's crown.[54] This tale is most revealing. Those who heard her words were amazed, and the countess's reaction was clearly thought to be exceptional. Mourning and protest were the expected responses of such women, and it was in fact the response of no less a person than Blanche of Castile, mother of King Louis IX of France. When King Louis proposed his 1244 Crusade, so De Joinville tells us, his mother "mourned as much as if she had seen him lying dead," and did all she could to persuade him to renounce his vow. He could, she maintained, argue that his original vow was taken under pressure of illness, and so easily escape its obligations.[55]

As in Matthew Paris's account of the reaction of the countess of Salisbury, the evidence of the opposition of women to the Crusade is often obliquely offered; but it is, when one looks for it, unmistakable. Take, for instance, the difficulties confronted by crusading preachers, such as St. Edmund Rich of Canterbury himself. The Pontigny *Vita* of St. Edmund describes how this saint reacted to the spirited actions of two other, humbler, women who clearly felt as Louis's mother did. St. Edmund was preaching the Crusade in France, and the two women tried to grab young men as they pressed forward to take the cross, and pull them back. The saint was in no doubt as to the proper response. He called upon his miraculous powers and struck one of them blind and withered the hand of the other, curing them only when they repented and let the young men go.[56] These measures were plainly provoked by a problem whose solution required the making of examples, or so Edmund's biographer implies; but the measures were extreme ones by any reckoning, and they suggest that the problem, too, was extreme. A further thirteenth-century example of a woman's opposition to the Crusade occurs in the *Dialogus Miraculorum* of Caesarius of Heisterbach (d. c. 1240). Master Arnold, preaching the Crusade at Over-Yssel, was jeered at by a woman. She died within three days, says Caesarius with satisfaction. A knight, on the other hand, who left his wife and children in spite of their protests, and went on Crusade, was taken directly up to heaven by the Virgin at his death.[57] A story is told in the *De Predicatione S. Crucis in Anglia* (written c. 1216) of the mother of Eustace of Flanders, which reveals the latter's attitude extremely clearly. Eustace, failing to wait for his brother Godfrey, had rushed into battle with the Saracens and been killed. When his mother heard of his death she gave thanks to God for preserving for her the son she loved the most.[58] The same theme runs through crusading songs and poems. There is often an expectation in these that wives and lovers will object to the departure of their loved ones on Crusade, and that the latter, for their part, will be doubly troubled.[59]

Record of the actual sermons of crusading preachers is curiously hard to find, for such sermons were rarely copied into liturgical collections, and few collections *ad status* have been published or even adequately identified. Occasionally, however, we can disinter them; and they convey precisely the same picture. I have found none which praise a woman's influence in favor of the crusading movement. Instead, such sermons stress how women either actively try to prevent their husbands or sons or relations from taking the cross or, by their very existence, render them unwilling to do so. Again, Jacques de Vitry is enthusiastic in the expression of such views. He tells, for instance, how the wife of a would-be crusader was so anxious to keep her husband from hearing a crusading sermon that she locked him into the house. He eventually jumped out of the window and took the cross.[60] How is it, Jacques asks the men among his audience, that you manage not to listen when your wife tells you to go to the devil, but you *do* certainly listen when she tells you not to go to God?[61] Jacques's experience as a crusading preacher may perhaps have done much to intensify his hostility to women. Another thirteenth-century crusading preacher, Odo of Chateauroux (d. 1273), had to stress again and again the renunciation required of those who would follow Christ (Luke 9:23), and apply it especially to the leaving of wives and loved ones. Moses, after all, left his wife and went wherever God wanted him to go.[62] Many called upon the old ways of discrediting the woman's voice. Eve gave entrance to that death the crusader must now avenge with his blood. Mary, Eve's counter, was willing to endure the necessary suffering and loss, and so therefore should modern woman be.[63] Against this background of discredit, there is an irony in the fact that preachers, when really pressed, employed stories of the mistreatment of women by the Saracens to excite the compassionate attention of men.[64]

The crusader's wife is represented especially often as an obstacle to crusading,[65] and indeed, she must have been so in reality, for Pope Innocent III (in a ruling which caused great anxiety to canonists) emended current law to allow a crusader to depart without his wife's permission.[66] Since the right to the payment of the "conjugal debt" was the only right which man and woman enjoyed equally within the original papal dispensation[67] and since Pope Urban II himself had, at the very beginning of the crusading movement, defended the woman's right to withhold her permission, this was certainly a serious emendation, and suggests that wives had been exercising their rights with some enthusiasm. Though her *Vita* only mentions the fact in passing, the impoverished widowhood of Elizabeth of Thuringia was in fact brought about by the death of her husband on the 1227 Crusade. Disasters of this order might easily have been foretold by wives. The 1252 extension of the crusading indulgence to abandoned wives and children reads, within this context, as a somewhat desperate contrivance, one rather indicative of the depth of the problem than likely to lead to its solution.[68]

The Crusades, then, offer us special evidence that many women were resistant to certain contemporary Christian views of, and demands upon, them, and with good reason. The problem of the intervention of violence and warfare in the cycle of childbirth and death is a universal human problem, applicable to all times and places; but the distress of a mother whose child meets a violent death in warfare for a cause with which she does not wholly sympathize is perhaps of a special order. We have only to glance at the press in times of threatened military deployment to see how important are the reactions of such mothers to the politics of warfare now. There was, therefore, I would aver, an urgent need in the thirteenth century for the conversion of women to the crusading movement above all. How might this be done?

POSSIBLE WAYS TO THE CONVERSION OF WOMEN

The men who wrote their *Lives* made great play with one apparent fact about the thirteenth-century women religious they hoped so greatly would be admired. Women religious were consumed, claimed these writers, by devotion to the vulnerability of the suffering Christ in the Eucharist, and to the blood He shed as the price of human redemption. This style of bloody sacrifice was held to have made an especial appeal to them: "Christ was apprehended in it [the Eucharist] as a man, a husband, a son, resplendent in vulnerable humanity, in the feminine principle, not as a judge, or as paternal, majestic or lordly."[69]

Thirteenth-century England seems to have been singularly short of holy women, or at least of written evidence of them.[70] There were recluses, certainly, but no movement resembling that of the Beguines of the Low Countries in either numbers or enthusiasm. We may advance several reasons for this deficiency. It may not be wholly unconnected with the state of affairs we reviewed earlier. We do have a small group of Continental *Lives* from the period, however, principally of northern European holy women, but arguably available in England. I have mentioned some of them, and we may call upon them again now as at least supplementary evidence of the appeal the largely male writers of these *Lives* thought the Precious Blood had for women. We may add to these materials from the so-called "Katherine Group" of *Lives* of women saints popular in thirteenth-century England, especially the Middle English *Life of St. Margaret,* a *Life* which appears to have been written specifically with English interests in mind.[71]

All tell the same story. Christian holy women were transfixed by the imagery of the Eucharist, the suffering Christ, and the Precious Blood. Jacques de Vitry himself, who, as we saw, had such trouble coping with the obstructive behavior of women, both elaborates on and apparently delights in this fixation. It seems to have given him hope. In his life of Mary of Oignies (d. 1213), for instance, a *Life* he wrote precisely to make his view of the strength of feminine devotion to the Precious Blood more widely known,[72] Jacques dwells especially upon the importance to Mary of the Precious Blood in the Eucharistic sacrifice: "The holy bread strengthened her heart; the holy wine inebriated her, rejoicing her mind; the holy body fattened her; the vitalising blood purified her by washing. . . . And when she was not able to bear any longer her thirst for the vivifying blood, sometimes after the Mass was over, she would remain for a long time contemplating the empty chalice on the altar."[73] Again perhaps rather hopefully, Jacques depicts Mary as supporting warfare against heterodoxy of all kinds, and as herself willing to die in battle for the faith. Reverence for

Christ's blood and for Christian warfare are here clearly connected.[74] It is worth remarking in this context that the crusading preacher Odo of Chateauroux himself took pains to procure a relic of the Blood for Neuvy-St.-Sépulchre, near Bourges, on his return from Louis IX's crusade.[75] The life of Mary of Oignies was extended by the Augustinian Thomas of Cantimpré, seemingly in much the same spirit. Thomas also wrote *Lives* of other female saints, expressing similar views through them.[76]

Each of these writers was, we should note, both pastor and preacher, and so would have been directly engaged in that conversion of women which, if I am right about it, was now dangerously overdue. It is of great importance to our understanding of the place of the devotion to the Precious Blood of Christ, therefore, to note that they all regarded the intensity of women's reverence for the Body and Blood and humanity of Christ as that which distinguished the springs of women's devotion from those of men, and as the ultimate key to female piety.[77] A great many treatises upon the humanity of Christ are in fact addressed during this period by men to women, and sermons on the Eucharist are surprisingly often directed to female audiences.[78] By this means, the sufferings and losses of women in giving birth and in consigning their children to Christian warfare are expected to be justified and given dignity. The life of Angela of Foligno, for example, describes the saint actually placing the heads of her sons within the wound in Christ's side.[79] Mary of Oignies cut pieces of flesh from her body in order the more vividly to be reminded of the bloodshed of Christ.[80] The life of St. Margaret associated Christ's bloodshed with Margaret's own impending martyrdom and also with the pain and anxieties of childbirth (of which she became the special patron).[81]

More than this, the direct experience of the shedding of Christ's blood was allowed to become a form of *imitatio Christi*: one in which women could almost attain to a form of priesthood.[82] A friend of St. Juliana of Cornillon apparently actually saw her, in a vision, assisting Christ himself to celebrate Mass.[83] The reception of the stigmata was thought to be an especially important sign of this *imitatio,* and the imprint of the five wounds of Christ upon women saints was in fact quite widely noted. The Cistercians took an active interest in proving that such female stigmata were genuine.[84] In that, furthermore, Christ had no human father, it could be held that all his humanity came from His mother;[85] that, in short, the female role was crucial not merely to His incarnation but to the perpetuation, through the Eucharist, of the results of that incarnation throughout the Christian world.

This special association between women, the Eucharist, and Christ's Precious Blood received reinforcement from the physiological association (widely believed in the thirteenth century) between blood and a mother's milk.

According to this theory, the menstrual blood of a woman, after feeding the child in the womb, was transformed into the milk which fed him or her externally, and so made the blood which sustained the child. In the case of Christ, therefore, the blood/milk of Mary produced his Precious Blood.[86] In the matter of their blood, moreover, women were considered the physiological equals of men, as they were not in any other respect.[87] The fact that men were so dependent on women for their blood rendered women, in this respect, their superiors.

These were great claims, and we may perhaps begin to see why there was such opposition to the Feast of Corpus Christi. Through the stressing of such devotion by the men who wrote their *Lives,* women were being helped towards a form of Christian equality, and of a right to be regarded as priestly and as central to the enactment and reenactment of the Incarnation. Women were, in short, being encouraged to "muscle in" upon an exclusively male preserve. Many members of the Christian priesthood and laity alike were unprepared for such a change.[88] There were, however, members of the church who actively assisted this preoccupation with Christ's Blood; specifically as a way, if I am right about it, of appealing directly to women. There were also at least two kings, Louis IX and Henry III, who united, rather than competed, in this aim. In short, some thirteenth-century rulers of both church and state were concerned for the conversion of resistant women, and they seem to have concentrated their attention precisely upon the potential appeal to all women of the Precious Blood.

The imagery was well chosen in a number of ways. Depictions of the female figure *Ecclesia* catching Christ's Blood in a chalice have a long ancestry, and the figure persists well into the thirteenth century.[89] Henry III's rebuilt Westminster Abbey (constructed c. 1245–53) may actually have had, on its north portal whereby laypersons were admitted to its shrines, a sculptured figure of this.[90] "Christian" women were, furthermore, constantly confronted with rulings about their blood. Menstruation was held to render them infirm and unapproachable by men, though the belief that the Virgin's menstrual blood fed Christ did much to rescue the process from stigma.[91] The blood that women shed in childbirth required them to be readmitted to the church by a special ceremony.[92] There are interesting independent signs that this ceremony was taken particularly seriously in thirteenth-century England, and that it may even be connected with a singular change in the design of churches. Lady Chapels came frequently to be built onto major cathedrals in this century, often at the extreme eastern end, behind the high altar and therefore, perhaps, to the immediate east of the major shrine.[93] Walter of Suffield, bishop of Norwich 1245–57 and enthusiast for the Precious Blood and Crusade as we have seen, built a splendid one at the east end of his own cathedral.[94] This interest in the building of Lady Chapels may have sprung, quite simply, from that increased devotion to the Virgin we have already marked, and from the need to accommodate that other thirteenth-century English Marian devotion, the daily Lady Mass.[95] The altar of the Lady Chapel, however, was possibly the preferred place for the churching of women. In the later Middle Ages many such women chose to present themselves and their newborn children before an image and/or an altar of the Virgin.[96]

We might mark, furthermore, that shrines in general seem certainly to have appealed to women, at least if we may judge by the numbers of miracles performed there on their behalf and by the journeys of such jolly figures as Chaucer's Wife of Bath. Shrines were attractive to women for many reasons, but a strong one may have lain in the relief they gave from the normal processes of confession to a known priest and in the offering of indulgence. This relief was contested (notably in clause 62 of the Lateran Council of 1215), but it remained real, and women were now being actively welcomed to these special places behind high altars of perhaps distant churches, and not merely in cathedrals but in Benedictine and Cistercian abbeys too—a great contrast to earlier monastic attempts to confine them to the narthex, Galilee Chapel, or north transept (well away from the cloister).[97]

The imagery of the Precious Blood was also well chosen in the face of the inadequacy of other possible attractions. This may well be the most important aspect of it of all. The Virgin Mary can be a doubtful ally to women, especially to laywomen who are not virgins, for all their apparent interest in her image for the churching ceremony. She was certainly no help to those who opposed Christian warfare.[98] Nor did she offer the least assistance to women who did not want to sacrifice their children; she deplored their resistance in fact.[99] And Mary was allowed to assume some singularly curious attitudes towards wronged married women, as we have seen. It is (and was) unwise, therefore, to assume that Marian imagery would have called strongly to all women, still more so to expect it to encourage women waverers to true conversion. In the little group of thirteenth-century *Lives* to which I have made my main appeal, Mary appears, certainly, but she does so to encourage the hard life of the holy woman, for which she offers a crown (but only after death), or a promise of intercession on the Day of Judgment.[100] There is little sign, in the thirteenth-century Marian literature I have examined, that she helps women greatly in those demands and travails of this life which most beset them, or that she is expected to do so. The Virgin could thus appear to them as yet one more collaborator with the objectionable forces of conformity.[101] Only through the image of the blood/milk of the *Virgo lactans* does she seem to draw reliably close to women; and this closeness is dependent upon the prior image of the Precious Blood. This same inadequacy is true of certain female saints—such, for example, as St. Etheldreda of Ely whose feast was apparently so shamefully displaced by that of the Precious Blood. Great royal abbesses of this type were, like the few female saints thirteenth-century England could produce, remote from the activities and disaffections of most women. The Precious Blood was far closer to these.

Finally, among the few saints who are known to have been attractive to thirteenth-century English women, the chief seem to have been St. Thomas of Canterbury and—judging at least by the circulation of the famous *Estoire de Seint Aedward le Rei*—St. Edward the Confessor. The original *Estoire* was most probably composed in the 1240s as a present for Eleanor of Provence, Henry III's queen. It, and an associated (but now lost) book of St. Thomas were enthusiastically received by the women of the court: Sanchia, countess of Cornwall, Eleanor of Castile (wife of Edward I), and Isobel, countess of Arundel.[102] The appeal of Edward the Confessor to certain women is not hard to explain. The Edward both of the Cistercian Ailred of Rievaulx's *Life* and of the *Estoire* was a singularly un-macho man. In the *Estoire* he was submissive to his wife, Edith, less than passionate about warfare unless it was clearly necessary, and given to Eucharistic visions and tearful devotions.[103] To combine, then, a shrine to the Precious Blood with a shrine to Edward the Confessor made excellent sense. As for the appeal of St. Thomas, there were, of course many reasons for this; but it is perhaps worth noting that that a unique cult of Thomas's blood began early at Canterbury, and that it was associated directly with the sacrifice of the Eucharist.[104]

POSTSCRIPT: BLOOD AND MAGIC

This starts another rabbit without a hope of tracking it to its burrow—but I should like just to touch upon another aspect of the reverence for the Precious Blood. This is its relevance to contemporary beliefs in magic, to the marginalization of magicians and heretics (among whom of course were women), and to the conversion of their followers. The thirteenth-century English church was much troubled by magicians, especially so, it seems, in London[105] and blood was a familiar constituent of magical practice. It looms large, in the magical treatises of the period; such, for example, as the *Liber de Angelis,* which claims that menstrual blood and the blood of one who dies by hanging or the sword are especially efficacious in the sowing of destruction or enmity.[106] Among the Cathar beliefs unearthed by the Inquisition was the belief that the soul resided in human blood.[107] Blood was thought also to be particularly treasured by Jewish magicians. It was a dominant consideration in the infamous legend of the murder of little St. Hugh of Lincoln in 1255, who was held to have been murdered precisely so that his blood and entrails might be used in magic.[108] Lastly, the power of blood was recognized in legal matters (themselves often the concern of magical practitioners), especially homicide trials.[109] This last remarkable, yet undoubted, fact shows how very deeply blood, its shedding and its potency, permeated late medieval consciousness.

Again, then, the special emphasis upon the Precious Blood at Westminster in 1247 may have been an attempt at compensation and attraction: at that sort of remodeling of habit and retranslation of revered substances which, I have suggested elsewhere,[110] was a most effective way of bringing the conversion of magicians about. Interestingly, the one medieval account we have of the arraignment of a witch before a court Christian involved a public procession between churches, with a condemned magical waxen image held high by the culprit, and an ascent to a raised place, on a scaffold, within the chosen church (here St. Paul's Cathedral) for sentence and punishment.[111] This was almost a parody of the procession conducted by Henry III when he took the Precious Blood to the raised shrine of Edward the Confessor. The similarities of movement, gesture, and even ascent only served to throw the contrast between unacceptable and acceptable "magic" into sharper relief.

CONCLUSION

We may perhaps summarize in short order the central argument I have tried to advance. The imagery of Passion relics in general, but particularly that of the shedding of Christ's Blood, was believed by certain male members of the Christian hierarchy (crusading preachers and Cistercians perhaps particularly) to be especially attractive to women.[112] Englishwomen were thought, furthermore, to be in particular need of such attraction, not least towards the Crusade. The encouragement of the devotion to the Precious Blood marked some movement, then, towards their supposed interests and immediate anxieties. Blood imagery was also relevant to the concerns of those who practiced certain forms of magic, and, especially, to the expectations of their followers. A shrine to the Precious Blood perhaps marked a concession to their interests too.

Did it work? A conclusion here must wait upon more research; but I doubt it. The tendency of women to support heresies and become witches suggests that it did not—but there is more. I have said that the conversion of mere "adherents" demands, ideally, two motions of appeasement from a would-be converter; some admission that all is not well within the church, and some effort to attend to those failings which offend the persons to be converted. In the case of women, there is very little sign of either of these motions, even among those who are so enthusiastic about the devotion of women to Christ's wounds. There was an element of compromise in allowing women a qualified access to the priestly function, and another perhaps in actually encouraging them to approach the raised shrines and eastern ends of great cathedrals and abbeys, but that is all. One of the more striking aspects of the *Lives* I have examined lies in the evident incapacity of Christian leaders and rulers truly to improve woman's lot. To take but one example, Christ's wounds alone saved Lutgard from sexual temptation and rape—as seemingly nothing else could have done.[113] The Precious Blood, in other words, was held, by her biographer, to have saved Lutgard from catastrophes against which no other recourse was offered, or likely to be. Thomas of Cantimpré tells the story as though sexual vulnerability was the normal fate of women and there was nothing to be done about it, unless, of course, they took to contemplating Christ's suffering and the religious life. Jacques de Vitry can offer only the Beguinage as a counter to the uncontrollable pressures of "rich men and secular prelates."[114] For such writers, an insistence upon the extreme piety of the few seems to compensate for their inability, or unwillingness, to confront the "Christian" conditions which beset the many. As for the Crusade, there is no evidence at all to suppose that the attitude of Englishwomen changed towards this, and some to suggest that it did not.[115] In the case of magical manipulators of blood, much work needs to be done, but it is perhaps no coincidence that they came to be equated so greatly with dissident women.[116]

The careful construction of shrines to the Precious Blood in thirteenth-century England should not be understood, then, as the inevitable outgrowth of Eucharistic and crusading enthusiasms already strong, but rather as a sign of dangerous weaknesses within the church. Nor should it be seen as a logical corollary of Marian devotion, but, instead, as a means of making up to women for deficiencies in that cult. It was in fact a singularly desperate attempt at the conversion of reluctant women and others to whom blood was known to make a powerful appeal. The English and French courts, and the Cistercian order, seem to have acknowledged these dangerous weaknesses more readily than did some of the bishops of the secular church; indeed the Cistercian order emerges as an important possible source of that compromise which, I have argued, is necessary to true "internal" conversion of the kind required here. Perhaps they saw, in this devotion, a means of reconciling ordinary laywomen to their lot. In that the attempt remained bound to a construct essentially unchanged, however, inevitably it fell short.

NOTES

1. H. R. Luard, ed., M*atthaei Parisiensis Monachi Sancti Albani Chronica Maiora,* vol. 4, Rolls Series 57 (hereafter RS), London, 1877), pp. 640–45; 5 (London, 1880), pp. 28–29; 6 (London, 1882), pp. 138–44. See further M. E. Roberts, "The Relic of the Holy Blood and the Iconography of the Thirteenth Century North Transept Portal of Westminster Abbey," *in England in the Thirteenth Century: Proceedings of the 1984 Harlaxton Symposium,* ed., W. M. Ormrod (Nottingham, 1985), pp. 132–37. I am deeply indebted to Dr. Nicholas Vincent for sharing with me his own impressive learning upon this subject.

2. W. Stubbs, ed., *Chronicles of the Reigns of Edward I and Edward II,* vol. 1, RS 76 (London 1882), p. 44.

3. Luard, *Matthaei Chronica,* 6:138–40.

4. He was a great proponent of the cult and wrote a letter of support to Juliana's friend and biographer, Eva of St. Martin; F. Callaey, "Documentazione eucharistica liegesi dal Vescovo di Liège Roberto di Torote al Papa Urban IV," *Miscellanea Pio Paschini,* vol. 1 (Rome, 1948), p. 215.

5. N. Denholm-Young, *Richard of Cornwall* (Oxford, 1947), appendix 5, p. 174, supported by M. Rubin, *Corpus Christi: The Eucharist in Late Medieval Culture* (Cambridge, 1992), pp. 185–96.

6. *Vita S. Julianae*; *Acta Sanctorum,* Aprilis I, iii, 460 (hereafter *AS).* All references are to the *Editio Novissima* of the *Acta Sanctorum* (Paris and Rome, 1867).

7. C. Hontoir, "Le septième centenaire de la Fête-Dieu: Sainte Julienne et les Cisterciens," *Collectanea Ordinis Cisterciensium Reformatorum* 8 (1946): 109–16.

8. C. Lambot, "L'Office de la Fête-Dieu; Aperçus nouveaux sur les origines," *Revue Bénédictine* 54 (1942): 71–81.

9. S. Roisin, "L'efflorescence cistercienne et le courant féminin de piété au XIIIe siècle," *Revue d'Histoire Ecclésiastique* 39 (1943): 342–78.

10. Interestingly, this phial had been authenticated by the future Pope Urban IV, supporter of the Feast of Corpus Christi, when he was patriarch of Jerusalem. See on all this the still valuable article by St. Clair Baddeley, 'The Holy Blood of Hayles," *Transactions of the Bristol and Gloucester Archaeological Society* 23 (1900): 276–84.

11. *Annals of Tewkesbury,* in *Annales Monastici,* ed. H. R. Luard, vol. 1, RS 36 (London, 1864), p. 98.

12. Richard compared the rewards accruing from his expenditure on Hayles with those accruing from his expenditure on his fortress at Wallingford, greatly to the latter's discredit. Denholm-Young, *Richard of Cornwall,* p. 76.

13. St. Clair Baddeley, "Holy Blood of Hayles," p. 278.

14. J.-M. Canivez, ed., *Statuta Capitulorum Generalium Ordinis Cisterciensis,* vol. 3 (Louvain, 1934), article 69, p. 149.

15. See, for instance, J. H. Rohling, *The Blood of Christ in Christian Latin Literature before the Year 1000* (Washington, D.C., 1932), and N. Vincent, *The Holy Blood* (forthcoming, Cambridge University Press). The earliest evidence of a Western relic of the Holy Blood comes, according to Dr. Vincent, from seventh-century Spain.

16. The first book of the *Dialogus Miraculorum* of Caesarius of Heisterbach (d. 1240) is devoted to conversion, and Caesarius, too, deals with stages which fall short of it, ending with his own definition: "Conversion is a turning of the heart, either from bad to good, or from good to better, or from better to best." *Dialogus Miraculorum* I.2, tr. H. von Scott and C. C. S. Bland, *The Dialogue on Miracles* (London, 1929), p. 8.

17. True, King Louis had a piece of the True Cross, the Crown of Thorns, the Holy Lance, and the Nails; but the Precious Blood was far greater than these, for this was the price of human redemption. The Cross itself and all the other relics owed their special status, he maintained, to their impregnation with the Blood. Luard, *Matthaei Chronica,* 6:142–43.

18. P. E. D. comte de Riant, ed., *Exuviae Sacrae Constantinopolitanae,* vol. 2 (Geneva, 1878), no. 79, pp. 134–35.

19. L. Carolus-Barré, "Saint Louis et la translation des corps saints," *Etudes d'histoire du droit canonique dédiés à Gabriel Lebras,* vol. 2 (Paris, 1965), pp. 1089–91.

20. Luard, *Matthaei Chronica,* 4:632, 646–47.

21. Described elegantly and accurately as "a kind of architectural parallel to the king's crusading ideal." W. C. Jordan, *Louis IX and the Challenge of the Crusade* (Princeton, N.J., 1979), p. 108.

22. S. Lloyd, *English Society and the Crusade 1216–1307* (Oxford, 1988), pp. 210–17.

23. N. Morgan, "Texts and Images of Marian Devotion in Thirteenth Century England," in ed. W. M. Ormrod, *England in the Thirteenth Century* (Stamford, 1991), pp. 69–103.

24. "Illud siquidem corpus Christi quod beatissima Virgo genuit, quod in gremio fovit, quod fasciis cinxit, quod materna cura nutrivit, illud, inquam . . . nunc de sacro altari precipimus, et eius sanguinem in sacramen-

tum nostrae redemptionis haurimus": I. Lucchesi, *Peter Damian, Sermons* (Turnholt, 1983), p. 267.

25. The best general summary of this preaching is still that in G. R. Owst, *Literature and Pulpit in Medieval England* (Cambridge, 1933), pp. 377–404.

26. "And Adam was not deceived, but the woman being deceived was in the transgression."

27. Owst, *Literature and Pulpit,* p. 493.

28. "Mulier . . . est hominis confusio, insaciabilis bestia, continua sol[l]icitudo, indesinens pugna, cotidianum dampnum, domus tempestatis, sollicitudinis impedimentum. Fugienda est ergo mulieris societas propter tria: 1, quia hominem illaqueat . . . 2, quia hominem commaculat . . . 3, quia hominem rebus et virtutibus spoliat": ed. J.–Th. Welter, *Le Speculum Laicorum* (Paris, 1914), p. 77.

29. R. Metz, "Recherches sur la condition de la femme selon Gratien," *Studia Gratiana* 12 (1967): 380–85.

30. *Fratris Johannis Pecham Tractatus Tres de Paupertate,* quoted by K. Kerby-Fulton, "Hildegard and the Male Reader: A Study in Insular Reception," in *Prophets Abroad: The Reception of Continental Holy Women in Late Medieval England,* ed. R. Voaden (Woodbridge, 1996), p. 15.

31. "And therefore oure ladie amended that was amys, that woman shuld not be ashamed in that she made Adam trespasse; therefore thorowe crist Adam was amended. For no man shuld have woman in despite; for it is no wisdam to dispise that God loveth." Owst, *Literature and Pulpit,* p. 20.

32. For instance that of Friar Arnold of Liège, under the rubric "Woman." C. Ribaucourt, "L'alphabet des récits; Pour parler des femmes," in J. C. Schmitt, ed., *Prêcher par exemples* (Paris, 1985), pp. 107–20.

33. D. D'Avray and M. Tausche, "Marriage Sermons in *Ad Status* Collections," *Archives d'Histoire Doctrinales et Littéraires du Moyen Age* 47 (1980): 71–119.

34. Ibid., pp. 104–5.

35. M.-C. Gasnault, "Jacques de Vitry: Sermon au gens mariés," in Schmitt, *Prêcher par exemples,* pp. 53–67.

36. D'Avray and Tausche, "Marriage Sermons," p. 89.

37. He does object to drunkenness and violence in husbands; ibid., p. 106. He nowhere stresses the faults of husbands as much as he does those of wives, however.

38. J. Greven, ed., *Die Exempla aus den Sermones Feriales et Communes des Jakob von Vitry* (Heidelberg, 1914), nos. 70 and 71, pp. 43–44.

39. T. F. Crane, *The Exempla or Illustrative Stories from the Sermones Vulgares of Jacques de Vitry* (London, 1890), p. 92.

40. Where he admits that matters are worse, for there women poison their husbands in order to be free to remarry. R. B. C. Huygens and G. Duchet-Suchaux, *Jacques de Vitry, lettres de la Cinquième croisade* (Turnholt, 1998), pp. 54–55.

41. P. D. Fleming, ed., *S. Bonaventurae Opera Omnia,* vol. 9 (Florence, 1901), p. 459. The passage is drawn originally from Maximus the Confessor.

42. "Quid est mulier nisi amicitiae inima, ineffugabilis poena, necessarium malum, naturalis tentatio, desiderabilis calamitas, domesticum periculum."

43. Ibid., p. 396

44. Francis "asserebat etiam, frivolum esse mulieris colloquium, excepta sole confessione vel instructione brevissima": ed. A. Lauer, *Legenda S. Francisci, S. Bonaventurae Opera Omnia,* vol. 8 (Florence, 1898), p. 517.

45. Such as Galatians 3:28.

46. Though it is still, in fact, imperfectly assembled. There is no complete edition, for instance, of the sermons of Jacques de Vitry.

47. P. Biller, "The Earliest Heretical Englishwomen," in *Medieval Women: Texts and Contexts in Late Medieval Britain,* ed. J. Wogan-Browne et al. (Turnholt, 2000), pp. 363–76. I owe this reference and much helpful discussion to Dr. Wogan-Browne.

48. Gasnault, "Jacques de Vitry," pp. 57–58.

49. *Siete Partidas* II.7, pp. 11–12.

50. For an introduction to these writings see M. Goodich, 'The Contours of Female Piety in Later Medieval Hagiography," *Church History* 50 (1981): 20–32; and B. Bolton, "*Vitae Matrum*: A Further Aspect of the Frauenfrage," in *Medieval Women,* ed. D. Baker (Oxford, 1978), pp. 253–73.

51. Lutgard, *AS,* Junii IV, i, 191; Lutgard's mother, we might note, seems to have been glad that the investment had been so unsuccessful, and aided Lutgard against her father). *Life* of Elizabeth by the Cistercian Caesarius of Heisterbach, in *Die Wundergeschichten des Caesarius von Heisterbach,* ed. A. Hilka, vol. 3 (Bonn, 1937), p. 363.

52. Goodich, "Contours of Female Piety," pp. 23–25.

53. *AS,* Januarii II, ii, 147.

54. Luard, *Matthaei Chronica,* vol. 3 (London, 1876), p. 173.

55. M. R. B. Shaw, trans., *Joinville and Villehardouin: Chronicles of the Crusade* (Harmondsworth, 1963), p. 191. At least one crusading propagandist found this attitude such an embarrassment that he replaced it by an admiring verse on the material assistance Blanche offered to the king; C. Th. J. Dijkstra, *La chanson de Croisade* (Amsterdam, 1995), pp. 135–36.

56. Pontigny *Vita S. Edmundi,* ed. E. Martène and U. Durand, *Thesaurus Novus Anecdotorum,* vol. 3 (Paris, 1717), pp. 1779–80.

57. *Dialogus Miraculorum,* IV.11, VII.56; Scott and Bland, *Dialogue on Miracles,* pp. 207, 541.

58. *De Predicatione S. Crucis in Anglia,* ed. R. Röhricht, in *Quinti Belli Sacri Scriptores Minores* (Geneva, 1879), p. 20.

59. J. Bédier and P. Aubry, *Les chansons de Croisade* (Paris, 1909), XXVII and XXVIII, pp. 283–91; *The Lyrics of Thibaut de Champagne,* ed. and tr. K. J. Brahney (New York, 1989), pp. 226–27, 230–33. My attention was drawn to this material by Professor William Chester Jordan.

60. C. Maier, *Crusade, Propaganda and Ideology* (Cambridge, 2000), pp. 120–21.

61. Ibid., pp. 122–23.

62. "Et signum est quod homo Deum diligat, qui mundum abjicit. Sic signum manifestum est, quod homo dilectione Dei ardeat et zelo propter Deum, qui patriam, possessiones, domos, filios, uxores derelinquit, vadens ultra mare in servitionem Jesu Christi": ed. J. B. Pitra, in *Analecta Novissima,* vol. 2: *Sermones* (Paris, 1888), p. 311. The reference to Moses is on page 313. ("The sign that man loves God is his rejection of the world. He shows most clearly his deep zeal and burning love of God who leaves his country, possessions, property, sons, wives [*sic!*], and travels across the sea in the service of Jesus Christ.")

63. Röhricht, "De Predicatione," pp. 6, 11–13, 25.

64. C. T. Maier, *Preaching the Crusade* (Cambridge, 1994), pp. 116–17.

65. Ibid., p. 119.

66. J. B. Brundage, "The Crusader's Wife: A Canonistic Quandary," *Studia Gratiana* 12 (1967): 427–41.

67. Metz, "Recherches," 386–87.

68. Jacques de Vitry supported this extension; Pitra, *Analecta Novissima,* 2:426.

69. Rubin, *Corpus Christi,* p. 168.

70. Only three are to be found in Goodich's list of thirteenth-century saints; M. Goodich, *Vita Perfecta: The Ideal of Sainthood in the Thirteenth Century* (Stuttgart, 1982), pp. 218–41. All are removed from the common run of womanhood. Ella (conversion date 1236) was the wife of William Longespée I, earl of Salisbury, and the mother of the crusader, William Longespée II; *Bibliotheca Sanctorum,* vol. 4 (Rome, 1964), p. 979. Margaret Rich (d. 1257) was the sister of Edmund Rich of Canterbury; ibid., vol. 8 (Rome, 1967), p. 802. And the elusive Matilda of Lappion was a daughter of the king of Scotland; *AS,* Maii I, 438–39.

71. F. Mack, ed., *Seinte Marherete the Meiden ant Martyr,* EETS 193 (London, 1934); E. Robertson, "The Corporeality of Female Sanctity in the Life of St. Margaret," in *Images of Sainthood in Medieval Europe,* ed. R. Blumenfeld-Kosinski and T. Szell (Ithaca, N.Y., 1991), pp. 268–87.

72. He says in the prologue that he wished it to have an effect similar to that of the *Vitae Patrum*; Bolton, "Vitae Matrum," pp. 253–54.

73. *AS,* Junii V, x, 568. I take the translation of this passage from C. W. Bynum, "Women Mystics and Eucharistic Devotion in the Thirteenth Century," *Women's Studies* 11 (1984): 179. This splendid study first drew my attention to this phenomenon.

74. *AS,* Junii V, x, 565.

75. Abbé Caillaud, *Notice sur le Précieux Sang de Neuvy-Saint-Sépulchre* (Bourges, 1865), pp. 14–27. I owe this reference to Dr. Nicholas Vincent. The church of Neuvy was close to one of the main pilgrimage routes to Compostella, and might reasonably have expected a visit from women pilgrims.

76. Mary of Oignies; *AS,* Junii V, 547–72. Thomas added the *Lives* of the excitable Christina of St. Trond (1150–1224), Margaret of Ypres (1216–37) and, in 1249, Lutgard of Aywières; *AS,* Julii V, 650–60 (Christina), Junii IV, 191–210 (Lutgard). The *Life* of Margaret of Ypres is edited by G. Meerseman in *Archivum Fratrum Praedicatorum* 18 (1948): 70–80, 106–30. The Premonstratensian Hugh of Florette contributed, in 1230, the *Life* of Ivetta of Huy (1157–1228); *AS,* Januarii II, 147–69.

77. That there truly was such a distinction is eloquently maintained by R. Kieckhefer, "Holiness and the Culture of Devotion: Remarks on Some Late Medieval Male Saints," in Blumenfeld-Kosinski, *Images of Sainthood,* pp. 288–305. I owe this reference to Dr. Julia Smith.

78. "Even in accounts by male authors written for male audiences, we find the eucharist and the attendant theme of the humanity of Christ associated especially with women." Bynum, "Women Mystics," pp. 182–83. See also C. Bynum, *Fragmentation and Redemption: Essays on Gender and the Human Body in Medieval Religion* (New York, 1991), pp. 194ff.

79. *AS,* Januarii I, 189, 206.

80. Ibid., Junii V, ii, 552.

81. Mack, *Seinte Marherete,* pp. 46–48. That late medieval tradition which connected Christ's lance-wound with the female pudenda increased the intensity of this devotional association. W. Riehle, *The Middle English Mystics* (London, 1981), pp. 46–47.

82. "[E]ucharistic ecstasy was a means by which women either claimed 'clerical' power for themselves, or by-passed the power of males or criticised male abuse of priestly authority"; Bynum, "Women Mystics," p. 193.

83. *AS,* Aprilis I, ix, 475.

84. Thus Abbot Philip of Clairvaux investigated those borne by Elizabeth of Erkenrode, and approved them. Goodich, *Vita Perfecta,* pp. 183–84.

85. Bynum, "Women Mystics," pp. 204–5.

86. B. Williamson, "The Cloister's Double Intercession: The Virgin as Co-redemptrix," *Apollo* 152, no. 465 (2000): 48–54.

87. T. Lacquer, "Orgasm, Generation and the Politics of Reproductive Biology," *Representations* 14 (1986): 8.

88. Albertus Magnus, for instance, thought those who encouraged this devotion to the Precious Blood were going far too far, and that frequent communion for women should be disallowed. Bynum, "Women Mystics," p. 186.

89. G. Schiller, *Ikonographie der christlichen Kunst,* vol. 2 (Gütersloh, 1980), figs. 365, 371, 450, 697, 710.

90. M. E. Roberts, "The Relic of the Holy Blood and the Iconography of the Thirteenth Century Transept Portal of Westminster Abbey," in Ormrod, *England in the Thirteenth Century,* pp. 141–42.

91. Honorius Augustodunensis, for instance, described menstruation as a "natural infirmity," during which time men may not have intercourse with their wives; *PL* 172: 867. Jacques de Vitry also stresses the need for such abstinence; D'Avray and Tausche, "Marriage Sermons," p. 97. C. T. Wood, "The Doctor's Dilemma: Sin, Salvation and the Menstrual Cycle in Medieval Thought," *Speculum* 56 (1981): 719–26.

92. A medieval rite for the churching of women is printed in E. Martène, *De Antiquis Ecclesiae Ritibus,* vol. 1 (Rouen, 1700), p. 639.

93. B. Singleton, "The Remodelling of the East End of Worcester Cathedral in the Earlier Part of the Thirteenth Century," *British Archaeological Association Conference Transactions* 1 (1978): 109–10. The Lady Chapel of Exeter Cathedral is a particularly fine surviving example of the genre.

94. E. C. Fernie, "Two Aspects of Bishop Walter de Suffield's Lady Chapel at Norwich Cathedral," in Ormrod, *England in the Thirteenth Century,* p. 52. Walter acquired a relic of the Precious Blood for his cathedral too; correspondence with Dr. Nicholas Vincent, who supplied the reference Ms. Magdalen College, Oxford, 53, fols. 212–20.

95. Insisted upon by William of Trumpington, early thirteenth-century abbot of St. Alban's, and then extended to "all the noble churches of England"; R. Bowers, "The Lady Chapel and Its Musicians, c. 1210–1559," *British Archaeological Association Conference Transactions* 20 (1998): 247–48.

96. E. Duffy, *The Stripping of the Altars* (New Haven, Conn., 1992), p. 181.

97. Durham, for instance, confined them to the "atria exteriora ecclesiae"—presumably the Galilee Chapel. J. Raine, ed., *Reginaldi Monachi*

Dunelmensis Libellus de Admirandis Beati Cuthberti Virtutibus, Surtees Society 1 (London, 1835), CXIX, p. 265.

98. The English *Lambeth Apocalypse,* for instance, contains (fol. 45v), a singularly revealing scene. In it, the Virgin Mary, wearing her crown and so possessed of all the joys, supports St. George, with his cross, in his battle against the infidel. She seems, indeed, to be actively strengthening his lance-arm. G. Henderson, "Studies in English Manuscript Illumination," *Journal of the Warburg and Courtauld Institute* 31 (1968): pl. 46b.

99. See the illuminating chapter on child sacrifice and the model of Mary in B. Newman, *From Virile Woman to WomanChrist* (Philadelphia, 1995), pp. 82–96.

100. Lutgard of Aywières, *AS,* Junii IV, ii, 202; Ivetta of Huy, ibid., Januarii II, xv, 154.

101. I have found so far only one Marian intervention against a violent husband; R. Blumenfeld-Kosinski, "Sexual and Textual Violence in the 'Femme D'Arras' Miracle by Gautier de Coincy," in *Translatio Studii: Essays by His Students in Honor of Karl D. Utti for His Sixty-Fifth Birthday,* ed. R. Blumenfeld-Kosinski et al. (Amsterdam, 2000), pp. 51–64. Even in this story, the Virgin intervenes belatedly and only after the woman has been forced to marry and has suffered physical mutilation at the hands of her husband. I owe this reference to Dr. Kosinski.

102. For an excellent discussion of the content and circulation of the *Estoire* see P. Binski, "Reflections on *La Estoire de Seint Aedward le Rei*: Hagiography and Kingship in Thirteenth Century England," *Journal of Medieval History* 16 (1990): 333–50.

103. "Churchmen are seen on horses in this manuscript, but never the king." Edward is depicted only eight times as standing up, and thirty lying down! Ibid., pp. 341, 344–45.

104. M. Caviness, *The Early Stained Glass of Canterbury Cathedral, circa 1175–1220* (Princeton, N.J., 1977), pp. 149–50.

105. See, for example, the mandate issued in 1311 by the bishop of London, Ralph Baldock, for the pursuit and prosecution of the many magicians in his diocese. F. M. and C. Cheney, *Councils and Synods with Other Documents Relating to the English Church,* vol. 2, pt. 2 (Oxford, 1964), p. 1349.

106. J. G. Lidaka, "The Book of Angels, Rings, Characters and Images of the Planets: Attributed to Osbert of Bokenham," in *Conjuring Spirits,* ed. C. Fanger (University Park, Pa., 1998), pp. 66–67.

107. J. Duvernoy, ed., *Le registre d'inquisition de Jacques Fournier évêque de Pamiers (1318–25),* vol. 1 (Toulouse, 1965), p. 260.

108. Luard, *Matthaei Chronica,* 4:546, 552. See also J. Trachtenberg, *Jewish Magic and Superstition* (New York, 1939), pp. 227–28.

109. A. Boureau, "La preuve par le cadavre qui saigne au XIIIe siècle," *Micrologus* 7 (1999): 247–81.

110. Valerie I. J. Flint, *The Rise of Magic in Early Medieval Europe* (Princeton, 1991), passim.

111. Stubbs, *Chronicles,* 236, 275–76.

112. Despite their quarrelsome, deceitful, lustful, naturally sinful natures, women could be compassionate, and feel for the shedding of blood. See, for instance, the *Exempla* of Friar Arnold of Liège (put together c. 1297–1308); C. Ribaucourt, 'L'alphabet des récits: Pour parler des femmes', in Schmitt, *Prêcher par exemples,* p. 110.

113. When an attractive young man attempted to seduce her (and very nearly succeeded), Christ appeared, showing his wounds running with fresh blood, and asked her to think more carefully about what precisely was true love. When, a little later, multiple knights and suitors tried to carry her off, Christ again rallied her strength by reminding her of His bloodshed: "[V]ulnus lateris ostendit, quasi recenti sanguine cruentatum dicens: Blanditias inepti amoris ulterius non requiras; hic jugiter contemplare quod diligas, et cur diligas: hic totius puritatis delicias tibi spondeo consequendas." *AS,* Junii IV, ii, 192. ("He showed the wound in his side, all red with fresh blood, and said: 'I do not ask the flattery of imperfect love. Look here at what you truly love and why you love it, and I promise you the delight of pure love.'")

114. J. Greven, "Der Ursprung des Beginenwesens," *Historisches Jahrbuch* 35 (1914): 43–47.

115. The carefully orchestrated cult of William Longespée II later in the century may be an indication of a sustained opposition to the Crusade which had constantly to be contested. S. Lloyd, "William Longespée II: The Making of an English Crusading Hero," *Nottingham Medieval Studies* 35 (1991): 41–69.

116. As they were, indeed, by Jacques de Vitry himself; J. F. Hinnebusch, *The Historia Occidentalis of Jacques de Vitry* (Fribourg, 1972), p. 82.

2

CONVERSION AND CONFORMITY IN THE EARLY FIFTEENTH CENTURY

JOHN VAN ENGEN

By the year 1400 Christian peoples had dominated the European landscape for centuries, in some southern and western lands for a thousand years. In most parts of Europe the christened knew only other christened peoples. Few ever witnessed a conversion to Christianity or met a convert—the world of Iberia standing out, in this respect, as exceptional. Still, images of conversion lived on vividly in people's imaginations, especially by way of saints' lives and epic stories of combat against the infidel. The cults of antique martyrs flourished anew in the later Middle Ages, their story lines rendered in graphic detail, now also in the vernacular languages and visual arts. Images of coerced conversion, with only the barest concession to the niceties of human will or baptismal vows, gained new force from desperate crusading propaganda, intermittent actions against Jews (in lands where they were still permitted to live), and an apocalyptic expectation that all peoples in the End would be brought into the Christian orbit. In 1375 Catherine of Siena appealed to Queen Joanna of Naples to join a planned crusade, to fire up her desire that the "land of our sweet Savior be taken out of the hands of the infidel," "their souls out of the hands of demons," so that they, "like us, might share in the blood of the little son of God."[1] Images of reverse conversion also circulated in some locales: fearful stories of apostasy to Jewish or Muslim communities, or allegiance to suspect groups. Actual conversions to Christianity, the hard bargaining over generations that went into the Lithuanians' choice for baptism, largely escaped widespread notice. When Aeneas Silvius Piccolomini (Pope Pius II) wrote the first book entitled "On Europe," in the 1450s, he noted simply that "Livonia" counted as the most recently converted (*ultima*) of the "Christian provinces" in his "Europe."[2]

People saw conversions all the same, indeed quite a lot of them, for this term had long since come to denote those who voluntarily took up more intense forms of religious life. Going back a thousand years to fifth-century Rome, a baptized person who "turned away" from the demands, desires, and distractions of ordinary human life, who "turned toward" a life apart, wholly intent upon God, toward, as they said, "religion"—that person was said to "convert." The notion became routinized, then institutionalized: it meant joining the monastic life, pledging to keep the Gospel counsels under the Rule of Benedict. And yet its life-changing force could never be contained, never fully reduced to a routine life-transition. During the religious reformations of the eleventh and twelfth centuries, after generations of recruitment to monastic life primarily by way of child oblation (like child baptism, an expression of parental or group will more than individual choice), adult converts appeared on the historical stage in numbers. Whether as adolescent students, adult clerics, or self-motivated women, each made their own way, took their own peculiar "turn," some remaining active religious innovators throughout their lives, some channeling that energy into new forms of organized religious life. Even unlettered peasants were now able to make this choice, conferring on "convert" a new meaning: lay brother. Whatever the social status of the person, the notion was reinforced, and revitalized: a "convert" turned away from ordinary Christian life, even peasant labor or a familial household, to pursue more intense forms of religiosity, freely chosen. A glance at any medieval dictionary, Latin or vernacular, will confirm this usage as common, springing to people's minds more readily than the idea of moving from one faith community to another. This reality they saw or even experienced.

The social powers of medieval Christendom, ecclesiastical and secular, could grow nervous over people who took such a "turn," especially over those who designed their own way. They preferred converts who settled into approved and regulated structures, religious houses subject to a rule and a superior. In 1215 Innocent III forbade the proliferation of new rules, lest this bring "too much confusion upon the church," and required that "a convert take up an approved rule."[3] Church lawyers framed the act of profession with legal conditions and understandings. For those who took vows, the word "conversion" came to function as a technical term, not unlike "betrothal." With conversion the professed entered upon a recognized legal estate, adopted a rule for their lives (*conversatio*), gained a measure of social prestige, and could look forward to a heavenly reward. As the ordinary word for transition into that estate, a lasting bond comparable to marriage,[4] the term carried, in itself, only modest religious overtones. The most widely read devotional works of the later Middle Ages invoked this routinized meaning. The *Horologium sapientiae* of the Dominican friar Henry Suso (a treatise from the early 1330s extant in some 250 Latin manuscripts, 70

Middle French, 70 Middle Dutch, and so on) focused entirely upon a self-conscious and intense turning of the heart to God. But the Latin word "conversion" appears only twice, its institutional meaning employed to warn against routine or late conversions, attempts to circumvent judgment.[5] The same holds for *The Imitation of Christ* (completed about 1420 and extant in some nine hundred Latin manuscripts alone), quoted here as it was first rendered into English about 1450–60: "oftetymes we feele the contrarye, for we fynde ourselfe better and purer in the begynnynge of oure conversion then after many yeres of profession."[6] This meaning could invoke strong feelings all the same, as an appeal or point of contestation. In a work influential among pre-Hussite reformers called the *Pomegranate* (*Malogranatum*), written at the Cistercian house of Königsaal in Prague during the second half of the fourteenth century, a monk reiterated the traditional case for conversion as entry into a religious house: putting it off was dangerous, and to attempt penance and conversion while still in the world doubly dangerous—all this evident from "experience," he said.[7] Whether he wrote to plead with wavering recruits or to reassure the already professed, his message sounded through: the only secure way to separate oneself from worldly distractions, to "convert," was to enter the security of a cloister.[8]

Not all converts took vows, however, especially not in the later Middle Ages. From the thirteenth century onward, many opted for more intense forms of religious life without vows: Beguines, Hospitalers, tertiaries, hermits, to name only a few. The presence of such converts, mostly in towns, though increasingly taken for granted, did not put their neighbors fully at ease. Churchmen, city magistrates, and lay parishioners alike worried about this self-styled "religion," even among the obviously sincere—its intentions and status, its precise *conversatio* in the absence of regular oversight. Lawyers and prelates, building upon a legal observation made in the 1250s by the canonist Cardinal Hostiensis, granted that certain lifestyles were "more holy" than those of ordinary lay people.[9] Individuals, lay or clerical, women or men, might join a pious society or take up a holy way of life without assuming the lifelong obligations associated with vows—or claiming all their privileges. Most imposed on themselves practices associated with the professed, such as fasting or prayer, often with greater rigor. Kaspar Elm has argued that these people were fitted into medieval society by stretching Hostiensis's teaching to accommodate such converts as a recognized status, the "semireligious."[10] His is a key insight, even if the term is modern. His teacher, Herbert Grundmann, had proposed, as the only long-term options for medieval converts, professed religion or persecuted heresy.

Still, in-between groups and "self-converts" lived in a precarious space, subject to suspicion and reprisal, with acceptance of their way of life ad hoc and tenuous.[11] They readily provoked sharp reactions from those charged with preserving order: the professed as the approved embodiment of the converted state, bishops as the keepers of discipline in their dioceses. And some resourceful "converts," as Duane Osheim has shown for Lucca, acted more as tax dodgers, claiming the status but hardly altering their lifestyle.[12] Still, most were sincere, and many had to negotiate for acceptance. Beguines, for instance, spread through much of north and central Europe from the early thirteenth century onward, became a familiar feature in many towns with the assistance of friendly pastors and urban magistrates, then faced condemnation after 1311, modified in the 1320s but its threat never fully lifted. Whenever their teachings appeared somehow suspect (usually spread in the vernacular), or their communities somehow troublesome (cadres of women vs. urban patricians, secular pastors vs. mendicant friars), they were liable to fresh attack. In 1405 a Dominican preacher in Basel named Johannes Mulberg—like the inquisitor Wasmod of Homberg at Mainz in the 1390s and the anonymous author of a vernacular "reformation treatise" in 1439 at Basel—attacked Beguines anew, this time, he said, for claiming a lifestyle holier than that of ordinary laypeople and a right to live from alms (reserved, he claimed, to friars and laypeople who were not "able-bodied").[13]

These systems for accommodating converts within a society of the converted—group understandings inherited and elaborated, ever shifting over time—proved unstable in the best of times. But a generation on either side of the year 1400, so this paper will argue, they nearly came undone: a turning point in European socio-religious history, potentially or actually, of the magnitude associated with the "reformation of the twelfth century." The era makes manifest a degree of effervescence and conflict that could not easily be tamped back down into the traditional forms—whose ramifications were felt into the early modern era. Past scholars, though invoking the notion of crisis with respect to the Black Plague or the Great Schism or endemic warfare, have tended not to see a "system" strained to its breaking point, for at least two reasons. First, the manifestations of trouble get put into distinct historiographical boxes: heresy, revolt, reform, prophecy, devotion, and so on. This essay, by considering three movements (others could have been included) attempts to criss-cross and shake up those categories. Second, scholars have not sufficiently reflected on conversion as a working system, and the conceptual-structural dynamics built into it. They have studied probingly the dynamics of conversion as the movement from one faith community to another, one cultic practice to another. But fewer have explored the dynamics latent in the far more widespread notion of moving from "ordinary" into more intense forms of religious life within the Christian community. By far the most and best work recently has gone into twelfth-century movements and figures, with attention as well to exceptional individuals and communities in the later Middle Ages.[14] This essay seeks to highlight notions of conversion, and the strains around the year 1400 that nearly shattered all the working systems for accommodating converts.

THE STRUCTURAL DYNAMICS OF CONVERSION

Each conversion, especially those that did not lead directly into profession at an established house, came with a story—some unique and historically fascinating, many stylized (at least in the telling, perhaps the doing) to accord with hagiographic conventions. Built into those stories, whatever their many temporal and personal permutations, was a dynamic, a set of presumptions about what was possible and not possible, how conviction and event came together, how culture and society shaped and were shaped by the experience. Each story began with the experience of a "turn," a break of more or less radical proportions with a society in which the hero had (usually) thrived. Rulman Merswin, for instance, a merchant from Strassburg, adopted a converted lifestyle on his own in 1347 and eventually founded the somewhat suspect "Friends of God." In his own vernacular telling, an account of the first four years, he initially launched out upon such debilitating austerities that he nearly undid himself physically and mentally. Tauler, a Dominican preacher and confessor, restrained him, lest he "go mad." Merswin understood his as a "turn" (*ker*) away from the "natural pleasures" of society, coming to the "single-minded view" that he "wanted to do penance for his sin," and so "boldly" gave up, an act of "free will," his trading and profit-taking.[15] Such personal turns were often conceived and presented as "taking up penance." Francis of Assisi offered the paradigmatic example in his *Testament*. Upon turning from youthful indulgence, according to his opening narrative, he moved not to "convert" (i.e. enter a religious house) but to "do penance"—his words here key and precise. His decisive act was to treat with mercy the polluted outcasts of urban society—lepers, the opposite of his own smart set. Then he "left the world."[16] Everyone, of course, was to do penance, ordinarily as a structured activity, once a year beginning on Shrove Tuesday and ending at the Easter feast. This was something different: voluntary penance, self-imposed, self-structured. Margery Kempe, in her personal account from the 1430s, reported going mad for a time after childbirth over an unconfessed sin, then entering upon a period of exhilarated ambition in the world, and finally making her "turn," marked, as she said several times, by "doing great bodily penance."[17]

Many factors played into such "turns"—illness, anxiety, troubles of all sorts. But why did converts speak of "taking up penance" or "making a turn"? Here history had intervened, over centuries, and transformed the meaning of key words and concepts. Medieval Europe was a society comprised mainly of the christened, the already converted (one meaning), while it privileged the professed as the social and legal embodiment of conversion (other meaning). To "convert" was thus to take vows and enter that socioreligious estate. The letters of Catherine of Siena, a wool worker's daughter writing in the vernacular, pleaded with people of all social ranks to adopt religious lifestyles, without, mostly, ever employing the word "convert." The importance of this goes beyond a note on the meaning of words: Key conceptual notions became socially and culturally ambiguous, their meanings confused and confusing. The christened made up the world, in this European view, and yet were called to stand over against it. Converts acted as the privileged, Christians over against Jews and infidels, the professed over against "seculars" (including clergymen), and yet also that which everyone was to be. The notion of conversion was preempted, and yet not contained–or containable. Its built-in claim to a higher, truer, more privileged state would inevitably break out in other ways. Its call to a personal or group "turn" operated still as an unpredictable catalyst.

A basic point, too easily lost sight of when this society gets read through the eyes of the converted, is simply this: converts generated tension. They might elicit admiration (nearly always presented positively in subsequent "lives"); and the professed might rank as the exemplary first order of society. But each act of conversion was an act of repudiation, a rejection, implicit or explicit, of surrounding society, meaning, the christened, the already converted. This provoked suspicion, scorn, resentment. Consider just one story. Master Geert Grote, founder of the Modern Devotion, experienced a life crisis in his mid-thirties, turned his parental home into a hospice for poor women, gave up his benefices, and as a deacon preached penance in market towns along the Ijssel River. In Zwolle one leading citizen, growing annoyed, reportedly objected, "Why, Master, do you upset our peace and introduce new customs? Cease from this preaching. Do not try to upset and terrorize our people." To this Master Geert replied, "I do not wish for you to go to hell." The town father indignantly answered, "Permit us to go to hell in peace!" And the Master answered, "I will not."[18]

When converts repudiated the "world" around them, they turned away from their families, neighbors, and countrymen, all baptized Christians. They left behind, as inadequate, the ordinary parish worship of their neighborhood. Every conversion, every plea for conversion, sprang from this negative dialectic, derived its power in part, implicitly or explicitly, from disparaging the ordinary life of the christened. Richard Rolle, who left Oxford to set up as a hermit, probably in the 1320s, says, in his impossible prose, that he himself wished for a world filled with Christians but could find not one ("non aliquem inuenimus"); all were full of vice, all his contemporaries cavalierly given to earthly delights ("omnes indifferenter ad delectabilia declinant").[19] But these same christened, denied the title of "religious" or "convert," were to fill parishes, pay tithes, submit to confession and communion at least once each year—and could still be found wanting. However proudly families may have donated a son or daughter to a religious house (and awaited their prayers in return), many parents, other stories tell, resisted, or retrieved their children, afraid to "lose" them to this otherworldly state. Tensions arose even more powerfully when it came to freeboot converts, so to speak, those who broke with society without entering the privileged estate of religion. Late medieval townspeople became annoyed with those who shirked their duties in arms or taxes or householding, indulging and cultivating their own religious selves in a leisure others could not afford—who became "able-bodied beggars," as Langland complained poetically of his contemporaries in the 1360s–80s, as critics at Basel said of Beguines in 1405, and the citizens of Dutch towns said of the Modern Devout.[20] Converts, on the other hand, found this world, all its customary and comfortable practices, distracting, devious, destructive. As Denis the Carthusian put it (mid-fifteenth century): Christians might not have had to flee the world at one time. But now it was "highly difficult" to "live well there and avoid mortal sin"—less so perhaps for lowly workers but certainly for the wealthy and those active in affairs.[21]

This tension makes sense only if the "world," in all its fullness, was still taken for granted as normal and satisfying, as the primary reality—that presumed "custom" which Master Geert's preaching so uncomfortably challenged. Most medieval christened did take it for granted. In the first chapter of his *Imitation of Christ* Thomas listed the "vanities" that consumed ordinary folks: wealth, honors and offices, desires of the flesh, hope for a long life, living for the present, loving things that quickly pass.[22] Catherine of Siena, in letters written a generation earlier, worked from a similar list: honor, pleasures, riches, comfort, solace among humans. These she likened, in a letter to a Florentine merchant, to a bad business deal: in the end they impoverished rather than profited.[23] This critique drew upon an ancient literature of *contemptus mundi,* and may be found everywhere in later medieval preaching and devotional literature. Accepted by laypeople, it seems, as commonplace, perhaps even fair, at least on the surface, it named those things for which, concretely, they had to do penance each Lent before Easter communion, or at death on facing judgment. Yet, plainly, "worldly" affairs ordinarily moved and preoccupied most of their time. The resultant tensions they had to live with or ignore, deal with fitfully or try to suppress. Most people, it seems, settled into some customary way of claiming Christianity, practicing its basic moral and cultic demands without becoming nonconformists in their own world. It was precisely this customary conformity that troubled converts no end. Rolle claimed to find people largely "indifferent" to the dilemmas he experienced so forcefully. Catherine characterized people in her time (also churchmen) as living in a state of "negligentia" (her Italian word). The Carthusian author Jacobus of Jüterborg saw his age as that of the fourth seal, the white horse, the reign of hypocrites, of people who slay with guile and false teaching, with vice protected by princes, of men and women whose sanctity is false, whose god is their stomach, who seek only honor and fame. Even churchmen supposed to be winning souls, this monk declared, operated under only the guise of uprightness.[24]

Those active in affairs found ways to account for this reality, these conforming customs, and not just as sinfulness or the lesser lay estate. With the help of Aristotle in particular, philosophers had expanded upon notions of the created order as a good in itself, while political thinkers described kingdoms and the social order as inherently good, even God-given. Human nature too, many recognized, was replete with its own dispositions and proclivities, mixed and diverse, a matter of psychology, humors, and the stars, not starkly spiritual or fleshly. In 1395 Master Henry of Langenstein, professor in Vienna, author of a treatise on the "discerning of spirits," noted that "habit" and "birth" ("a nativitate ex complexione seu ex constellatione") played enormous roles in shaping people's lives. Some were simply (and strongly: *fortissime*) inflamed with corporal pleasure by nature, some utterly bound to things worldly and fleshly by force of "long-standing custom and habitation."[25] Recognition of nature, custom, and habit as potent and "normal" forces may certainly be found richly represented in later medieval literary texts, but no less in vernacular devotional literature. A simple example: a woman who joined the Sisters of the Common Life in Deventer (Master Geert's House), as another of her sisters recalled in a posthumous memorial, was "by nature" of a "lively" and "airy" disposition. This meant that the devout way of life and her nature did not comport well, and she had initially much to suffer.[26]

Converts broke with this custom and conformity. As they or their biographers report, they set out consciously to break their own natures, to set desire against desire, one kind of satisfaction against another. Though descriptions could become highly stylized, the "turns" were often very personal. In his alliterated prose Richard Rolle tells how, as a young man encountering the powers of love ("adolescens extiteram amplissimo affectu; dum essem etate aptus amori; quam impetuosus, quam uiolens, sit uis amoris"), he came to perceive the world as only so much empty glory and lust ("vanitas et venus"), and to spurn it ("spiritu spirante spurciciam spernebam"), specially the allures of women, in order to pursue a safer course, in poverty, as a hermit. For all the impossible language here, some crisis over love likely precipitated this conversion ("cor a carnalibus curis conuertit"), and another love/Lover ("ut diligerem cum delectacione dulcissimum dilectum") now became his constant theme.[27]

If Rolle converted from human love to divine, Geert Grote of Deventer, about 1375, moved from clerical book-learning to devotional reading. His crisis came in his mid-thirties, over university life and clerical ambition, after nearly twenty years spent in their pursuit. In a remarkable document he set out a series of personal resolutions. "The first thing," he began, "is to desire no further office or benefice," and to give up "forbidden learning," by which he meant forms of astrology and black magic. As for learning itself, "Through the lucrative arts," he says, "a man becomes wholly tainted." "Take no degree in medicine"—he plainly had studied it—"because you intend neither gain nor profit." His self-reproach goes on: "Study no liberal art and write no book to spread your own fame and the renown of your learning." Again: "Avoid and abhor every public disputation held to score a triumph or make a good appearance, such as those disputations of theologians and artists in Paris." Again: "Never study to take a degree in theology, because you do not want to pursue gain or benefices or fame, and you can have the learning just as well without the degree." And he added: "In general it is a carnal subject, and all of them think very carnally." Yet he remained a passionate lover of books—*avidus et peravidus* he says in one letter. He frenetically spent family wealth to acquire them, organized a devout household to copy them, traveled round as a preacher of penance with a barrel full of them (in case he met resistance or heretics), and wrote letters and tractates in Latin and Dutch. He also drew up a new canon of readings, books recommended for devotion.[28]

Whatever fostered conversion, the turn reoriented each "toward God," an experience of divinity. Merswin, the merchant of Strassburg, after four years, achieved a breakthrough into "peace," an experience of God's presence beyond telling, he said, so powerful it nearly caused his heart to burst and him to "shout out in jubilee"[29]—an exalted cry associated with Beguines, in his day sometimes thought suspect. Richard Rolle, for his part, spent a lifetime writing, driven by love ("urget igitur amoris habundancia"), and found, after he withdrew as a hermit, his bitterness of spirit turned rather into song, a melody so rich he hardly dared show its fullness.[30] This became his mark, his solace, a divine "hum" (*canor*) he found indescribably compelling beyond any earthly song or love, which almost never left him (and which he may have tried to communicate in his unusual prose). He grew full of critique for the sanctimoniously religious—by which he meant local priestly leaders, as well as the professed—who did not have this experience or the knowledge to guide others. When they turned on him in irritation, he found peace within, again in jubilant song.[31]

The ordinary term for the benefit that came with conversion was *consolacio,* comfort, solace from God, the experiential return or blessing. Converts focused on spiritual solace, the reward for a more intensive religious life, often distinctly experiential in character. This same term, however, applied fully to another kind of solace, the more ordinary or customary kind, the comforts and goods of earthly life. In the *Imitation of Christ* Thomas frequently played out the calculus of returns from competing earthly and heavenly *consolationes*: "What seculer man is ther that wolde not gladly have spiritual consolacion and gladnes, yf he might have hit ever? For spirituel consolacions passeth alle the delyces of the worlde and alle fleisshely voluptes."[32] He argued from the stuff of ordinary life. Why do people talk and gossip so much? To comfort themselves: "Therfore we talke so ofte togydres, fo bi suche spekynge togydres we seke counforte every of other, to relieve the herte that is made wery with dyverse thoughtes. . . . but alas, oftetymes veynly and unfruytfully. For suche outward counforte is a grete hynderar of inwarde and hevonly consolacion."[33] And he made another point: The convert's break meant replacing one custom with another: "And the more that thou withdrawest thee fro consolacion of all creatures, the swetter and the myghtier counfortes thou shalte fynde in me. . . . The olde used custume wol withstande, but hit shal be overcomen bi a better custume."[34] The realism in these appeals should not be missed. Converts understood fully the force and appeal of the customary comforts, and could proceed themselves only by consciously breaking away from them.

CONVERTING THE CONVERTED: THE CHALLENGE
TO THE ORDERS

The force of conversion threatened unpredictably. Churchmen had managed to stabilize it in the twelfth century by way of influential new monastic orders, and in the thirteenth by way of mendicants in towns, each acting as spiritual and intellectual exemplars for a century or more. Still, there were men who did not fit, who went their own way, and always women denied a place, or options befitting them. By the mid-fourteenth century, mendicants, always subject to envy and attack from laypeople and the secular clergy, faced fresh waves of satirical and critical reproach for their importunate begging, their intellectual sophistry, their pastoral raiding, their international privileges—all of it deeply annoying. Religious houses, following the disastrous population losses of the plague in 1348–49 and again in the 1370s and the 1390s, found it harder to recruit and retain people in sufficient numbers or of satisfactory quality. When labor costs soared, while rents and staples held steady or declined, they also found it hard to manage budgets, just as a taste for better housing and clothing, more ornamentation and music, was growing. These conditions weighed heavily. But no less important was the mood. If we listen to contemporary converts, most of the christened lived in a terrible state of negligence, with cloistered life fully as worldly as life in a household or street, and religious houses difficult to enter, requiring connections or "gifts." Johan Busch, chronicler of the Modern Devout, claimed that hardly a house could be found where the rules were kept, hardly a place be found in his region (the northern Low Countries) where a serious convert could go.[35] So also Denis the Carthusian: The whole church, from the people to the clergy, extending to the religious, had become a ruined city, all its gates and walls thrown open to the enemy, no longer affording any spiritual security.[36] Laypeople in the 1420s, by one report, saw the Hussite revolt as sprung from the corruption of the orders.[37] What could be expected of the christened if the converted were corrupt?

Such complaints were not new. Calls for reform recycled through the whole medieval period. But to dismiss this mood in that way is to miss the force and particularities of this historical moment. Between the 1370s and the 1420s nearly every religious order experienced convulsive shake-ups, led by individuals or groups called "Observants."[38] The Carthusians, the most eremetic and contemplative of orders, underwent unparalleled expansion, Charterhouses were founded not in the "desert" but on the outskirts of cities, where they attracted men from schools and the clergy and where their writings, increasingly in the vernacular, reached an interested urban populace. Observants also attracted unusually able and innovative leaders, some of the most influential writers and preachers of the fifteenth century: Raymond of Capua, San Bernardino, John of Capistrano, Savonarola, even Martin Luther. But in the early days they rarely succeeded in reforming existing houses or transforming an entire congregation. They had to settle for the occasional house, new or reformed, with networks linking the likeminded together, clusters of "observant converts" within the body of the officially "converted." Some Observant houses enjoyed success with the laity, if not with the rank and file of their own orders: territorial princes and urban governments favored these zealous ascetics and preachers—think of Henry V's Sheen outside London, and cases across Europe, especially in the

Low Countries, the Empire, and Italy. But if these local powers found the existing religious arrangements for their citizens or children satisfactory, they would work to keep the fanatics at bay. The Strassburg preacher, Geiler of Kaysersberg, claimed that the Council of Basel had no power to change one house if local magistrates resisted and "stuck with their women."[39] All the same, the force of this appeal must be recognized, and the way its ideals threatened to undo the inherited association of the converted with the professed. Converts turned on converts, and after the 1370s every order, independently, was nearly torn apart.

Resistance was strong. Within houses the battle was cast as a dialectic between "converts" and the "worldly," both "religious," both professed converts. Those accused of being "worldly" protested that they did not find it unreasonable or irreligious to have private chambers or chests rather than a communal dormitory, to keep up continuing contact with friends and relatives and to receive occasional gifts from them rather than to have all contact controlled by their abbot, to wear clothing or eat food or sing music or possess books that befitted their rank in society rather than be reduced to the lowest and grossest standards. John Nyder, a leader of Observant Dominicans in the German Empire, heard the arguments for "immemorial" customs, an easy conformity, and reviewed them in a widely circulated book of about 1431 called *De reformatione monasteriorum*. The traditionalists claimed it was contrary to nature to live so austerely, too risky to give up the monetary arrangements carefully worked out to support a house; houses had already lost too many people and resources to plague and disruption. People of ability and distinction, further, would not join such a harsh life; reformers were merely restless innovators, upsetting traditional practices; and so on.[40] As Nyder conceded, "total reformation" of the religious life was impossible, even individual houses (*particularia*) unbelievably hard to remake, because the will for it was not there in the members and prelates positively blocked it ("tum quia voluntas bona in subditis deficit, tum quia illud prelatorum malicia impedit").[41] The going could get tough. A reforming prior of canons regular in Bavaria, in a letter he had not dared write earlier ("hucusque nulli unquam audebam scribere"), reported in 1456 that for promoting Observance he was twice locked up (presumably in his house), also exiled for ten weeks, and not successful until he had made his case twice to secular powers, whereupon five resisting brothers were driven out.[42]

All this issued in a paradox, even a contradiction, of which many contemporaries were fully aware. The "converted" lived now in a reversed conversion: while the married used property prudently to meet their needs and build a legacy for their heirs, Denis the Carthusian pointed out, religious, with no heirs or cares, indiscriminately spent through the goods granted them ("rebus sibi concessis valde multoties immoderate utuntur"). Private ownership was the poison root from which these evils grew ("ex proprietate seu peculio tanquam ex uenenosa radica multa peccata proueniunt").[43] So the converts now needed converting. Reformers lashed out at *proprietarii* ("possessors") in countless tractates and sermons, most still unedited and unstudied, scourging those who claimed these as age-old customary practices.[44] In origins, the Carthusian Henry Egher of Kalkar explained, religious houses were endowed to support common usage. Greedy prelates now shared out the proceeds in "burses" (prebends), allowed the professed to draw upon individual or family wealth, and forced poorer members to find resources as best they could[45]—all corrosive of charity, community, and fervor.

To get at the unruly force of this challenge, this worry from within, we may examine the life of someone who anticipated it, the Dominican friar Henry of Suso. He had entered the friary in Constance at age thirteen, probably about 1308. His spirit remained unfocused, distracted, he remembers, until a turn (*abker*—rhetorically, the final word of his introduction!) in his eighteenth year, troubled by the pesky thought that it might be easy to begin this way of life but hard to finish. To rein in his unruly spirit, (*wilder mut*), he turned away from those in the cloister who seemed loftily self-indulgent (*upiger gesellschaft*), who then heckled him about his "strange ways" and predicted he would "come to no good end."[46] Suso's experience, one of conversion from within the converted estate, eventually produced the first "autobiography" in German, partly for (and with the help of) a nun, Elizabeth Stagel, who saved up his written counsel and stories.[47] He told of experiencing raptures, entering into marriage with Wisdom, carving the Name of Jesus into his chest, pursuing ascetic austerities to their extreme, then coming under instruction from Eckhart to find release in detachment, a baring or emptying of the self before God, and then being suspected of heresy—all to attain conversion within the converted state. Could such a lifelong experiment in testing the extremes, regarded as fascinating but also bizarre, seriously challenge the first order of society? It touched a nerve. People read his writings in huge numbers, and in many languages; they imagined their way into his experiences; they appropriated his teachings by way of a handy short form he offered as "one hundred points." What he attacked was conformity, privilege, ease. And he did so in such a way that his desires recalled themes and tones found in vernacular poems: no love, by an ancient decree, apart from suffering, no real suitor unless he is a sufferer, no real lover unless he is a martyr.[48]

The rhetoric heated up after the 1370s. Those who took vows and did not observe them, some said, were worse than those who took no vows at all. Those who led lax and unobservant lives, given to leisure and chatting and worldly vanities, lived in sin rather than religion, gave offense rather than honor to God.[49] Observants attacked from two different angles, a pincer movement in its effect. To counter what they saw as signs of deviance and self-indulgence, of easy conformity to privileged customs, they demanded that the rules be kept "ad ungam," an idiomatic phrase meaning literally "down to the toenails," with absolute precision. A letter from Franciscan Observants to Parisian masters in early 1410 represented their party as "those who desire and aspire to observe the rule of St. Francis to the letter according to the apostolic utterances."[50] So too twelfth-century Cistercians had wanted Benedict's Rule kept to the letter, thirteenth-century friars had argued over the words and intentions of Francis. Enthusiasts for Observance, however, faced a different world, on the macro and the micro levels. They recognized perforce the great diversity of rules among religious and diverse customs within each order. On the local level they might dispute in detail the interpretation of a rule or seek to regulate the minutest items. But at the level of principle, above the local fray, they stood for "strict observance" as a generic principle. Leaving the world thus meant a vigorous keeping to the rules in every detail, a deliberate overthrowing of customary arrangements, however old, whatever their rationale. Moreover, the ecclesiastical life was now more institutionalized, with lawyers commonly governing affairs. So a call for observance came as a legal challenge, statutes and precepts to be enforced. Those resisting, the great majority for the first generation or two, had no choice for their part but to defend existing practices as also legitimated by law, by long-held "customs" or "privileges." Observant tractates could therefore resemble legal briefs, their threat directed against monetary arrangements, private rooms, social contact, books, clothing, music, all to be subjected to strict regulation. For territorial princes or urban magistrates attempting in this era to bring order by statute to people and practices within their jurisdiction (think of sumptuary legislation, for instance), this approach must have appeared quite intelligible, even necessary. John of Capistrano helped work out what observance meant for Franciscan women, and turned each chapter of Clare's rule into "precepts," her twelve prose chapters yielding 115 (!) mandates defining correct observance.[51] Of the eighty-two men's houses that made up the canons regular of Windesheim, twenty or so added a vow of permanent enclosure, regulated in an elaborate public document specifying exactly when and how often brothers could leave the cloister complex, for what reason, how far they might walk on what occasion, and so on.[52]

The Observants perceived that force alone, rhetorical, ascetic, or legal, could not carry the day, and might even, as Suso learned personally, bring ruin to a person or a community. If people only applied violently the bodily disciplines, Denis the Carthusian conceded, it would "more likely destroy them, because they proceed imprudently and take as their point of departure outward rigor and bodily observances."[53] The professed would be terrified of the rule's rigor, and find it hard to give up their customary ways (*consueta*). So Observants appealed at the same time to the other end of human motivation: to evoke an interior point of departure, of movement towards the good out of love or fear ("nec tamen proficiunt, quia non habent intra se principium motionis ad bonum, utputa timorem Dei aut caritatem") as well as an experiential point of arrival. a heavenly solace and spiritual sweetness ("supernam consolationem experientur, et diuinam ac spiritualem dulcedinem sentient").[54] This inner drive, born of love or fear, cast by Suso as desire, was not called "conversion." How could it be? That term was co-opted. They had first to dispose their interiors, and then act ("onus et devotus homo opera sua prius intus disponit que foris agere debet").[55] An avalanche of devotional tractates, some of considerable literary distinction like Suso's, others derivative, set out to move hearts, instill intentions, kindle desire. These spread with unprecedented rapidity, many in the vernacular, often on paper (then new), then in print (also new).[56] The emblem for all is the *Imitation of Christ,* quoted just above and (deliberately) frequently in this paper. Its spread between the 1420s and 1480s may serve as a red thread tracing the movement. Thomas of Kempen wrote other pamphlets than the four assembled as the *Imitation.* In his *De disciplina claustralium* he took for granted, from his opening lines, the observant emphasis on cloistered discipline as yielding perfection and eliciting grace of devotion: "Disciplina claustralis, si strennue seruetur, ad magnam perfectionem ducit. . . . Ubi disciplina custoditur, ibi adest gracia celestia, ibi deuocio floret. . . ." But he devoted his third chapter, uniquely, to "true conversion," which, he said, must be continuous, daily ("opus est ergo cotidiana conversione ad deum"). It is not enough to change the habit; for "true and religious conversion" there must be a constant battle "turning the heart from all things visible and material."[57]

All this yielded a paradox straining with tension: to convert the converted required that hearts be moved daily from deep within, more than ever through private devotional reading, also in their own tongue, and at the same time that life be regulated strictly from without, more than ever by law and statute. The resistance, human and institutional, was massive, in part because the extremity of the demands, from either end of human experience, potentially threatened the institutionalized state itself. Observants, moreover, were not afraid to take this message to the people, in their language, and even to ask the same of them (San Bernardino, Savonarola). They were, for all their relentless rigor, remarkably attuned to their contemporaries, moving easily between Latin and the vernacular, men and women, image and word, assimilating a woman teacher like Catherine of Siena or new devotions like the cult of the Holy Name. Dominicans made of Catherine their patron. She, a woman writing in Italian, urged their cause with the pope and their general chapter. She also called laypeople to observance, visible in some four hundred extant letters circling out from her "familia," her adherents. She urged a merchant and senator in Siena to turn away from the satisfactions of conforming life, to "observe" the commands of Christ as his rule or law. She worried about interior motivation, that people be spirited in observance ("acciò che siamo più animati ad osservarli"), out of love but also fear ("questo amore el fondaremo in uno timore santo di reverentia").[58] Carthusians collected, wrote, and distributed devotional tractates, some routine, some skirting the edge of the acceptable (Margaret of Porete, for instance). We must not miss the force of all this: Enforcing precept while deepening intentions, each pushed to its extreme, could collapse all middle ground, implode the customary practices of the ordinary christened as well as the professional converts.

"True Christians" as the Converted:
The Lollard Challenge

Some around 1400 lost confidence entirely in the professed as embodying the converted state. Laypeople and secular clerics had long resented these privileged claims, but critiques came in different forms, and it is important to hear each in its own time and place. The Italian humanist Lorenzo Valla wrote a dialogue "On the Profession of the Religious" about 1441, probably directed against Observant Franciscans, possibly even San Bernardino, though addressed formally to a learned jurist and lay magistrate. Valla attacked the very status of the professed as "the religious." As people who withdraw to think and live apart from others, they are rather a "sect." For what is a "religious" other than a "true Christian"?[59] Why add a "second promise" to that made at baptism to live an upright and holy life?[60] Why beg from others for your living? Better not to give up all you have, and carry out your duties in society![61] Most pointedly, Valla disputed the common view that vows entailed greater merit and a greater reward. The vow itself entailed nothing. It only created legally binding obligations—a mere promise would be better. We are in fact equals, he argued back, or indeed perhaps the professed deserve less reward, for they (a swipe here at the new Observant emphasis) pursue virtue under obligation. If we are all in pursuit of virtue and religion can there be any point to vows except to bind the bad?[62]

Despite its charged rhetoric, Valla staged his argument among elites, in polished Latin, though he did not fear to reiterate his stand when called to account three years later: "I thus believe that all who keep the Christian religion are 'religious,' and that properly not the professed alone can call themselves the only 'religious,' since others may be such and indeed no less than they."[63]

Things went very differently in England in the 1380s: there a university master's critique of doctrine and practice, ecclesiastical power, and exclusive religious claims issued in a broad revolt that aimed to reorganize the church. Interpreting this revolt has been taken up in recent years more by literary than church historians; my purpose is to consider it under still another rubric. At the same moment that Duffy found "traditional religion" flourishing in the parishes,[64] others came to see in the Lollards, ignored by Duffy and traditionally treated under the (loaded) rubrics of "heretics" or "pre-Reformers," a fundamental and "popular" subversion of the whole socio-religious system.[65] The "party" (*secta*) of the Lollards and the party of prelates (lords temporal and spiritual) each accused the other of "false teaching," of subverting the Christian community. One apologetic Lollard tractate reviewed sixteen "points" alleged by the bishops ordinary against them, seeking to help "true Christian people" answer these points in English "advisedly" (with learning), "truly," and "meekly" (without a brashness that would provoke more trouble). These "True Christians" now saw the whole church, people and priests, as become "blind and leprous by sustaining a proud prelacy, born up by the flattering of private religion," everyone stuck in a "stubborn and customary breaking of God's precepts."[66] Prelates persecuted, but people resisted too, comfortable with the practices of christening they knew, wary of this up-ending challenge. So if the great majority of the christened were tainted with customary and conforming law-breaking, if prelates were corrupted ("dotty": *began to dote in temperalte*) by power and possessions, if "converts" merely pursued "private religion" as "sects" protecting their privileges, what way stood open, what means or language, for the "true Christian people"? How do you set about turning round a whole community that falsely thinks of itself as converted?

Lollards initially had more confidence in lay government transforming the realm than prelates, and foresaw parishes transformed rather than elite bodies of the converted. They were themselves driven underground soon enough as a "sect" and formed their own "conventicles," but they saw the professed religious as the real "sects" in their society. This sense of things they expressed in the final paragraph of the Disendowment Bill, perhaps presented to Parliament in 1395, and in any case widely distributed in Latin and English:

all the true commoners desire for the worship of God and to the profit of the realm that these worldly clerics, bishops, abbots and priors that are such worldly lords be made to live by their spiritualities, for they do not live so now, nor do they perform the office of true curates as prelates should, nor do they help either the poor or the commoners by way of their lordships as true secular lords should, nor do they live in penance or by manual labor as true religious should by their profession. . . . the life and evil example of all these has been vicious so long that all the common people, both lords and simple commoners, are now become so vicious and infected through the arrogance of their sin that hardly anyone fears God or the Devil.[67]

Lollards never attacked the ideals associated with "conversion": living in penance and poverty, cultivating the fear and love of God, practicing almsgiving and charity. They charged prelates and "private religious" with perverting rather than exemplifying these things, betraying everyone, specially the commoners, turning false practice into conforming custom. Scholars have fit this attack into broad patterns of late medieval anticlericalism and antimendicancy, and rightly so. But this was a more comprehensive vision of "turning," whence authorities found it so unsettling. Rooted in conversion, it did not speak of "conversion," term that had come to define a whole corrupt class.

In a sermon preached at St. Paul's Cross in London about a decade after the Disendowment Bill, on 21 November 1406, William Taylor urged people to recognize, first, that the whole church, priests and people, had fallen away from the love and especially the "law" of God; nearly all the baptized were now hypocrites.[68] In such a state of confusion how could anyone tell friend from foe anymore, servants of Christ from servants of Antichrist?[69] Taylor set out particulars, for instance, that penance at Lent (structured conversion) was a mere sham ("as men weren wont aftir feyned turnyng in lente turne agen to her synne").[70] Clergy are at the heart of the problem: "For if the clergie . . . is turned into derknesse, how shal the puple conteyne hem in the weie that ledith to hevene . . . ?"[71] The only option is to effect a reversal, that is, "that there be a contrarie turnyng, that is to meene that derknesse be made light."[72] Taylor's notion of a "contrary turn," to reverse the momentum toward hypocritical and customary "law-breaking," stands in for "conversion." For Lollards a "turn" and a "re-turn" were needed. But since stubborn hypocrisy possessed the "possessioner" class in particular, the prelates and the religious, all the ordinary avenues of conversion were disgraced, even become "satanic." Their false claims had to be exploded, these religious orders smeared as "sects." Surveying all the English Wycliffite sermons, Gradon and

Hudson concluded: "The most frequent subject of polemical attack in the sermons are the *new sects, four sects, new religious orders,* and the attacks are undoubtedly the lengthiest single subject in these sermons."[73] Not, notably, the theologically explosive issue of the Eucharist or the politically sensitive issue of disendowment, but a relentless attack on those supposed to mediate and exemplify "religion." Lollards foresaw instead a "turning" of all people and priests, with no place left for a private class of "religious."

Wycliffe himself, a secular priest and university master, first led the repudiation of "private religion," the professed who set their privileged state over against the "common Christian religion." "Sects" put some new head (Benedict or Augustine or Francis) above the "common abbot Christ," ("Christus abbas tocius christiani ordinis"), also their rules above the perfect law of Christ ("and so mannys lawe groweth and Godus law is lettyd, and specially by lawis of these newe ordres").[74] Because their holiness was feigned or self-serving, because it substituted their rule and example for Christ's, such "new orders" or "sects" of "private religion" had to be avoided, in fact adjudged "heretical": "thei dele not with thes newe ordris but supposon hem heretykus, be their monkis, be their freris."[75] Lollard rhetoric frequently invokes, over against these false rules, or against conformity, the "true law of Christ," an ambiguous phrase which means at once the Scriptures and the Lollard understanding of faith and practice. This is a mood that in some striking ways echoes that of the Observants. Both set "true law" against customary or false practice; both take aim at a well-endowed church, setting themselves against the symbiosis of religion and possession. Indeed Lollards, too, understood themselves as those who singularly knew and pursued the truth ("men and women that loven truth, and heeren or known of this pursuyng that now is in the chirche," that is, their movement); who were rigorous in self-imposed penance ("we moten taken upon us and usen scharp penaunce contynuelli"); who were forced to stand up to a false establishment ("by my sodeyne and unwarned apposynge and answeryng, that all thei that wolen of good herte withouten feynyng . . ."); who faced "persecution of their bodies" from the "enemies of truth" in order to uphold truth and righteousness ("for her lyvynge, and for her trewe knowlechyng of truthe, and for her pacient, wilful and glad suffrygynge of persecucioun for rightwisnesse"); and who might therefore expect an inheritance of heavenly bliss.[76] But for Lollards this was the way of the "meek" who followed "poor priests" in the people's language and simple parishes, not the private and privileged way of professed converts. Indeed one interpretation of Wycliffe's complex teachings on religion and the social order would hold that only those not in mortal sin—only the truly converted—could have command over people or things. As the Observants resembled princes and city magistrates in calling for a legal enforcement of the moral order, so Lollards, the community of true Christians, initially hoped that lay princes would effect such a reordering by legislative fiat, turning out all sinful "possessioners," as Observants now turned against the "proprietarii."

The Lollard approach to Christian life radically repudiated the special estate of the converted and yet also radically appropriated it. The Lollards were born along, at least initially, by a kind of zealous and visionary optimism that the whole realm, and specially each parish, could be so transformed. It was just in this period that historians can first see the parish truly functioning locally, with the coming of churchwardens, the maintaining of the fabric, the roles of societies and side altars, sometimes even a voice for parishioners in the naming of rectors.[77] Here, in some odd way, Duffy's thriving parishes and these dissenting subversives come round to meet at the extremes: The vigor of contemporary parish life, however seriously they critiqued it for its misguided and customary ways, enabled Lollards to imagine a religious community which put them, not the professional converts or the prelates, at the center. The essential mark after all is "observing the perfection of the Gospel." There might be, Wycliffe concedes in one work, a "private religion" given to this end. But a Christian keeping this outside the cloister cannot be called "worldly" or "lay" (secularis) for Christ and the apostles lived this way. The two are, or can be, equal, as there are also "imperfect" people and practices equally inside and outside any cloister.[78] In a more radical mood, some Lollards imagined a single head or "abbot" in Christ, a single Gospel law, a single way of life, a singular poverty aimed only at supporting "poor priests" who served their communities and lived on gifts, a singular preaching aimed only at edifying. In the language of Wycliffe, no other "sect" was necessary than that of Christ, no other "law" or rule than that of the Gospel.[79] The orders, with their notions of observance, only obstructed the observance of Christ's law.[80] The only solution was to "convert" the orders (!) to this true sect ("ad puram sectam Cristi per suam graciam convertantur"). Owing to their inherently poisonous state, however, Wycliffe observed, this would require a miracle from God, like the conversion of Paul; better, more simply, to purge them to keep the body healthy.[81] The Lollard vision turned the inherited christened world inside out.

This fundamental insight can be extended to other elements in the Lollard outlook. True conversion, at almost every turn, requires reversal, away from customary practices and powers. The bread of the Eucharist is *not* converted; the heart must be turned to union with Christ. Confession with the mouth to a priest is *not* necessary for forgiveness; the heart must be turned to God in true contrition. Power (*dominium*) is *not* built into social structures, neither over possessions nor people; it turns upon hearts, not in mortal sin, committed to just actions and usages. Pilgrimage is *not* a matter of touring with the body, but of turning the spirit to right belief and contrition. In each case a radical critique of established structures rests upon an inner turn to God, away from the customary practices of the merely christened (or in Wycliffe's heavy theological language, the *praesciti*, the foreknown).

"PRIVATE RELIGIOUS" AS THE CONVERTED: THE CHALLENGE OF THE NEW DEVOUT

At exactly the same time, across the water in the Low Countries, the "Modern Devout" promoted a vision of conversion in still another form, not suppressed in the end, but also disputed at the beginning. Both Master John Wycliffe and Master Geert Grote sparked controversy in the later 1370s with their pointed critique of the church and churchmen, and the teachings of both masters, despite their awful academic prose, extended influentially into the vernacular and drew in people of all social stations. Both found themselves at odds with most "religious" and variously dissatisfied with parish life, but they developed different stances toward conversion. Master Geert's crisis, as noted above, issued in a written resolution, a *propositum* rather than a profession, widely imitated by the later Devout. He wrote out personal notes, detailing what he was repudiating in the world (benefices, office, study, influence), what resolutions he now adopted as his own (a plan of reading, devotions at Mass, fasting, and so on). Others might "convert" to a suitable religious house (and Grote spent time with Carthusians); but he self-consciously chose to "remain in the world but not of it." He conceded that his way was "perhaps foolish," but he had reasons: Most "religious" were of the "world" and hated the truly devout.[82] Master Geert acted as a private citizen rather than a religious under vows, owned and acquired books to pursue his ends (as Valla advocated over against his Observant adversary), embodied devotion in a communal household rather than a cloister, preached as a deacon rather than a priest. This was a form of devotion "new in our day," thus "modern" in the sense of "present-day"— this a contemporary designation. Partly it was an ardent devotion that drew self-consciously on supposed older models for the "present day"; partly it was "devotion" in the "present day" in the face of all the "laxity" that the Devout saw round them in parishes and cloisters.

The convert had thus to carve out a distinct space, in some ways a new space, between the world and the religious, the parish and the cloister, at the risk of provoking both. Brothers or sisters lived on ordinary city streets, walked with people to church and to market, maintained relations with family and friends; and yet lived a life apart in religious practice, in dress, in social structure. A Dominican inquisitor sought to shut down these households in the 1390s—first the women, then the men. For the Devout heirs of Master Geert, the inquisitor had to be kept at bay, adherents confirmed in this way, the bishop persuaded of its legitimacy, neighbors mollified. Despite recognition extended by the local bishop in 1401 and a successful defense of their way of life at the Council of Constance in 1417, the Devout never entirely overcame recrimination. How could they act as a commune and an urban household at the same time? As late as the 1450s one of their number pulled together several apologetic arguments, a *Satisfactio nostra*. It was nothing new, he said, to be called names for wanting to live differently than all the worldly people living "carnally" around them.[83] Some said they were sliding into the "Bohemian heresy" (Hussitism). Some objected simply because they looked different from "the common ways of" all the others called "Christian." Still others said their ways implicitly impugned ordinary parish priests doing their duties, this made worse by their constant invocation of the early church.[84] The Devout answered with an explicit critique of custom: People inevitably conform to the company they keep, so those aware of their own fragility and these evil times need to flee the society of the undisciplined.[85] To the obvious retort that they should then join "religion," the Devout, building upon a position more or less articulated at Constance by Jean Gerson, declared that the "Christian religion" was the most fundamental and approved form, with Christ as its chief lawgiver, not Benedict or Francis or any other. No such "religion" need be added in order to observe the "Christian religion."[86] These lesser "religions" were not "established" by the church, merely "permitted"—this taken explicitly from Gerson. Besides there existed hardly any good houses to choose from, and none nearby! These arguments echo those put forward by Lollards, and yet with such a different ideal in mind: one of distinct households of the converted, men and women living separately in communes, supporting themselves with the work of their own hands (including book-copying), rather than an ideal of parishes made up of "poor priests" and "true Christians."

To stave off prosecution, the Devout successfully mustered arguments and authorities from canon law.[87] In the later 1390s Gerhart Zerbolt of Zutphen, a thirty-year-old Devout brother, moving between wily defense and creative invention, turned the legal brief into an apologetic tractate, *consilium* into counsel. His remarkable work, assembled as a hundred-page tractate in eleven parts, is unintelligible apart from its defensive stance; it is intriguing, however, in its positive apologetic, its ability to expand legal positions by sleight of hand into rhetorical assertions. He envisioned a way of being religious without professing religion, and thereby unsettled critics and a Dominican inquisitor. The Devout get most attention for their spiritual return to the ideal of the early church, as projected by Cassian, the Desert Fathers, Jerome, and Augustine. But it required an even greater legal and social reorientation to imagine ordered communal religious households outside orders. For this Gerhart turned to the language of a private "society," introduced into church law from Roman law. Societies had the right to organize; what better than a society whose purpose was devotion? Societies could manage their own goods; how better to handle them than on the communal model of the early church and natural reason? Household societies could establish internal customs; what better than a like-minded household of devout people acting together? Christians could admonish, teach, counsel, and correct one another; how better than in a household society that performed voluntary works of charity and offered guidance in the people's own language? All the obligatory structures of the church and the orders, so the Devout protested, remained untouched and unchallenged. So too the whole lay world could continue in its earthly business. But their communal household, a private society based on mutual charity and material commonality, would pursue its ends "in between"—that is, in the social and legal spaces left by the civic and ecclesiastical worlds: they would be a household organized as religious, its members wearing garb neither lay nor religious that bore "middling" appearance, using language that mediated the spiritual and the lay. Gerhart located the Devout, legally and conceptually, in the interstices of medieval urban and ecclesiastical society.

Joining such a communal society came with legal paperwork to protect the household—a deeding over of property and of all future claims, a last will and testament—but with no vows, no legal or social shift into the category of the "religious."[88] So "conversion" was not a point in time, a single act. It was, in some sense, continuous, constantly cultivated and reaffirmed. Thus Thomas: "Every day we owe to renewe oure purpose and styrre oureselfe to fervoure, as thoughe we had this day be furste converted. . . ." Further, since there was no cloister wall, no separation in law or estate, theirs had to be a self-conscious turn inward and away. Protecting this private interior space was a greater achievement than working miracles, as Thomas also insisted: "Better hit is a man to be hydde and take cure of himselfe, thenne takynge none heede of himselfe to worche wonders." For real conversion meant a turn toward peace within: "Oure Lorde seithe that the reawme of God is withein you. Turne thiselfe to God with alle thi herte and forsake this wrecched worlde, and this soule shal fynde reste. Lerne to despise outwarde thinges and to converte thee to inwarde thinges, and thou shalt see the reaume of God come into thee. For the reawme of God is pees and ioye in the Holy Ghoste." So, then, even as their households fought for a legal place between religion and the civic world, so the mental and spiritual life of Brothers and Sisters hung always on the edge, always faced testing: it had ever to turn inward to break with the outward conformity all about them. Not so surprisingly, a sense of spiritual alertness and even anxiety pervades their writings, a significant element in the *Imitation of Christ*: "Hit is good that sumtyme we suffre ayeinsayars and that men feele of us yvel and unperfetly, yea thoughe we do welle and mene welle. . . . For then we seke better the inwarde wyttenes, God, when we ar litel sette by outwarde of men, and litel credence is yiven to us. Therefore a man owed to ferme hymselfe in God, so that hym neded not to seke any consolacions outewarde."[89] An amusing story about Egbert, later rector in the house at Deventer, captures this tension. He was walking across town, eyes down, bringing food to someone. A female cousin saw him in the square and greeted him, to which he made little response. She knocked the plate out of his hand in annoyance, and exclaimed: "What kind of a Lollard have you become!"[90] Within a communal household members were forever "watching" and "admonishing" one another on a private basis, forever testing and cultivating their individual conversions, their outlook captured in proverbial sayings.[91]

The "sayings" in Devout communities are replete with admonitions to "resign yourself" through the day to God, examine yourself each evening, send up short prayers as you work—in sum, a life of constant "exercises."[92] But these exercises, like their readings, they designed and implemented themselves, in their own copybooks, in their own rooms. So while this could appear burdensome, and was—they could never rest, had always to be on guard, never secure ("nunquam sit securus")[93]—it was a life they took upon themselves. Why? There is no simple answer, but the theme every-where in these sayings is plain enough: peace within, solace (*consolatio*) without. So, Thomas again in the *Imitation*: "ther is no pes in the herte of the fleysly man, ner in hym that is al yiven to outwarde thinges, but in the fervent spirituel man." The goal is a *mens* or *vir pacificus,* a person no longer distracted, troubled, disappointed: "Yf thou forsake outwarde counforte, thou shalt more beholde hevonly thinges and oftetymes have iubilacion withinforthe."[94] Sometimes the call is forceful, as in this word from Florens, first head of the house in Deventer: Flee to your cell as to your friend; coerce and force yourself because there you are secure.[95] But force was only to start: "If we wolde in the begynnynge put to a litel violence, we shulde mowe do alle thinges aftirwarde with esines and gladnes. . . . Withstande thine inclynacioun and unlerne yvel custome. . . . O, if thou woldeste take heede how much pees thou sholdest get to thiselfe. . . . " Such a stance required

a continuous keeping watch over yourself, a *custodia sui ipsius,* as they called
it: "An inwarde man before al other cures taketh cure of himselfe. If thou
wolte have pees and very onehede, thou must sette alle aside and onely have
thiselfe before thine yen."[96] These sayings, too easily skimmed over as plat-
itudes, called in their own way for a rebellious stance, a kind of personal
violence within on the part of the convert, a taking possession of the self, a
continuous breaking with customary life.

The Devout generated a vision that opened this interior, private conversion to others. Theirs was not the wholesale "contrary turning" of the
Lollards, transforming practice and belief across society, touching even matters
so sensitive as Christ joined to the Host in the Eucharist and the church
joined to its immense material wealth. Nor was theirs any expectation that
they would convert all their urban neighbors, or indeed all the professed
religious (as their friends among the Observants hoped). The Devout accepted the inherited socio-religious dialectic that rendered the existing
Christian world harmful and dangerous, customary practices largely beyond
change. They perceived this, however, in personal terms: adults hardened
into the ways of the world by custom and care, their sensibility shaped by
carnal images and experiences. They hoped to draw in a few malleable
adults, by their example and their vernacular teaching. Increasingly, however, they turned to young people. Deventer was a market town with a significant school population. The Devout looked on these boy-clerics, about to
be ruined by adolescence and clerical ambition, as in some sense innocent,
"blank slates" not yet fouled or hardened. "For whoever passes his days in
a worldly manner up to adulthood, as is usually the case, or in carnal
affections or in worldly cares and distractions, they so fill their mind with
images of bodily matters both seen and experienced that they are less able
to grasp or understand the spiritual matters put forward in the teaching of
faith and virtue; because the understanding of young people, since it is like
a blank slate on which nothing is depicted, can more easily grasp and
understand such things."[97] So they set out to form (*instituere*) them in a
religious *conversatio,* by housing and overseeing them, by guiding them in
studies and in devotions. They saw in them hope for a fresh start.

This was to "convert the youth." Some, or many, among their fellow
citizens objected; hence four tractates on the subject, probably written in
the 1420s (all still unedited), by the then leader among the Devout, Dirk
of Herxen, rector in Zwolle. The christened dared not attack directly the act
of "young people being drawn to Christ," but they disparaged such a conversion operation ("eorum conversione derogant uel non magnipendunt").
Adolescents are too fickle and inconstant to make such a choice, they protested. Moreover, those who have gained experience in the world prove

nobler converts later in the spiritual life. Some conceded that it was good to preserve innocence, but thought it also good to experience the world ("cum possibile sit hominem seruata innocencia experiri secularia"). Dirk retorted that this was "possible but rare." He also imagined, or had heard, a stronger objection, that this whole tack insulted the customary practices of the christened.[98] Dirk answered: they should open their eyes and look round at the state of the christened in their day ("status modernus christianorum"). One whole tractate defended the zeal of those anxious to "rescue" young souls and prepare them before it was too late. Dirk saw "private admonition" and conversation, along with example, as far more effective than preaching or the confessional, and the encouragement of youthful comrades as the most effective tool of all.

The anonymous author of the *Satisfactio nostra,* celebrating the success of the Devout in turning many young boys away from the world, noted too that, supported by copying books, they conversed with these students and thus drew them toward religious life.[99] Earlier Jean Gerson had, in a brief tractate, defended his vision of shaping youth in Paris and then sending them out to transform the world. So too Dirk, in Zwolle, believed this possible not just in Paris, but at any site boasting schools and a large number of youths and effective personal guides (meaning the Devout).[100] The world of the christened, adults hardened in their ways, could hardly be turned round. Custom and conformity proved too powerful. But youth could be guided and molded, as Gerson envisioned it, into "teachers" for the whole of Christendom. In like manner the author of the *Satisfactio nostra* saw the forming of Devout households and the converting of youth as a small *reformatio* in their distant part of the world, a tiny contribution to an effort everyone cried for and no one effected.[101]

CONCLUDING REMARKS

How people came to see or act upon "conversion," within this European society of the christened, depended in good part upon how they perceived custom and conformity: whether within that world they could act safely and satisfactorily as "true Christians," avoid mortal sin, cultivate devotion, secure salvation. For if the whole world appears or claims to be converted, and is not, what are the religiously intense, the converts, to do? And if the power of nature, habit, and hypocrisy is overwhelming, how is their hold to be broken? Those who chose to break with the conforming christened were necessarily extraordinary, whether despised or admired, typed as eccentrics or saints, zealots or the devout. Historical interpreters, it seems to me, find themselves in a hard spot: we can admire the energies, the zeal, the powers of critique and self-critique displayed by the converts, without which this society would have been ever so much more stagnant; and we can empathize too with the christened whose ease with custom and conformity seems normal, even appealing. And we inevitably find ourselves telling the story from one vantage point or the other (often the convert's, self-consciously or no), when a significant part of the energy and the action, even the culture and the religion, springs from the tension between the two.

Converts could attempt to go their own way, find personal solace in God—and many did. Especially in later medieval society, more found their own niche, with varying degrees of acceptance. But the dynamic of conversion around the year 1400 threatened to spill over in uncontainable ways, to unhinge the entire system within and without. Among Observants, those recognized as converts broke with the customary privileges and practices of their comrades, gave up a lifestyle regarded as self-indulgent, tried to enforce the rules without, called for an ever deepened devotion within—and appeared to call the whole institutionalized ideal into question. Others, resentful and suspicious of the professed, seeing them more as the perverted than the converted, tried to make a "contrary turning," to transform entire parishes and ultimately an entire society, as the Lollards proposed (and also the Hussites)—to repudiate "private religion" as privilege and not conversion, to consolidate communities around "poor priests" living off gifts, to instill in all a common upright practice, to disendow the propertied church. Or those less hopeful about change in either the professed or the christened might attempt to create their own separate societies, located between religion and the world, in the form of communal households of converts. Other options, in my view, were probably also animated by this dialectic: that of humanists, for instance, who turned to new forms of piety by way of letters and speech and private sodalities.

Recent historians are not nearly so comfortable as they once were with invoking a generalized "crisis" to explain European society in the later fourteenth and fifteenth centuries, whether to account for social change[102] or to describe its religious ferment. Any simple causal links must fail to satisfy. Here the emphasis has been upon the dynamic of conversion itself, its latent but explosive force, in a society of the christened. Around the year 1400, the intensity of that dynamic accelerated, generating widespread experimentation. The *Imitation of Christ,* compiled by Thomas of Kempen about 1420, captured this mood. It spoke to people's sense of heightened alertness and spiritual need, whence its enormous success. Thomas grew to adulthood in the schools and Devout household of Deventer, absorbed fully the tension of living in the world as one converted (though he eventually made profession as an Observant canon regular), appropriated the impulse to express this in memorable "sayings," and reflected on it again as novice master in his house. In these gathered sayings, he codified the sense that, for a convert in a conforming age, the first care had to be watchfulness over one's self (*cura sui ipsius*), hence the deep and persistent turn inward. This alone could yield "peace" and "quiet" and "solace" of a kind not found in the tempests and disappointments everywhere else. But it meant constant self-examination, ever living on the edge, ever steeling one's self against the easy turn to custom. Though he plainly wrote with the Devout and the religious of his time in mind, he captured an outlook cherished by Observants, cultivated later by Jesuits and by lay parishioners alike, even appropriated by early modern Protestants. What he offered in his proverbial sayings, if I may borrow the phrase, was a powerful means of "self-fashioning," born of converts forging a way for themselves, a private way, through a world overwhelmed by custom and conformity.

NOTES

For probing questions and stimulating conversation, I am indebted to all members of the Davis Seminar in the academic year 1999–2000, a wonderful experience. And for a thoughtful critique of the revised paper, I am specially indebted to Kathryn Kerby-Fulton.

1. *Epistolario di santa Caterina da Siena*, ed. Eugenio Dupré Theseider (Rome, 1940), no. 32, p. 136. Suzanne Noffke, *The Letters of Catherine of Siena*, 2d ed., vol. 1 (Tempe, Ariz., 2000), p. 122, places this letter in the first week of July 1375.

2. *Cosmographiae: De Europa*, c. 28, in *Aeneae Sylvii Piccolomini Opera quae extant Omnia* (Basel; reprint ed., Frankfurt 1967), p. 419. For an introduction to the complex subject of Lithuania's conversion, see Rasa Maseika, "Bargaining for Baptism: Lithuanian Negotiations for Conversion, 1250–1358," in *Varieties of Religious Conversion*, ed. James Muldoon (Gainesville, Tex., 1997), pp. 131–45.

3. Lateran Council IV c. 13 (*Ne nimia*), included in the canon law as *Decretales* 3.36.9, ed. Aemilius Friedberg (Leipzig, 1879), 2:607.

4. For the explicit comparison in law, see my "Religious Profession: From Liturgy to Law," *Viator* 29 (1998): 323–43.

5. "Debeo paenitere? Debeo me convertere? Nonne vides angustias mortis me prementis? . . . O felix paenitentia et conversio matura, quia secura. Qui autem tarde paenitentiae se committit, dubius and incertus erit, quia nescit utrum vere an ficte paeniteat. . . . Propositum bonum sine inchoatione,

voluntas sine operatione, promissa bona sine executione perdiderunt me."
Horologium Sapientiae II.2, ed. Pius Künzle, Spicilegium Friburgense 23
(Freiburg, 1977), pp. 531–32.

6. *The Imitation of Christ: The First English Translation of the 'Imitatio
Christi,'* ed. B .J. H. Biggs, Early English Text Society 309 (Oxford, 1997),
p. 14. This English version, done thirty years or so after the Latin original
while Thomas of Kempen was still alive, renders the Latin nearly word for
word (I.11): "e contrario sepe sentimus ut meliores et puriores in initio
conversionis nos fuisse inueniamus quam post multos annos professionis."
The same usage appears a little later (I.23): "Utinam per unam diem bene
essemus conuersati in hoc mundo! Multi annos computant conuersionis, sed
sepe paruus est fructus emendationis."

7. "Sed in seculo multe sunt occasiones per quas homo trahitur ad uicia
et retrahitur a sancta conversione, ut docet experientia." See Manfred Ger-
wing, *Malogranatum oder der dreifache Weg zur Vollkommenheit* (Munich, 1986),
p. 161 n. 10.

8. Ibid., p. 160 n. 9.

9. Here the technical term is not "convert" but what a convert became,
"religious": "Largo modo dicitur 'religiosus' qui in domo propria sancte et
religiosus uiuet, licit non sit professus. . . . dicitur talis 'religiosus' non
ideo quod astrictus sit alicui regule certe sed respectu uite quam arctio-
rem et sanctiorem ducit quam ceteres seculares, qui omnino seculariter,
idest dissolute, uiuent." Hostiensis, *Summa Aurea* (Venice, 1574), p.
1108.

10. An argument he has developed through a lifetime of work and presented in a rich article: "*Vita regularis sine regula*: Bedeutung, Rechtsstellung
und Selbstverständnis des mittelalterlichen und frühneuzeitlichen Semireli-
giosentums," in *Häresie und vorzeitige Reformation im Spätmittelalter,* ed.
František Šmahel (Munich, 1998), pp. 239–73.

11. I have argued this in "Friar Johannes Nyder on Laypeople Living as
Religious in the World," in *Vita Religiosa im Mittelalter: Festschrift für Kaspar
Elm zum 70. Geburtstag* (Berlin, 1999), pp. 583–615.

12. Duane J. Osheim, "Conversion, *Conversi,* and the Christian Life in
Late Medieval Tuscany," *Speculum* 58 (1983): 368–90.

13. See now Sabine von Heusinger, *Johannes Mulberg OP (gest. 1414): Ein
Leben im Spannungsfeld von Dominikanerobservanz und Beginenstreit* (Berlin, 2000),
with earlier literature, and an edition of Mulberg's *Tractatus contra Beginas et
Beghardos.*

14. In a very large literature, allow me to cite only two representative
volumes, the important synthetic study of Giles Constable, *The Reformation*

of the Twelfth Century (Cambridge, 1996), and the essays gathered in Daniel Bornstein and Roberto Rusconi, eds., *Women and Religion in Medieval and Renaissance Italy* (Chicago, 1996).

15. *Rulman Merswins Buch von den vier Jahren seines anfangenden Lebens,* ed. Philipp Strauch, Altdeutsche Textbibliothek 23 (Halle, 1927), p. 3.

16. *Testamentum* 1, ed. K. Esser, Sources chrétiennes 285 (Paris, 1981), p. 204 (hereafter SC).

17. Lynn Staley, ed., *The Book of Margery Kempe* (Kalamazoo, Mich., 1996), p. 25.

18. Thomas, *Chronica montis sanctae Agnetis* 1, in *Opera omnia,* ed. Michael Joseph Pohl, 7 vols. (Freiburg, 1902–22), 7:336.

19. Richard Rolle, *Le chant d'amour (Melos amoris)* 34, ed. Arnoud, 2 vols., SC 168–69 (Paris, 1971), SC 169:20.

20. This first studied by Jean-Claude Schmitt, *Mort d'une hérésie: L'Eglise et les clercs face aux béguines et aux béghards du Rhin supérieur* (Paris, 1978), and now by Von Heusinger, *Johannes Mulberg.* For the Devout, see the tractate edited by Marcel Haverals, "*Contra detractores monachorum* alias *De utilitate monachorum* van Dirk van Herxen," in *Serta Devota in memoriam Guillelmi Lourdaux* (Louvain, 1992), pp. 241–87.

21. Denis the Carthusian, *De arcta via salutis et mundi contemptu* 24, *Dionysii Carthusiani Opera omnia,* vol. 39 (Tournai, 1910), p. 462.

22. Thomas, *De imitatione Christi* I.1.

23. Catherine, *Epistolario, no.* 33, ed. Dupré Theseider, p. 138.

24. Jacobus, *De septem statibus ecclesie,* in *Fasciculus rerum* (London, 1690), 2.102.

25. Thomas Hohmann, *Henrichs von Langenstein 'Underscheidung der Geister' Lateinisch und Deutsch* (Munich, 1977), pp. 108/110.

26. *Hier beginnen sommige stichtige punten van onsen oelden zusteren,* ed. D. de Man (The Hague, 1919), p. 127.

27. *Melos amoris* 34, 24, ed. Arnoud, SC 169:24, 168:282.

28. See now Thomas Kock, *Das Buchkultur der Devotio moderna* (Frankfurt, 1999), pp. 112–47. For a translation of Grote's complete *propositum,* see my *Devotio Moderna: Basic Writings* (New York, 1988), pp. 65–75.

29. *Rulman Merswins Buch,* p. 7.

30. *Melos amoris* 1, SC 168:100.

31. Ibid., c. 7, SC 168:146.

32. *Imitation of* Christ, II.109, ed. Biggs, p. 53.

33. Ibid., I.10, pp. 12–13.

34. Ibid., III.12, pp. 81–82.

35. Johan Busch, *Liber de origine moderne devotionis* 47, in *Johannes Busch,*

Chronicon Windeshemense und Liber de Reformatione Monasteriorum, ed. Karl Grube (Halle, 1886), p. 373.

36. Thus, representatively for dozens of texts, Denis the Carthusian, *De arcta via salutis ac mundi contemptu* 17, *Opera Omnia* 39:450–51.

37. "All laygen rüffent und sprechent, daz der Hussen ketzery uf erstanden sig von dem, daz die pfaffhait und münch und frowen in clöstern nit reformiert sin. . . . So sprechen erst die layen: Uss münchen und nunnen komt kain gutes, die Hussen verderbent sy denn zu grund." See Johannes Meyer, *Buch der Reformacio,* ed. B. M. Reichert (Leipzig, 1908–09), pp. 62f.

38. See Kaspar Elm, ed., *Reformbemühungen und Observanzbestrebungen im spätmittelalterlichen Ordenswesen* (Berlin, 1989), and his programmatic essay, "Verfall und Erneuerung des Ordenswesens im Spätmittelalter: Forschungen und Forschungsaufgaben," in *Untersuchungen zu Kloster und Stift* (Göttingen 1980), pp. 188–238. Despite a large literature on the Observant movement, little of it, outside Elm's work, integrates the subject into historical and cultural contexts. See now the thoughtful overview offered by Dieter Mertens, "Monastische Reformbewegungen des 15. Jahrhunderts: Ideen—Ziele—Resultate," in *Reform von Kirche und Reich zur Zeit der Konzilien von Konstanz (1414–1418) und Basel (1431–1449),* ed. Ivan Hlaváček and Alexander Patchovsky (Constance, 1996), pp. 157–81.

39. Cited here from Johannes Helmrath, *Das Basler Konzil 1431–1449: Forschungsstand und Probleme* (Cologne, 1987), p. 131 n. 214.

40. There is no proper study or edition of Nyder's work, but see Eugen Hillenbrand, "Die Observantenbewegung in der deutschen Ordensprovinz der Dominikaner," in Elm, *Reformbemühungen,* pp. 222ff.

41. Johannes Nyder, *Formicarius* 1.7, ed. Hans Biedermann (Graz, 1971), p. 25 (reprint of the incunable edition).

42. Bernard Pez, *Bibliotheca ascetica antiquo-nova,* vol. 8 (Regensburg, 1725) 576–77.

43. Denis the Carthusian, *De reformatione claustralium* 16, *Opera omnia* 38:236.

44. This is the subject of a dissertation by James Mixson at the University of Notre Dame, "Professed Proprietors: Religion, Property, and the Origins of the Observant Movement" (2002).

45. A. P. Orbán, ed., *Die Korrespondenz und der* Liber Exhortacionis *des Heinrich von Kalkar,* Analecta Carthusiana 111 (Salzburg, 1984), p. 170.

46. *Seuses Leben,* Prologue, c. 1, ed. Karl Bihlmeyer, in *Heinrich Seuse, Deutsche Schriften* (Stuttgart, 1907), pp. 8, 9, 10.

47. Despite a substantial literature on Suso, there is no single work on how to interpret him as a writer, religious, mystic, and preacher. Good introductions in English now by way of Frank Tobin's Paulist Press translation, *Henry Suso: The Exemplar with Two German Sermons* (Mahway, N.J., 1989), and Jeffrey Hamburger, "Medieval Self-Fashioning: Authorship, Authority, and Autobiography in Suso's *Exemplar,*" in his *The Visual and the Visionary: Art and Female Spirituality in Late Medieval Germany* (New York, 1998), pp. 233–77.

48. *Seuses Leben,* c. 3, p. 13.

49. Thus, representatively, Denis the Carthusian, *De reformatione claustralium* 6, *Opera omnia* 38:221.

50. ". . . regulam beati Francisci secundum declarationes apostolicas ad literam cupiunt et aspirant observare." P. Oliger, "De relatione inter Observantium querimonias constantienses (1415) et Ubertini Casalensis quoddam scriptum," *Archivum Franciscanum Historicum* 9 (1916) 38.

51. Friar John began thus, supposedly to set their consciences at rest, probably alluding to anxiety and scrupulosity on issues of observance: "In primis ad omnem sororum ambiguitatem tollendam de mentibus et conscientiis earumdem, noueritis non obligari sorores ad alia consilia evangelica quam ad ea que in regula exprimuntur preceptorie, inhibitorie, uel aequipollenter." D. van Adrichem, "Explicatio primae regulae s. Clarae auctore s. Ioanne Capistranensi (1445)," *Archivum Historicum Franciscanum* 22 (1929): 344.

52. No good modern study, but a representative document presented by R. de Keyser-Paul Trio, "De *inclusio* van Melle uit 1447: Beidrage tot de insluiting van Windesheimse kloosters," in *Serta Devota,* pp. 189–202.

53. ". . . magis destruunt eos, quia indiscrete procedunt et ab exteriori rigore corporalique observantia sumunt exordium." Denis the Carthusian, *De reformatione claustralium* 21, *Opera omnia* 38:242.

54. Ibid., 6–7, 38:221–23.

55. *Imitatio Christi,* I.3.

56. For the likely role of Observants and related groups in the spread of fifteenth-century manuscripts and the coming of print, see Richard and Mary Rouse, "Backgrounds to Print: Aspects of the Manuscript Book in Northern Europe of the Fifteenth Century," in their *Authentic Witnesses* (Notre Dame), pp. 449–66.

57. Thomas, *De disciplina claustralium* 1, 3, L. M. J. Delaissé, *Le manuscrit autographe de Thomas à Jenous et 'L'imitation de Jésus-Christ'* (Brussels, 1956) pp. 407, 418–19.

58. ". . . scrivo a voi e racomandomivi, con desiderio di vedervi sempre osservatore de' santi comandamenti di Dio, senza e' quali neuna creatura

può avere in sé la vita della gratia, e non è neuno che per gentilezza nè per ricchezza nè signoria nè per prosperità nè grandezza si possa ritrare nè scusare che non sia servo, a servire 'e ad osservare questi dolci e santi comandamenti, e' quali sono dati a noi dalla prima e dolce verità, el quale fu regola e via nostra, e così disse egli: 'Io so' via e verità e vita.' O reverendo padre, reguardate al nostro doce Salvatore, che fu datore della legge, che perfettamente la volse ossservare in sé!" *Epistolario,* no. 43, ed. Dupré Theseider, p. 172.

59. Mariarosa Cortesi, ed., *Laurentii Valle De professione Religiosorum* (Padua, 1986), pp. 18–19. The introduction to this edition is exceptionally good on contextual matters.

60. Ibid., pp. 45–46.

61. Ibid., pp. 51–54.

62. "Et enim omnis ratio voti, omnis indictio ieiunii, omne iusiurandum, omnis denique lex (est autem professio lex quedam), propter metum inventa est, idest ut apertius loquar, propter malos. Et tu te magnanimitatis et tolerantie iactas!" Ibid., p. 62.

63. "Ego sic sentio omnes qui christianam religionem servant esse religiosos, nec recte se professos esse solos religiosos dicere, cum alii tales sint et quidem non minus quam ipsi." From Valla's "defense," quoted by Cortesi in her introduction, p. 1.

64. Eamon Duffey, *The Stripping of the Altars* (New Haven, Conn., 1992).

65. There is an ever-expanding literature on Wycliffe and the Lollards, with much differentiating of distinct threads in the movement and many scholarly disputes. The basic work remains Anne Hudson's *The Premature Reformation* (Oxford, 1988). See now, with additional literature, David Aers and Lynn Staley, *The Powers of the Holy: Religion, Politics, and Gender in Late Medieval English Culture* (University Park, Pa., 1996).

66. *Twelve Conclusions,* in *Selections from English Wycliffite Writings,* ed. Anne Hudson, (Cambridge, 1978), p. 24.

67. "The Lollard Disendowment Bill," ibid., p. 137.

68. "And thanne [in the days of the early church] was the puple as the preestis ful feruent in the loue of God and keping of his lawe, where now as the puple so the prestis ben fallun into obstynat and custromable biekiiig of the comaundementis of God. . . . so now cristen ypocritis, defoulid or infect with the sourdow of fariseis that is ypocrisie . . . boosten of her bodily baptym, not chargynge the baptym of soule from al unclennesse." Anne Hudson, ed., *Two Wycliffite Texts* (Oxford, 1993), pp. 6–7.

69. "But now whom shal a man caste out, or from whom shal a man hide him? For alle ben frendis and alle ben enemyes, alle nedeful and alle aduersaries, alle of houshoold and noon pesible, alle neigheboris and alle seken

that that is hers, mynystris of Crist and seruen antecrist. Woo to this generacioun. . . ." Ibid.

70. Ibid., p. 10.

71. Ibid., p. 11.

72. Ibid.

73. Pamela Gradon and Anne Hudson, *English Wycliffite Sermons,* 5 vols. (Oxford, 1983–99), 4:121.

74. Sermon 36, ed. Gradon and Hudson, 1:374. Or Sermon 40: "As men of thes foure sectis that puttyn bihynde Cristis lawe, and takun hem a newe patroun and newe reule withoute Crist: thes men be ypocritis that Crist hatith most of alle." Ibid., p. 644.

75. Sermon 123, ibid., 2:342.

76. William Thorpe, in Hudson, *Two Wycliffite Texts,* pp. 26–28.

77. For important new work on the late medieval parish, see, representatively, with literature, Katherine French, *The People of the Parish: Community Life in a Late Medieval English Diocese* (Philadelphia, 2001).

78. ". . . sicut est religio privata claustralis perfectorum, sic est vel potest esse religio privata secularis sive exclaustralis perfectorum. Et a pari est vel potest esse religio privata, tam claustralis quam exclaustralis imperfectorum." Wycliffe, *De religione privata* I.8, in *John Wiclif's Polemical Works in Latin,* ed. Rudolf Buddensieg (London, 1883), pp. 515, 516.

79. Wycliffe, *De ordinatione fratrum* 3, ed. Buddensieg, pp. 95–96.

80. Ibid., p. 96.

81. Wycliffe, *De oratione et ecclesiae purgatione* 5, ed. Buddensieg, pp. 352–53, where similar language is repeated several times.

82. "Eciam, secundum meum uidere, non auderem vobis consulere quod intraretis religionem. . . . Desiderium meum est, secundum cor meum (forte fatuum), ut maneatis in mundo et non sitis de mundo, quia odibit uos mundus, et multi nomine religiosi, quia de mundo sunt et sua querent, et uos odient." Geert Grote, *Epistola,* ed. W. Mulder (Antwerp, 1933), pp. 229–30.

83. This little tractate is preserved only in Emmerich, Stadtarchiv, MS 13. I am editing it.

84. Ibid.

85. "Cum enim persuasum habeatur, ut qui a uiciis in quibus laborat human fragilitas—ne dicam malicia horum temporum—abstinere uoluerit, fugiat frequencias hominum indisciplinate uiuencium, et abstractam pocius eligat uitam, proprie infirmitatis conscius, cum talis quisque efficiatur qualium societate perfruitur." Ibid.

86. "Religio enim christiana, que prior et maior est omnium religionum, approbatissima est, utputa a Christo summo legislatore instituta et approbata

et a fidelibus deinceps observata, nec indigens aliqua approbatione sedis apostolice. . . . Ad quam obseruanciam conciliorum Christi non requiritur quod superadditur alia religio. . . ." Ibid. The Devout drew upon a position worked out at Constance in their behalf by Jean Gerson; see *Oeuvres complètes,* ed. P. Glorieux, vol. 10 (Paris, 1973), pp. 69–72. Obviously this has striking parallels with Wycliffe's position as well, which scholars have not investigated in detail.

87. Here I draw upon the results of my lengthy study, "Devout Communities and Inquisitorial Orders."

88. For the novel institutional dimensions of this communal life, see my "Managing the Common Life: The Brothers at Deventer and the Codex of the Household (The Hague, MS KB 70 H 75)," in *Schriftlichkeit und Lebenspraxis im Mittelalter,* ed. Hagen Keller, Christel Meier, and Thomas Scharff (Munich, 1999), pp. 111–69.

89. *Imitation of Christ,* I.19, I.20, II.1, I.12, ed. Biggs, pp. 23–27, 40–41, 15.

90. *Vita Egberti* 1 (I am editing this text). See Gerhard Dumbar, *Analecta seu vetera aliquot scripta inedita* (Deventer, 1719), pp. 162–63.

91. See my "The Sayings of the Fathers: An Inside Look at the New Devout in Deventer," in *Continuity and Change: The Harvest of Late Medieval and Reformation History. Essays Presented to Heiko A. Oberman on his 70th Birthday,* ed. Robert J. Bast and Andrew Colin Gow (Leiden, 2000), pp. 279–302, with "A Working Edition of the *Dicta patrum,*" pp. 303–20.

92. "In istis duobus cotidie te exerce, scilicet, quod memoria semper sit occupata sacra scriptura et mens erecta et intenta amori dei et proximi. . . . Semper sis uigilans circa temptationes et motus passionum. . . . Nunquam sis otiosus, sed sancta precipue occupatione implicitus, dirigendo affectiones tuas et omnes operationes ad Deum." There are two versions of "sayings" attributed to Florens Radewijns (d. 1400), first rector of the Brothers' house in Deventer. Thomas of Kempen compiled the "tamer" version, a kind of appendix in his *Dialogus noviciorum* III, ed. Pohl, *Opera Omnia* (Freiburg, 1922) pp. 198, 207.

93. Ibid., p. 208.

94. *Imitation of Christ,* I.6, II.1, ed. Biggs, pp. 10, 40–43.

95. *Dialogus noviciorum III,* ed. Pohl, pp. 201–2. Compare: "Bonus discipulus, quamtumcumque potest, diligat et custodiat cameram suam. Et si contigerit aliquando ipsum abesse, tamen cor suum sit continue in ea, et festinet quantum ualet ad eam."

96. *Imitation of Christ,* I.11, II.5, ed. Biggs.

97. Dirk of Herxen, "De laudibili studio eorum qui nituntur instituere iuuenes in uita" (unedited; I have an edition in progress). See, for orienta-

tion, Georgette Epiney-Burgard, "Les idées pédagogiques de Dirc van Herxen," in *Serta devota in memoriam Guillelmi Lourdaux,* vol. 1 (Louvain, 1992), pp. 295–304.

98. Ibid.

99. ". . . ubi propter exuberanciam uictualium crebriora sunt studia que dicuntur particularia et copiosior confluxus scolarium, per presbiteros et clericos . . . cernere est negocium dei actitari. Nam cum in opere scripture diatim se exerceant ut uictui neccesaria conquirant . . . bene uacat eis familiariter ipsos scolares alloqui cum incitamento, ut a lubrico carnis se abstineant, latas huius mundi uias deuitent, et semitas iusticie et seruitutuis dei apprehendant." *Satisfactio nostra.*

100. For Gerson's *De parvulis ad Christum trahendis* and *Pro pueris ecclesiae Parisiensis* (as yet, little studied), see *Oeuvres complètes,* vol. 9 (Paris, 1973), p. 669–89.

101. *Satisfactio nostra.*

102. See now especially Howard Kaminsky, "From Lateness to Waning to Crisis: The Burden of the Later Middle Ages," *Journal of Early Modern History* 4 (2000): 85–125; and Peter Schuster, "Die Krise des Spätmittelalters: Zur Evidenz einer sozial- und wirtschaftsgeschichtlichen Paradigmas in der Geschichtsschreibung des 20. Jahrhunderts," *Historische Zeitschrift* 269 (1999): 19–55, partly anticipated by the essays in Ferdinand Seibt and Winfried Eberhard, eds., *Europa 1400: Die Krise des Spätmittelalters* (Stuttgart, 1984).

3

"TO THE POINT OF SHEDDING YOUR BLOOD"

THE BIBLE, COMMUNITIES OF FAITH, AND MARTYRS' RESISTANCE TO CONVERSION IN THE REFORMATION ERA

BRAD S. GREGORY

In your struggle against sin you have not yet resisted to the point of shedding your blood.
—*Hebrews 12:4*

The resistance to conversion finds its limit in martyrdom. Nothing bespeaks more dramatically the refusal to adopt different religious beliefs, practices, and values than the willingness to die for those that one currently embraces. Christians under Roman rule were killed for spurning pagan deities; medieval Jews suffered death rather than accept a forcibly imposed Christianity. In sixteenth-century Europe, Western Christendom itself comprised an extensive arena for martyrdom, in which the judicial executions of Protestants, Roman Catholics, and Anabaptists as either heretics or religious traitors accounted for the deaths of some five thousand people.[1] In this essay I will examine three of these execution victims, one from each of these traditions. One of these, Thomas More, is probably the most famous Christian martyr of the sixteenth century. The other two, Jacob Hutter and Pierre Brully, are for the most part known only to specialists. This essay explores the ground for and character of their resistance to conversion, based on their own writings. Different and incompatible claims to true doctrine separated Catholics, Protestants, and Anabaptists from one another, and further subdivided Protestants and Anabaptists among themselves. Nevertheless, Christian martyrs in the Reformation era shared a biblical hermeneutic—a way of reading and applying Scripture to their particular circumstances—and were embedded in their respective communities of belief.[2] My recent book, *Salvation at Stake*, analyzes Christian martyrdom in early modern Europe as a comparative, cross-confessional whole.[3] This paper treats three martyrs in more detail than was possible in the full-length study, with particular reference to their resistance to conversion. Such an exploration will permit the questioning of certain assumptions common in recent scholarship on early modern Christianity, and indeed on religion in general. Before analyzing the writings of our three protagonists, however, we need to know something about the respective circumstances of their resistance.

Jacob Hutter was an Austrian hatmaker, a native of the Puster valley in the South Tirol born around 1500, who from 1528–29 until his execution in 1536 was the most important Anabaptist leader in Austria and Moravia.[4] The South Tirol lay within the jurisdiction of the diocese of Brixen and was subject to the temporal authority of Ferdinand I, the Habsburg king of Bohemia and Hungary. He assumed the crown in August 1526, just after the waves of central European peasant revolts were crushed. Rattled by the insurrection and mindful of his duty to protect Catholic institutions and teachings, Ferdinand issued a series of severe anti-heresy measures beginning in August 1527.[5] Accordingly, Hutter's conversion and his entire career as an Anabaptist leader occurred under the continuous threat of capital punishment. Apprehensions and executions of co-religionists punctuated his years as a "servant of the Word." As early as mid-1529 Habsburg authorities in Innsbruck identified him as the most important Anabaptist leader in western Austria.[6] Despite the variegated penalties stipulated by the royal edicts, there is little question that as a leader he faced certain execution in the event of capture. Indeed, this constant danger led him soon after his conversion to seek refuge among feudal nobles in Moravia, who traditionally had thwarted Habsburg overlordship. At Austerlitz in 1529 Hutter and his colleague, Christoph Schützinger, reached an agreement to join with a like-minded group of nonresistant Anabaptists who practiced community of goods. Beginning in 1530, Hutter organized dangerous treks of refugee Anabaptists from the South Tirol to Austerlitz, then after the spring of 1531 to nearby Auspitz, where his followers moved after the first of two significant schisms within the community. The second split, in 1533, was followed by another collective relocation, this time to Schakowitz, which also proved to be precarious. Between 1529 and 1535, Hutter himself shuttled between the beleaguered South Tirolese Anabaptists and the repeatedly uprooted community in Moravia. In July 1535, with the intensification of imperial efforts to capture him, he returned to the Puster valley for what would be the final time. Apprehended on 1 December 1535, Hutter was taken to Brixen, then to Innsbruck, where after several rounds of interrogation and torture, he was publicly burned in the city square in mid-March 1536. Before he was captured, however, Hutter wrote letters to absent followers during his back-and-forth travels: seven epistles survive, including four written between late July and late November 1535, in addition to an eighth letter sent to Johan Kuna of Kunstadt, the governor of Moravia, in the spring of 1535. These letters were preserved and copied in sixteenth-century Hutterite codices after his death, from which they were edited and published in the twentieth century.[7]

Thomas More's resistance assumed an altogether different trajectory, the context of which is well known.[8] An erudite friend of Erasmus and other humanist scholars, the author of *Utopia* as well as numerous works attacking heresy, More capped a brilliant career as a London lawyer, a royal advisor, and a diplomat when Henry VIII named him the lord chancellor of England in late October 1529, a position he held until he resigned it in May 1532. Yet less than two years after his resignation More was imprisoned, then in 1535 executed as a traitor for his refusal to swear the oath that acknowledged Henry VIII to be "the only supreme head in earth of the Church of England."[9] This astounding reversal of fortune, a fall from the kingdom's highest civil office to beheading for treason, stemmed from Henry's inability to secure a papal dispensation annulling his marriage to Katharine of Aragon and permitting him to wed Anne Boleyn. This impasse precipitated the undoing of England's ecclesiastical allegiance to Rome. However widespread was sympathy for the spurned queen, loyalty to the king proved stronger, especially when it was backed by the threat of capital punishment for treason. More was the only layman among a handful of men who, in 1534 and 1535, persisted in their refusal to take the Oaths of Succession and/or Supremacy. Famously, More declined to give the reason for his refusal lest he incriminate himself, but it is clear from correspondence with Thomas Cromwell, as well as from his trial, that his reticence was due to the implicit denial of papal supremacy that taking the English oath would have entailed.[10] As he sat in the Tower of London between April 1534 and his death on 6 July 1535, More annotated his psalter and book of hours and wrote two lengthy treatises, *A Dialogue of Comfort against Tribulation* and *De tristitia Christi,* as well as thirteen surviving letters and several prayers.[11] These sources permit us significant access to the roots of his resistance to the king's demands.

Pierre Brully's experience prior to his execution differed yet again from that of Hutter or More.[12] The only clergyman among the three, Brully had been a Dominican in Metz before he became a Reformed Protestant and left the order in 1540 or 1541. He proceeded to Strasbourg, where John Calvin, exiled from Geneva in 1538, had been learning from Martin Bucer the delicate art of successful city reformation.[13] As a francophone minister in a Germanic town, Brully lived with Calvin before the latter's return to Geneva, then succeeded him as pastor to the growing number of French and Wallonian refugees in Strasbourg. By early 1544, however, Valérand Poullain was imploring Calvin on behalf of the faithful in Tournai and Valenciennes to send them someone to conduct worship, preach, and serve their pastoral needs, as well as to ward off the influence of Anabaptists and "libertines" in the region. So at Bucer's behest, disguised as a merchant, Brully set out with a party from the safety of Strasbourg for Tournai in September 1544. In so doing he entered lands subject to the anti-heresy placards which the emperor Charles V had issued repeatedly since 1521, edicts which had grown especially severe after the Anabaptist Kingdom of Münster in 1534–35.[14] After ministering discreetly to the Reformed Protestants in Tournai, Brully spent time with the fledgling Protestant communities in other Wallonian towns, including Valenciennes, Douai, Arras, and Lille, before he returned to Tournai in late October. Magistrates in the town had got wind of his presence and offered a reward for his capture, which occurred on the night of 3 November 1544, and was followed by the arrest of several co-religionists. Attempts by the magistrates of Strasbourg to intervene on his behalf were rebuffed, in part by the emperor himself, and Brully was tried for violating the imperial placards. Repeatedly interrogated and tortured in an effort to make him disclose information about other Protestants in Wallonia, he refused all attempts to make him recant his beliefs. In February 1545, shortly before his execution, he wrote three letters (two to fellow Protestants and another to his wife) as well as an account of his interrogations that is essentially a Calvinist confession of faith. Brully was burned in the marketplace in Tournai on 19 February 1545. Jean Crespin, the future Protestant martyrologist and printer whom Brully might well have met in Arras, included Brully's prison writings in his martyrology from the first edition (1554) onward.[15]

Three men, three incompatible views of Christian truth, three different paths of resistance that led to execution: Hutter's entire Anabaptist existence was precarious, More fell from the pinnacle of high politics to the ignominy of treason charges, and Brully left a Protestant haven to minister in hostile territory. Does it make sense to characterize the actions of all three as "resistance to conversion"? Hutter and Brully, it might be argued, were not so much resisting attempts at conversion to Catholicism as they were resisting attempts by Catholic secular authorities to force them into outward religious conformity. After they were captured, repeated attempts to secure their recantations and to "convert" them hardly mattered, one might say, since as heretical leaders they faced virtually certain death whether they abjured their views or not. Moreover, it might seem strange to call More's actions an example of resistance to conversion. Doing so would

imply that the large-scale swearing of the Oaths of Succession and Supremacy constituted not simply an act of political obedience to their king, but
rather a mass conversion of the English people to a different religion. Is this
what happened in England in the mid-1530s?

Once Hutter had converted to Anabaptism and Brully to Reformed Protestantism, their persistence before imprisonment is better viewed as resistance to *re*conversion than as resistance to conversion. As among early
Christians in the Roman Empire who sought to avoid relapse into paganism, the conversion that mattered to them had already occurred. It remained only to resist the pressures to reconvert—-including those measures
applied once they were captured. Even if we assume that as heretical leaders
their deaths were a foregone conclusion, however, it would be a serious
interpretive error to underplay their unflinching resistance. As virtually
all sixteenth-century Christians believed in some manner and to one degree
or another, right doctrine was a prerequisite for the possibility of eternal
salvation. According to Protestants and Anabaptists, this prospect would be
lost were they to recant and return to the papist errors implied even in
external conformity, a compliance that they regarded as rank idolatry. On
the other side, the same concern for true doctrine made the imperative to
secure the abjurations a pastoral duty for the Catholic clergy who interrogated heretics, whatever propaganda value also attached to recantations:
they might yet save the stubborn for eternity even if they could not prevent
their deaths.

My impression is that most historians today tend to construe resistance
in modern political (in the broad sense) terms, seeking to discern the techniques and strategies that were employed to gain or preserve rights or
influence, to fend off threats to identity or interests. The success of resistance is measured in terms of whether power relations budged, cultural
identities were sustained, social practices changed, self-determination was
promoted. Depending upon the questions one asks this is fine as far as it
goes, but it fails to capture all past criteria of successful resistance—in this
case, most notably, the criteria of the martyrs themselves. If one's horizon
extended beyond death, for example, as it did for early modern Christians,
then the nature and implications of resistance will appear very differently,
and modern secular categories of analysis will fail to do justice to past
experience. Precisely when Hutter and Brully faced certain death, their
resistance to reconversion mattered most. Indeed, any and all previous resistance paled by comparison to their perseverance then and there.

The character of More's resistance was different: he simply persisted in
the religion he had known all his life. In contrast to English contemporaries
who accepted the royal supremacy, More and the other Henrician Catholic

martyrs stand out because they *did* regard the swearing of the oath as a religious conversion disguised as an act of political obedience. To acknowledge Henry's authority over the English church was not like Augustine's epiphany in the garden alongside Alypius, not like Paul's conversion en route to Damascus, but it was no less real for being so apparently innocuous. According to More, the supremacy denied Christ because it denied the authority of his vicar, his church, and his tradition, and in so doing jeopardized in principle all the teachings and practices of true Christianity, notwithstanding the king's hostility to Protestantism. What would happen should a Protestant become the sovereign? Implicitly, English Catholics were being told to change the basis for what they believed, to turn from an implicit acknowledgment to the explicit disavowal of papal authority within the "common corps of Christendom."[16] Hence More's refusal to accept this mandate is rightly understood as a resistance to conversion. No less than Hutter and Brully, More believed that without persistence in resistance he would forfeit hope of heaven.

Let us now turn to the writings of these three men in order to discern the basis for and character of their resistance to conversion. Their writings make clear that this resistance was grounded in religious belief: that is, minimally, in a trust and conviction that a particular view of reality was true. If we bear this in mind, their resistance through death makes perfect sense; if not, it becomes opaque if not unintelligible. Belief supported the ways in which all three men, regardless of their differences concerning the content of Christian truth, understood and used the Bible in their writings. They viewed Scripture as the authoritative expression of God's will, laced with multiple admonitions directly relevant to their circumstances, and with eternal ramifications. Logically distinct but experientially related to this, their resistance was social in nature, because each man stood firm not for his own individual view of Christian truth, but rather for convictions shared with others in a community of faith. Accordingly, others encouraged these martyrs to persist, and the martyrs maintained links to fellow believers despite persecution or imprisonment. The martyrs' letters both presupposed and reinforced already existing social relationships.

Whether he was writing from the mountains of Austria or from Moravia, Jacob Hutter repeatedly expressed deep care and concern for fellow Anabaptists in his letters. Indeed, every one of his letters is laced with phrases redolent of a tight social solidarity, forged through the self-selecting radicalism of Anabaptist separatist commitment. "I know that all the time you long for us, as we do also for you," he stated near the outset of a letter from the South Tirol to the Anabaptists in Moravia in 1530. Writing from Moravia three years later, he exclaimed, "we greet you firmly and deeply

from our hearts many thousand times, in genuinely holy and godly, broth-
erly, burning love with the holy and heavenly kiss of our Lord Jesus Christ."[17]
Many times he expressed compassion for the brothers and sisters, likening
himself, for instance, to "a devoted father anxious about his most deeply
beloved children (*Herzallerliebsten*) who are far away from him and in great
distress."[18] In five letters he greeted particular members of the community
by name and/or conveyed greetings from individual Anabaptists with him.
Separation strained solidarity, so Hutter wrote, "I embrace you with the
arms of my heart and soul," though his affection could not satisfy his desire
for contact: "O, you devout, Christian hearts, that God might grant me a
single day or a single hour among you, that my voice might gratify, refresh,
and restore you in the Lord."[19] Such expressions flow effortlessly in Hutter's
prose; their repetition reflects the inextricably social nature of Hutterite
religiosity. Messengers carried letters back and forth, extending lifelines of
news and tenderness across the three hundred miles between the Tirolean
mountains and the Moravian towns. Clearly, Hutter's resistance to reconversion was not that of a heroic individualist.

Reciprocally, Hutter thanked others from the community for their encouragement and consolation. Writing from Auspitz in November 1533,
for example, he told Anabaptists in the Etsch valley that "we cannot marvel
enough nor sufficiently commend and praise the Lord for all the messages
and letters, plus all the grace-filled (*gnadenreiche*) and loving, friendly and
comforting greetings and warnings, which you sent us both by writing and
by word of mouth. These I disclosed and read aloud with the greatest
diligence before the entire community of God."[20] Back in the South Tirol in
the summer of 1535, Hutter told the "beloved brothers and children of the
living God" in Moravia that "we are heartily and well comforted by your
message," which the Austrian brothers and sisters had "diligently and faithfully considered, again and again, with the greatest earnestness."[21] More
than once, drawing on Paul's comment in 2 Cor. 3:2, Hutter referred to a
messenger who brought word of beleaguered believers as a "living letter"
(*lebendiger Brief*), a phrase that captures the community's textually mediated
social life.[22]

The Bible was the text that grounded this community. The conviction of
its truth as God's word, of its foundational authority for Anabaptist belief
and action, is implied on every page of every letter that Hutter wrote. "I
have often said and pointed out to you," he stated in his last surviving
letter, "that you should listen to and seize upon and write the word of God
in your hearts with the greatest diligence." That way, should any of them be
separated from one another "through imprisonment, tribulation, or death,
or by some other means," they would be able to draw "from the treasure of

their hearts what they had heard and gathered together and received from God."[23] Hutter was keenly aware that much might be heard, gathered, received, and internalized from Scripture when it came to resisting reconversion and persisting in God's truth.

Hutter's 1534 letter to fellow believers imprisoned in Hohenwart, in Lower Austria not far from the Moravian border, contains dozens of densely packed biblical passages applied directly to their circumstances. It is worth quoting at length to convey the way in which Hutter piled verses one upon the other:

> We should rightly remember if we meet with such things [as persecution and tribulation] for the sake of truth, that we are not therefore God's enemies but rather his friends and dear children, as the Lord himself says, "I discipline those whom I love" [Prov. 3:12, Rev. 3:19], and "every son whom the Father receives he chastises" [Heb. 12:6]. . . . "Blessed are you when the crowd or people insult you on my account, rejoice and be glad, for your reward will be great in heaven. For in the same way they persecuted the holy prophets who came before you" [Matt. 5:11–12], which is so often said, as if Christ intended to say (als wollte Christus sprechen): In this way you shall clearly note and recognize that you are made holy and very dear and pleasing to God, for he has made known and shown you to be among those who love him. Therefore Christ says about his own only that they will be crucified, persecuted, chastised, reviled, killed, and murdered, robbed, driven out, captured, and tortured [cf. John 16:33, Matt. 10:17–22]. Thus holy Paul says, "through much suffering and tribulation must we enter the Kingdom of God" [Acts 14:22], and again he says, "if we are fellow sufferers, we shall also be fellow heirs; if we endure with Christ, we shall also rule or reign with him" [Rom. 8:17], yet once more he says, "to you alone it has been granted not only to believe in Christ but also to suffer with him and to fight the same fight that you have seen in me" [Phil. 1:29–30].[24]

Fundamentally, the letter is an applied biblical concordance with interspersed glosses by Hutter. Unequivocally it urges resistance to reconversion, if necessary through death, which would in any case be the gateway to eternal life. Both in this letter and in others, Hutter invoked perhaps the single most pointed verse for Christians facing possible torture and death, 1 Cor. 10:13: "God is faithful, and he will not let you be tested beyond your strength, but with the testing he will also provide the way out so that you may be able to endure it."[25] The promise of heaven would enable Anabaptists to endure anything for the truth's sake, in the tradition of the persecuted prophets and apostles.[26] The imperative to persevere could hardly have been clearer, considering that one who holds firm "is worth more according to God and before God (*gilt mehr bei Gott und vor Gott*) than many hundreds of thousands of godless and unfaithful men. . . . Yes, let us see and follow such a man in the Lord."[27] Hutter combined the biblical admonition to persist with his love for members of the community, declaring in several letters his willingness to die for them if God so willed it. "I thank and praise God for entirely taking fear away from me (*die Furcht gar treulich von mir aufgehoben*); I trust in my God that fear can never harm me," he wrote. "I have entirely and completely delivered, surrendered, and offered my body and my life to the Lord, and with my whole heart am willing to suffer and die for the sake of the Lord and his truth."[28]

It was otherwise with Thomas More. In contrast to Hutter's bold willingness to die, More distinguished between eager and timid martyrs and placed himself clearly in the latter camp. The contrast comprises a central theme in *De tristitia Christi,* More's heavily revised, nuanced exegetical reflection on the agony of Christ in Gethsemane before his apprehension.[29] According to More, Jesus too was hesitant rather than courageous, notwithstanding his divinity, and for good reason. The Gospels record his grief, his fear, his desire to "let this cup pass," all noted for the sake of the many persecuted Christians who afterwards would find themselves similarly stricken with fear. Hence Jesus, "having made himself weak for the sake of the weak, he might take care of other weak ones by means of his own weakness."[30] The passages that More flagged and glossed in his psalter, too, are consistently those of someone seeking strength in troubled times. In the margin next to Ps. 23:4, for example—"For even if I walk in the midst of the shadow of death, I will fear no evil, for you are with me"—he wrote "fiducia trib[ulatione]," "confidence in tribulation."[31] Similarly, he scrawled "in tribulatione magna" next to Ps. 69:1–2: "Save me, God, for the waters have come up to my neck. I have sunk into the deep mire, and there is no support."[32] And More persistently meditated on Christ's Passion, a practice central to late medieval devotion, in part to resist the fear of bodily pain and death that he knew lay in his path. As the nephew Vincent complained to his uncle Antony in More's *Dialogue of Comfort,* "the pinch is in the pain," and "all the wisdom in this world, can never so master pain, but that pain will be painful [in] spite of all the wit in this world." Antony concedes the point, yet in the work's final chapter counsels meditation on the "incomparable kindness" of Christ in his Passion, "that we should find our self not only content, but also glad and desirous to suffer death for his sake, that so marvelously lovingly letted not to sustain so far passing painful death for ours."[33]

God's mercy notwithstanding, More was well aware that the Bible he knew so intimately did not have separate commands for the hearty and the fearful. At the end of his holograph of *De tristitia Christi* are twenty-eight pages of biblical verses about the endurance of suffering and persecution, clearly written at different times, some of which he glossed.[34] His resistance to Henry's demands is linked to Scripture no less explicitly than is Hutter's resistance to Ferdinand's edicts. One of the most frequently repeated passages in his *Dialogue of Comfort* is Matt. 10:32–33: "Everyone therefore who acknowledges me before others, I also will acknowledge before my Father in heaven; but whoever denies me before others, I also will deny before my Father in heaven."[35] According to More, the denial of Christ's vicar implicit in the Oath of Supremacy was at once a denial of Christ himself. The equally explicit parallel verse of Matt. 10:28/Luke 12:4–5 recurs in More's prison treatises and correspondence: "Do not fear those who kill the body but cannot kill the soul; rather fear him who can destroy both soul and body in hell."[36] Like Hutter, who also quoted Matt. 10:32–33, More drew strength from 1 Cor. 10:13, Paul's dictum that God would not let one be tempted beyond one's strength, and would provide a way out.[37] More's reliance on Scripture in all his Tower writings is extensive, pervasive, and unmistakably tailored to his concrete circumstances. The psalter he annotated in the Tower is of course the Latin Vulgate version of the Book of Psalms; the *De tristitia Christi* is a deeply autobiographical commentary on precisely that part of the New Testament most relevant to More's anxiety about death; and the *Dialogue of Comfort* contains almost five hundred specific quotations from and references to Scripture, nearly two per page.[38] Since he was preparing to die for God's truth, it made perfect sense to rely on God's word.

At first sight, More's social isolation seems to have set him apart from Hutter no less than his fear of martyrdom is to be distinguished from the Anabaptist leader's alacrity. Without question More appreciated the sociability of friendship, a theme that runs throughout his life and letters. Yet his family members understood neither his refusal of the oath nor his unwillingness to disclose the reason for his actions. They did not encourage him to hold fast, nor did he benefit from a strong stream of support from fellow Catholics. To the contrary, More flagged the margin of Ps. 38:11: "My friends and those near me draw away and stand back from me because of my affliction, and my neighbors stand far away from me."[39] By December 1534, the family's financial distress drove More's wife Alice to implore Henry VIII for relief and to request her husband's release,[40] a far cry from spousal approval of his course of action. Meanwhile his daughter Margaret, permitted to visit her father, repeatedly urged him to take the oath, which so many other learned and good men (as More himself admitted) had done. More reiterated the necessity of standing by his conscience lest he jeopardize his soul, just as they would have to stand by theirs. He jested with Margaret about whether "mother Eve" sought "to offer father Adam the apple yet once again."[41]

Yet it would be overreaching simply to contrast Hutter's social support with More's social isolation. More was a member of multiple communities, of which his family, however dear to him, was only one.[42] Friendship and familial support as such could not outweigh his place in the Body of Christ, the church. More's salvation depended on sustained membership in the latter community, not on acquiescence to personal social pressures. And so More stayed put in "the general council of Christendom," despite the familial exhortations and political inducements from within "the council of one realm."[43] At the same time, he was not entirely bereft of epistolary contact in the Tower. He exchanged letters with the imprisoned bishop of Rochester, John Fisher, who described them ten days before his own execution as "exhortations to patience, and prayers to God for grace."[44] To Antonio Bonvisi, a friend who had sent him gifts in prison, More wrote a letter praising "the sweetness of this marvelous friendship of yours," "the felicity of so faithful and constant friendship in the storms of fortune."[45] And despite her efforts to change his mind and bring him home, Margaret's letters and presence delighted him. He gushed his appreciation: "Your daughterly loving letter, my dearly beloved child, was and is, I faithfully assure you, much more inward comfort unto me than my pen can well express [to] you."[46] In his final letter, written to Margaret the day before his execution, he told her frankly, "I never liked your manner toward me better than when you kissed me last, for I love when daughterly love and dear charity hath no leisure to look to worldly courtesy."[47] So More was not forgotten or abandoned even by his family, regardless of how much he baffled or frustrated them.

Pierre Brully fared rather better than More in garnering the support of family and fellow believers. Shortly after 4 February 1545, Brully wrote the first of two surviving letters to persecuted co-religionists in Wallonian towns, three months after his apprehension.[48] The lapse of time, he told them, derived not from a lack of desire to write, but from a previous lack of pen and ink.[49] There seems little question that during Brully's imprisonment in Tournai he maintained his ties to fellow Protestants, including members of his family, and that they reciprocated. "My dearest sister in Jesus Christ," he wrote to his wife in recounting his interrogation, "I have seen your letter that you sent me by way of Marguerite, which deeply touched my heart, inasmuch as you and all the brothers care about and are solicitous towards me."[50] Aware of the tribulations faced by his Protestant addressees, he expressed solidarity with them: "I participate with you, and drink from the same drink that you do, and as for myself, I expect nothing other than cruel death at any moment."[51] In the final letter to his wife, penned the day before his execution, Brully articulated most fully the wealth of his relations with family and friends, and the comfort that they afforded him. Letters from his father and father-in-law, written in his wife's name, delighted him with news of her joy "that this good God and Father has given you a husband whom he has chosen to endure for his name, and for the Gospel and his son Jesus Christ." He knew what lay ahead and told her exactly what it entailed: he would be burned, his body reduced to ashes and then scattered. His wife would be widowed, which would enable her, following Paul (1 Tim. 5:5), to devote herself wholeheartedly to God—or to receive another husband, if it was his will. As Brully reminded her, she still had her mother and father, a brother and her sisters, Brully's own brothers, and their go-between Marguerite, who had told Brully that she wanted to withdraw with his wife "and to serve our Lord for the rest of her life." His wife would not be alone after his death. "Greet the church in my name," he wrote near the end of his letter, "but especially your parents and mine."[52] As with Hutter and More, the radical nature of Brully's actions did not betoken a man striking out on his own.

Still, however important Brully's relationships were to his resistance, in themselves they cannot account for it. The willingness to die as a martyr was not simply the product of belonging to a religious community. Like Hutter and More, Brully's resistance was based on an uncompromising belief, which in his case included the conviction that Calvinist Christianity was true.[53] Dense with biblical paraphrases and allusions, Brully's letters show how tightly he fitted relevant scriptural passages to his circumstances, both as a prescription and as an explanation of his predicament. Such texts were certainly no less important to a *sola scriptura* Protestant who had lived in Calvin's house than they were to an Austrian Anabaptist leader or an erudite Roman Catholic layman. "Surely, my brothers," he stated near the beginning of his first letter, "[God] has given you from on high not only to believe in [Christ], but also to suffer something for him, which is not given to all those who believe, but is a special gift from God, as holy Paul witnesses in his letter to the Philippians" [Phil. 1:29].[54] We have seen Hutter quote the same verse. Echoing Peter and seamlessly blending him with Paul, Brully urged others suffering persecution not to be troubled "by our crosses and adversities, as if something strange were happening to us, but on the contrary, we should greatly rejoice when various afflictions and attacks occur [cf. 1 Pet. 4:12–13], knowing that tribulations engender endurance, and endurance patience, and patience hope in God, which does not fall short, because the love of God for us is poured into our hearts by his Holy Spirit" [Rom. 5:3–5]. Again, the biblical hermeneutic shared by all three martyrs involved not technical exegesis per se; rather, it applied scriptural admonitions to concrete circumstances of persecution. Since the living God continued to bestow his grace and to speak through his word, his word was no less relevant in the sixteenth century than it had been when he first revealed it.

Brully seems to have been more confident than was More about the calling to martyrdom. As he told his wife, "it now pleases God to accomplish in me that which I have many times desired, as you well know: namely, that he grant me the grace to die for his Gospel, to the edification of his people."[55] He was joyful and thanked God for the suffering he was enduring for Christ's sake.[56] Like Hutter and More, Brully drew strength from his sense of standing in a venerable tradition of unjustly persecuted men and women, which he could trace back through the early Christian martyrs to the apostles of the New and the prophets of the Old Testaments. He encouraged fellow believers to reflect on them, as he had done, that they might see the close correspondence between themselves and these predecessors.[57]

Beyond predicting persecution and prescribing resistance, the Bible recounted stories of flesh-and-blood resisters from the Maccabees to Stephen. Brully's key paradigm was Christ himself, just as it was for More. While Brully left no elaborate reflections on Christ's agony in Gethsemane, he made clear the centrality of a Protestant *imitatio Christi* to his experience, an understanding also rooted in scripture. "You have learned in [Christ's] school that in the first instance his child must deny himself, and take up his cross, and follow him [cf. Matt. 16:24]. Whoever fears these things, and in order to avoid them shrinks back (*se retirera arriere*) and dissembles before the world, thinking that one can be a good disciple of Christ without carrying the cross, loses one's self (it's not I who say it, it's the Master himself)."[58]

This parenthetical phrase—"ce n'est point moy qui le dit, c'est le Maistre luy-mesme"—implies the entire structure of faith, worldview, and practical hermeneutic, one shared across mutually antagonistic Christian traditions. The martyrs did what they did because they believed that God had commanded it. Without taking them on their own terms, it becomes difficult if not impossible to account for their actions, assuming that one shuns analytically useless categories such as "fanaticism." I submit that nobody, whether now or in the sixteenth century, is willing to endure horrific death for what they themselves consider to be mere subjective opinions, or cultural constructions, or doubtful doctrines.

Now let us move from the experience of three men to a much wider domain. If Hutter, More, and Brully, as well as so many other martyrs, were willing to resist conversion to the point of death because of their religious belief—-if their faith is what explains their behavior, in the sense that it accounts for why they did what they did—-then the implications for the history of religion in general could be considerable. Of course it would be wholly unjustified, based on the experience of articulate believers willing to die for their religious commitments, to infer anything about the large majority of Christians in early modern Europe. Many ordinary men and women, far from evincing such convictions, seem to have resisted intraconfessional clerical attempts to convert them even to a self-conscious Christian morality and devotion—a resistance to conversion worlds away from that of the martyrs' willingness to die. The martyrs cannot absolve us from doing the social history of early modern Christianity, from investigating the ways in which men and women across the cultural spectrum and the social hierarchy responded locally to the Reformations. Yet the social history of Christianity also encompasses (or should encompass) the reformers who sparked the Reformations, the authorities who enforced them, and the committed Christians of whatever group who embraced them. Here martyrdom should provoke significant rethinking. For the worldview and beliefs of the martyrs—the whole picture of creation, revelation, redemption, divine sovereignty, and salvation in Christianity—are apparent in countless early modern works of theology, controversy, devotion, and liturgy, not to mention sermon collections and catechisms. If religious belief explains the martyrs' willingness to die, it might also explain much more within early modern Christianity than recent historiographical trends in the field would suggest.

If religious belief could move the most committed Christians to prefer painful death to (re)conversion, then it might also have been the overriding factor that moved even less devout Christians to act in any number of less extreme ways. If such Christians were preachers, religious belief and pastoral concern might have prompted them to warn people from the pulpit of the danger of hell, imploring them to avoid the sins that jeopardized salvation. If they were devout Catholic princes or godly Protestant magistrates, religious belief and answerability to God might have led them to rule such that their states or cities would reflect the glory of God's created order—a concern all the more pressing in a divided Christendom. If they were pastors or missionaries, religious belief and awareness of the dangers of heterodoxy bred by ignorance might have moved them diligently to catechize, admonish, and oversee the lives of the men, women, and children in their care. If they were husbands and fathers, religious belief and the knowledge of Paul's biblical injunctions about the family might have led them to expect obedience from their wives and children; if they were wives and children, the same knowledge might have inspired them to obey their husbands and fathers. If the martyrs were willing to die as a result of what they believed, then religious belief is plausible as the principal motivation for all these patterns of action. Certainly all can be supported along these lines by abundant evidence from the period.

If such a reading sounds strange—or "naïve"—that is because it runs counter to what has become, it seems to me, the dominant postconfessional interpretation of early modern Christianity. Fundamentally, according to the latter, historians of religion should employ a hermeneutics of suspicion as their chief interpretative assumption, seeing self-professed religious motivations as an ideology for the exercise of power and the assertion of self-interest. In general, the sermons, the missionary efforts, the regulation and surveillance, the state's support of churches, the emphasis on obedience, should be understood as means by which authorities sought incrementally to discipline and control a relatively unruly late medieval population through confessionalization. In this crypto-Foucauldian narrative of religion as social control, wherever human interactions *can* be interpreted as the exercise of power, they *should* be, with "faith" and the entire discourse of Christianity construed as a means of domination. Only where religion was adopted as the language of protest or resistance—in the early evangelical movement or the Peasants' War of 1525, for instance, or among vulnerable Anabaptists— might it merit interpretation as a premodern aspiration to some form of social progress, political autonomy, or cultural self-determination.

Martyrdom undermines the assumption behind this approach, with far-reaching implications. The combination of martyrs' beliefs and behavior should elicit a nonreductionist interpretation of religious belief vis-à-vis martyrdom from scholars otherwise inclined to reduce belief to something else. There was nothing "in it" for the martyrs in any ordinary social or political sense; they simply resisted (re)conversion and died gruesome deaths. Accordingly, the general assumption that belief *must* be reduced to something more fundamental is rendered untenable. And if the general assumption is untenable, then even in those instances where religion and power coincided—-in the words and deeds, say, of confessionalizing princes or ecclesiastical courts or patriarchal husbands—-it is not enough to demonstrate the coincidence to show that religion was being "used" rather than simply lived. Upon reflection, this should not be especially surprising, insofar as the Bible's practical applicability, to the extent that it was believed to be God's word, extended to every domain of life on which it could be brought to bear. The same Scriptures that inspired Christians to endure death also asserted, for example, that "there is no authority except from God, and those authorities that exist have been instituted by God" (Rom. 13:1). Or again, "obey your leaders and submit to them, for they are keeping watch over your souls and will give an account" (Heb. 13:17). The issue is not whether such verses could be and were interpreted in diverse and mutually contradictory ways (as they clearly were), or whether other passages or theological reasoning could have been taken to trump them, as sometimes happened (think of the emergence of Calvinist resistance theory, or Catholic justifications for tyrannicide). The issue is rather whether there are any compelling reasons to think that such passages could not have been applied any less sincerely than were passages about the endurance of suffering. If committed Christians were willing to die in accordance with biblically based convictions in contexts of vulnerability, should we doubt that they could seek to live in accordance with them in contexts of responsibility and control? Had Thomas More been any less religiously motivated in opposing heretics than he was in readying himself for execution?

This critique of reductionist presumption does not imply that every self-proclaimed religious profession or action should be taken at face value. Such a position would indeed be naïve, since people have resorted in the past and continue to resort in the present to all sorts of rationalizations and justifications for their actions. Nor does this critique propose that religion be studied in isolation from social relationships, political institutions, or cultural practices; we have seen how contextually embedded was the resistance to conversion by Hutter, More, and Brully. The point is rather to problematize purported answers to the question of why past people did what they did, with a nominalistic openness that transcends a crypto-Foucauldian cynicism toward the early modern past. The latter attitude, whatever postmodern trappings it might receive, serves a besieged but still dominant and largely approved liberal narrative of secular modernity, in which early modern individuals and groups gradually freed themselves from the shackles of hierarchy and tradition. In this account, traditional religion and the societies that it informed, with their dogmas, morals, prescriptions, and sanctions, comprised perhaps the single greatest impediment to the individual freedoms engendered by the institutions and ideologies of Western modernity. Hence the politically intelligible—but analytically unjustified—tendency to ascribe self-professed belief to base motives wherever it offends modern or postmodern secular sensibilities. Yet why in fact people did what they did centuries ago has nothing to do with whether anyone happens today to like or dislike their behavior or its roots. The lives and values of past people have no logical connection to any metaphysical or moral convictions in the present. Between naïveté and cynicism lies a critical analysis open to sincerity as well as manipulation on a case-by-case basis, which separates the understanding of past people from both modern value judgments about them or intellectual assumptions that distort them.

NOTES

1. This figure, which is approximate, is derived from data in William Monter, "Heresy Executions in Reformation Europe," in *Tolerance and Intolerance in the European Reformation,* ed. Ole Peter Grell and Bob Scribner (Cambridge, 1996), pp. 48–65; Geoffrey F. Nuttall, "The English Martyrs 1535–1680: A Statistical Review," *Journal of Ecclesiastical History* 22 (1971): 191–97; and E. De Moreau, *Histoire de L'église de Belgique,* vol. 5 (Brussels, 1952), pp. 172–206. By "religious traitors" I mean those Roman Catholics executed as traitors in Britain for their refusal to repudiate allegiance to the papacy.

2. For the purposes of this paper, any number of martyrs for whom sufficient source material survives could equally well have been chosen. I have selected these three in part because they were put to death within a fairly narrow time span (1535–45) and, in their respective ways, had a significant influence after their deaths.

3. Brad S. Gregory, *Salvation at Stake: Christian Martyrdom in Early Modern Europe* (Cambridge, Mass., 1999).

4. This paragraph is based largely on Leonard Gross, "Jakob Hutter: A Christian Communist," in *Profiles of Radical Reformers: Biographical Sketches from Thomas Müntzer to Paracelsus,* ed. Hans-Jürgen Goertz (Scottdale, Pa., 1982), pp. 158–67; Werner O. Packull, *Hutterite Beginnings: Communitarian Experiments during the Reformation* (Baltimore, 1995), esp. pp. 66–67, 166–67, 187–96, 198–203, 214–40, 242–55.

5. For the decree of 20 August 1527, see *Österreich,* pt. 1, vol. 11, ed. Grete Mecenseffy, in *Quellen zur Geschichte der Täufer* (hereafter *QGT*) (Gütersloh, 1964), pp. 3–12.

6. See *Österreich,* pt. 2, vol. 13, ed. Grete Mecenseffy, in *QGT* (Gütersloh, 1972), pp. 263–65.

7. The letters are included in Hans Fischer, *Jacob Hutter: Leben, Froemmigkeit, Briefe* (Newton, Kans., 1956), pt. 3, pp. 1–72.

8. The body of scholarship on More is immense, as is that on the Henrician Reformation. In my opinion, Peter Ackroyd's recent biography of More is the most successful full-length study, avoiding the fulsome admiration of Chambers as well as the tendentious psychologizing of Marius. See

Peter Ackroyd, *The Life of Thomas More* (New York, 1998); R. W. Chambers, *Thomas More* (1935; reprint ed., Harmondsworth, 1963); Richard Marius, *Thomas More: A Biography* (New York, 1984).

9. 26 Henry VIII, c. 1, 13, in *The Tudor Constitution: Documents and Commentary*, ed. G. R. Elton (Cambridge, 1972), pp. 62, 355.

10. For the correspondence, see More's remarks on papal primacy in the last letter he wrote to Cromwell prior to his imprisonment, in Elizabeth Frances Rogers, ed., *The Correspondence of Sir Thomas More* (Princeton, N.J., 1947), no. 199, March 5, 1534, esp. pp. 498/200–500/283; for the trial, see J. Duncan M. Derrett, "The Trial of Sir Thomas More" (1964), in *Essential Articles for the Study of Thomas More*, ed. R. S. Sylvester and G. P. Marc'hadour (Hamden, Conn., 1977), pp. 55–78.

11. See Thomas More, *A Dialogue of Comfort Against Tribulation*, vol. 12 in *The Complete Works of St. Thomas More* (hereafter *CWTM*), ed. Louis L. Martz and Frank Manley (New Haven, Conn.,, 1976); More, *De tristitia Christi, CWTM* 14, pts. 1–2, ed. and tr. Clarence H. Miller (New Haven, Conn., 1976); *Thomas More's Prayer Book: A Facsimile Reproduction of the Annotated Pages*, tr. Louis L. Martz and Richard S. Sylvester (New Haven, Conn., 1969); and Rogers, *Correspondence*.

12. This paragraph is based chiefly on Gérard Moreau, *Histoire du Protestantisme à Tournai jusqu'à la veille de la Révolution des Pays-Bas* (Paris, 1962), pp. 90–111.

13. On the importance of Calvin's period in Strasbourg under Bucer's tutelage, see François Wendel, *Calvin: Origins and Development of His Religious Thought*, tr. Philip Mairet (Durham, N.C., 1963), pp. 57–68.

14. Paul E. Valvekens, *De Inquisitie in de Nederlanden der zestiende eeuw* (Brussels, 1949), pp. 164–91, 205–33; James D. Tracy, "Heresy Law and Centralization under Mary of Hungary: Conflict between the Council of Holland and the Central Government over the Enforcement of Charles V's Placards," *Archiv für Reformationsgeschichte* 73 (1982): 288–301.

15. The letters appear in all the folio editions of Crespin, the first of which was published in 1564. I have used Jean Crespin, *Histoire des vrays Tesmoins de la verite de l'evangile, qui de leur sang l'ont signée, depuis Jean Hus iusques au temps present* (Geneva, 1570), fols. 134v–140. On Crespin's editorial reliability in printing the martyrs' letters, see Gregory, *Salvation at Stake*, pp. 21–22; on his reliability with respect to Brully's letters in particular, see Moreau, *Protestantisme à Tournai*, pp. 97–98 n. 2.

16. On More's ecclesiology, which was essential to his resistance to conversion, see Brian Gogan, *The Common Corps of Christendom: Ecclesiological Themes in the Writings of Sir Thomas More* (Leiden, 1982).

17. Fischer, *Hutter*, pt. 3, no. 2, November 1533, p. 18. For the dating of the letters, see Packull, *Hutterite Beginnings* pp. 242–49.

18. Fischer, *Hutter*, pt. 3, no. 5, late July/early August 1535, p. 36.

19. Ibid., no. 6, after 24–25 August 1535, p. 52; no. 8, 20–25 November 1535, p. 69.

20. Ibid., no. 2, p. 6.

21. Ibid., no. 5, p. 45. See also no. 7, [late October?] 1535, p. 54: "Weiter . . . ist uns bald hernach eine Botschaft gekommen von euch durch euren und unseren lieben Bruder Hänsel. Dieselbe Botschaft und Brief habe ich, Jakob, gehört, verlesen und auch zukund getan allen Kindern mit Fleiß."

22. Ibid., no. 5, p. 36; no. 8, pp. 63, 71. 2 Cor. 3:2: "You yourselves are our letter, written on our hearts, to be known and read by all" (NRSV).

23. Fischer, *Hutter*, pt. 3, no. 8, p. 66.

24. Ibid., no. 3, 1534, p. 23.

25. Ibid., no. 3, p. 22; no. 5, pp. 33–34; no. 8, p. 72. The translation is from the NRSV.

26. For the stress on the joys of heaven supported by clusters of scriptural verses, see ibid., no. 5, p. 42; no. 7, pp. 58–59, no. 8, pp. 69–70; for the Hutterites as standing in the same tradition as the prophets and apostles, see ibid., no. 8, p. 64.

27. Ibid., no. 6, p. 47.

28. Ibid., no. 5, p. 35. For expression of the same willingness, see this passage in the same letter, p. 38: "O ihr meine herzallerliebsten Geschwister, o wollte Gott, daß ich solche Trübsal mit meinem Leib möchte ablegen, wie gar gern und williglich wollt ich meine Wangen und mein Rücken und alle meine Glieder dem Schlagenden darbieten und meinen Leib geben in alle Marter und Pein durch die Hilfe Gottes." For similar passages, all in the letters from 1535, see pp. 39, 43; no. 7, p. 55; no. 8, pp. 64, 68, 70.

29. More's holograph of the treatise survives and is preserved in the Royal College and Seminary of Corpus Christi, Valencia. It is photographically reproduced in *CWTM*, vol. 14, pt. 1. For painstaking analysis of More's composition and revisions of the work, see Clarence H. Miller, "Introduction" to *De tristitia Christi*, in *CWTM*, vol. 14, pt. 2, pp. 745–76.

30. *De tristitia Christi*, in *CWTM*, vol. 14, pt. 1, pp. 107/7–109/2 (English). More's Latin reads: "quo uidelicet infirmis infirmus factus / infirmos alios sua infirmitate curaret." Ibid., pp. 107/7–109/1 (Latin). I have used Miller's translation throughout in references to *De tristitia Christi*, occasionally with slight emendations. Similar frank admissions of fear or frailty are to be found in the prison letters. See, for example, no. 206, Margaret Roper to Alice Alington, [August 1534], in *Correspondence*, p. 531/640–644 (his daughter's report on one of their prison conversations); ibid., no. 210, More

to Margaret Roper, 1534, p. 543/125–132; ibid., no. 211, to Margaret Roper, 1534, p. 545/44–47.

31. More, *Prayer Book,* p. 51.

32. Ibid., p. 113.

33. More, *Dialogue of Comfort,* pp. 292/17, 20–22; 312–13, quotation at 313/3, 4–7. I have modernized the spelling of More's English. More wrote a separate treatise on Christ's Passion, most likely in the early months of 1534, before his imprisonment began, although he perhaps completed it in the Tower. See Garry E. Haupt, "Introduction" to More, *Treatise on the Passion, Treatise on the Blessed Body, Instructions and Prayers,* vol. 13 in *CWTM* (New Haven, Conn., 1976), pp. xxxvii–xli. For references to meditation on Christ's Passion in More's prison letters, see *Correspondence,* no. 202, to Margaret Roper, [May? 1534], p. 509/19–22, 40–46; ibid., no. 214, to Margaret Roper, 2 or 3 May 1535, p. 552/66–68. On late medieval devotion to Christ's passion in England, see Ellen M. Ross, *The Grief of God: Images of the Suffering Jesus in Late Medieval England* (New York, 1997).

34. More, *De tristitia Christi,* pp. 626–80 (fols. 156–169v in the Valencia MS).

35. More, *Dialogue of Comfort,* pp. 109/2–7, 198/5–7, 247/9–10, 290/15–25. He also quotes this verse in the *De tristitia Christi.* See *CWTM,* vol. 14, pt. 1, pp. 271–73. The translation here and in the following note are from the NRSV.

36. For some examples, see More, *De tristitia Christi,* pp. 53/4–6, 133/11–135/5, 267/6–269/1; idem, *Dialogue of Comfort,* pp. 298/9–17, 303/5–15; idem, *Correspondence,* no. 210, to Margaret Roper, 1534, p. 542/97–98.

37. See More, *De tristitia Christi,* pp. 69/6–71/2, 105/5–7; idem, *Dialogue of Comfort,* p. 247/13–21; idem, *Correspondence,* no. 206, Margaret Roper to Alice Alington, [August 1534], p. 531/630–35. For the quotation of Matt. 10:32–33 by Hutter, see Fischer, *Hutter,* pt. 3, no. 3, p. 24.

38. Frank Manley, "Audience," in More, *Dialogue of Comfort,* p. cxlviii, based on Germain Marc'hadour, *The Bible in the Works of St. Thomas More,* vol. 5 (Nieuwkoop, 1972), pp. 191–95.

39. More, *Prayer Book,* p. 74.

40. More, *Correspondence,* no. 212, Alice More to Henry VIII, [c. Christmas 1534], pp. 547–49. See also her letter to Thomas Cromwell, ibid., no. 215, May 1535, pp. 554–55.

41. For the fullest account of their exchanges, see ibid., no. 206, Margaret Roper to Alice Alington, [August 1534], pp. 514–532, quotation at p. 529/560–563.

42. Soon after his incarceration, More expressed to Margaret his deep concern for her and the rest of his family: "A deadly grief unto me, and much more deadly than to hear of mine own death, . . . is that I perceive

my good son your husband, and you my good daughter, and my good wife, and mine other good children and innocent friends, in great displeasure and danger of great harm thereby." More, *Correspondence,* no. 202, to Margaret Roper, [May? 1534], p. 509/19–25.

43. For the quoted phrases, see ibid., no. 200, to Margaret Roper, c. 17 April 1534, p. 506/128–129.

44. *Letters and Papers, Foreign and Domestic, of the Reign of Henry VIII,* vol. 8, ed. James Gairdner (London, 1885), no. 858, p. 332.

45. More, *Correspondence,* no. 217, to Antonio Bonvisi, 1535, p. 562/28–29, 39–40. Here I have used the English given in the 1557 Rastell edition of More's works. For More's Latin, see ibid., p. 560/23–24, 30–31.

46. Ibid., no. 211, to Margaret Roper, 1534, p. 544/1–3. See also ibid., no. 210, to Margaret Roper, 1534, p. 540/1–4.

47. Ibid., no. 218, to Margaret Roper, 5 July 1535, p. 564/22–24.

48. For the dating, and the identification of this letter as "vn escrit que i'ay fait ces iours passez à mes freres prisonniers," to which Brully refers in his account of his interrogation, see Moreau, *Protestantisme à Tournai,* p. 109 n. 2. For the quotation, see Crespin, *Histoire,* fol. 135v.

49. Crespin, *Histoire,* fol. 138.

50. Ibid., fol. 135.

51. Ibid., fol. 139.

52. Ibid., fol. 139v.

53. In the account of his interrogation, Brully gave an unmistakably Calvinist definition of faith: "I'ay respondu que foy est vne certaine asseurance qui nous est donnee par le sainct Esprit, de la misericorde de Dieu, & de sa bonne volonté enuers nous, contenue aux promesses de l'Euangile, lesquelles sont accomplies en son Fils Iesus Christ." Ibid., fol. 136v.

54. Ibid., fol. 137v.

55. Ibid., fol. 139v.

56. Ibid., fols. 137v, 138.

57. "Certes, tesmoin Iesus Christ, parauant ses Apostres ils auoyent persecuté les Prophetes qui auoyent precedé, comme ils ont fait les Apostres. Et apres les Apostres, les Euangelistes, les Martyrs & bons Pasteurs, qui ont esté la primitiue Eglise. & generalement tous ceux qui dés le commencement du monde iusqu'au definement dernier, ont voulu viure selon Dieu, ont tousiours esté affligez des mauuais, des mondains & charnels." Ibid., fol. 138. After this passage, Brully listed the respective biblical models appropriate for those whose brothers and neighbors, children, and wives were persecuted.

58. Ibid., fol. 138v.

4

Translating Christianity

Counter-Reformation Europe and the Catholic Mission in China, 1580–1780

R. Po-chia Hsia

In their dialogue on the art of eloquence, Jean-Denis Bredin of the Académie française and Thierry Lévy exchanged these words:[1]

Lévy: Cet instant, là, celui des premiers mots de notre dialogue, je l'attendais depuis longtemps. Dans le même temps, je vérifie ce fait, que j'ai eu l'occasion d'observer à maintes reprises, c'est qu'en présence d'un visage—même s'il s'agit, comme c'est le cas aujourd'hui, du visage d'un ami cher—monte une crainte, une anxiété qui est sans doute un élément important de la parole. Nous sommes tous les deux ici, à la campagne, sous les arbres, comme il faut être pour dialoguer, en prenant le temps, sans subir les contraintes de la vie professionelle. C'est le printemps, le climat est doux, le soleil n'est pas loin. Nous savons que tout à l'heure nous irons nous promener . . .

Bredin: Le dialogue dont tu rêves, c'est le dialogue fondé sur l'amitié, c'est le dialogue voulu par Ciceron, celui de la parole souverainment libre, franche, affectueuse, généreuse . . . , le dialogue né d'une parole qui parle réellement à quelqu'un, à quelqu'un qui vous écoute, à quelqu'un qui ne cesse d'être disponible pour vous, qui est avec vous engagé dans une aventure commune, précisément celle du dialogue. Mais il y a . . . beaucoup de faux dialogues.

This brief exchange, in a different time and space, captures the spirit of the early Catholic enterprise in China. For the European missionaries, conversion necessitated conversation and discussion, using words to persuade in an atmosphere of "free, frank, affectionate, and generous" discourse, ideally in the presence of one or more interlocutors, friends and acquaintances, not infrequently in gardens, banquets, and reception halls.

What I propose to examine in this paper is precisely this technique of conversion: conversation. It seems particularly important because there is no word in Chinese to signify "conversion." People "became Christians," or "believed in the Laws of the Lord of Heaven," or simply accepted baptism to enter into a ritual community. There exist but a handful of personal accounts as to why people believed in Christianity. Even the most important literati converts of the late Ming dynasty—Xu Guangqi (1562–1633), Yang Tingyun (1557–1627), and Li Zhizao (1565–1630)—prominently named by Matteo Ricci and in the early Jesuit sources, were less than effusive in documenting their personal spiritual journeys.[2] One searches in vain in the writings by Chinese Christians for an Augustinian model of conversion. The *loci communes* of Christian conversion are all absent: the struggles between the Old Self and the New, the gradual ascent toward God, a spiritual journey marked by real or imagined violence, and, above all, a postconversion narrative reordering of memory. Stories of "conversion" in China were much less dramatic. Even told by the Jesuits, these narratives are short, fragmented, and lacking, seemingly, in psychological relief. These stories of adherence to Christianity suggest rather a continuous and not a disruptive narrative, whereby Christian doctrines, symbols, commandments, and representations are inserted into a larger field of meaning that appears coherent for the convert, but problematic for the missionary. The reluctance to destroy Buddhist and popular Chinese statues, for example, even among those who adhered to Christian law and faith, struck the Jesuits as particularly troublesome.[3]

But convert they did, and in no small numbers relative to the paucity of European missionaries in sixteenth- and seventeenth-century China. Why did they become Christians? The answer, as we shall see, is complicated. To help us understand the different paths to Christianity, I propose to focus on the most important technique of the missionary: words. In this essay, I shall sketch out a dialogical history of the Catholic missionary enterprise in China between the advent of Matteo Ricci in 1583 and the suppression of the Society of Jesus in the 1760s and 1770s. I shall argue that an initial dialogical model gradually gave way to a second one between the 1680s and 1720s as the Mission grew rapidly in success before encountering the crisis of the Chinese Rites Controversy. The characteristics of this initial dialogical model were generally the ones praised in the dialogue between Bredin and Lévy: conversation as a free, frank, affectionate, and generous exchange of sovereign words between friends, *en face*, with an indeterminate subject, between Jesuit missionaries and Chinese scholars. The dialogical model that replaced it manifested increasing signs of unequal exchange. We hear more from the missionary interlocutor: in sheer number of words and in the intensity of his tone; we hear less from his Chinese interlocutor. The subject of conversation became more focused, intensified, and less varied. Our scene is not one of conversation between friends, but a totally unequal exchange of words, between the Qing emperors and their Jesuit servants, and between European clerical masters and their Chinese pupils. The Ciceronian dialogue gave way in this second phase to a discourse of polemics and catechism.

I

The first task of a missionary was to learn Chinese. For Ricci, the difficulty of the Chinese language was compounded by its representation in an extremely complex field of social rituals:

> There are other customs also in their way of talking and writing in which they differ greatly from us, and these are increased in number by the difficulties involved in their language. When two are conversing they never use the grammatical second person. . . . The pronoun of the first person is not used when one is talking about himself. . . . In conversation they have as many ways of avoiding self-praise as they have of lauding others. . . . It will appear quite evident from this that one must be well acquainted with the different formulas for expressing his ideas if he is not to appear uncultured or ignorant and if he hopes to understand what is being said or written.[4]

A missionary who did not speak Chinese, or could not express himself eloquently, was useless. Such was the experience of Michele Ruggieri and António Almeida, two of Ricci's earliest companions in China, who were invited in 1586 to visit Shaoxing in Zhejiang province by mandarin friends the Jesuits had made in their first residence in Zhaoqing. They spoke of the Faith but made little impression and were eventually asked to return to Zhaoqing.[5]

A superb linguist, by contrast, Ricci saw his fame increase as his proficiency in the Chinese language and literature deepened. His long apprenticeship of thirteen years (from his first arrival in Zhaoqing in 1583 to success among the ruling elites in Nanchang in 1596) depended on both talent and hard work. Success came in the wake of numerous visits and conversations with mandarins and literati, as his network of friends and acquaintances spread ever wider. Not for nothing was his first published

Chinese work entitled "On Friendship," *Jiao you lun* (1595); and his keen observations of social etiquette and rituals among the literati were carefully recorded in his memoirs.[6]

If Ricci was impressed by the elaborate rituals of conversation among the Chinese literati (very little was eaten at formal banquets, for example, which were occasions for serious conversations), they were equally impressed by him. In his preface to Ricci's *Ji ren shi pian* (Ten Chapters of a Remarkable Person), Zhou Bingmo recalled his first impression of Ricci, "a most remarkable person (*Ji ren*) ."[7] Perhaps Ricci's most brilliant performance was at the banquet in the early months of 1599 in Nanjing at the home of Li Yuzheng, a mandarin steeped also in Buddhist texts. Some twenty scholars were invited to a banquet "because the Chinese . . . carry out all their disputations and discussions at the table while they eat and drink."[8] Present at the colloquy was a well-known Buddhist monk, whose "twisted logic" crumbled before his eloquence, according to Ricci's report. It was less his logic that impressed at this dinner than Ricci's ability to summarize diverse arguments, simultaneously expressed in excited exchange by many present, that particularly impressed.[9] He was, in other words, a brilliant conversationalist, who became a topic of conversation himself.[10]

Crowning his stunning career was the permission in 1601 to reside in the imperial capital of Beijing. Ricci became a veritable sensation, whom everyone in the ruling class must visit. A Chinese manuscript, written by a Jesuit missionary (possibly Ricci himself) and dated from the early seventeenth century, gives us a vivid description of the hectic social life Ricci must have experienced in the capital. Entitled *Shi ke wen da* (Answers to Visitors' Questions), this dialogue begins with a scene of scholars visiting one another as well as famous people in the capital; of a host who is very busy; it writes of visitors leaving their calling cards when the host is not at home and of return visits; it describes in detail the polite conversations during these visits—the admiration of someone's fame and their writings, etc. After the formal greeting and questions as to the place of origin, the conversation turns to one driven by the curiosity of the Chinese visitors about the West:

> How many countries are there in the West? Do they go to war? What do the officials wear: do they wear mandarin robes of round collars and wear mandarin headgear? What do the common people wear? How do they wear their hair? Do the men have beards? Are the women beautiful? Do they bind their feet? And what shoes and jewelry do they wear? How do people marry? Can one remarry? How big is your esteemed country? Are there prostitutes? (Answer: few, they are not

tolerated in the cities; to which the Chinese scholar said this was precisely the custom in our ancient times). How long is the journey? How are the ships constructed? What are the dangers of sea travel? Are there sea monsters? How many people can travel in a ship and what do they eat? How many countries does the European pass through on the way to China? Then follow questions about Africa, to which the Jesuit replied in rather disparaging terms, except that they thought the Africans were ready to do good if properly civilized; moreover, they danced and traded gold and silver for glass. Questions then about India were posed: about food, customs, peppers, eating with hands, and the written languages. Is China the middle of the world? To which the Jesuit had to disappoint his visitor and said politely that the equator was. Why did the venerable master not take the land route? (Difficult route on account of Muslims). There follows a long conversation on Chinese porcelains and European glass. After which, the visitor's curiosity turns to the salaries for officials in the west: in Europe, a prime minister makes more money (sixty to a hundred thousand taels of silver a year). Are Western officials greedy? Are there civil service examinations? Does one get an appointment after passing the examination? Can one sit for a subject in military science? To which the answer is no, but then there is medicine, and the subject of the humanities is the learning of the Lord of Heaven. The conversation turns to astronomy, fortune-telling, Western medicine and pharmacy, before the Chinese visitor indelicately asks about money: How do your friends send money? The point of this query, after the visitor found out that money was sent via Canton, was the legend of alchemy; and the visitor confessed that "I have never believed the saying that your Venerable use magic to get silver." The subject of alchemy led to the monetary system in Europe and to poverty and charity. Are there bandits? How are they punished? What are houses like? Are there hereditary rulers? Are there cities and fortifications? The conversation meanders now to European weaponry and horses before ending with several disparate subjects: tribute-bearing, palaces, geomancy, and how one captures lions. Religion is not mentioned.[11]

"To be all things to all men for the sake of Christ," as Ricci described his aim, meant also to converse on all manners of subjects, until the interlocutor was drawn into the fishermen's net and won over to the Faith.

This one visit and conversation, reproduced in manuscript, stands for thousands of encounters that Ricci and the other Jesuits experienced in their missionary work. In fact, "Answers to the queries of visitors" became a standard genre in the writings of European missionaries and their Chinese converts. Recorded in texts, conversations supplied the material for a growing corpus of Chinese-language Christian books. The very earliest Catholic book in Chinese, the *Tianzhu shengjiao shilu* (A Concise Treatise on the Doctrines of the Holy Religion of the Lord of Heaven), written by Michele Ruggieri in 1584, is written in the form of a dialogue between a Confucian scholar who seeks out a Jesuit to inquire about the truths (*li*) of the afterlife.[12] Most were produced by Jesuits, such as the *Tianzhu jiaoyao xulun* (The Essential Doctrines of the Religion of the Lord of Heaven) written by Ferdinand Verbiest in 1670, who explained in his preface that "many visitors ask me what Christianity is; and many Christians follow the commandments of the church but cannot explain them, so I have set them out in an orderly fashion."[13] Verbiest then proceeded to compose a short answer in elegant classical Chinese. Other Jesuits wrote in the vernacular for the common people, an example being the *Sheng jiao yuanliao* (Origins of the Holy Religion), attributed to the Portuguese Jesuit Rodrigo de Figueiredo (1594–1642), a dialogue between a Chinese and a Jesuit, explaining the sacraments, Mass, and holy images.[14] The other missionary orders readily picked up this genre as well. The Spanish Franciscan Pedro Piñuela published one in 1680 under the title *Chuhui wenda* (Conversations at a First Meeting).[15] In spite of his apology for his poor style, Piñuela managed to compose in reasonably good classical style a dialogue between himself and a Chinese visitor curious about Christianity.

While these dialogues reproduced the experiences of conversation between Europeans and curious Chinese visitors, the texts by Chinese Christians reflected similar conversations, in which their families, friends, and acquaintances showed their curiosity about the Europeans. *Sheng shui jiyan* (A Dialogue at the Holy Water Confraternity), a manuscript written by Sun Xueshi in the 1610s, introduces two interlocutors: Yuan the Christian, given the epithet "Know Much Sir," and Yang the Zen Buddhist, given the epithet "Know Nothing Sir." Yang asks Yuan what kind of people the Jesuits were, to which Yuan answered, echoing the title of Ricci's book, that they were "remarkable persons" (*ji ren*).[16]

Curiosity about Europeans soon turned to their teachings. A great scholar addressed all sorts of questions and doubts about Christianity to Yang Tinyuan, in the words of Ricci, one of the three pillars of the early Catholic Church in China. The scholar asked Yang to explain the Christian notion of "Heaven" (*Tian*), and how Christian concepts of heaven and hell differed from those of Buddhism. He was skeptical that Europe could have more books than China and about how the Jesuits could have traveled such a long distance. He even uttered the fear that the Jesuits might be in collusion with Japanese pirates. To all these doubts Yang replied: "Whoever visits them is always received with respect; whoever knows them for a while does not fail to admire them. Those who doubt and castigate them are people who have never met them and merely repeat rumors."[17]

In still other dialogues between Chinese Christians and their fellow literati, curiosity and doubts turned to outright criticisms and disapproval. In *Wei tian ai ren ji lun* (A Radical Discourse on the Fear of Heaven and the Love of Man), a manuscript written in 1628 by the convert Wang Zheng, the following conversation takes place:

> A friend visits Wang and says, I have heard that you were determined to learn from the sages, are things different now? Please tell me the truth and do not hide anything. The visitor said he heard that Wang had studied Buddhist and Taoist texts, and also the I-ching, but now he is obsessed with the Learning of Heaven [i.e. Catholicism]. "How can you have abandoned so lightly the learning of tradition for foreign learning?" reproached the visitor. Moreover, Wang, according to his friend, was so imbued with his new learning that he would discourse endlessly on it, ignoring whether his interlocutor was interested or not, ignoring the disapproval of family, country, and society.[18]

The critique of Christianity as an alien faith also appeared in the 1647 dialogue written by Han Lin, which recorded a schoolmate of Han questioning him about Catholicism, and reproaching him and other Chinese scholars for adhering to a foreign faith.[19]

II

Indeterminancy was the essential character of these conversations. By this I mean that both the form of the dialogue and its subject matter flowed freely within the confines of amicable discourse. A conversation between a missionary and a Chinese visitor turned easily from questions about European clocks and books to doctrines of the afterlife. Conversations could be about dreams: the Italian Jesuit Giulio Aleni recalled a conversation about dream interpretation with a Chinese scholar by the name of Zhang, and used the occasion to translate into Chinese a dialogue between the soul and the body by St. Bernard.[20] Missionaries and their Chinese interlocutors talked about dictionaries: the Belgian Nicholas Trigault and a Chinese scholar discussed the differences of linguistic representations between East and West, and whether dictionaries classified by sounds rather than by the Chinese system of radicals were easier to use.[21] They reflected on sublime matters: the Portuguese Manoel Dias the Younger counseled a visitor who sought the Jesuit out to discuss his spiritual ills, still uncured after years of reading Buddhist texts, and gave him a crash course in Christian doctrines.[22]

The indeterminacy of form and subject extended to the time and place of conversation. As we have noted from Ricci's memoir, the banquet in the house of a mandarin or scholar was perhaps the most frequent occasion. Conversations also took place during visits to the residences of the missionaries and while the Jesuits were traveling on boats. Often it was simply a matter of serendipity. Interested in the fame of the Jesuits in ethics and astronomy, the father of Wang Yuantai asked his son to visit the Europeans because he himself was too old to travel. Wang did not manage the trip until more than two decades later in 1633. He and two friends had been summoned by the Imperial Court to Beijing to emend the calendar and one of the group fell off a horse en route and was forced to stay in Hangzhou to recuperate. During the forty days that he was held up, Wang by chance finally met the Europeans in Hangzhou and accepted their faith.[23] For Zhu Jianshi, it was the rain that favored him. When the Italian Jesuit Martin Martini was passing through Lanchi where Zhu lived, they waited for the rain to stop in a mountain house and ended up talking about friendship for five days, and this resulted in a small book of aphorisms on the subject.[24]

Conversations, even disagreements, could continue while the interlocutors were touring natural and manmade landmarks. In 1632 Aleni traveled with two of his Chinese disciples to Longxun in Fujian province, where they were invited to dine by a former superintendent of schools, Lin Taishi, a non-Christian. A few days later Lin again invited Aleni to a pagoda to the south of the city, in spite of the fact that they had disagreed about polygamy during the banquet. At the pagoda, the good host pointed to the Nine Fairies Mountain to the west, with a rock shaped like a Buddha, to which his guest retorted politely: "Why not say it resembles a saint?" Before Aleni's departure, Lin invited him yet again to a banquet where the conversation turned to the less controversial subject of European instruments.[25] It was clear that Ricci was right when he observed that "the Chinese are not nearly as interested in the honor they believe to be due to their gods as they are in the courtesy they believe to be due to a friend."[26]

Referring to one another in Chinese, the Jesuits called their socios *huiyou* (Friends of the Society). To their Chinese acquaintances, friends, admirers, and even detractors, they represented perhaps not "all things to all men," but certainly more than just missionaries of the Christian faith. They were

Western sages, European literati, alchemists, dream interpreters, magicians, scientists, learned foreigners, and seditious barbarians. By exorcising demons, curing illness, promising eternal life, attacking Buddhism, praising Confucianism, teaching arithmetic, translating geometry, admonishing virtue, adjudicating quarrels, publishing books, giving gifts, displaying clocks, casting canons, furnishing new rituals and religious images, and being ever ready to converse on Christian doctrine and on a multitude of subjects, the very persons of the Jesuits represented the most eloquent and powerful signifiers for the Chinese. Bi Gonggen, the Italian Alfonso Vagnoni, was an amazing philosopher, who discoursed on stars, astronomy, storms, rains, the body, nature, physics, plants, animals, and voices.[27] The subject of numerous encomia, Ricci impressed even those who disagreed with him. Li Zhi, the radical Confucian philosopher turned Buddhist, who met the Jesuit toward the end of his life, described the Western scholar to a friend:

> You asked after Ricci: he is a Westerner from the Extreme West, and traveled for over a hundred thousand *li* to reach China, sailing at first to south India, where he first learned of Buddha. . . . When he reached Canton and the South Sea, he found out that our Great Ming realm has had the virtuous kings Yao and Shun and the sages Zhou and Confucius. He lived in the south and in Zhaoqing nearly two decades, reading every book of our nation, asking teachers to help him note the pronunciations and meanings of the words . . . so that now he is fluent in speaking and writing our language, and following our rituals. He is a most urbane person. He is most intricate and refined in his interior (*zhong ji linglong*),[28] and very plain and modest in his exterior; and listening to scores of people debating nosily, he can follow and recapitulate their arguments in order. I have never seen anyone more impressive. People are either too critical or too flattering, either showing off their brilliance or coming across as too dull. But I have no idea why he is here. I have met him three times already and still do not know his intention in coming here. Perhaps he wants to study our Confucian learning, but surely this is a stupid guess, which probably does not reflect his real intention.[29]

Li Zhi and Ricci parted on good terms—Ricci received a poem in his honor from Li—even though they disagreed on Buddhism and Christianity. Was their conversation an exchange of sovereign words between interlocutors engaged in a common venture, or was it a false dialogue?

In June 1595, a mandarin friend politely but firmly turned Ricci away from Nanjing, fearing any association with foreigners during the Japanese invasion of Korea. Saddened in spirit, Ricci returned to Nanchang, musing over the perils and labor he had endured. He recalled in his memoirs that

> Falling into sleep, he saw a strange man who said to him: "Is this the way you wander about this vast kingdom, imagining that you can uproot an age-old religion and replace it with a new one?" Now, it so happened that from the time of his entrance into China he had always kept his ultimate design as an utter secret. So he answered, "You must be either the Devil or God himself, to know what I have never revealed to anyone," to which he heard the reply, "By no means the Devil, say rather God.[30]

Whereupon Ricci besought God with tears, who consoled him with the words, "I shall be propitious to you in both of the royal cities." Indeed, Ricci was to enjoy triumphal receptions later in Nanjing and Beijing. No amount of pleasant and serious conversation with the Chinese literati could console Ricci more than this Ignatian moment of inner dialogue.

III

Revealed to no one, suspected by Li Zhi, and known only to his inner interlocutor, the true intention of Matteo Ricci was made manifest after his successful installation in Beijing. In 1603, two years after establishing the Beijing Jesuit residence, Ricci published his first catechism, the *Tian zhu shi yi* (A Treatise on the True Nature of the Lord of Heaven). Consciously forgoing the mysteries of Holy Scripture and the conventional format of European catechisms, Ricci employed natural reason and copious citations from the Confucian Four Classics to argue his case.[31] Enormously successful and admired for its elegant style, Ricci's *Tian zhu shi yi* launched a conversion effort based on the harmony of Christianity and Confucianism.

When Ricci died in 1610, others took his place. Both Jesuits and Chinese Christians composed books to demonstrate the concord of Christian ethics and Confucian moral philosophy. For Xu Guangqi, Yang Tingyun, Li Zhizao, and other literati, there was but one truth in East and West, one conscience guiding Chinese and European scholars; and the laws of the Lord of Heaven were being promulgated "to cleanse China of Buddhist errors and supplement the teachings of Confucianism," as Xu Guangqi put it in a memorial to the throne.[32]

Arriving in China one year after Ricci's death, Giulio Aleni, more than any other Jesuit missionary in China in the mid-seventeenth century, took on the mantle of the Western-Confucian sage. The author of a celebrated

biography of Ricci in Chinese, Aleni, after working in the interior provinces, extended the mission to Fujian province, where he wrote and lectured
from 1625 until his death in 1649.[33] Adapting himself expertly to the
institutions of the literati of the late Ming—the colleges (*shu yuan*), the
lectures and discussions (*jiang xue*)—Aleni became a celebrated scholar-
master with scores of Chinese students, who carefully recorded his sayings
and teachings, and his many visits to the literary elites of one of the provinces that supplied the Ming dynasty with the largest number of successful
civil examination candidates. In a biography written by his disciple Li
Sixuan, *Taixi Sijiai xiansheng xingshu* (Acts of Master [Aleni] of the Far
West), published in 1689, Li recorded that Aleni lectured to hundreds of
students in his San shan (Three Mountain) College. A veritable sage, Li
recalled, "Master [Aleni] is most informal in meeting people . . . and loves
to give to charity . . . and never tires of helping others. . . . He had a
magnificent countenance that shone on the hearts and eyes of others, and
whenever he discoursed on the ultimate truths, he did it in an orderly way.
. . . He never scolded anyone in public and only admonished them at night
in private."[34]

Aleni died in the tumultuous years of the mid-seventeenth century. The
China Mission, however, survived the destruction and slaughter of peasant
rebellions and Manchu invasion. After a momentary persecution in 1662
under the new Ching dynasty, Christianity flourished under the emperor
Kangxi (r. 1661–1723), reaching its greatest achievement with the promulgation of the Edict of Toleration of Christianity in 1692.[35] From the handful of Jesuit pioneers the European presence grew to scores of missionaries
from all Catholic countries and religious orders, including one, the Missions
Etrangères, established in Paris principally for work in the China Mission.
Not all emulated the Jesuits. In fact, the Dominicans and the Missions
Etrangères were resentful of Riccian methods and Jesuit preeminence. Nonetheless, the Society of Jesus remained the principal vehicle for the propagation of faith in China. Within the Jesuit mission, the Portuguese
preponderance gave way to French numerical superiority with the arrival of
French fathers in the 1680s. Sent under Louis XIV at the instigation of
Colbert, "[who] regarded the conversion of China as one of the most glori-
ous enterprises for France under the reign of the king,"[36] the French Jesuits
began to assume a dominant position in the China Mission under Kangxi.
They did not forget Aleni's example. Giving advice to new French missionaries to China, Jean de Fontaney wrote in 1704 that

a missionary should have a serious and grave demeanor, which he must
retain always even in the inside of his house, if he wants the esteem of

the Chinese and that his words may make an impression on them. For this reason Father Jules Aleni, one of the greatest men who had worked in this mission . . . always put on a visiting robe whenever a Christian wanted to speak to him. By this composed exterior, he immediately inspired respect, and with his sweetness and affability in conversation, he then won their admiration and confidence.[37]

The Riccian method of proceeding was still held as exemplary; and the French Jesuits followed Ricci's footsteps in the conquest of the Chinese language and literature. A very few, notably Joseph Prémare (1666–1736), excelled in classical Chinese and composed works that matched Ricci's in elegance; several more—François-Xavier Dentrecolles (1664–1741) comes to mind—wrote fluently in colloquial Chinese for a less-elevated readership; still others, such as Jean-François Gerbillon (1654–1707) and Joachim Bouvet (1656–1730), preferred the tongue of the ruling Manchus, an Altaic language with an alphabet that seemed much easier than the Chinese writing.[38] For the majority, however, their experience resembled more that of Jean-François Fouquet (1665–1741), who wrote in a letter of 1702 to the Duke de la Force: "I can assure you there is no labor more difficult or more off-putting than [learning Chinese]. These Chinese characters are an unreadable scribble, and at first, it is impossible to decipher them. However, if you continue to stare and exhaust your imagination and memory, things become clearer, and one begins to see them clearly."[39] Fouquet became nonetheless quite proficient in his knowledge of Chinese letters.[40] For his confrère Langlois de Chavagnac (1670–1717), who spent eight hours every day for five months learning the language (forty-five thousand letters in the alphabet! he wrote), acquiring enough knowledge only to administer the sacraments and preach simple sermons, there was another method far more efficacious in preaching the faith.[41]

For the propagation of faith, books were potentially far more efficient than conversations. By its very nature, dialogue is unstable, flexible, and sumptuous in its use of words; a good conversation depended on setting, gestures, attire, as well as on the eloquence of speech. For a missionary, a conversation was barren if it yielded no interest in the Faith: in the arithmetic of salvation, dialogues were economically unsound, as words were squandered in mere social rituals. The Belgian François Nöel reported to the general of the Society in 1703 that the mandarins and officials in Beijing were mostly very friendly with the Jesuits. They would converse with them about ethics and faith, and professed admiration for their religion, but they would not pursue the conversation whenever the Jesuits broached the subject of conversion.[42] By contrast, books made conversions.

In 1702, fifteen scholars paid a courtesy visit to Fouquet in Fuzhou; they had come for the provincial civil service examination. The Frenchman conversed with them and presented them with Chinese books written by Jesuits, particularly Ricci's *Tian zhu shi yi,* which made an excellent impression. Another favorite Jesuit book was Aleni's *Wanwu zhenyuan* (The True Origins of All Things, 1628), which inspired many conversions. Fouquet knew one scholar in Fuzhou who became a Christian after reading it; he had heard of another mandarin in Beijing converting after reading a Christian book given to him by Adam Schall. For Fouquet, books were "mute preachers."[43]

Not only did these "mute preachers" discourse more eloquently than real preachers who spoke bad Chinese, they enabled an enormous leap in the production of evangelizing dialogue. For every polite conversation between a missionary and a mandarin-scholar, during which the Faith might never be broached, the book could create hundreds of mute dialogues between reader and text. Ricci realized this early on and, once established in Beijing, turned his attention to writing and publishing books.[44] Moreover, books had other advantages. On visiting the mountainous rural areas of western Fujian, Jean Baborier baptized an eighty-three-year-old scholar who was almost deaf and did not understand Baborier's spoken Chinese, but was so impressed by reading the books the Jesuit gave him that he accepted baptism.[45]

With books, one could dispense with missionaries altogether, at least initially. In 1724, a Manchu prince of the imperial line saw a Christian book at a book fair in Beijing. His curiosity aroused, he had his servant purchase the title and read it with great interest. Failing to find similar books in bookstores, the prince was told about the library at the Catholic church. He sent his servant to buy more books and the servant returned with a bundle given away but not sold by the Jesuits. The Manchu prince later told the fathers: "I read [the books] as fast as I could; I was charmed by the order, the clarity, and the solidity of the reasoning that prove the existence of a sovereign being, creator of all things, such that one could not imagine anything more grand and more perfect. The simple exposition of his magnificent attributes gave me so much pleasure, that I found this doctrine in conformity with the ancient classics."[46] He sought out the Jesuits, learned the doctrines, and "submitted his reason to the yoke of the faith."

IV

From the modest beginning of half a dozen titles in the first years of the seventeenth century (almost all by Ricci), the library of Catholic books in the Chinese language grew to over two hundred works a century later by scores of Jesuit and Chinese authors, as well as dozens of translations of European books. The imperial capital, Beijing, was the publishing center: together, the two Jesuit residences (the Portuguese and the French) held wood blocks for 212 book titles, the majority (123) on religious subjects (doctrines, liturgy, catechisms, breviaries), as well as 89 on natural and moral philosophy, calendrical and scientific subjects, and the lives of leading missionaries and Chinese converts. Outside of Beijing, the Jesuits had also established two other publishing centers, at their residences in Fuzhou (51 titles) and Hangzhou (40 titles), which happened to be centers of Chinese publishing as well.[47] To this substantial corpus must be added a small number of manuscripts composed by Chinese Christians that circulated in handwritten copies, and a much smaller number of Chinese books published by other religious orders.[48]

The growth of book production was accompanied by the institutionalization of Catholic printing. As in Europe, Catholic authors submitted their books to ecclesiastical censorship. For the Jesuits, this usually meant the imprimatur of the residence superior; and after the 1670s all Jesuit works were published with the names of the author as well as the censors and readers. For the Dominicans, it often entailed getting the works approved in Manila; and for the other religious orders, censorship and imprimaturs were provided by their members in the China Mission.

With printing, the spoken word at each and every conversation was rendered into visual signs, standardized and reproduced over time and space. With the expansion of the mission, dialogues yielded in significance to published texts subject to ecclesiastical authority and control. Disciplined by the printed text, conversations lost their indeterminacy as the spoken word came under the authority of authorship and censorship. Two examples should suffice to demonstrate this dialogical change.

In 1694 the Italian Augustinian Bonavente published a work in colloquial Chinese, *Shi ke wen* (Answering Visitors). Summarizing the many questions from visitors, Bonvaente arranged the answers according to the subjects of a catechism while preserving the format of a dialogue. What was being reproduced, in this work that seemed to echo the style of a well-established genre, was not the experience of any one conversation between our Italian friar and a particular Chinese visitor, but an abstract dialogue that served to explicate Christian doctrines.[49] Conversation has been institutionalized into catechism.

Our second example concerns the French Jesuit Placide Hervieu (1671–1746), who was stationed in Jiujiang in Jiangxi province. Hervieu wrote of a habitual visitor, a Chinese scholar, who asked for books to read every time he came to the Jesuit residence. On one visit, sometime in 1718, Hervieu was editing de Chavagnac's manuscript for posthumous publication. His visitor asked to read this latest work, but Hervieu replied that the Society's rules prohibited unpublished and unauthorized works to circulate. Instead, they set down to discuss the meaning of the term *Shengjiao* (Holy Religion). When the visitor took his leave, he again expressed his hope to have the chance to read de Chavagnac's book after it had been edited.[50] There was no longer a continuous flow between conversation and reading, for it was interrupted by textual authority and ecclesiastical censorship.

In fact, de Chavagnac himself was rather disenchanted with conversing with the Chinese when he first arrived in China. He landed in Canton on 1 September 1701 and in a letter written only four months later to the superior of the Paris house, le Gobien, he complained:

> The Chinese are not capable of listening in the space of a month to what a Frenchman can say to him in an hour. One must suffer without anger and not become impatient with this languor and this natural indolence, in order to speak about Religion, without getting discouraged, to a people who are afraid only of the emperor, and who love nothing but money, and are consequently excessively indifferent to all things that touch on eternity.[51]

Be that as it may; one wonders, how much Chinese de Chavagnac was able to speak in an hour after studying the language for four months. One can only surmise that de Chavagnac spoke from experience, but that his repertoire of conversation, limited only to the Christian religion, and restricted by his vocabulary, could hardly have interested an interlocutor.

De Chavagnac thought better of the Chinese later on, spending fourteen years in Jiangxi province where he died in 1717. Like other missionaries of his generation, de Chavagnac turned to the common people to preach the Gospels. The common people, namely those not of the literati and mandarin elites, had always constituted the majority of the Chinese Christian population, if only because of their overwhelming majority in the general population. A careful reading of Ricci's memoirs yields this impression; and the figures reported by the Jesuits in their annual reports (*Litterae Annuae*) of the early seventeenth century amply confirm this sociology of conversion.[52]

Things had not changed much in 1703, when François Noël wrote his annual report: the majority of converts were common people; only one Manchu prince had converted with his entire household; there were some scholars and literati among the Christians, but very few mandarins, and only at the Bureau of Mathematics (where the Jesuits themselves were appointed).[53] In 1715 Dentrecolles reported that in Jiangxi province artisans and workers formed the greatest part of the Christian community. The French missionary was touched by their fervor and their poverty, which forced some to sell their children. While he counted several friends among the literati, no one had converted. In general, Dentrecolles lamented, the literati scorned Christianity, even though the mandarins knew of the Kangxi emperor's benevolent disposition.[54] In the provinces, the Jesuits were finding that the rural folk and urban artisans much more amenable to evangelization than the scholars and mandarins. In their enthusiasm to welcome the simple folk into the embrace of the church, some entered dangerous ground. In 1730, the French Jesuit Etienne Le Couteux baptized a former White Lotus sectarian with his entire family of twenty while traveling by boat throughout the province of Huguang.[55] The charge that European missionaries plotted sectarian rebellions, just like the heterodox White Lotus Buddhist sect, first raised in the persecution of 1616–20, would haunt them for generations to come.

In the imperial capital, all hopes were pinned on converting the emperor. If this looked imminent in the 1690s, when Kangxi enjoyed a close rapport with several Jesuits at court—at least according to the all too optimistic Jesuit letters—it was still not impossible to imagine during the early years of the eighteenth century, when the storm of the Chinese Rites Controversy was gathering force. But with the papal prohibition of Chinese rites involving the veneration of ancestors and Confucius, and Kangxi's 1715 edict requiring all European missionaries to subscribe to the methods of Ricci, all hope was dashed for a Chinese Constantine. The breakdown of diplomacy between Rome and Beijing resulted eventually in the prohibition of European missionaries in the provinces as well as of Chinese becoming Christians. Both edicts, enforced by sporadic persecutions, retarded but did not choke off the growth of the mission.[56] The successors to the imperial throne, Yongzheng in 1723 and Qianlong in 1735, both repeated these earlier injunctions against Christianity. The only Europeans legally tolerated were those at the imperial court, in the service of the emperors as musicians, mathematicians, painters, and interpreters. The Jesuits, formerly Western literati and friends of the mandarins, became almost like the *bao-yi,* the bondservants of the Manchu service class pledged in perpetual loyalty to their liege lord.

In the eighteenth century, the European missionaries had no friends. True, they had many acquaintances, even among the mandarins and scholars; and they enjoyed personal friendships, even with the exalted personages of Manchu princes of royal blood. But they did not have friends in the Ciceronian definition of the term: of sovereign souls united in a common venture, engaged in dialogue, open to one another in a frank, affectionate, and generous exchange. After the treatises by Ricci and Martini on friendship, published in 1595 and 1647 respectively, no other work was written on the subject by European missionaries.[57] The idea of friendship, which animated literary and political discourses in seventeenth-century Europe, had gone out of fashion by the eighteenth century. In China, the literary associations, the framework of friendship networks among the scholars in the late Ming dynasty, wilted in the cold wind of literary persecutions under the Yongzheng emperor.

In the eighteenth century, the European missionary had a master and pupils. The Jesuits acknowledged the emperor as their master and looked upon the Chinese Christians in their charge as pupils. As conversation gave way to catechism, friendship yielded to hierarchy. An anonymous manuscript, written in colloquial Chinese around 1700, describes the meeting of a newly arrived European missionary and a Chinese visitor in the form of a dialogue between master and pupil. The missionary receives his Chinese visitor, who reverently addresses him as *laoye* (Old Master), a term servants used to address their household masters, and as *laoshi* (Teacher). The Chinese visitor offers the seat of honor to the missionary and kneels down to kowtow to the foreigner, as one would to a superior.[58] Kowtowing was of course what the court Jesuits in Beijing performed in the presence of the emperor. As vicars of the King of Kings in a pagan country, the missionaries in the provinces seem to have expected the same ceremony of deference.

In the first half of the eighteenth century, Chinese works published by European missionaries came to be dominated by catechisms and liturgical works. More of them were written in colloquial Chinese, reflecting the reality that the mission had changed its target audience to the common people and the lower social classes. These later catechisms, written by members of all the religious orders, confirmed an earlier alternative missionary strategy practiced by the Spanish Dominicans in the coastal province of Fujian, where they concentrated on evangelizing the common people. Critical of the Jesuits for their oversubtle accommodation to Confucian teachings, the Spanish Dominicans resorted to direct and uncomplicated explication of Christian doctrines, which seemed to have served them well enough in the Americas and in the Philippines. A catechism, *Tianzhu shengjiao rumen wenda* (Questions and Answers for Entering the Holy Religion of the Lord of Heaven), graced with a frontispiece of the Dominican Rosary, gave short and precise questions and answers:

Q: Who made Heaven?
A: God made Heaven.
Q: Is Buddha a good person?

A: Buddha is also a human created by God. Since he was created by God, he should have worshiped the Lord of Heaven. But not only did he not worship God, he wanted others to serve him instead....He was the greatest sinner in history.

Q: Is it a sin to have sex with your own hand?

A: It is a pretty bad sin.[59]

Crude perhaps, but effective in its economy of language. After all, unlike Ricci, the Dominicans never tried to dissimulate their true intention. To the horror of the Jesuits, some friars would come in on Chinese vessels from Manila and land on the coast in Fujian, holding up large crucifixes, and walk into the nearest village or town to preach the Gospel, whereupon, escorted by astounded Chinese civilians to the magistracy, they were usually imprisoned and expelled.

The Jesuits had reason for anxiety, for while the Qianlong emperor favored his court Jesuits, he frowned upon unauthorized European missionaries in the provinces. In the mid-Qing, the Jesuit-Confucian of the late Ming dynasty was replaced by the Jesuit-courtier, who tried to intercede on behalf of his fellow missionaries working in the shadows of the provinces. Court gossip and conversations filled the pages of Jesuit reports, whether occasioned by the promulgation of Kangxi's so-called Edict of Toleration in 1692, which came after several formal petitions and private pleadings by the court Jesuits, or by the visit of Portuguese embassies. These were not conversations that meandered the pathway of friendship, but palace gossip, formal petitions, and private pleadings.[60] With the outbreak of persecutions in Fujian and Chiangnan in 1754, the Mission seemed shaken to its foundation, and the Jesuits at court pinned their hopes on the visit of a Portuguese embassy, headed by Francisco Xavier d'Assis Pacheco Sampaio. The ambassador was received with great distinction by Qianlong, who seemed to have taken a personal liking to him, but the visit achieved only temporary relief from persecutions. No one at court dared to speak openly about the dangerous subject of Christianity.[61] When Qianlong ordered Jean-Denis Attiret, a Jesuit brother and court painter, to fashion a portrait of the ambassador for his European portrait gallery, Attiret and Giuseppe Castiglione, the emperor's favorite painter, seized the opportunity. Throwing themselves before Qianlong, they pleaded on behalf of Christianity and begged the emperor to stop persecutions. Surprised and slightly irritated, Qianlong simply replied, "zhi dao le," literally "all right, I know," an expression that indicates the speaker's desire not to listen any longer to the subject.[62]

The long conversation begun by Ricci on Europe and China, on Christianity and Confucianism, finally came to a close; and when that dialogue resumed in the early nineteenth century, it became a harsher and less interesting one.

NOTES

1. Jean-Denis Bredin and Thierry Lévy, *Convaincre: Dialogue sur l'éloquence* (Paris, 1997), p. 9.

2. See Willard J. Peterson, "Why Did They Become Christians? Yang T'ing-yün, Li Chih-tsao, and Hsü Kuang-ch'i," in *East Meets West: The Jesuits in China, 1582–1773,* ed. Charles E. Ronan and Bonnie B. C. Oh (Chicago, 1988), pp. 129–52.

3. See the comments by Ricci in *Storia dell'introduzione del Cristianesimo in China,* ed. Pasquale M. D'Elia, 3 vols. (Rome, 1942–49), here vol. 2, bk. IV, chap. 18, p. 218: "E assi, sem embargo de fazer altíssimo conceito de nossa Santa Fé e lei, reparavão porém geralmente todos neste ponto, assi por lhes parecer sem rezão, como por ser cousa que seus antepassados lhes deixarão por tradição; a qual deixar—se hé tido por crime de desobediencia." Hereafter cited as Ricci, *FR.*

4. Ibid., 1:73. English translation from Louis J. Gallagher, trans., *China in the Sixteenth Century: The Journals of Matthew Ricci: 1583–1610* (New York, 1953), p. 61. Gallagher's translation is based on Nicholas Trigault's 1615 Latin translation. Any variation from his translation is based on Ricci's original text and is so marked.

5. Ibid., p. 229: "Con questa occasione cominciorno anco a parlare delle cose della nostra Fede; ma non si potette far niente, per nessuno de' doi Padri sapere la lingua cinese, e menare un interprete non molto a ciò, per esser vecchio e puoco spedito."

6. Ibid., bk. II, chap. 7.

7. Introduction to *Ji ren shi pian* by Zhou Bingmo, edition of Bibliothèque Nationale de France (hereafter BNF), Fonds Chinois 6832, fols. 4a–5b.

8. Ricci, *FR,* 2:75. For the banquet-colloquy see pp. 75–80.

9. Ibid., pp. 77–78: "Venuti tutti gli invitati, si posero a sedere alle tavole. . . . E nel mezzo del convito cominciorno i letterati a trattar tra se stessi una questione molto ventilata nell scuole della Cina: se la natura humana di se stessa è buona, o mala, o indifferente. . . . Il Padre stette tutto questo tempo in silentio senza dir niente, e pare che molti pensavano che non intendeva questa questione per esser molto sottile, o almanco che non stava attento a quello di che si parlava; e desideravano tutti udirgli parlare qualche cosa. Per questo, facendo segno che egli voleva parlare, tacquero

tutti e si voltorno a lui con molta attentione. Cominciò il Padre prima a ripetere in somma tutto quanto avevano detto della natura humana. . . ."

10. Ibid., pp. 72–73, on Ricci's donning the dress of a Confucian scholar: "E per questo si parlava molto di questo fra la gente principale, e dicevano essere il Padre il vero letterato che non si imbruttava niente con la setta degl'idoli . . ." And on Ricci's brilliant performance at the banquet, p. 80: "Di questa disputa si parlò molto per tutto Nanchino . . ."

11. BNF Chinois 7024, *Shi ke wenda,* 37 leaves, unfoliated. The text cited is a précis of the work.

12. There are four copies in BNF Chinois 6816–6819.

13. BNF Chinois 6972.

14. BNF Chinois 6882/6883.

15. BNF Chinois 7014.

16. BNF Chinois 6845.

17. *Dai yi pian* (A Reply to Doubts), BNF Chinois 7093, fol. 33a.

18. BNF Chinois 6868, fols. 1a–2a.

19. *Shengjiao xinzheng* (Proof of the Holy Faith), BNF Chinois 6903, preface by Han Lin.

20. *Sheng meng ge* (Song of Holy Dream), written in 1637, attributed to Aleni. BNF Chinois 6885.

21. The dialogue is appended to a dictionary *Xi ru er mu zi* (A Visual-Aural Aid for Western Scholars), containing fourteen thousand Chinese characters classified under vowels, diphthongs, and triphthongs). BNF Chinois 9081.

22. *Tianxue juyao* (Selected Essentials of the Learning of Heaven), BNF Chinois 6900/6901.

23. In Wang's preface to "On Charity," written by the Italian Jesuit Giacomo Rho, BNF Chinois 6869, fols. 1a–2a.

24. *Qiu you lun* (On Friendship) (1661), composed by Martini with an introduction by Chu. BNF Chinois 3415.

25. *Kou dou ri chao* (Written Notes of Oral Teachings), Giulio Aleni, compiled by Zhang Geng et al., 8 juan, 1631, juan 3, fols. 14b–16b.

26. Ricci, *FR,* vol. 2 bk. V, chap. 4.

27. *Fei lu da hui* (A Compilation of Answers to Diverse Subjects) (1636). conversations of Vagnoni compiled and edited by Gao Yizhi, with introduction by Bi Gonghan. BNF Chinois 3394.

28. Li Zhi's adjective to describe Ricci's personality, *linglong,* echoes the term for the armillary (*linglongyi*) at the Nanjing Observatory.

29. Li Zhi in x*u fen shu* (Book to be Burned: A Continuation), juan 2.

30. Ricci, *FR* 1:355–56, trans. Gallagher, p. 273.

31. Ibid., 2:293.

32. Sun Shangyang, *Mingmo Tianzhujiao yu Ruxue de jiaoliu he chongtu* (Exchange and Conflict between Catholicism and Confucianism at the End of the Ming Dynasty) (Taibei, 1992), p. 167.

33. The only biography of Aleni is by Eugenio Menegon, *Un solo cielo: Giulio Aleni, S.J. (1582–1649): Geografia, arte, scienza, religione dall'Europa alla Cina* (Brescia, 1994). See also the conference volume, Tiziana Lippiello and Roman Malek, eds., *Scholar from the West: Giulio Aleni, S.J. (1582–1649) and the Dialogue between Christianity and China* (Brescia, 1997).

34. BNF Chinois 1017, Part I is the acts; and part II is a compilation of the teachings. This citation is from juan 2 of part II.

35. See R. Po-chia Hsia, "L'édit de tolérance de Kangxi et la mission chrétienne en Chine," in *Tolérance: L'Edit de Nantes 1598–1998* (Nantes, forthcoming).

36. Charles Le Gobien, preface to *Lettres edifiantes et curieuses écrites de missions etrangères, par quelques missionnaires de la Compagnie de Jesus,* 1. Recueil (Paris, 1717), fol. A5r.

37. *Lettres edifiantes,* 8. Recueil (Paris, 1708), pp. 239–40.

38. Ibid., 7. Recueil (Paris, 1701), p. 176.

39. Ibid., 5. Recueil (Paris, 1708), pp. 229–30.

40. His superior rated him as "profectus in litteris sinicis: non exiguus, sed novitatem amans." See Joseph Dehergne, *Répertoire des Jésuites de Chine de 1552 à 1800* (Rome, 1973), p. 99.

41. *Lettres edifiantes,* 9. Recueil (Paris, 1711), pp. 333–34.

42. Ibid., 6. Recueil (Paris, 1707), p. 90.

43. Ibid., 3. Recueil (Paris, 1713), pp. 166–72.

44. Ricci, *FR,* vol. 2, bk. V, chap. 2.

45. *Lettres edifiantes,* 8. Recueil, pp. 95–100.

46. Ibid., 17. Recueil (Paris, 1726), pp. 14–16.

47. See BNF Chinois 7046 VII for a list of the titles.

48. The largest collection of Chinese-language Catholic books, at the BNF, has many examples of books printed by the mendicant orders and by the Missions Etrangères.

49. BNF Chinois 7023.

50. Preface by Hervieu to de Chavagnac, *Shengdao zizheng* (Evidential Proofs of the True Doctrine) (1718), fols. 1a–8a. BNF Chinois 7047.

51. *Lettres edifiantes,* 3. Recueil, p. 156.

52. See the annual reports of 1636 and 1643–49, in António de Gouvea, *Cartas Ânuas da China,* ed. Horácio P. Araújo (Lisbon, 1998), passim.

53. *Lettres edifiantes,* 6. Recueil, pp. 87–90.

54. Ibid., 13. Recueil (Paris, 1718), pp. 315–27.

55. Ibid., 22. Recueil (Paris, 1736), pp. 157–60.

56. See Zhang Ze, *Qingdai jin jiao qi de Tianzhujiao* (The Persecution of the Catholic Church during the Qing Dynasty) (Taibei, 1992).

57. Cf. Louis Fister, *Notices biographiques et bibliographiques sur les Jésuites de l'ancienne Mission de Chine 1552–1773,* 2 vols. (Shanghai, 1932–34).

58. BNF Chinois 7046, sec. 4, "Conversations between a Newly Arrived Priest and a Visitor."

59. BNF Chinois 6902. On the Dominican mission in China, see Jose Maria Gonzalez, *Misiones Dominicanas en China (1700–1750)* (Madrid, 1958). The author, a Dominican, blames the "Riccistas" for losing China.

60. On the Edict of Toleration, see Charles Le Gobien, *Histoire de l'édit de l'empereur de la Chine, en faveur de la Religion Chrestienne: avec un eclaircissement sur les honneurs que les Chinois rendent à Confucius et aux Morts* (Paris, 1698).

61. *Lettres edifiantes,* 28. Recueil (Paris, 1758), p. xiii.

62. *Litterae Annuae Sinensis 1754,* fol. 318r. Fugger-Archiv, Dillingen, Akten 1.2.148.

5

TWISTING A PAGAN TONGUE

PORTUGUESE AND TAMIL IN SIXTEENTH-CENTURY JESUIT TRANSLATIONS

INES ŽUPANOV

CONFUSION OF NAMES

When Henrique Henriques (or Anrique Anriquez), a missionary among the Parava fishing communities in south India, chose to employ *tamil* both as an adjective and a noun in his pious compendium of Christian saints and festivals, printed in 1586 in the Tamil language and in Tamil characters, he created an instant semantic dislocation, both subtle and gigantic.[1] His choice, as I propose to demonstrate in this essay, is a symptom of a linguistic, strategic, and national epistemic, though subterranean, rupture between Portuguese "colonial" and Jesuit "spiritual" conversion enterprises in Asia. On the surface, the uneasy cooperation continued until the middle of the eighteenth century, when the Jesuits were made to pay for all the failures of the Portuguese "empire" in Portugal and beyond, but the relation between the secular and spiritual arms in the grand project of Christianization of Asia remained one of contained mistrust.

To the extent that Asia, or some geographical pockets of it, was haltingly converted to Christianity, the Portuguese language, the extolled medium of religious conversion, was eclipsed and replaced by local languages. In the regions distant from leading administrative and military centers such as Goa, efforts at downplaying or effacing Portuguese claims to sovereignty over the Asian Christian word (and world) were further facilitated after the 1580s, under the rule of the Spanish Habsburgs.[2] Some prominent Jesuits, many of them Italians—as the opponents of their "accommodationist" method of conversion never failed to mention—such as Alessandro Valignano, Matteo Ricci, and Roberto Nobili, at times openly dissociated themselves from Portuguese religious patronage.[3]

In the introductory story of Henriques's *Flos Sanctorum* in Tamil, in addition to the absence of Portugal and Portuguese, Christianity itself appears without its "European" origins. Thus he divides the religious world into Muslim, Jewish, Christian, and Tamil. The meaning of "Tamil" clearly extends to include all "pagans." Another "confusing" word is present in the title of the chapter, *cuṇṇattu,* which stood for "circumcision." This Arabic term referred to a Muslim practice, making Henriques's statement oddly anachronistic, since he first claimed that "at the time of the birth of our Lord Jesus Christ as a man, except for Jews and Tamils, there were no Muslims. As soon as he was born, an angel appeared and made known the news of his birth to the Jewish shepherd. In that manner, as soon as he was born, a star appeared to the three Tamil kings."[4]

By translating, or rather in his case substituting, key terms such as *gentio* or *ethnicus*—commonly used terms in Portuguese and Latin texts for a Gentile or a heathen—with a proper noun designating a language and a people inhabiting a particular south Indian region, Henriques hoped to produce for his Tamil Christian readers a resonant past and a sense of difference vis-à-vis their non-Christian neighbors. To make somebody come to (*varuttu*) the Christian path/religion (*kiricittiyāṇi maṟkam*), as he paraphrases the act of conversion, meant stepping out of Tamil identity and assuming a new one. A "true Christian religion" is therefore opposed to "false Tamil religion," the latter ambiguously combining late antique paganism and Indian religious practices encountered in the sixteenth century.[5] In this scheme of things, can we venture to say that for Henriques and his like, conversion meant a total loss of previous identity, of cultural and social substance? Another linguistically and socially hegemonic move might furnish additional proof that the Jesuit conversion strategies aimed at total annihilation of their converts' past experiences. In the same story of Christ's circumcision, Henriques insisted on regulating the attribution of personal Christian names. Not only were the Parava converts to choose Christian names for themselves and their children to replace Tamil names, but also, he added— betraying that the opposite was often the case—to actually use them: "If anybody calls you by your Tamil name, do not respond."[6] The directory of suitable Christian names was the *Flos Sanctorum* itself. Untranslatable *stricto sensu,* these were transliterated Portuguese names deformed at times beyond recognition through Tamil script and further adaptation to Tamil phonetics. Thus St. Lucy became *su. uluciyāḷ,* St. Matthew *su. mattēsu.* Over the course of time and in the course of geographical dispersion, some saints began to resemble local deities both in name and in powers. St. Mary or *su. mariyal* blended at times with *mariyāmmaṇ* and other manifestations of the Goddess. (Known under various local names, the Goddess is the most important south Indian divine person, feared and worshipped for her ability to inflict and cure illness, especially smallpox. Even the name of St. Francis Xavier, Henriques's famous predecessor and superior of the mission, engendered *cāverimuttu* (the pearl of Xavier), which is still a popular Tamil Christian name.[7]

It appears, then, that if discursively unbraided, the *Flos Sanctorum* might serve as an exemplary school text for studying the articulation of religious linguistic colonialism. Arbitrary choice of words, confusion of names, and anachronistic borrowings are only the most conspicuous and heavy-handed tricks of the trade. However, in spite of the fact that both religious conversion and/or linguistic translation were valuable adjuncts and accessories of colonialist/imperialist ambitions, it has also been successfully argued that "translation and conversion produce the vernacular as that which simultaneously institutes and subverts colonial rule."[8] The inherent instability of the framework in which conversion and translation were to take effect made the encounter, in our case between Portuguese, the source language of missionary enterprise, and Tamil as well as other Asian vernacular languages, the receptor languages, a turbulent space for cultural transference.[9] Given that translative practices are unavoidably metaphoric activities, the displacement of meaning from one semantic site to another is endlessly threatened by willful or unselfconscious human agency and arbitrary discursive moves. The operative field in which the translation is carried out is in itself a no-man's-land of otherness up for grabs by political, national, cultural, ecclesiastical, mystical, and "scientific" interventionists.[10] In a similar, although not identical, manner, religious conversion as improvised in the Jesuit missionary field in Asia under the Portuguese *padroado* was an invitation to cultural nomadism, "refugee" movements (like the so-called "Rice Christians"), social dissent, and political extremism.[11]

By looking closely into more than half a century of linguistic experiments in the first Jesuit mission in India, established by St. Francis Xavier on the southernmost stretch of sandy coast from Cape Comorin (Kanyakumari) to Rameswaram, my intention is to chronicle the gradual failure of Portuguese linguistic "colonialist" domination.[12] Ironically, or inevitably, the Jesuits, initially sent by the king of Portugal, João III, to extend the Lusophone and Christian world in Asia, "went native," on the level of *parole,* if not of *langue.* Therefore, the effects of "treachery" inherent in the act of translation affected both Portuguese and Tamil at the site of their encounter. Treacherous undercurrents, narrative deviations as well as cultural reconstruction, are to be found in various written documents produced by Henrique Henriques (printed or in manuscript) such as the *Flos Sanctorum, Confessionairo, Arte Malauar, tampirān vaṇakkam,* and *kiricittiyāṇi vaṇakkam.*[13]

If Parava pre-Christian identities were irreparably lost, new identities were eventually forged which successfully combined Christian religious imagery and ethics with Tamil cultural and linguistic expression.

Hence, by the end of the sixteenth century the unstable Christian linguistic territory of south India—while remaining staunchly Catholic—had decisively slipped out of Lusophony, which had in fact reflected the apogee of Portuguese "imperial" intentions in Asia. Without acquiring extensive territorial possessions, except coastal trade enclaves, and with a feeble presence of Portuguese native speakers, both the language and the "empire" diminished, disappearing by the end of the eighteenth century. Goa and Macau remained, of course, as feeble reminders of earlier ambitions. But in the beginning of the sixteenth century when rapid mercantile expansion was gaining momentum, Portuguese linguistic pretensions were rising high, along with political appetites.

EXCHANGE AND CAPTURE OF FOREIGN WORDS

At least four decades before the arrival of the missionaries, the first linguistic encounters between Portuguese and other European languages and various Asian languages were cast in narratives of exchange and capture. European travelogues and logbooks provided the first dictionaries of words and set phrases to facilitate mutual comprehension. Predictably, salutation formulas, verbs of perception, often in imperative or infinitive forms like "look," "hear," or practical verbs and nouns referring to actions and things vital to subsistence, such as "food," "to eat," "to drink," and terms designating titles or functions pertaining to the local social hierarchy and mercantile commodities, appeared in European print and manuscripts of the late fifteenth and early sixteenth centuries. The words were also perceived as booty, conquest or possession by which to enrich one's language. An example of this wishful "imperialist" thinking is João de Barros, a famous Portuguese Renaissance polymath with a panoptic view of the role of the Portuguese language in Asia.[14]

> . . . as we can see in all those words that begin with *ál* and *xá,* and in those that end with *z,* all of which are *mouriscos.* And now, from the conquest of Asia we took *chatinár* for trading, *beniaga* for merchandise, *lascarim* for warrior (soldier), *cumbáya* for reverence and courtesy, and other *vocábulos* that are already so natural in the mouth of the people who go to those parts, just like their own Portuguese.[15]

These exotic borrowings were unquestioningly subjected to Portuguese linguistic sovereignty. The ultimate "glory," Barros maintained, was to see Ethiopians, Persians, and Indians, in the midst of their temples and "pagodas," learning the Portuguese language through which they could be converted to Christianity.[16] Thus, linguistic expansion leads naturally to religious conversion. Furthermore, the exotic peoples who inhabited Portuguese Asia, according to Barros, were no better than uninstructed children because they did not speak Portuguese.[17] For that reason, his *Gramática,* printed in Lisbon between 1539 and 1540, was not only, in his own words, intended for children, but also for foreigners. Under the general title of *Gramática da língua portuguesa com os mandamentos da Santa Madre Igreja,* four distinct works are included: (1) a *Cartinha,* or primer for learning basic literacy skills with a short catechism; (2) a grammar of the Portuguese language; (3) *O diálogo em louvor da nóssa linguágem* (Dialogue in Praise of our Language); and (4) *Diálogo da viçiosa vergonha* (Dialogue of Defective Shame). Reading and studying his *Gramática* was, in Barros's opinion, an enterprise much larger than the simple apprenticeship of letters and grammatical rules, it was also a way of learning Christian prayers and catechism, moral and ethical precepts, as well as theological and philosophical implications embedded in linguistic questions. And, most importantly, as a written and codified document, *Gramática* could operate and produce from afar effects which, without temporal and material constraints, were more resistant to the corrosive force of time. "Portuguese arms and memorial stones (*padrões*), planted in Africa and in Asia, and on thousands of islands beyond the three parts of the world, are material and time might spoil them, but it will not spoil the doctrine, customs and language that the Portuguese have left in those parts."[18] The comparison with the Roman empire that naturally follows merits closer attention, containing as it does both an open self-congratulation and a subtle warning against Portuguese overexpansion. Because the Romans insisted that the people they subjugated speak their language, Latin remained the only "eternal signal" of their past achievements when their empire crumbled.

Like Antonio de Nebrija, who presented his grammar of Castilian, the first grammar of a modern European tongue, as a gift to the Spanish royal family to enable them to use their national language as an "instrument" or a "partner" of their empire, Barros made a similar claim for his *Gramática* half a century later. In the dedication to the Portuguese prince and future king (*príncipe e rei em esperança*), he specifically underscored that the Asian nobles were also recipients of his grammatical gift and that four Indian "chieftains" were already studying Portuguese at the "House of Santo Elói" in Lisbon.[19] They came from the Malabar country, where fifty-seven thousand souls had been converted and where "St. Thomas with so much labor and martyrdom left this life for celestial glory." In spite of Barros's geographical and ethnographical imprecision, it is possible, though not certain, that these four "chieftains" belonged to the Parava pearl-fishing community from the Fishery Coast, converted nominally in the early 1530s, and converted for the second and final time by St. Francis Xavier in the early 1540s.[20] It is most probable that the four "chieftains" in Barros's dedication returned home as *línguas* (tongues)—a common name for "colonial" interpreters—or as catechists, even diocesan priests. Regardless of their individual destinies, the point he was making was that they were brought to Lisbon on wings of love for the Portuguese language, "love which brings them thousands of miles" from home. In the 1580s, Henriques's three kings (*mūvi rācākkal*), who made their entrance into the holy city of *vellem* (Belem, Bethlehem) in the pages of the *Flos sanctorum,* were also Tamils far from their native country, but they had no intention of learning Portuguese. The truth is, however, that some "relics" of Portuguese and Latin words remain in the text to remind us of Barros and his overenthusiastic theory of linguistic expansion. While the first "Malabar" words were captured (along with their speakers) by Vasco da Gama's crew and brought to Lisbon, some eighty years later in Henriques's translations into Tamil, Portuguese words appear as captives rather than captors.[21]

TAMIL VOICES IN LATIN SCRIPT

A small masterpiece of early Portuguese typography, the *Cartilha em Tamul e Português, impressa em 1554 por ordem do Rei,* published by Germão Galhardo, a French master printer in Lisbon, is a curiously hybrid text in which Portuguese and Tamil appear to be engaged in an indecisive tug-of-war.[22] The quarto edition of some forty pages in red and black Gothic lettering with seventeen small engravings was of "mixed" authorship. According to the prologue, Vicente de Nazarethe, Jorge Carualho, and Thome da Cruz, three "Índios," translated the "doc(t)rina xrãa" into Tamil by order of the king of Portugal and under the supervision of João de Villa de Conde, a Franciscan from the province of Piedade, who had spent some time in India. The polyphony of voices—Latin, Tamil, and Portuguese—caught in the printed text, demanded multiple authorizations, and the authorizing was done through a series of exterior sightings. From the royal to the final inquisitorial approval ("visto pola sancta inquisiçam"), the gazes of secular and religious officials criss-cross with those of the authors, who know very well that their expertise is only linguistic: "because we know all three languages."

The *cartinha* or *cartilha* belonged to a pedagogical literary genre that combined the learning of reading and writing (the primer) with basic prayers and religious teachings (the catechism). It seems that from the beginning of the sixteenth century *cartinhas* were in demand in Portugal and in the colonies, as well as *mestres de ler,* teaching the basic skills of reading and writing. In Lisbon, from thirty schools that taught children to read (with some thirty-four teachers) in 1553, the number grew to sixty in 1620.[23] The printed word was thus trickling down to illiterate metropolitan Portuguese, but also, and very early, to the overseas territories in order to teach the "natives" to speak. In 1512, Afonso de Albuquerque wrote to the king that he had discovered in Cochin a chest full of *cartinhas* and had given it to a *casado* to teach some boys to read and write.[24]

After almost half a century of Portuguese presence in India, when hundreds of *cartinhas* had been sent to promote the metropolitan language, the *Cartilha* of the three Indians, with typically Parava Christian names—and who might have been, according to Charles Boxer's speculative identification, the "chieftains" of João de Barros's *Gramática*—is the first reliable witness to the internal fracture in the linguistic "imperialist" dream. Meant to produce literate colonial actors and subjects who could go on with the important work of Portuguese commercial and cultural expansion, the *Cartilha* brought back home a "pagan" vernacular and juxtaposed it with Portuguese and with Latin.

What made the *Cartilha* possible, and at first sight unproblematic, was the confidence which its various authors felt and the consensus that they shared concerning the role of Portuguese vis-à-vis Tamil, or any other newly "discovered" language. Compared to Portuguese, these languages were less perfect and some, like Tamil, had a long way to go before catching up. While Barros felt compelled to juxtapose Portuguese and Latin in order to tease out a favorable comparison for the former, the *Cartilha* operates in a similar vein. Tamil is made to appear poor, inefficient, and impure. As the three Indians point out in the prologue, Tamil possesses

> two limits (*extremos*) in the enunciation (*pronunciação*). The first is that it is poor in vocabulary/ it cannot explain certain things by its own words and speaking styles (*estilos de falar*)/ especially that which this work contains and of which nothing is known in India, and it begins sometimes where the Portuguese end theirs/ and it begins where they end it: and sometimes the opposite: we search for circumlocutions that correspond to the sentence: without being in discord/ as can be seen in

the declaration [*declaração*—that is, a word-by-word translation] placed on top in red. The second is that it is so barbaric that certain elocutions (*dições*) cannot be pronounced by any of the Latin characters (*com nenhũs carateres latinos se podem pronunciar*).[25]

In addition, Tamil is accused of being flawed in terms of theological content and phonological substance. The passage from oral Tamil into written Portuguese was indeed resolved quite successfully, but without any reference to the Tamil writing system and script. The group of sounds that the three Indians fixed upon for their Portuguese audience was, however, incomplete. It was completely "purified" of difficult, unpronounceable sounds such as the retroflex stops (*ṭ, ṇ*) and semivowels (*ḻ, ḷ*), and was therefore converted and normalized for regular Indo-European vocalics.[26] Correspondingly, lexical choices were equally reductive. Most technical Christian categories were inserted into the Tamil text in their original written form, for example, *sacramentos, baptismo, charisma, confissam, comunham,* as well as the names of the Apostles. Moreover, Tamil had a number of additional sounds that were disregarded by the translators, while other, nonexistent sounds were added, such as the fricative (*f*) as in *confissam* or *cathólica fé,* which is regularly replaced with the labial (*p*) in the Tamil script. In Henrique Henriques's translations printed in Tamil script, "I confess" became "*kompecarikkiren*," a hybrid locution but fully respectful of the Tamil rules regarding both conjugation and phonology.

Transliteration of Tamil, as it was fabricated in the *Cartilha,* reterritorialized this puzzling, pagan language within the ambit of European linguistic dominion, showing a typical "imperial" casualness about disconcerting details. However, when detected, differences are explained through inversion—the Tamil sentence begins where the Portuguese ends; or absence—Christian concepts/words are nonexistent in Tamil. The solution to these problems came providentially from the printer's workshop. The choice of lettering, color, and graphic design succeeded in both underscoring and containing the difference, as well as reassuring the audience with a perfectly "analogical" translation/transcription. Romanized Tamil thus found itself squeezed between an interlinear word-for-word translation in red above (the *declaração*) and a syntactically correct translation in black beneath.

Eu___peccador_ meu peccado a deos___ [red]
Nan pelleali enpillei tambiranoru [black]
Eu peccador e errado me confesso a deo [black]

digo_____: assi___aa sancta_____
xolurren: ápari puniauálatiána
e ha virgem sancta_____maria

virgem ____maria_____a sam _____Pedro___
caniastri mariatincaniastri mariatinrôum/puniaualánana pedrunó
_____a sam ___Pedro_____

_____: assi _____a sam _____Paulo:_____a
rum: áuuanam puniaualánana paulunorum: pu
_____a sam _____Paulo _____a

The interlinear translation was not a new method. From medieval manuscripts to the polyglot Bible printed in Alcalá, it was one of the accepted ways of juxtaposing originals and translations. The Jesuit missionaries on the Fishery Coast reported having used it for preaching as early as 1548, when Henriques transliterated a palmleaf manuscript ("ola") from "malavar" to Latin script and wrote above each word "the declaration (*la declaración*) so that when it is read in the church, a father or a brother who was there present, could have a translation and could hear what was read."[27] How Henriques's interlinear translation looked on the palmleaf manuscript we may never know, but in the printed version of the *Cartilha,* Tamil appears as an inefficient language.[28]

Partly because it was printed in larger letters, the Tamil spreads along the lines without leaving any empty spaces, as the two Portuguese lines do. Red and black horizontal lines are, therefore, introduced to fill in the voids between Portuguese words. The visual effect is that the Tamil transcription looks as if imprisoned by Portuguese lines, as if making sure that no "pagan" substances transgress into the pages of this pious book. Fear of contamination or a convenient graphic solution, or both? On the other hand, in spite of the empty spaces between Portuguese words, the Portuguese sentence appears to contain an excess of meaning compared to the Tamil, or rather the Tamil sentence seems to be talking more and saying less. The complicated black and red graphic carries a very simple message— "I the sinner confess my sins to the Lord." The Tamil text, on the contrary, does not convey all that needs to be said. The verb denoting the act of confession is conspicuously absent from the word-by-word translation above where one finds a simple "peccado . . . digo" ("I tell my sins"). This omission does not seem to be necessary since a few pages later, *confissam* is present in the Tamil text as a noun, not a verb. More likely, the subtext warning is that confessing in Tamil is not quite as appropriate and efficient as confessing in Portuguese, as if the translators themselves were trying to caution their readers not to mistake similarity for identity. While in Portuguese, words stood for things (actions, thoughts), in the Tamil translation, they were only unavoidable "new" clothes which, although not fitting perfectly, at least did not compromise the ultimate meaning.[29]

Besides simply reproducing the key concepts of the "sacred" Christian doctrine in order to avoid accidental incorporation of what was feared as Tamil "pagan" phonological substance, the Tamil translation was geared to simplicity and, as its visual/graphic presentation amply confirms, to transparency. However, in spite of these precautions and translators' complaints about the poverty of the Tamil language (in expressing Christian *veritas*), local linguistic praxis made it virtually impossible to avoid contamination. In choosing an appropriate lexical fabric, the principle of "similarity" or "adequacy" was replaced by the principle of "authority." The words that ultimately made their way into the *Cartilha* to denote, for example, "faith," "sacred," the Holy Spirit, came straight out of what would later be denounced as the local "religious" register. *Xudammana xitan* (the Holy Spirit), *punia* (sacred, merit, holy), *vizvasam* (faith), *mamdrangal* (prayers), *agajam* (heaven, sky), and many other terms were also used by Hindu religious specialists, but seem to be taken implicitly by the translators as providing only a "neutral" phonological husk for the Christian concepts, while at the same time preserving something of an authorial mystique culturally inherent in these words. This complicated linguistic "conversion" reveals another important aspect, which made translation a nightmare for zealous European missionaries in south India. Most of the key technical words evoking Christian "truths" turned out to be taken from Sanskrit. Complex layering, with Sanskrit neatly woven through linguistic patterning, is a basic feature in most Indian languages.[30] Briefly, the use of Sanskrit was an unmistakable sign of a legitimating move. With all the twisting and turning of Tamil words in order to squeeze out a workable relation with Portuguese meanings, the truth of the matter is that the *Cartilha* is not, as might at first seem, a dialogic text at all. The translators claimed that it was written "in two languages, Tamil and Portuguese, so that everybody can profit"; but who would have or could have profited from this booklet is an open question. Since primers were mainly intended for those who wanted to learn to read and eventually to write, one could, perhaps, learn to read Portuguese from the syllabary presented on the very first page of the *Cartilha,* but not Tamil. Furthermore, it was not helpful to those who wanted to learn basic Tamil, although for those Indian Christians who had already mastered some Portuguese, it could have served as a useful reminder of Latin prayers. In the prologue, it is also underscored that this *doctrina* should be taken to various nations (*nações*), that is, it should be shipped out of Portugal to the overseas colonies.[31] Thus, in fact, the *Cartilha* was geared to convert, gradually and by means of a bilingual manual, Tamil native speakers into Portuguese "naturalized" Christian speakers and, ideally, subjects. Barros's idea of Lusophone Asia still loomed large behind this project.

Nevertheless, the *Cartilha* is the product of a considerable translating effort. Tamil, in spite of its unsatisfactory phonetic transcription, is a real, if "defective" language arrested in its effort to transpose and interpret Portuguese meanings (themselves transpositions from Latin). For the first time, Tamil was exposed to the Portuguese metropolitan view and could be read, heard, and voiced. It remained, of course, safely locked in orality and devoid of "self-reflection," unlike the double Portuguese version which figures simultaneously as a source language and a receptor language. The role of the *Cartilha* was primarily to force its readers to pronounce what was written, to memorize it, and only incidentally to understand it. Language and knowledge (self-knowledge included) obviously did more (or less) than accompany each other in this early game of translation from Portuguese into Tamil, in which the writing appears to have served mostly to recycle knowledge back into orality.

FROM APOSTOLIC GESTURE TO CHRISTIAN TAMIL

While Franciscans threaded behind Portuguese military and diplomatic expeditions against Sri Lankan sixteenth-century kingdoms and while the three Parava students in Lisbon composed the *Cartilha,* on the other side of what some historians prefer to call the *Mar de Ceilão,*[32] Tamil was used by the Jesuits not as an exotic language of missionary "exposure," but as a refined tool of conversion. The first missionary figure to cast doubt on the usefulness of the "imperialist" linguistic policy in Asia and to reject Portuguese as a language of conversion had been, in fact, implicitly sent to enforce it. Not a native speaker of Portuguese himself, Francis Xavier (1506–52), the first Jesuit missionary in Asia, was ready to teach the world Portuguese if that was how the Christianization of the world was to proceed, but he was also "indifferent" enough—in the Jesuit sense of the word—to adopt and adapt any other language if necessary. In Lisbon and initially in Goa, Portuguese appeared as a natural choice, and among the many books given as gifts to Xavier and Simão Rodrigues during their visits to the court of João III, Barros's *Gramática* was probably one.[33]

Once in Goa, in 1542, Xavier wrote his *Small Catechism,* a basic prayer book in Portuguese, a large part of which was taken verbatim from Barros's *Cartinha.* The *Small Catechism* would in the course of time grow into the *Big Catechism* with the addition of the "Declaration of the Articles of Faith," which Xavier wrote around 1546–47 during his stay on the island of Ternate.[34] The latter version of the text was then copied and sent to all Jesuit missionaries as a manual for teaching Christian doctrine and, in 1556, with the introduction of the printing press in Goa, it became one of the first books printed in southern Asia.[35] Portuguese was, therefore, around the middle of the sixteenth century considered as the master language for the teaching of the Christian doctrine in Asia. It was, of course, a lingua franca of the merchant communities involved directly or indirectly in trade with the Portuguese.

"Speaking half black and half Portuguese," if not only in words and through their meaning, Xavier nevertheless could make himself understood everywhere and left an impression on his audience.[36] His theatrical "actions" were performed at public places in the Portuguese colonial enclaves—prisons, churches, streets, marketplaces, the viceroy's palace—as well as in private homes, *portas adentro* ("within doors"), as this particular "action" seems to have been called. In the evening after confessing prisoners, according to the habitual scenario he walked the streets and summoned the faithful with a little bell (*campainha*)—his imitators in Europe called it "mos Indicus"—shouting loudly according to one of the witnesses in Melaka, the Jesuit Francisco Pérez, "Christianos, mandad vuestros hijos y hijas, esclavos e esclavas a la predicación de la fee!"[37] When some three hundred people had gathered around him, Xavier led them in a procession towards one of the designated churches in the town. With the polyphonic orchestration of sounds—prayers, exclamations, and tearful sighs—he tried to conjure up an interior *lingua sancta,* a universal language, a mother tongue of mystical ecstasies. The "method" of Loyola's *Spiritual Exercises* is clearly visible in Xavier's approach—from sensual experience to interior "ripening" of word and image, from cognitive experiment to mystical certainty, from indecision to clear discernment of the will.[38] The combination of images and words that staged a specific Jesuit experiential/experimental language was to become a new and powerful tool of public introspection. Xavier introduced this sort of mixed media into the missionary field with considerable success. Schurhammer is probably right to point out that the mixture of "black" and "Portuguese" refers to a particular mixed vernacular, a Creole Portuguese in basic syntax and variously garnished with Konkani vocabulary in Goa, or any other indigenous language elsewhere. The mixture of linguistic registers produced multiple and changing versions of *crioulos* (Creole Asian dialects based on Portuguese), some of which have survived into the twentieth century. Linguistic creolization is in many ways an ideal colonial situation in which the language of the masters is never completely the language of the slaves or subjects. Although the "natives" were quick to speak or curse back in Portuguese, their speech was endlessly "interrupted" by communicative sequences (phonetic, morphological, and syntactic) borrowed from "alien" tongues.[39] Creolization was also particularly useful to the missionaries because a *crioulo* was taken for a language "without a grammar," a "young," still unformed language, or simply for no language at all, but rather a "corrupted" Portuguese. The burden of translation was, therefore, lighter since the most important decisions as to how to translate the terms and categories of the doctrine become unnecessary. Key words in Portuguese or Latin, usually nouns and verbs, although at times slightly deformed, remained basically unchanged. Their "kingly" state inspired João de Barros to explain his theory of universal language through the rules of chess, a theory which prefigures linguistic theories from Port-Royal to the generative grammar of Noam Chomsky.

> Two kings are needed just as in the game of chess, one of one color and the other of another, and each of them keeps his pieces stationed in their own houses (*cásas*) and arranged, with obligations (*leies*) that each of them has to fulfill (according to the office given to it): in this way all the languages have two kings, different in kind, and equal (*concórdes*) in office: one is called Noun and the other Verb. Each of the kings has his own queen, that of the Noun they call Pronoun, that of the Verb they call Adverb. Participle, Article, Conjunction, Interjection are all pieces and principal captains who have under their jurisdiction many foot soldiers, i.e. modes of expression (*dições*).[40]

Barros's grammar was intended to be an *Arte* which would enable the teachers of language (*artistas*) to successfully mold the minds of their students.[41] The early "translations" of the doctrine into non-European languages, therefore, proceeded by substituting words considered as neutral, such as adverbs, prepositions, etc., while retaining as far as possible the "two kings" in their Portuguese form. Thus, a particular type of *crioulos* came into being, fabricated specifically for the purpose of religious teaching and conversion. It was these "syncretic" languages that Xavier cultivated in his various Asian missions.

These "kings" were crucial for the first generation of Jesuit missionaries in Asia. From his experience Xavier knew that "if from our Company came some foreigners who do not speak Portuguese, it is necessary that they learn

to speak, because otherwise there will be no *topaz* to understand them."[42]
The *topaz* or interpreter who, according to the etymology proposed by
Paulinus à Sancto Bartolomeao, knows two (*do*) languages (*bhashya*), is the
same type of linguistic intermediary usually called *língua* in Brazil and
other Portuguese colonies.[43] This sort of translator—and often traitor, as the
popular adage goes—was the peon or the foot soldier in the Portuguese
linguistic invasion without whose initial help no understanding was possible. After trust comes aggression, and in the course of time, all "errors" of
translation were duly laid to the account of the *topazes*.[44] In the long run,
the linguistic strategy of the Jesuits was to avoid their services altogether,
or to train and turn their most ardent converts into *topazes* or, inversely,
topazes into reliable converts.

The three Parava authors of the *Cartilha* printed in Lisbon in 1554 were,
technically, *topazes*. On his way from Goa to the Fishery Coast, Xavier was
also accompanied by three "natives," two of whom, Gaspar and Emmanuel,
were deacons, who spoke both Portuguese and their own language.[45] The
translation of his *Small Catechism* into Tamil was the work of these or similar
specially trained local helpers.[46] After only two years of initial fieldwork
outside Goa and away from direct Portuguese administration, Xavier had
learnt a most important lesson that would not be forgotten—that the Christianization of Asia was not identical with Portugalization. The linguistic
opening became inevitable and indispensable.

FROM IMPURITY OF BLOOD TO PURITY OF LANGUAGE: THE FIRST JESUIT TAMIL LANGUAGE SCHOOL

In 1549, at least three missionaries showed real linguistic talent and were
able to speak without interpreters—Antonio Criminali, Paulo do Valle, and
Henrique Henriques—while others either still spent their time learning. or
at least managed to learn by heart the basic prayers.[47] Since by a twist of
fate two of them died shortly after, Henriques became the pivot of all
linguistic activity in the mission. In a letter to Ignatius of Loyola, Henriques hinted at the fact that learning Tamil was a heroic endeavor.[48] He did
not dare present it as a kind of "white" martyrdom, although he could have
done just that, as a number of Jesuits—Paulo do Valle and Adam Francisco
among them—were believed to have died after a few years in the mission
because of their extraordinary physical efforts, of which language learning
was one. His "subliminal" or between-the-lines message to Ignatius concerning the unexpectedly quick mastery of this "most laborious (*muy traba-*

josa), language," as well as the "recovery" of his "normally" weak health, is that these were proof of the special "forces (*fuerças*)" which "Our Lord gives me to work."[49] Learning languages thus becomes a thaumaturgic act as well as an act of Providence soon to be linked to a new Pentecostal miracle.

In Henriques's Jesuit missionary career, linguistic expertise had, perforce, a special place. As an "*asás bom letrado*" who had studied philosophy and theology in Coimbra, he was a perfect candidate to join the Society, except for a "small" biographical detail. He belonged to a family of *cristãos novos* from Vila Viçosa in the archdiocese of Évora, and thus had to endure all the civic and religious disabilities that this "impurity of blood" entailed. In the 1540s and early 1550s, a thought-out Jesuit policy of recruitment or internal gradation was neither in place nor fixed, and Henriques was not alone in finding himself in limbo between being accepted and not being confirmed. For this reason his early letters to Ignatius read like so many "statements of purpose" for his various linguistic projects: a Tamil grammar to be used for learning the language; translations of the doctrine and various other religious manuals; as well as homilies against and refutations of Hindu "paganism."

Behind the scenes Henriques was, nevertheless, pulling strings as best as he could and not without reason. Unlike in Europe, where Ignatius encouraged Jews and New Christians to join the Jesuit ranks, in India the situation was entirely different.[50] In one of his late instructions to Barzeus (6–14 April 1552) Xavier recommended that those who were "of Hebrew lineage" not be admitted, a decision that obviously went against the Jesuit policy defined in Rome. This was probably less of a personal decision than a question of yielding to the pressures building in India, especially with the arrival of a larger contingent of Portuguese Jesuits who easily confused Portuguese colonial and "national" priorities with missionary imperatives. Thus when, in 1549, the army of "Badagas" decapitated António Criminali, the missionaries on the Fishery Coast unanimously elected Henrique Henriques as their superior, because "he was most sufficient for that (*mais sufficiente pera isso*) and knew the language, and the Christians got along well with him."[51]

It was this position of authority that brought Henriques more trouble than recognition. His desperation is clearly visible in his repeated pleas to do something about his *impedimento*.[52] Although the impediment is not mentioned in the letter itself, it could not have been his New Christian origin, since there was no such provision in the Jesuit official documents. Technically, Henriques's problem was that he had briefly been a *capochino,* as Nicolò Lancillotto, an Italian Jesuit stationed on the Malabar Coast in Kollam, reported to Rome in 1548—that is, a member of the Franciscan reformed order of Piedade province, but was dismissed when his Jewish ancestry was revealed.[53] However, in another letter in 1551, Lancillotto again clearly spelled out the reason behind Henriques's "persecution": "He excused himself from being superior, because he was of the New Christian lineage (*casta de christãos novos*) and because the Portuguese would be scandalized to see a New Christian in charge of other Fathers."[54]

Ignatius's absolute refusal to subscribe to the "racial" theory of *limpieza de sangre* and his staunch belief that conversion could clean even the "dirtiest" of blood were positions progressively hammered into the very heart of the Society of Jesus.[55] The rejection of biology in favor of culture did not, however, in any way mean the introduction of toleration of religious difference. On the contrary, initial openness was no more than a strategy or a method of conversion, a way of carving an entrance into the community in order to bring it "out" as Christian. Individual converts were especially considered as cherished Trojan horses to be installed among their kith and kin, or to be sent elsewhere as missionaries.

Although Ignatius of Loyola conferred the status of spiritual coadjutor on Henriques, a permanent doubt about his religious and missionary vocation must have remained among "nationalist" Portuguese Jesuits.[56] As plans to set up the Inquisition were progressing, especially after Xavier's passionate plea to João III to establish the Holy Office in Goa, Henriques had to shore up his professional identity in increasingly menacing circumstances.[57] It was his gift of languages that enabled him to effectively defend his "spiritual" innocence, orthodoxy, and divine election.

THE ART OF SPEAKING: THE FIRST TAMIL GRAMMAR

Henriques's self-discovery of linguistic talents is shot through with a dose of mystic and providential fantasizing, as demanded by a budding Jesuit literary convention. He was barely able to restrain his enthusiasm for what he probably considered the real discovery—his ability to crack open the grammatical structure of Tamil.

> I had a sort of a grammar (*arte*) to learn it, because just as in Latin we learn conjugations, I made an effort (*trabajé*) to learn this language, [and] I conjugated the verbs; and to arrange (*allar*) preterits, futures, infinitive, subjunctive, etc., cost me great work; also to learn accusative, genitive, dative, and other cases; and as well to learn what comes first, the verb or a number or a pronoun, etc.[58]

The key to this point-to-point mapping of grammatical forms was its perfect fit with something he already knew—Latin grammar, or "the Grammar." This discovery, or rather confirmation, of the basic underlying unity of all languages may also have further enhanced Henriques's linguistic and hermeneutic motivation. A space of fixed grammatical rules to be uncovered and followed was also a space of certainty, unlike the unpredictability of social rules in his doubly hostile environment—paganism on the one hand and the Inquisition on the other. In fact, Henriques's almost obsessive concern with rules and orders was frequently remarked by his Jesuit superiors, not as a positive virtue of obedience, but as an excess of "scruples."[59] He resurfaces in his letters as a dogged writer of "petitions," asking permission for the minutest trivia.

His Tamil grammar was not about trivia at all and one can glimpse in the written manuscript his titanic effort to subject a "pagan" tongue to the rules of grammar.[60] It is important to note that what he did to Tamil was what João de Barros had done to Portuguese only eight years earlier, and in an indirect way he did acknowledge his debt to the *Gramática* by stating that, "in order to easily understand this grammar (*arte*) it is important to know Latin grammar, and those who do not know Latin have to read a Portuguese grammar made by Yoaõ dBairros."[61] Although their philological project is identical, namely the description and prescription of grammatical rules of a given language, the difference in pedagogical articulation is obvious. Literacy is the primary goal of Barros's compendium. From learning the *ars recte scribendi* of their own mother tongue, children and other *idiotae* were to gradually assimilate higher ethical and intellectual precepts.[62] Henriques's is an *ars recte loquendi* of a foreign language and, given its rudimentary form, it is not a grammar at all, but a shortcut manual enabling missionaries to "say the right thing" to their Parava converts and to impress the "pagans."

The text is scattered over 157 sheets and resembles an open notebook, as if additions were to be included as they were discovered, formalized, verified, and approved. To a certain extent even the unitary authorship is in question, as the manuscript bears no signature and the Tamil inscriptions seem to have been added only after the version in Latin characters was completed. This unfinished, open-ended form agrees with the picture we get concerning its composition from Henriques's correspondence. For almost twenty years, in practically each and every letter sent to Europe, he reports on improvements he has made in the initial text. From his letter to Loyola in 1548 announcing the plan to write a grammar of Tamil to his letter to another New Christian, and general of the Society of Jesus, Diogo

Lainez, in 1564, mentioning his grammar as finished (*grammatica feita*), it is clear that the process of establishing the grammar was fraught with difficulties.[63]

The pronunciation of certain Tamil sounds/letters was most certainly one of the major problems for the missionaries. The *Cartilha em Tamul e Português* (1554), mentioned the unpronounceable "dictions" (*dições*), that is, those sounds that escaped the fixed grid of the Latin characters. "So barbarous" was Tamil, according to the prologue, that printers even lacked accents for marking its unpronounceable phonological features. From Lisbon, the three Tamil native speakers, possibly Paravas themselves, echoed a predictable metropolitan view. From the Fishery Coast, Henriques's perspective was entirely different. Since each "strange" sound has its own letter in Tamil, the Latin characters appear as lacking descriptive force. Thus for certain sounds, such as the retroflex (*ṭ*) and (*ṭṭ*), and especially the lateral flap (*ḻ*), this linguist *avant la lettre* invents particular signs such as "ḻ, with a line through l."[64] It is an accepted fact among contemporary linguists that the Dravidian languages—of which Tamil is one of the most prominent examples—contain a number of striking features compared to other world languages and often lead to a "notational nightmare."[65] According to Henriques, "sometimes, not all of them understand me, and because of that many times when I preach in the church, I say words in the same Malabar language and make another one say the same, who is like a *topaz,* so that everybody can better understand."[66] The doubling of the preaching voice points to the fact that it was the missionary tongue that had to be twisted in order to produce meaningful sounds. Nevertheless, the *topaz*'s acoustic organ was all a missionary needed. The real substance (the content and linguistic material) of the sermons was closely controlled by Henriques, because "here there is no *topaz* who can explain the things of the faith; when a father says one thing, they [the interpreters] often say the other."[67] The *topazes* were, therefore, increasingly seen as those who distorted while translating the "glad tidings" of the Christian faith. The fault was no more a simple *lapsus linguae,* but was increasingly seen as originating either in malice or in basic misunderstanding. It was the "pagan" mind that needed to be twisted before it could accommodate the "sacred" truth. Henriques's doctrinal texts and the confession manual were made just for that, but before undertaking the labor of turning the other's mind inside out, a missionary had to acquire the best possible linguistic competence.[68] The goal, as was often repeated in Jesuit letters, was to speak better than the "natives," and to make "them" believe that this could not be achieved by human means.

Short as it is, and in spite of its various defects, *Arte Malauar* is not simply a grammar; it is a Christian grammar, or if one may add a subcategory, a Christian missionary grammar, since the choice of its interior linguistic apparatus is geared to keeping the conversion machine going. It comes as no surprise, then, that the verb employed to demonstrate the Tamil conjugation paradigm—the equivalent of the *amo, amare, amavi, amatum* of Latin grammars—was *vicuvadi,* "to believe." On more than thirty sheets, this verb spreads faith in all its forms—participles, verbal nouns, imperatives, conditionals, etc. Sentence examples in Tamil and Portuguese translation cover almost all that can be said and done with the word "to believe," in two languages and often in two scripts. For example:

como se a de crer (Portuguese)
vichuuadiquiravagu epirhi (transcription of Tamil into Latin characters)
(how to believe—present-day scholarly transcription would be " viccuvatikkiṟavaku eppiṭi")

crer nos pagodes he tamto como crer nos demonios
pagaudiaei vichuuadiquiradu paeae vichuuadiquira mathiram
(believing in "pagodas" (pagan gods) is the same thing as believing in demons)

em lugar de crer em deus cree nos pagodes
tambiranaei vichuuadiquiraducu pagauadiai vichuuadiquran
(instead of believing in God he believes in "pagodas")

According to Bror Tiliander, *vicuvācam* (Sanskrit *viśuvāsa*), in its theological signification of faith is absent from Hindu Tamil theistic literature and appears to be "a property of Christian Tamil."[69] Henriques is at the beginning of this Christian genealogy, according to Tiliander, although technically it was Xavier who introduced it, in his corrigendum of the Tamil prayers, by replacing the verb *vēṇṭum* with *vicuvācam.*[70] The question of etymology and of borrowings is more often than not a terrain of shifting sand, but one thing is certain: in defining the relation between the divine and the human, the combined richness of the Sanskrit and Tamil languages had more than enough words to accommodate Christian theology. When a "native" category in Tamil or Sanskrit was deemed to be too close to a "pagan" practice, another one was chosen from what the missionaries (often confusedly) thought were the profane or secular linguistic registers. The etymology of *viśuvāsa* referring back to the act of breathing, besides its additional meaning of trust and confidence, and its absence from the daily religious practice of the "pagans," was certainly decisive for its inclusion in Tamil Christian terminology.

Henriques's grammar is a curious enterprise in at least one more sense. Due to its contrastive structure, incessantly opposing two languages, it is an embryonic comparative grammar and, therefore, contains two grammars— one of Portuguese and the other of the Tamil language. As in the game of *mise-en-abyme*, Latin grammar still works from within the Portuguese. Whatever Henriques's difficulty in precisely describing and fixing the rules of Tamil, his method of teaching was a complete success. His residence in Punnaikkayal turned into a language school for the missionaries, who were given six to ten months to learn Tamil well enough to preach and, more importantly, to hear confession.

By 1552 Henriques's linguistic appetites had grown wild. In a letter to Loyola, he claimed that, "if I'm not wrong, but by the goodness of God, I feel (*sinto*) the manner by which in a short while (*em breves dias*) the declensions and conjugations of any language from these parts can be extracted... To have good interpreters would be enough."[71] In the course of time he would try his hand at Malayalam (*maleame*)—which is as close to Tamil as Portuguese is to Spanish—and at Konkani and Telugu (*badaga*).[72] Henriques was persuaded that he could do the same for Japanese, Ethiopian, Chinese, or any other language.[73] The 1560s, after the Council of Trent and with Francisco de Borja at the head of the Society of Jesus (1565–72), were particularly propitious for the writing of grammars and other linguistic works. From 1565, the Jesuit authorities in Rome actively encouraged missionaries not only to learn local languages, but also to compose grammars and dictionaries (*algún vocabulario o método*) and to send copies of such works to Europe. With Everard Mercurian, who replaced Borja as a general of the order (1573–80), and the arrival of Alessandro Valignano—first as visitor of the province (1573–83), later as provincial (1583–87), and then again as visitor until his death in 1606—a veritable linguistic offensive took place in the missions in India, China, and Japan.[74] It was an offensive against "paganism" but also against Portuguese. In 1577, Mercurian, addressing missionaries in the East and West Indies, reminded them that learning local languages was part and parcel of the "divina voluntad," and that the divine grace would help those who did.

TAMIL IN PRINT: THE JESUIT LINGUISTIC OFFENSIVE

For Henriques, this new Jesuit priority meant partly a recognition of his work and partly an additional effort. In 1575, the first Provincial Congregation that took place in Goa spelled out very clearly that translations of doctrinal literature (catechisms, confession manuals, lives of saints, etc.)

were to be printed in the local languages.[75] Although catechetical activity in Tamil and Konkani was of long standing, only after Valigano's administrative shake-up did a series of authorized translations come from the presses. Four of Henriques's major works printed in Cochin and Kollam in Tamil characters, especially cut for them, have survived in one or two copies in the European archives.

The texts themselves bear witness to very close cooperation between Parava Christans and Jesuit missionaries in crafting Tamil Christian language, liturgy, sociability, and affects. That the missionaries, including Henriques, were at every step helped by the local "sábios" or "poets," is amply corroborated in the existing Jesuit correspondence. According to the second page of the small catechism *Doctrina Christam* or *tampirāṇ vaṇakkam,* printed 20 October 1578 in the *Collegio do Saluador* in "Coulam" (Kollam or Quilon), the co-author of the booklet (sixteen pages in all) was a certain Padre Manoel de São Pedro, who neither appears in the Jesuit catalogues nor is ever mentioned in their letters. His name and his title suggest that he was a secular priest and a Parava. Brushed aside by Jesuit historians as mere "native priests," these "local" intermediaries were in fact crucial in the construction of the Jesuit linguistic edifice.[76]

During the final decades of the sixteenth century, Parava interpreters with increasing sophistication in matters of Christian doctrine appeared and replaced the former *topazes* or *linguas,* some of them non-Christian. Most of the new interpreters came out of missionary schools in Cochin, Goa, and even Lisbon and Coimbra.[77] Already in 1551, these new "vines of the Lord" knew by heart Latin prayers such as the Paternoster and the Ave Maria and pronounced them "reasonably well," even better than the Portuguese who settled on the Fishery Coast.[78] A year later, according to Lancillotto, most of the thirty consecrated churches in the mission possessed Henriques's book entitled *A Small Compendium in Malavar Language about the Creation of the World, about Angels and Men, about Hell, Heaven, about Sin, about Grace, and about Demons.*[79] In addition, paintings depicting sacred events "from the beginning of the world until Judgment Day" were made in Goa by a Portuguese who then brought them to the Fishery Coast. These represented, wrote Henriques to Loyola, "a book by which those with less knowledge could easily learn the things of the faith."[80] Christian imagery finally invaded oral literature with local bards weaving together local stories, such as Xavier's miraculous resurrections and the like, with the biblical master narrative.[81]

Henriques's printed texts were, therefore, no simple translations from Latin or Portuguese into Tamil; they contained the already tested, negotiated, and appropriated "eloquence" of the Parava Christian community. Just as stone churches replaced earlier mud and palmleaf structures, printed books replaced paper manuscripts and *olai* (palmleaf strips).[82] However, unlike the *Cartilha em Tamul e Português,* which exhibits Tamil translation as an object of wonder and exoticism, the *Doctrina tampirāṇ vaṇakkam,* printed in Kollam in 1578, presents Portuguese as a curious "intermediary" language which needs "protection." On the second page, a diamond-shaped sign is introduced in order to shelter Portuguese and Latin words appearing in the text, except for titles such as *Pello Sinal, Credo, Os Mandamentos,* etc., which stood alone and apart from the Tamil text.[83] Unlike the *Cartilha,* the *tampirāṇ vaṇakkam* does not claim to be a primer, although it is in fact an ABC of Christian doctrine with all the principal vocabulary used in other, longer and more elaborate printed works. It was in the *Doctrina Christam/ kiricittiyāṇi vaṇakkam,* a translation of Jorge Marcos's Portuguese catechism published a year later (1579) by the Collegio da Madre de Deos in Cochin, that the Christian Tamil categories come to life as dramatized figures.[84] Marcos's *Doutrina Christã* seems to have been in use and "performed" already in the early 1570s in Cochin, together with Xavier's Small Catechism.

> The Christian doctrine is done (*se faz*) in this college, as is the custom, every day and sometimes in the town squares (*polas praças desta cidade*). On Sundays, two of the teachers walk through the town with a bell; they bring more than a thousand children and slaves who fill the whole church where they are made to do the doctrine in dialogue and that of *P.e Mestre Francisco,* of holy memory. Father Rector often does it or another father in his place, and then they sing on the street as they go."[85]

Henriques's *kiricittiyāṇi vaṇakkam* must have served, at least on special occasions, the same purpose—that is, as a libretto for an open display of religious zeal under the guise of the procession of children. The space of "education" and religious ritual was thus collapsed into a public spectacle. The quick exchange of dialogues between a teacher (*vāttiyar*) and a student (*cīcaṉ*), following the recitation of each prayer as a kind of simple hermeneutic appendage, grows in the course of the text from a classroom drill to an inquisitorial questioning. The basic method (*muṟai*) of the doctrine, translated as *vaṇakkam,* which technically means "salutation," is the ladder (*yeṇi*), as Henriques explained: "By this ladder our deeds climb from this earth to heaven and stand before God (*tampirāṇ*) and our deeds speak for us."[86] The language of the deeds that spoke to *tampirāṇ* was obviously Tamil, while each and every step climbed on this spiritual ladder was made of words, words to be memorized, as the student says, "in our lotus hearts (*yirutaiy tāmaraikkuḷ*) . . . in order to remove bad thoughts and bad behaviors."[87]

Tampirān vaṇakkam and even more so *kiricittiyāṇi vaṇakkam* remain tied to the Portuguese and Latin "originals"; but, at the same time, the end result of the translational movement is the creation of intervening spaces, imperceptible and secret at first, in which newly planted words ripen and assume meanings of their own. Linguistic conversion cannot happen suddenly. It takes place between the two breaths needed to pronounce the *Padre nosso* in the title and the *vāṇangaḷil/irukkiṟa/engalpitāve* . . . which follow. The problem (or the solution) is that once on the other side, or "outside of itself," in Loyola's spiritual vocabulary, the convert, that is, the Tamil language in this case, begins a "new" life of its own.

This is precisely the moment at which, paradoxically, the Jesuits won the battle and lost the war. First of all, from around the 1560s, the Paravas contributed money directly for the upkeep of the Jesuit mission. They paid the salaries of the church employees, bought new "ornaments" for the altars, and finally themselves financed the printing of at least some of Henriques's books.[88] In the preface to the *kiricittiyāṇi vaṇakkam,* an interesting (and symptomatic) circle of spiritual and secular (i.e. financial) involvement between the missionaries and their converts is disclosed: "You have desired to have several books which will teach you and your descendants the path to heaven and therefore you have contributed large sums of money to the press. Therefore we are giving you this book as a gift."[89] Converts who desire and are ready to pay for a "gift" of a (Christian) book are obviously the ideal missionary products. Parava demand, according to Jesuit letters, surpassed missionary supply. Thus the churches were crowded and there was a lack of qualified confessors.[90] In the years to come, the Jesuits also recorded with wonder and gratification the extraordinary enthusiasm for confession among their Parava converts.[91] The *Confessionairo* printed in Cochin in 1580 and the *Flos Sanctorum* in 1586 were offered, therefore, to the audience of devoted Parava Christians who fervently demanded fortifying pious literature, and probably also paid the printing costs. Resounding with the converts' desires for "explanation," "consolation," "method," these texts contain "standard" doctrinal Tamil vocabulary established and fixed earlier. And while untranslatable words from Portuguese and Latin and proper names continue their sheltered presence within diamond-shaped shields, the rich worlds of cultural adaptation open on the pages of these two exceptional books—the two longest printed texts in a non-European language (and script) to have come from the sixteenth-century European printing presses in Asia. These two works are, in fact, both witnesses and instruments of a "second" conversion, that is, the conversion that occurs when the "translated' utterance is made to act on and discipline the minds and the bodies of converts. Christian Tamil in print is, therefore, made to "do what it says."[92] In *Confessionairo* it probes forcefully into the convert's mind in order to test and purify his or her inner will or intention. Besides the psychological dislocations that it operates, *Confessionairo* also functions as a proto-regulatory document, containing "laws" and defining penal, legal, and moral jurisdiction within the Parava caste organization. In this respect it is perfectly complementary to the *Flos Sanctorum* in which ethical, theological, and community principles pose as accomplished narrative events, as overinflated *exempla* of correct behavior, righteous thinking, and spiritual edification. Through these figures, plots, and legends, universally known in the Christian West, Henriques, and through him his Parava informants, told stories about their own local Christian (or non-Christian) world. If Henriques turned the three Magi into Tamil kings (*mūvi rācākkaḷ*), this was no simple linguistic adaptation (or conversion). The behind-the-scenes ramifications were much more important; they enabled Paravas to establish for themselves a "royal" lineage that reflected both their enhanced status in the region as a Portuguese client pearl-fishing and pearl-trading community, and their place in local south Indian political and social networks. By the time the three Tamil kings entered the holy city of *vellem* (Belem), almost nothing except the diamond-shaped shields remained of the Portuguese language and of the linguistic imperialism envisaged by João de Barros.

CONVERSION: ARRESTING THE WORK OF RETURNING

As the three Tamil kings reached and themselves experienced—with the help of Henriques's textual time machine—the moment and the site at which Christianity originated, the break with European and Portuguese spiritual guidance was accomplished. According to de Certeau's explanatory "rectangle," as soon as they were positioned within Christian history (*temporality*) and Christian narrative (*writing*), the Tamils necessarily and simultaneously acquired Christian *identity* and Christian *consciousness*.[93] From the "barbarian" state to which the writers of the *Cartilha em Tamul e Português* had consigned Tamil language (and culture), the *Flos Sanctorum* and the *Confessionairo* converted it into a modern vernacular, as capable of handling Christian concepts as any other. In this scheme of things, Latin or Portuguese words could continue to function as vestiges of "sacred" utterances— to be learned by heart and uttered on ritual or liturgical occasions—or as the memorial stones (*padrões*) of an imaginary linguistic possession. Parava Christian culture and imagery would, henceforth, develop within its own semantic field, guided by its own imperatives.

The Jesuit gift to their Parava converts of the book, or rather the gift of "printing" in their own language and script, arrested the "work of returning" which is, according to de Certeau, one of the principal operators of ethnographic (ethnocentric) production. Ignatian spiritual conversion proceeds with exactly the same "ethnographic" logic. Endlessly transforming/translating the "out there" into "over here," this regressive, narrative, descriptive, and cognitive movement opens as much as it bridges distances; it poses as "hermeneutics of the other," but brings home only the simulacra of the same. And yet, Henriques's translations, in fact, bring nothing back home. They leave everything "out there" in Tamil, for the Tamils and, whether deliberately or not, they relinquish control over the written/printed word of the receptor language. What was repatriated, or rather repatriable, was the Jesuit Tamil grammar, returning to where it originated—to the rules of Portuguese or Latin grammar—but remaining endlessly unfinished, imperfect. On the other hand, the conversion of the Paravas was completed by the end of the sixteenth century with undoubted success, since they are the oldest Catholic convert community in Asia and still thriving. The perfect translation/conversion from Portuguese to Tamil appears to necessitate a sacrifice of the former. The Jesuit missionaries discovered early enough that the source language has to be renounced in order for the receptor language to produce freely its own signification, imagery, cognitive patterning, esthetic and religious identity. The strategic, economic and political inability of the *Estado da Índia* and the *padroado* to prevent the gradual erosion of the Portuguese language in the Asian missionary fields made this linguistic sacrifice even easier.

NOTES

This work was presented before various audiences: in Paris at the Ecole des Hautes Etudes en Sciences Sociales; in Princeton at the Shelby Cullom Davis Center for Historical Studies; in New Delhi at the Centre for Historical Studies, Jawaharlal Nehru University; and in Tirunelveli, at the Manonmaniam Sundaranar University. I thank Sanjay Subrahmanyam, Catherine Cléwmentin-Ojha, Kenneth Mills, Anthony Grafton, Peter Brown, Charlotte de Castelnau, S. Arokanathan, and James Walker-Tai for their comments and insights. An abbreviated Italian version of this text will appear in *Etnosistemi*.

1. Henrique Henriques, *Flos sanctorum eṉṟu atiyar varalāṟu,* ed. S. Rajamanickam (Tūttukuṭi, 1967). The original (342 folios) is kept in the Vatican Library. J. Wicki, S.J., "O 'Flos Sanctorum' do P. H. Henriques, impresso na língua tamul em 1586," *Boletim do Instituto Vasco da Gama* 73 (1956): 42–49.

2. Fernando Jesús Bouza Álvares, *Portugal no tempo dos Filipes; Política, cultura, representações (1580—1668)* (Lisbon, 2000).

3. For the Indian accommodationist mission headed by Roberto Nobili, see I. G. Županov, *Disputed Mission; Jesuit Experiments and Brahmanical Knowledge in Seventeenth–Century India* (New Delhi, 1999). Roberto Nobili, in particular, endeavored to efface the derogatory title *Parangi (Frangue, Frangui, Firingi,* etc.) applied to his mission in the heart of Tamil country to Portuguese and their converts. Parangi is a Tamil version of an old and often-used term *Farangii (Firanji, Frank,* etc.), designating a generic European and Christian in Asia. For Tamils, it also meant a person of low caste due to "polluting" habits of drinking alcohol and eating meat. See S. R. Delagado, *Glossário Luso-Asiático,* 2 vols. (Coimbra, 1919–21). Still unsurpassed is the book on Matteo Ricci by Jonathan D. Spence, *The Memory Palace of Matteo Ricci* (New York, 1983).

4. *Flos Sanctorum,* p. 7.

5. Ibid., p. 507.

6. Ibid., p. 6.

7. Xavier called the Paravas his pearls. Sebastião Gonçalves, *Primeira parte da História dos Religiosos da Companhia de Jesus e do que fizeram com a divina graça na conversão dos infieis a nossa sancta fee catholica nos reynos e províncias da India Oriental* (1614), ed. and introd. J. Wicki, S.J. (Coimbra, 1957). There are two manuscripts of this text: one in the Biblioteca Nacional, Lisbon (Fundo Geral 915); and the other in the Archivum Romanum Societatis Iesu, Rome (Goa 37). On Parava conversion and Christianization see S. Bayly, *Saints, Goddesses and Kings* (Cambridge, 1989) and I. G. Županov, "Prosélytisme et pluralisme religieux: Deux expériences missionnaires en Inde aux XVIe et XVIIe siècles," *Archives de sciences sociales des religions* 87 (Jul.–Sept. 1994).

8. Vincente L, Rafael, *Contracting Colonialism: Translation and Christian Conversion in Tagalog Society under Early Spanish Rule* (Durham, N.C., 1993), p. xv. See also Stephen J. Greenblatt, *Learning to Curse: Essays in Early Modern Culture* (New York, 1990).

9. G. Steiner, *After Babel* (1975; reprint ed., Oxford, 1992). p. 29.

10. Michel de Certeau, *La fable mystique,* XVIe–XVIIe siècle (Paris, 1982), pp. 156–215.

11. "Rice Christians" was a derogatory name for those converts who were purportedly attracted by economic rather than spiritual gains. It was especially applied to Portuguese Catholic converts by the British colonial authors. M. N. Pearson, *The Portuguese in India* (London, 1987).

12. Conversion of coastal people in south India (to Islam first, then Christianity) becomes a rule in this period. Throughout the sixteenth century there was a permanent low-intensity war on the Fishery Coast where lucrative pearl fishing kept attracting commercial and military predators

and invaders. Georg Schurhammer, S.J., "Die Bekehrung der Paraver (1535–1536," *Archivum Historicum Societatis Iesu* 4, (1935): 201–33. See also Georg Schurhammer, S.J., *Francis Xavier: His Life, His Times,* trans. M. J. Costelloe, S.J., 4 vols. (Rome, 1977), 2:286–359.

13. Joseph Wicki, S.J., ed., *Documenta Indica,* 18 vols. (Rome, 1948–88), 12:716 (hereafter *DI*). It was in 1582 that a Jesuit father from the Fishery Coast, João Rodrigues (Bustamante) was sent to Goa in order to oversee the printing of the *Flos Sanctorum*. The printing of the *Flos Sanctorum* was completed in Goa in 1586; the *Confessionairo* was printed in Cochin (1580), *tampirāṇ vaṇakkam* in Kollam (1578), and *kiricittiyāṇi vaṇakkam* in Cochin (1579). *Arte Malauar* remains in manuscript in Biblioteca Nacional, Lisbon, Reservados, ms. no. 3141.

14. Maria Leonor Carvalhão Buescu, *O estudo das línguas exóticas no século XVI* (Lisbon, 1983), and *A galáxia das línguas na época da expansão* (Lisbon, 1992).

15. João de Barros, *Gramática da língua portuguesa: Cartinha, Gramática, Diálogo em louvor da nóssa linguágem e Diálogo da viçiosa vergonha,* ed. Maria Leonor Carvalhão Buescu (Lisbon, 1971), pp. 401–2.

16. Ibid., p. 405.

17. He worked in Lisbon as treasurer of the Houses of India, Mina, and Ceuta (1525–28), and factor of the India and Guinea Houses (1533–67). See Charles. R. Boxer, *João de Barros: Portuguese Humanist and Historian of Asia* (New Delhi, 1981).

18. Barros, *Gramática,* p. 405.

19. Ibid., p. 240.

20. Unless they were St. Thomas or Syrian Christians, converted according to legend by the apostle himself, or early converts Christianized by the Portuguese from the region around Cochin.

21. See Álvaro Velho, *Roteiro da primeira viagem de Vasco da Gama,* ed. Neves Águas (Lisbon, 1987), and Sanjay Subrahmnayam, *The Career and Legend of Vasco da Gama* (Cambridge, 1997).

22. António Joaquim Anselmo, *Bibliografia das obras impressas em Portugal no século XVI* (Lisbon, 1926), pp. 160–92. Galhardo left 117 works during his long professional life (1509 or 1519–61).

23. Fernando Castelo-Branco, "As cartinhas quinhentistas e o humanismo," in *O Humanismo Português* (Lisbon, 1988), p. 138.

24. *Cartas de Affonso de Albuquerque,* vol. 1 (Lisbon, 1844), pp. 44–45, cited by Fernando Castelo-Branco, "As cartinhas para ensinar a ler," *Boletim bibliográfico e informativo* (1971): 309. Literally "a married man," *casado* means a merchant and Portuguese settler in Asia.

25. The slashes in the text of this document are a seventeenth-century version of commas.

26. See J. Filliozat *Un catéchisme tamoul du XVIe siècle en lettres latines* (Pondicherry, 1967).

27. *DI* 1:286–88, 31 October 1548, from Vembar.

28. There is no reason to think, as Donald Lach does, that it was Henriques who "invented" the system of Tamil transcription used in the *Cartilha*. Jesuits were probably not even consulted by the authors of the *Cartilha*, since even the Portuguese original does not correspond to the text made canonical by Xavier. See F. G. Perry Vidal, "São Francisco Xavier: Catecismo Grande," *Brotéria* 22 (1936): 250–65; Donald F. Lach, *Asia in the Making of Europe*, vol. 2 (1977; reprint ed., Chicago, 1994), p. 495.

29. On problematic identity between meaning and words present in the common "clothing" topos and Erasmus's argument privileging social context, see Mary Jane Barnett, "Erasmus and the Hermeneutics of Linguistic Praxis," *Renaissance Quarterly* 49 (1996): 542–72.

30. For politics and poetics of a particular mixture of Sanskrit with Tamil (and/or Malayalam, a regional language in Kerala), the Manipravalam, see Rich Freeman, "Rubies and Coral: The Lapidary Crafting of Language in Kerala," *Journal of Asian Studies* 57, no. 1 (February 1998): 38–65.

31. Disregarding the Tamil text in the middle, the *Cartilha* could have been used as a simple, monolingual Portuguese primer.

32. Jorge Flores introduced the term in order to underscore the close ties developed between Sri Lanka and other islands and the maritime regions at the extreme south of Indian peninsula. Jorge Manuel Flores, *Os Portugueses e o Mar do Ceilão (1498–1543)* (Lisbon, 1998).

33. G. Schurhammer and J. Wicki, eds., *Epistolae S. Francisci Xaverii*, 2 vols. (reprint ed., Rome, 1996), 1:94 (hereafter *EX*).

34. Ibid., letter no. 58.

35. G. Schurhammer and E. A. Voretzsch, *Ceylon zur Zeit des Königs Bhuvaneka Bahu und Franz Xaver, 1539–1553* (Leipzig, 1928).

36. *DI* 3:336.

37. *EX* 1:126, 2:93, *DI,* 1:372; *Monumenta Xaveriana*, 2 vols. (Matriti, 1899–1912), pp. 461–62, 467, 504. For the first books printed in Goa, see M. Saldanho, "A primeira imprensa em Goa," *Buletim do Instituto Vasco da Gama*, no. 73 (1956). During the celebration of Xavier's canonization in Lisbon in 1620 the bell was honored as an important relic. See Schurhammer, *Xavier*, 2:218; A. Prosperi, *Tribunali della coscienza* (Turin, 1996), p. 627.

38. The term "method" appears to be often affixed to the titles of seventeenth–century devotional works. See M. de Certeau, *The Writing of History*, trans. Tom Conley (New York, 1988), p. 196.

39. See *Contracting Colonialism*, p. 65, and his adaptation of Benjamin's "principle of interruption."

40. Barros, *Gramática,* pp. 293–94.

41. See Buescu's remarks in Barros, *Gramática,* p. 234n.

42. *EX* 1:293.

43. H. Yule and A. C. Burnell, *Hobson-Jobson: A Glossary of Colloquial Anglo-Indian Words* . . . (reprint ed., New Delhi, 1979), disagrees with this etymology, and derives the word from Turkish *topi* (hat), p. 933; compare Delagado, *Glossário Luso-Asiático,* 2:381. Paulinus a Sancto Bartolomeo or Ivan Filip Vezdin (1748–1806), of Croatian origin, was one of the most important pioneer Sanskrit scholars in addition to being a Carmelite missionary in Kerala.

44. *DI* 1:287; 2:158–59, 381.

45. *EX* 1:127, 147.

46. Schurhammer, *Xavier,* 1:308–10.

47. *DI* 1:234.

48. Ibid., pp. 276–300.

49. Ibid., p. 298.

50. John W. O'Malley, *The First Jesuits* (Cambridge, 1993), pp. 188–92.

51. *DI* 1:488–89.

52. Ibid., 2:4–6.

53. Ibid., 1:438.

54. Ibid., 2:147.

55. Francisco de Borja Medina, "Ignacio de Loiola y la 'limpieza de sangre,'" in *Ignacio de Loyola y su tiempo,* ed. J. Plazaola (Bilbao, 1992), pp. 579–615.

56. *DI* 2:312, 325.

57. *EX* 1:346–47.

58. *DI* 1:285–86.

59. According to Nunes Barreto (in 1560), Henriques was not only "escrupuloso" but also always doubting everything, indecisive and inefficient in negotiations. Ibid., 4:516.

60. The manuscript contains no signature. It was identified as Henriques's grammar by Jeanne H. Hein, "Father Henriques' Grammar of Spoken Tamil," in *Indian Church History Review* 11 (1977): 127–57. The manuscript was published by Hans J. Vermeer, *The First European Tamil Grammar* (Heidelberg, 1982).

61. Vermeer, *First European Tamil Grammar,* p. 5 (fol. 6v).

62. Maria Leonor Carvalhão, in her preface to Barros's *Gramática,* denies that it was meant to be used as a tool for teaching foreigners, p. xxiii.

63. *DI* 1:287, 6:396.

64. Vermeer, *First European Tamil Grammar,* p. 4 (fol. 5v).

65. K. V. Zvelebil, *Dravidian Linguistics* (Pondicherry, 1990), pp. 1–15.

66. *DI* 1:286.

67. Ibid., p. 287.

68. See Nobili's Tamil works, and Županov, *Disputed Mission.* Also see S. Arokiasamy, S.J., *Dharma, Hindu and Christian According to Roberto de Nobili* (Rome, 1986).

69. Bror Tiliander, *Christian and Hindu Terminology* (Uppsala, 1972), pp. 227–33.

70. *EX* 1:196.

71. *DI* 2:305.

72. *DI* 5:688, 6:375.

73. Ibid., 3:598.

74. Jesuit linguistic zeal in Brazil was not without problems. Resistance of the young Jesuits to learning Brazilian Indian languages, as detected by Charlotte de Castelnau, is not present, at least not in the same form, in the Indian Jesuit province. See the essays by both Ines G. Županov and Charlotte de Castelnau in the collective contribution of the Groupe de Recherches sur les Missions Religieuses Ibériques Modernes at the Ecole des Hautes Etudes en Sciences Sociales, "Politiques missionnaires sous le pontificat de Paul IV: Un document interne de la Compagnie de Jésus en 1558," *Mélanges de l'Ecole française de Rome, Italie et Méditerranée* 3, no. 1 (1999): pp. 295–310.

75. *DI* 10:218. The printing press arrived in Goa in 1556.

76. Georg Schurhammer, S.J., "The First Printing in Indic Characters," *Orientalia* (1963): 321.

77. *DI* 5:27–28.

78. Ibid., 2:156.

79. Ibid., pp. 373–74.

80. Ibid., p. 308.

81. See the Portuguese rendering of an epigram in Tamil celebrating the Cross, ibid., 12:718.

82. The first stone church was built on the island of Mannar in 1571. Joseph Thekkadath, *History of Christianity in India* (Bangalore, 1982), p. 166.

83. The same principle of demarcation is present in all four of Henriques's printed texts.

84. Jorge Marcos's catechism *Doutrina Christã* was printed in Braga in 1566 by António Mariz, See Anselmo, *Bibliografia,* nos. 469, 843. For Borja requesting that the book be sent to Rome and published there, see *DI* 6:522.

85. From Salvador Cortez's letter it is not clear what language was used in the following church and street "performance." *DI* 10:649. *Tampirāṇ vaṇakkam* is considered by some authors as almost identical to Xavier's *Small Catechism* in Portuguese.

86. *Doctrina Christam/kiricittiyāṇi vaṇakkam* (*Padre nosso*), Bodleian Library, Oxford, Reading Room, Oriental Department, Vet. or Tam f. 1, p. 22.

87. Ibid., p. 14.

88. *DI* 5:14–21.

89. *kiricittiyāṇi vaṇakkam,* page without numeration.

90. *DI* 5:677–89, 7:164–75.

91. Ibid., 7:419, 557, 8:510.

92. J. L. Austin's "performatives" belong to this category of linguistic acts. See J. L. Austin, *How We Do Things with Words* (Cambridge, 1962).

93. Michel de Certeau, "Ethno-Graphy: Speech, or the Space of the Other: Jean de Léry," in *The Writing of History,* p. 210.

6

CONVERTING THE ANCESTORS

INDIRECT RULE, SETTLEMENT CONSOLIDATION, AND THE STRUGGLE OVER BURIAL IN COLONIAL PERU, 1532–1614

PETER GOSE

INTRODUCTION

This paper will examine conversion as a cultural project that was central to Spanish colonial rule in Peru. Far from being monolithic, however, conversion was pursued through many strategies that had diverse and sometimes contradictory consequences. I will discuss these strategies in two generic groupings, each of which contained significant internal variation. One approach sought Andean precedents for Catholicism and therefore worked through indigenous forms, although it frequently distorted them beyond recognition. These strategies predominated during four decades of indirect rule that followed the Spanish invasion in 1532, but remained important into the seventeenth century. Another approach rejected the colonization of indigenous social and religious forms, and tried to replace them with Spanish institutions. Viceroy Francisco de Toledo's policy of settlement consolidation (*reducción*) established this strategy in the 1570s and articulated a repressive approach to the persistence of Andean "religion" known as the "extirpation of idolatry." Even under this new regime, however, Spaniards continued to rely on native political authorities (*kurakas*) for the extraction of tributary labor and many other key tasks of colonial government. Indirect rule persisted, if less visibly, and so did the rituals that maintained native rulers' authority, particularly the worship of mummified ancestors. Mortuary ritual also helped consolidate the newly formed settlements, so many Spaniards were concerned when Andean people clandestinely disinterred their dead from church floors and installed them in "pagan" mortuary sites. These "idolatries" directly affronted Catholic eschatology, and belied conversion, at least as many Spaniards understood it. Andean people, however, seldom considered Catholic and ancestral devotions to be mutually exclusive, as Mills has rightly insisted.[1] By exploring how such different understandings of this specific issue were possible, I will emphasize the ambiguous and ultimately contradictory nature of conversion as a cultural project.

In making these arguments, I will not use conversion as an analytical concept. It forecloses too many interesting questions by dichotomizing, codifying, and objectifying religious traditions, whether or not such a dynamic is endogenous to them. It further implies that the stuff of traditions, and the boundaries between them, are obvious, given by the facts of history or geographical separation. Such traditionally conceived cultural differences did exist between Spaniards and Andean people. Yet they were not absolute, and changed as all parties acted on them according to diverse understandings. Discursive representations of cultural difference (and similarity) therefore mattered, as all orienting frameworks do. I will examine how various authors claimed the Andean past for Christianity, constructing it as providential preparation or scrutinizing it for signs of apostolic revelation. All these authors fervently hoped for Indian "conversion" yet partially destabilized the notion by portraying the Andean past as already somewhat Christian. In so doing, they started a debate about how or whether the Andean should be understood as a tradition separate from Christianity, one that modern scholars have barely begun to explore.

CONVERSION AND INDIRECT RULE

Alexander VI's papal bull of 1493 made Spanish rights of conquest in the New World conditional upon converting the natives to Catholicism.[2] The Spanish crown initially appointed trustees (*encomenderos*) from among the conquistadores, paired them with provincial Andean rulers (*kurakas*), and granted them access to the labor of Indian tributaries. In return, *encomenderos* were to discharge the crown's missionary obligation to Indians.[3] Thus, it was particularly religious conversion that was "entrusted" to the *encomenderos,* who with greater or lesser zeal constructed churches within their jurisdictions and paid those priests they managed to recruit. The colonial state's institutional weakness and lack of territorial control forced *encomenderos* to rely on Andean political authorities and the descent groups (*ayllus*) they ruled in completing these and all other tasks.[4] Such dependence was not an insurmountable problem for evangelization. Andean *ayllus* were used to invading outsiders settling in their midst and bringing their deities with them. Usually these situations resolved themselves into reciprocal worship of ancestral deities between local and intrusive groups, from which a degree

of assimilation followed.[5] The early colonial church interpreted this openness as conversion, without realizing that it implied no intention to renounce existing forms of worship. Even as it articulated the exclusivity of
monotheistic commitment, the church committed a category mistake in
assuming the transparent universality of its notion of "belief," since Andean
societies did not give religion a doctrinal form or institutionally separate it
from the state or the *ayllu*. It was not clear exactly what Andean people
were supposed to abandon as they "converted," particularly when the colonial state otherwise relied on indirect rule through their institutions.

Indirect rule necessarily had its evangelical counterpart. The practicali-
ties of early missionaries' work required concessions to indigenous forms,
whether or not they shared Las Casas' apologetic view of indigenous religions as an application of "natural reason" to civic affairs and a providential
preparation for reception of the True Faith.[6] Initially, missionaries had little
choice but to work through Andean languages when trying to convert the
natives, which enmeshed them in the very understandings they were trying
to alter. For example, many began by trying to determine the Andean
names of God and the Devil in order to preach the Gospel. Since no real
counterparts for these notions existed, they had to select from terms that
were already available, but whose meanings they only partially understood.
Many concluded that the natives knew the one true God as "Viracocha" and
the Devil as "Supay," names that largely stuck and apparently derived from
Andean ancestral narratives and soul concepts. Viracocha was a name that
applied to an entire class or cohort of primordial ancestors who emerged out
of Lake Titicaca, and dispersed across the landscape to populate localities.[7]
Although Viracochas were decisively plural in their Andean form, Spanish
missionaries nonetheless managed to singularize them, presumably by asking Andean people who their creator was. When the answers they elicited
were filtered through a monotheistic grid, "Viracocha" was transformed
from a title that attached to the remotest founders of local groups to an
immaterial prime mover and universal creator.[8] A similar process led to the
designation of the Devil as "Supay." Although the Christian appropriation
of this term was early and overwhelming, it also continued to refer to a soul
that departed the body on death, and undertook a subterranean journey that
retraced the steps of the founding ancestors, frequently back to their ultimate origins in Lake Titicaca.[9] Missionaries must have deduced that supay
were devils by seizing on their subterranean existence, and equating it with
hell. Thus, the Spanish colonization of Andean ancestral and mortuary traditions began with the first linguistic footholds of the evangelical project.

Spaniards also appropriated Viracocha as a wandering apostle, either St.
Thomas or St. Bartholomew, who entered the New World and conducted a

primitive evangelization there.[10] Again, there was only the slimmest Andean pretext for this Spanish interpolation. Possibly the countless Andean myths that featured venerated tutelary ancestors who came from afar evoked the apostles' prodigious journeys. Certainly many Spaniards believed that a pre-Columbian statue in the town of Cacha depicted a man in priestly or apostolic garb.[11] These convictions were essentially a priori, however. Speculation about the visit of an apostle to the New World began as early as 1493,[12] and was well developed by the time of such early chroniclers as Betanzos and Cieza. It was grounded in the doctrine that the apostles had gone out to preach throughout the world and in traditions that gave Bartholomew and Thomas the most easterly assignments, hence those closest to the New World. The hypothesis of a pre-Columbian evangelization was, among other things, an attempt to reconcile the "discovery" of the Americas with a Christian universalizing history.[13] It also allowed Spaniards to account for similarities they perceived between Catholicism and the "idolatries" they observed among Andean people as the result of an initial exposure to the True Faith that had subsequently degenerated in the absence of the church.

Such Christian appropriations of Andean ancestral figures were more than just an imaginary exercise, but neither did they comprise an officially sanctioned conversion strategy. At a time when the Counter-Reformation was gathering force, the church could not overtly promote doctrinal experimentation in its approach to conversion, even if such experimentation proliferated in practice and was the inevitable result of attempts to make sense of Andean "religion" in Christian terms. This partial alignment of traditions arose when the overriding concern was the formal incorporation of Andean people into Christendom through baptism. It allowed a certain degree of practical solidarity between colonizers and colonized, but no real consensus about the socio-religious order they were building. As long as Andean people could view their relationship with Spaniards as an alliance, and their commitment to Christianity as nonexclusive, both were at least tolerable. To sustain this initial orientation, however, Andean people had to remain insulated from how Spaniards understood their relationship in terms of conquest and conversion. By the 1560s, as Stern has argued, both parties to this colonial encounter had learned enough about the other that it was no longer possible for either to proceed blithely, as if its own understanding of the relationship was shared by the other.[14] The most dramatic expression of this change was the Taki Onqoy movement that began around 1564. Adepts of this movement sang and danced until some went into trance and were possessed by important deities (*huacas*), who announced that they had afflicted their Andean subjects with devastating plagues since the Spanish invasion because they no longer received proper sacrifices. Thus, they counseled Andean people to avoid all contact with Spaniards and things Spanish, particularly Christianity. This separatist message is particularly interesting in relation to the Spanish attempts to colonize Andean ancestral deities discussed above. It suggests both a recognition of this strategy, and its potential to subvert the relation between Andean people and their deities. Negatively, then, the Taki Onqoy confirms that Christian colonization of Andean ancestral narratives was consequential, and could not be ignored.

The Taki Onqoy's separatism and its understanding of the recurring epidemics that ravaged Andean people resurfaced in later sixteenth-century movements, and are also present in many mid-seventeenthh-century "extirpation of idolatry" documents.[15] Yet separatism was never the only indigenous response to Christianity, and seldom if ever the dominant one. Although Spaniards would clearly never conform to the traditional Andean formula of reciprocal ancestor worship as a way to integrate conquerors and conquered, neither did Andean people abandon this search for reconciliation. Some of the most interesting attempts to achieve it came from early seventeenth-century mestizo and indigenous chroniclers, who tried to steer the Spanish appropriations of their ancestral religion that we have just considered toward a greater recognition of Andean religious achievements.

The most famous case is that of Garcilaso de la Vega, who vigorously sided with Las Casas' providential position. His opening argument was that the preeminence of the sun in Inca religion prepared Andean people for the True Faith.[16] However, the Incas also "perceived by the light of nature the true supreme God our Lord, the maker of heaven and earth." His name was Pachacamac, "he who gives life to the universe" in the same immaterial way as the soul does to the body.[17] Thus, a more respectable form of monotheism lay behind Inca sun worship. Apparently feeling the need to reconcile these objects of Inca devotion, de la Vega further specified that worship of the sun was exterior and worship of Pachacamac was inward. Although Pachacamac supposedly lacked temples and a cult, and was considered an unknown god, he nonetheless received greater veneration than the sun.[18] A more finely honed intuition of the True Faith would be hard to imagine. Only revelation was missing. De la Vega was somewhat more rigorous than Las Casas in dismissing the notion of an apostolic evangelization. He cites at length a passage from Valera, in which the latter scathingly dismisses purported Maya foreknowledge of the Holy Trinity as "pure invention and fiction on the part of the Spaniards." If the Maya had such knowledge, Valera argued, they would have learned the mystery of the Trinity more readily from missionaries than they actually did.[19] This argument is based on explicitly providential criteria: the past is to be evaluated by how it disposes people in the present.

Valera and de la Vega had good reason to feel that their providential position on religion was incompatible with an apostolic evangelization. Providentialism reinforced not only the neophyte status of Indians in the True Faith, but a respect for the rationality and morality of their social institutions. By contrast, the apostolic evangelization hypothesis suggested that Indians had been exposed to the True Faith, but were backsliders or renegades, against whom even Las Casas believed it was just to wage war.[20] Valera and de la Vega were apparently well aware of these implications, and constructed their accounts accordingly. Their Andean contemporaries did not necessarily draw the same conclusions, however. Santacruz Pachacuti, a *kuraka* from Canas, accepted that St. Thomas had evangelized the Andes and linked him to a mythical Viracocha named Tonapa or Tarapaca.[21] He describes the apostle's Andean peregrinations much as had preceding Spanish chroniclers, but adds an important innovation. There was one *kuraka* named Apo Tambo who sheltered the apostle and heeded his teachings. In return, the apostle left him with a rod cut from his staff, upon which were inscribed the Ten Commandments and the Seven Precepts: only the names of God and Jesus Christ were missing. As the narrative continues, it turns out that Apo Tambo was none other than the father of the siblings who went on to found the Inca empire. On the birth of Manco Capac, his first son, the staff that the apostle left turned into pure gold, as did two cups from which he drank. Eventually, when Manco Capac's seven younger siblings were born and their parents had died, he led them on their journey to Cuzco, bearing the relics that the apostle had left. They and their descendants went on to found the Inca empire, which became a powerful force against idolatry in the Andes, and prospered as long as these apostolic relics were remembered.[22] Only under Gyuana Capa, the last Inca sovereign to die in possession of the empire, did idolatry make significant inroads. Had missionaries come during the time of Capac Yupanqui, Santacruz Pachacuti observed, they would have fared very well.[23]

The fundamental message of Santacruz Pachacuti's narrative is that despite some backsliding into idolatry, the Incas were a powerful force for the establishment of the True Faith in the Andes. Yet he also makes their defeat intelligible as a result of their spiritual degeneration after the reign of Inca Yupanqui. In short, the narrative concedes just enough to the Incas' Spanish critics to count as "reasonable" while still maintaining that despite their weaknesses, the Incas were essentially an instrument of divine will. Santacruz Pachacuti acknowledges the necessity of outside missionary influence, and regrets its absence during the propitious reign of Capac Yupanqui. Thus, he gives external agency the primary role in conversion and makes local agency secondary. Ultimately, the historical challenge was to synchronize the efforts of foreign and local agents, which finally happened in the period of indirect rule following the Spanish invasion. This triumph was prefigured, however, in the original compact between the apostle and the *kuraka* Apo Tambo. Santacruz Pachacuti's entire treatise was a parable that sought to reinforce and dignify this collaboration by writing its imagined history in a manner intelligible and acceptable to all parties. Under different historical circumstances, he was doing the same work of reconciliation that had occurred in pre-Columbian times, when conquerors and conquered coordinated their ancestral traditions and ritual lives to establish a local modus vivendi. Yet Santacruz Pachacuti also wrote in a different historical moment than the Spaniards who pioneered the apostolic evangelization thesis. Whereas they sought to integrate the New World and its religious manifestations into a narrative of Christian revelation, he had to address a heightened rejection of things Andean under the Toledo reforms and the extirpation of idolatry. He might well have been trying to re-create or intensify that earlier moment of greater Spanish recognition by writing an even better historical charter than they had managed to do.

Guaman Poma was the other major indigenous chronicler who accepted the apostolic evangelization of the Andes, and he meticulously grounded his account of the Andean past in Christian historical time. One of his spectacular feats in this regard was to treat the first inhabitants of the Andes, the *Uari Uira Cocha Runa,* as passengers on Noah's ark. No less astonishing, however, is his identification of these primordial Andean ancestors as Spaniards. Trading on the (by then) well-established designation of Spaniards as *viracochas,* Guaman Poma reasoned that because these original inhabitants of the Andes were also so designated, they must have been descended from Spaniards.[24] The claim is not merely that Andean people descended from Noah, were part of the Judeo-Christian tradition, and therefore had a rightful claim to membership in it. Rather, Guaman Poma claims that Andean people were nothing less than a lost tribe of Spaniards: an identical twin separated at birth, whose inherent virtues shone through in a different environment, where revelation was largely (but not entirely) absent. Guaman Poma describes a succession of four ages in the Andes during which its inhabitants became technologically and politically more sophisticated, but insists that they remained devout monotheists until the rise of the Incas, when the licentious Mama Huaco introduced idolatry.[25] During the reign of the second Inca monarch Sinchi Roca, however, Christ was born, and three wise men came to pay their reverence: Melchor, who was an Indian; Baltazar, a Spaniard; and Gaspar, a black. After the Crucifixion, the Holy Spirit sent the apostles out to preach the gospel across the whole world. It was St. Bartholomew's lot to come to the Indies. During this apostle's Andean travels, the first miracle that God performed was in Cacha, where he saved the saint with celestial fire from idolatrous townspeople whom his teachings had offended. From there, Bartholomew continued south to Collao, where he silenced the devil who spoke through idols. As a sign of this deed, the saint left the Cross of Carabuco, which God intended and provided as the second miracle in Collao.[26]

Although Guaman Poma and Santacruz Pachacuti disagreed sharply over the historical role of the Incas, their accounts are otherwise remarkably similar. Both used the notion of an apostolic evangelization to defuse the panic over Andean idolatries that was orchestrated in 1609, and was such a prominent part of the context in which they wrote. While neither went quite so far as to claim that Andean people qualified as "Old Christians" in the peninsular sense, both portrayed them as experienced in the True Faith. Thus, both used their mytho-histories to depict an evangelical partnership between Spaniards and Andean people, one that appears to recall the inter-ethnic alliances of the postinvasion decades. Obviously, however, they operated in a different and much less favorable context. Implicitly, both addressed the breakdown of this partnership as Spanish colonial power became consolidated and more exclusionary. It is no accident that racial themes emerge in Guaman Poma's insistence that one of the three wise men was Indian and that Spaniards and Andean people were ultimately one and the same. These arguments would only make sense in a context where the religious and racial status of Indians was under significant downward pressure. Let us now identify and explore what this context was.

SETTLEMENT CONSOLIDATION AND THE EXTIRPATION OF IDOLATRY

The term *reducción* designated a second and far more sweeping strategy of conversion. Its defining feature was the consolidation of dispersed Indian settlements into church-based towns. By relocating and rebuilding Andean towns, advocates of *reducción* hoped to reconstruct their inhabitants similarly, and replace indirect rule with Spanish fiscal, administrative, and religious organizations. Early modern Spaniards, whose intellectual culture strongly linked ideas of urbanism, civilization, and religious propriety,[27] readily saw an intimate connection between consolidated settlements and the True Faith. The same concatenation of ideas existed in the semantic field of *reducción* during the sixteenth and seventeenth centuries: core meanings of ordering, rational persuasion, religious conversion, and political subjugation subsumed the particular emphasis on physical incorporation and consolidation.[28] The most obvious consequence of defining conversion in this way was that it became inseparable from the larger package of Spanish colonialism, part of a holistic project of civilization. Although more ambitious than purely religious understandings of conversion, *reducción* was also more realistic about the magnitude of the task involved, and eventually became colonial policy.

Declarations and limited enactments of *reducción* date to the beginnings of Spanish colonialism in the Americas.[29] Although Carlos V ordained settlement consolidation throughout the Indies in 1549, the pace of implementation continued to be desultory in Peru as elsewhere. Fraser shows that the regularities of Spanish colonial town planning derived less from royal decrees than from established cultural premises, presumably those encoded in the term *reducción* itself.[30] Yet by the 1560s, the political will to enforce *reducción* was emerging specifically in Peru due to the chronic state of civil war that had afflicted the colony since its conquest. The Spanish crown sought to curb the local power of its trustees, who, when not in open revolt, frequently allied with Andean political authorities to deprive the crown of revenues. Settlement consolidation became a vehicle for reorganizing the local level in the crown's interests, as part of a broader process of administrative reform and institution building.[31] The crown introduced a spiritual component to these reforms when it charged *encomenderos* with neglecting their duty to evangelize the Indians on its behalf. Parish formation received extensive discussion in the Second Council of Lima in 1567. However, it was not until the arrival of Viceroy Toledo in 1569 that the administrative and evangelical components of *reducción* fused into a single, sustained, and centrally organized policy initiative. Toledo issued instructions for the *reducción general* of the Peruvian countryside in 1569–70, and continued to amend, refine, and repeat these ordinances during the following decade. The sheer volume of his writings on *reducción* precludes anything but the most cursory summary here.

Toledo oversaw the creation of *reducciones* on a general tour of inspection (*visita general*) that also established the tributary obligations for each newly created town. Thus, construction of the churches and municipal buildings around which these settlements cohered was often the first tributary project that the inhabitants of these new towns undertook.[32] Each *reducción* was to establish its own community coffer (*caja de comunidad*) to meet the cost of local improvements and tributary payments. By 1575, as an incentive for completion, Toledo remitted a half-year's tributary obligations in those jurisdictions where *reducción* was still ongoing. He then ordered the remaining half-year's tribute deposited in the community coffers.[33] Eventually, however, Indians assumed their tributary obligations to the crown. Indians' religious status as neophytes figured in most rationalizations of tribute, most commonly by presenting it as what they owed temporally in return for their spiritual salvation, but also as penance for their idolatrous past, or preparation for their gradual entry into Catholic civilization. However, as Abercrombie observes, *reducción* involved an attempt to discipline and reshape Andean society that went well beyond the collection of tribute, and considerable expenses that would have been avoided if the only goal were to extract wealth.[34] Let us therefore take a closer look at what comprised this program.

New towns were to be built as far away as possible from the shrines that were the centers of pagan settlements. Once the construction of these new settlements was underway, the "old towns" were to be destroyed, not only to salvage building materials but also to make *reducción* definitive and irreversible. The new towns were to take form on a grid pattern, with a central plaza, onto which were to face the church and buildings for the community, the town council, court, and jail. Additional buildings for the priests were also stipulated. Indians were to construct their houses within the blocks laid out on the grid plan so that their doors led out onto the street. The house of the *kuraka* (local Andean political authority) was to be wider than the others and equipped with meeting chambers for the discussion of public business, a large kitchen, and separate dormitories for the *kuraka* and his wife, their girls and female servants, and their boys. Ordinary Indians were also to have such segregated dormitories, sleep on raised platforms, and keep their floors well swept. For what were considered to be public health reasons, no fields or irrigation canals were to be allowed within the town, and houses were permitted only a small kitchen garden. Finally, a full set of officials was to be chosen for the town council (*cabildo*), thus involving the Indians in Spanish modes of self-government.[35] The goal was clearly not just to consolidate Indian settlements for administrative convenience, but to make them embody an entirely different and more elevated way of life, involving Catholicism, urbanity, public order and rational governance, improved personal hygiene and morals.

Abercrombie notes the emphasis on visibility in this new regime and argues that *reducción* inaugurated techniques of surveillance that other colonial regimes implemented only in the nineteenth century.[36] The temptation to invoke Foucault here is understandable, but risks mistaking the will to inspect and correct, which is amply evident in Toledo's writings, for their actual achievement on the ground, which was at best episodic. By the end of the 1570s, many Andean people had already found *reducción* to be insufferable, and were escaping it by fleeing to remote areas, other indigenous communities, or the private service of individual Spaniards. By the end of the sixteenth century, official correspondence was already suggesting the failure of *reducción*.[37] Reports that Indians were abandoning the *reducciones* continued unabated into the second half of the seventeenth century.[38] Although many were alarmist, these reports clearly had significant grounding in fact.[39] Viceroys and archbishops blamed Indian flight on abusive local officials and priests, and accused *kurakas* of hiding Indians for their own service in remote areas.[40] Alliances among these local figures had been overt in the early colonial period of indirect rule. They continued in the era of *reducción,* but were redefined as corruption. Endless reforms were proposed, but almost all had the fatal flaw of requiring cooperation from the very local interests they were meant to curtail.[41] In short, *reducción* did not magically transform the institutional weakness of the colonial state. However much the intentions behind it may have anticipated the panopticon or the iron cage, the policy was never fully enforceable and produced only modest measures of surveillance and containment.

It was not just the capacity of the colonial state to conduct surveillance that was at stake here, but also the nature of the surveillance itself, which obviously drew more on the Inquisition and Counter-Reformation than modern forms of governance. When Toledo announced the policy of *reducción* in his instructions of 1569–70, it was with the following preamble:

> the principal cause of the *visita general* is to give order and a way for the Indians to have competent religious instruction and be better versed in the things of our holy Catholic faith, and can have the sacraments administered to them with greater facility and comfort, and so that they can be maintained in justice and live politically like people of reason and like the rest of His Majesty's vassals, and for all this to be effected, it is desirable that the Indians who live dispersed and scattered be reduced to towns with layout and order . . . [42]

Religious indoctrination is clearly the primary goal here, although Toledo links it to political order and consolidated settlements. Ostensibly, the general tour of inspection's main goal was to convert the Indians and learn their religious doctrines in order to refute them better.[43]

On 8 September 1571, Toledo issued the first of several additions to the instructions for his inspectors. He began by reminding them that the main reason for their *visita* was the failure of settlers and *encomenderos* to provide adequate religious instruction to the natives.[44] Later, however, he identified Indian "idolatries" as one of the principal obstacles to the successful realization of *reducción,* and added that "the principal effect of the general inspection and of my personal inspection was to extirpate idolatries, sorcery, and dogmatizers so that the evangelical teaching would fall well disposed upon ground where it could bear fruit."[45] He further specified that the ecclesiastical judge ordinary must punish idolatrous Indians, and ensure that they receive intensified religious instruction:

> And should it occur that an infidel dogmatizer be found who disrupts the preaching of the Gospel and manages to pervert the newly convert-ed, in this case secular judges can proceed against such infidel dogma-tizers, punishing them with death or other punishments that seem appropriate to them, since it is declared by congresses of theologians and jurists that His Majesty has convened in the Kingdoms of Spain that not only is this just cause for condemning such people to death, but even for waging war against a whole kingdom or province with all the death and damage to property that reults.[46]

In this ordinance, Toledo was clearly compensating for the fact that the Inquisition did not have jurisdiction over Indians, a situation that he even-tually tried to change.[47]

These same provisos reappeared verbatim in a communication promoting religious instruction that accompanied a revised set of instructions concern-ing *reducción,* both issued on 6 March 1573. In the revised instructions, Toledo acknowledged that some officials were reluctant to enforce *reducción* and that Indians resisted it out of attachment to the drunken festivities, vices, and idolatries that they were free to pursue in their old towns.[48] Perhaps for this reason, he appointed Cristóbal de Albornoz, the principal extirpator of the Taki Onqoy movement, to implement *reducción* in the provinces of Chinchaysuyo. Apparently Albornoz pursued settlement con-solidation and extirpation simultaneously during his inspections.[49] These policies would again converge in seventeenth-century "extirpation of idola-try" campaigns, which often justified themselves as the necessary means to the unquestionable end of *reducción.*[50] Some contested this argument, but nobody denied that the eradication of "idolatry" required *reducción.* Only when priests began to live among Indians in church-based towns was it possible to hope that they could systematically detect and extirpate idola-tries. The only question was whether intensified religious surveillance and correction would speed the conversion of rustic Indian idolaters into civi-lized, quasi-urban Christians, or derail that project by emphasizing the negative. To the extent that the extirpators prevailed against their oppo-nents, however, *reducción* and the extirpation of idolatry did become succes-sive, mutually implicated phases of the missionary project.

On 7 November 1573, Toledo issued further instructions concerning *reducción,* warning inspectors against the danger of *kurakas* who wanted their own hamlets to become sites for consolidated settlements, and adding:

as you will already know and have understood from your instructions, the principal point of which you will have to be aware when making said *reducciones* is that said Indians be removed from the places and sites of their idolatries and burials of their ancestors, out of respect for which, and on the pretext of piety, they have tricked and are tricking inspectors into not moving them from where they are, which is in great detriment to their souls and against that which His Majesty has decreed.[51]

To counteract this perceived ill, Toledo announced a series of fines and other penalties for any inspectors who let themselves be talked out of enforcing *reducción,* for *kurakas* who tried to prevent or subvert it, and for priests who spoke against or otherwise attempted to undermine it. Of note is Toledo's growing awareness that these officials were allying with each other to block *reducción*'s execution. While Toledo only insinuated that corruption was responsible for their noncompliance, there can be little doubt that this was among his concerns. His realization initiates the long run of recrimination over the perceived failure of the *reducciones* mentioned above, one that became progressively louder and more accusatory. Toledo continued to revise his instructions concerning *reducción,* in part to refine the policy, but also to reiterate it in a context of noncompliance. In linking the greed and corruption of Spanish petty officials to the failure of *reducción* and the persistence of Indian idolatries, this passage anticipates the analyses of Archbishops Lobo Guerrero (1609–22) and Campo (1625–26), who not only led initiatives to extirpate idolatry but also tightened surveillance of their own clergy in a broader package of reform.

The 1573 passage specifically blames Indians' attachment to their mortuary sites for their reticence to accept *reducción*. Predictably, Toledo followed this analysis with his ordinances of 6 November 1575 on the proper manner of death and burial. Indian mayors were to take testaments from dying Indians in the manner of the Spaniards, setting aside property not only for their children, but also for pious bequests and suffrages for their souls: Toledo even provided a standardized form for such testaments.[52] As he neared the end of his term as viceroy in 1580, Toledo again denounced Andean mortuary idolatries:

. . . these Indians had as a very celebrated religious observance among themselves the adoration of the dead from whom they directly descended, ignoring the first cause of their creation as they did in all their other opinions, and thus they had their tombs by the roads, distant and separated from the towns, and in other places inside of them, and in others in their very houses, for in this they had different customs, and to avoid this said damage, I order and command that each magistrate ensure that in his district all the tower tombs be knocked down, and that a large pit be dug into which all of the bones of those who died as pagans be mixed together, and that special care be taken henceforth to gather the intelligence necessary to discover whether any of the baptized are buried outside of the church, with the priest and the judge helping each other in such an important matter, and that they take great caution in the doors of the temples since they remove and take them [the baptized dead] from the sepulchers at night when they are authorities and important people for said effect [clandestine burial], and they kill some women and Indian men saying that they will serve them in the other life.[53]

As we will see below, such clandestine disinterments were common. In this passage, Toledo assumes, but uncharacteristically fails to stipulate, that Christian Indians should be buried in the floors of their churches. Perhaps he refrained from pronouncing this requirement since the First Council of Lima had already done so in 1551,[54] but this was a viceroy who had no aesthetic reservations about repeating orders. Toledo probably took church burial for granted as an integral part of *reducción*, as indeed it was. Occasionally, reports show the existence of outdoor graveyards in some Andean villages,[55] but church burial was the norm. It not only facilitated the surveillance that Toledo recommended, but further consolidated churches as the new settlements' ritual centers.

Peter Brown's classic study shows that the rise of the cult of the saints in late antiquity involved bringing the dead, who had previously been banished to the periphery, into churches at the heart of the city.[56] Saintly relics were physically and categorically associated with the altar, which radiated grace not only to the living, but also to the dead interred in the church and awaiting resurrection. Over a millennium later and an ocean away, *reducción* continued to insist on this same basic pattern: the church was to be a mortuary space at the center of Christian settlement. Thus, colonial functionaries sometimes referred to this theological dimension of *reducción*. For example, Archbishop Lobo Guerrero described church burial as an act of compassion for those who die in the Lord, one that confers grace and a great many benefits on them, according to the "doctrine of the saints."[57] Similarly, in the only argument for church burial to be made in an idolatry trial, a vicar is said to have exhorted his parishioners not to disinter the dead "so that they may enjoy the suffrages of the church and that among them there could be many who might have been saved."[58] Despite these fundamental long-term continuities in the Christian tradition, the Spanish mediation and its intervening history also deserve some attention.

Ironically, a recent study of death in medieval Spain suggests that the church struggled with its laity to prohibit burial *ad sanctos*. Eventually it gave in, and allowed interments in church floors covered with flat memorial stones, while trying to ban elaborate raised monuments. Only members of religious confraternities had a right to church burial, although the privilege soon became available to others if they pledged an offering to the church, half of which was due on the day of the funeral, and the other half on the day of a subsequent votive mass for the soul of the deceased. As the concept of purgatory emerged during the twelfth century, however, it made the souls of dead Christians increasingly dependent on the ministrations of the living, and hence, the spiritual benefits of church burial only grew. In the process, there was a greater elaboration of suffrages: acts of penance through which individuals might shorten their stay in purgatory. These acts might include prayer and fasting but also posthumous pious donations and sponsorship of masses arranged through a person's will. The conceptual basis of both suffrages and church burial was to be found in a doctrinal revision of the communion of saints.[59] Indulgences were one way the living could help those in purgatory, but an even more effective vehicle was the Eucharist, the one sacrament that could reach beyond the living.[60] Those whose bodies lay near the altar could benefit fully from the performance of the Eucharist there, and quicken their progress through purgatory. These benefits diminished as distance from the altar increased. People eagerly sought burial places close to the altar, and while the church could not sell them outright, substantial pious donations and mass sponsorships in one's will might secure them.[61] Such practices established the church as a redemptive organization based on the circulation of grace across the boundaries of heaven, earth, and purgatory. A Christian community was never solely comprised of the living, but required a broader accumulation and distribution of members in these other domains, a process in which burial was key. This is the most basic reason that church and crown insisted on the sanctity of Christian burial in colonial Peru. Thus, *reducción* applied not only to the living but also to the dead, as a woman in one idolatry trial realized when she confessed to hiding the body of her husband "so that they not reduce it to the church."[62]

Spaniards had another, somewhat more specific set of reasons for emphasizing church burial. In Spain, both Jews and Muslims tended to bury their dead outside town in graveyards, hence burial in urban churches set the Christian community apart. Although Christians had their own consecrated graveyards, these progressively fell into disuse as the Reconquest of Spain progressed. By the sixteenth century, nearly all Christian burials were in churches.[63] Similar strategies of differentiation from Jews and Moors existed in mourning customs. Late medieval Christians explicitly attenuated their attentions to the corpse, and frowned upon exaggerated displays of grief during interments, which betrayed a lack of faith in resurrection.[64] Thus, church burial became one of several ways that Christians used death to make an ethnic statement, marking their particular affiliation within the religious plurality of late medieval Spain. Furthermore, by burying their dead in the centers of settlements, when Jews and Moors buried theirs outside them, Christians claimed a certain preeminence within these multiethnic settlements. Their religious life became more fully invested in Spanish towns than did that of Jews and Moors. Undoubtedly, this contributed to the strong identification between urbanity, civilization, and Christianity that had emerged by the sixteenth century in Spain, which the very meaning of *reducción* embodied.

As Jews and Moors converted to Catholicism during the fifteenth century and became "New Christians," their burial practices were closely monitored. The Council of Alcalá, convened in 1481, prohibited all differences in the burial practices of Old and New Christians. Even after their conversion, some New Christians of Toledo apparently continued to bury their dead in unconsecrated ground in the countryside, perhaps because their ancestors had always been buried there, or perhaps because Old Christians denied them burial in urban churches. A previous archbishop of Toledo had ordered New Christians to bury their dead in the cemetery of the sanctuary (*hermita*) of San Bartolomé, outside the city walls of Toledo, both to legitimate and to control this continuity with past practice. But this compromise still led Old Christians to speculate that the newly converted were reverting to their old religion. Hence it was overturned, and the New Christians were ordered to bury their dead in the city, and told that any new marble mortuary stones outside its walls would be taken down and donated to local parish coffers. The object here was not to persecute the newly converted but rather to cease treating them as descendants of Jews and Moors by including them in the communion of the saints. Thus, this same set of ordinances anathematized, in the name of the unity of the church, any confraternities that refused to accept New Christians.[65] The same universalist motives arguably informed Spaniards' insistence on church burial for Indians in the Andes.

Contemporary with such decreed inclusion, however, were more powerful currents of exclusion. In 1483, the Council of Alcalá's measures were repealed, only two years after their enactment, during the Inquisition's inaugural attack on New Christians.[66] By allowing a return to mortuary segregation this annulment also reinforced a parochialized understanding of the communion of saints that emerged during the *reconquista*, according to which Spanish Old Christians saw the Church Suffering and the Church Triumphant as their own carnal ancestors who had transmitted the true faith to them while fighting the infidel. Questions of ancestry subtly displaced those of grace and redemption in a universalizing faith. This peculiarly Spanish version of the communion of the saints began to generate or converge with the proto-racist ideology of "purity of blood" (*limpieza de sangre*), according to which an individual's religious disposition was hereditary and racialized.[67] Old Christians received the grace of the true faith from their ancestors, and therefore were "pure." By contrast, New Christians received only the "stain" and "infamy" of religious error from their ancestors. Despite the watchful eye and firm hand of the Inquisition, it was uncertain exactly how many generations it would take to remove this stain. Even the more moderate exponents of "purity of blood" expressed at least some degree of racial pessimism about the possibility of true conversion for New Christians.

In a passage that evoked the peninsular language of "purity of blood," the Jesuit intellectual José de Acosta transposed this pessimism onto Peruvian Indians:

> . . . one would have to think that we are dealing with a hereditary illness of idolatry which, contracted in the mother's very breast and nursed upon suckling her very milk, made robust by paternal example, and familiar and fortified by long-standing custom and the authority of public laws, has such vigor that it cannot be cured except by the very abundant sprinkling of divine grace, and the assiduous and indefatigable work of the evangelical doctor.[68]

Reducción was to be the centerpiece of this "cure." Only by rebuilding Indian life from the ground up, educating, and preventing (with force if necessary) the return to idolatry, could the missionary arrest these hereditary inclinations and modify them over time. Even Spaniards who rejected the racializing overtones of Acosta's analysis could agree on this course of action. There was also consensus that the most pernicious of the vast panorama of Andean idolatries was the "cult of the dead." Spaniards commonly interpreted indigenous oracular consultations of the dead as veiled communion with the Devil.[69] Worse still, however, was the natives' proclivity to clandestinely disinter their dead kin from the floors of churches and take them to be with their ancestors in pagan mortuary sites. This practice epitomized the quasi-hereditary intergenerational transmission of idolatry that Acosta identified. It directly undid the good example of *reducción* and frustrated the formation of a proper church in which grace, not error, could circulate between the living and the dead. Not surprisingly, it became a flash point.

CLANDESTINE DISINTERMENTS

One of the earliest reports of clandestine disinterment dates to 1541.[70] In 1551, the First Council of Lima also acknowledged this practice when it stipulated punishments for burying Christian Indians outside consecrated ground. First-time offenders were to be jailed for three days and given fifty lashes in public, with escalating penalties for subsequent offenses. The bodies of any Christians who had secretly requested burial outside church or cemetery were to be burned publicly. When burying Christian Indians, priests were instructed to check the face of the deceased to make sure that another body had not been substituted for it. They were instructed not to charge Indians for burial, however, to encourage acceptance of Christian mortuary rites. Pagan Indians were to bury their dead in a designated area within view of the settlement. Any Christian Indians with pagan dead in their houses or in large sepulchers were to rebury them in the pagan burial ground, with no more than one day of mourning. The council also stipulated that henceforth, excess clothing and offerings of food and drink were not to be included in Christian graves. Above all else, priests were instructed to prevent the successor of a dead *kuraka* from allowing the sacrifice or self-immolation of his predecessor's wives or servants, and to insist that Christian *kurakas* be buried in church or cemetery.[71] Collectively, these ordinances suggest not only a will to monitor and regulate Andean funerary practices, but also some experience with them. In 1566, still before settlement consolidation, a local priest reported clandestine disinterment of Christian Indians in Huaylas, and an inspection of the northern Peruvian highlands in 1567 portrayed the practice as widespread.[72] Similarly, Polo noted that Indians commonly disinterred their dead in secret, taking them from churches and graveyards to pagan shrines (*huacas*), mountains and plains, old sepulchers, and houses, where their kin and associates gathered to give them food and drink, and to perform songs and dances for them.[73] As we have already seen, Toledo denounced similar practices in 1580. Another report of clandestine disinterment emerged in 1584 from Albornoz's investigation into the Taki Onqoy,[74] although mere disinterment necessarily took a back seat to the more spectacular "heresies" of that movement. Far from being incidental, these reports were part of an emerging pattern.

Aullagas, 1588: An Inquisitorial Ethnography

Bartolomé Alvarez, an obscure priest who worked in the parish of Aullagas in what is now Bolivia, wrote an early account that contextualized clandestine disinterments extensively in a broader understanding of Andean socioreligious life.[75] In his lengthy and often bitter letter to Felipe II, Alvarez's main goal, following Toledo, was to make the Indians answerable to the Inquisition for their idolatries and sins against the sacraments. He observed that his Indian parishioners were likely to take bodies, particularly those of local *kurakas,* from any unguarded church or graveyard for reburial in pagan tombs (pp. 114–15). When his vigilance made it impossible for them to remove a body from its Christian place of burial, they would take hair and nail clippings instead, tie them in a bundle of cloth with coca leaves, and take them to the pagan tomb as a substitute for the body during acts of ancestor worship (p. 116). Alvarez reported that they would also reopen graves to give the body a mortuary mask, and the articles it had used in life, including clothing, footwear, adornments, musical instruments, tools, and implements for eating, drinking, and cooking (pp. 114–15). Sometimes they would even try to slip these items in during Christian burial itself (p. 263).

Although he was certainly in favor of forcibly preventing Andean people from engaging in their traditional funerary practices, Alvarez immediately added:

> I do not pretend to insinuate that the baptized ones are really Christians, and that therefore they ought to be buried in the churches and enjoy holy or blessed ground and the sacrifices of the Holy Church: from this I would have them as deprived as their grandparents who did not hear of the faith nor knew the name of God. I only wish to make it understood that it is necessary to put an obstacle in the way of this evil [of traditional burial]. (p. 98)

By his own account, Alvarez actually did refuse Christian burial to at least some Indian bodies, and in so doing, induced confessions of idolatry from their living kin (p. 175). Before proceeding, he asked whether the dead presented for burial were baptized, which often they were not (pp. 172–74). Yet no baptismal records existed, and frequently Indians claimed to have been baptized by priests who had subsequently died or left the area. Proving them wrong was almost impossible. Alvarez discovered in confession that certain individuals were not baptized. When asked publicly to bury them in the church, however, he reluctantly complied because he could not betray the privacy of confession, nor did he wish to face the possibility of his parishioners complaining to the ecclesiastical inspector (pp. 174–75). This quandary severely vexed Alvarez, and not only led him to vent his considerable displeasure with the Indians, but to channel it into an investigation of their "beliefs" (*doctrina*) and "rites" (*ritos*), particularly those regarding death and ancestors, which I will now summarize.

Before the arrival of the Spaniards, the people of Aullagas built stone tower tombs on hills and plains, their height proportional to the dignity and nobility of the dead housed in them. Other tombs were subterranean and contained basins for offerings: their doorways faced east and were covered with hefty stone slabs. Founding ancestors were placed in the lowest levels with offerings, and more recent *kurakas* higher up, with clothes and insignia, where the cold air perfectly conserved them (pp. 92–93). When a *kuraka* died, his concubines were enclosed in the tomb with him, given food and drink, and then killed to serve their lord in the afterlife: Alvarez cited the case of a woman who fled to a priest to avoid this fate (p. 94). With the arrival of Spaniards eager to loot the tombs for silver offerings, and priests anxious to destroy their holy objects, people began to build new hidden subterranean tombs for their dead, and transferred the ancestral mummies to them, arranging them in order of seniority before carefully covering over the entrances, disguising them with vegetation to look like undisturbed ground. In these tombs, according to Alvarez, fathers buried sons, sons buried fathers, and brothers buried brothers, as before, and often with the tacit consent of Spanish priests (p. 95). Although Alvarez polemicized against Acosta, he nonetheless joined him in seeing the intergenerational continuity of such idolatries as a racialized habit that required breaking (pp. 83, 110). He recounts how a five-year-old boy told him of a tomb that contained the body of Auqui Penchuca, the local founding ancestor, and his venerated descendants, more than sixty in all, including some who were young and recently buried, with their bodies intact (pp. 108, 96). Alvarez also describes how he took the children off to look for another hidden subterranean tomb in the "old town," kept them there three days until he found it, and then whipped them to confess who the bodies were and what the *kurakas* did there: among the bodies were some who had been baptized (pp. 108–9). "It is necessary to order the burning of all the dead that there are in the countryside and fields," he concluded, thus suggesting the multiplicity of such mortuary sites in his parish (p. 96).

These tombs and the dead they contained were considered sacred, and called *huaca,* a generic term that referred to both deities and their shrines (p. 103). In pre-Conquest times, every province, town and descent group (*ayllu*) placed statues of its most revered *huacas* atop high mountains. These they took with them when moving to new lands, or in war (p. 75). With the arrival of the Spaniards, priests found and destroyed most of the statues and shrines on lower mountains, so people dismantled bridges and other accesses to high mountain shrines. Some said, though, that the statues were moved and buried in lower, more accessible places, including town plazas and cemeteries, where people still worshiped them, and assigned them estates from which their sacrifices were culled (pp. 74, 81, 87). These statues were of stone, and represented dead Incas or *kurakas,* who might give oracles, or generate the appearance of more closely related dead who would speak (pp. 75–76, 82). Thus, Alvarez opined that the dead and their deities were actually the same thing, since it was primarily through the dead that the Devil appeared to Indians (pp. 155–56). He notes that in contrast to the mundane Aymara word for cadaver, *amaya,* a more specific term *çupay* designated the venerated ancestors who received sacrifices (p. 103).[76] Other, less venerated ancestors lacked deity status and seemingly did not belong to the *çupay* category (p. 89). Like so many churchmen of his era, Alvarez firmly believed that *çupay* was none other than the Devil. He struggled to reconcile this *ideé fixe* that *çupay* was necessarily malevolent with his parishioners' view that as founding ancestor and tutelary deity, it could also be benevolent (p. 103).

Although Alvarez's account of the ancestors is thoroughly demonizing, additional details of what we may suppose to be their Andean character nonetheless manage to filter through. Local tradition held that the ancestors emerged from a high snowcapped mountain named Ancocaua (Anconcagua, in modern Chile); elsewhere, people called these ancestral origin points *pacarinas.* Ancestors like Auqui Penchuca traveled in cohorts, stopping off at several such points as they dispersed across the landscape toward the various localities they were to colonize.[77] These founding ancestors were the most revered of all the mummies and statues contained in Andean tombs and shrines. People called them "creators of men" and gave them such honorific titles as "condor" (*mallku*), which also passed down from one *kuraka* to the next (pp. 77, 79–80, 94). In this way and many others, political authority was intimately tied to notions of ancestorhood.[78]

Turning to the nature of ancestor worship, Alvarez mentions that the Indians sacrificed camelids to the dead by their tombs, and gave them offerings of toasted maize, cooked food, corn beer, feathers, gold, silver, and coins (pp. 90–91, 116). Apparently people made these offerings at specific points in the agricultural cycle. Just before sowing (i.e., September to November), each *ayllu* congregated at its principal shrine where its members confessed one by one (and in some areas, collectively) to their ministers, who exhorted them to tell all, or else the *huaca* would punish the group with sickness, drought, frost, or hail. The ministers then did coca leaf divinations to determine whether the participants had confessed truly and threw out the sins, embodied in the coca leaves and fat collected from each confessor, onto a mountain or in a gully. Next, a minister collected offerings and engaged the *huaca* in oracular communication, sacrificing a dog and four guinea pigs for the crops (pp. 100–102). He wrung the guinea pigs' necks, stripped their hides from their carcasses, stuffed them with straw, and hung them on poles atop four high mountains that formed corners enclosing the fields. The dog was similarly sacrificed amid the fields. These hide sacrifices were to the *huacas,* whereas the flesh and bones of animals were buried as a sacrifice to the earth (*pachamama*). As this was their principal celebration, excessive feasting and corn beer drinking followed, with dancing and singing to flute and drum, punctuated by the reciprocal offering of drinks until, as Alvarez so delicately put it, they fell vomiting "like filthy pigs" into the arms of their concubines (pp. 103–5). After insisting that the entire ceremony was about nothing more spiritual than getting enough to eat, and their false confessions merely a means to deliver them from sickness, Alvarez returns to ethnographic mode. He notes regional variation in these observances. For fear of being detected by the priest, he continued, people did not always perform them publicly. Sometimes the rituals occurred indoors or at night, or in remote areas with rigorous internal vigilance for Christian informers and sentinels posted to prevent outsiders from approaching unseen (pp. 105–6).

Alvarez then describes an observance that took place at the end of the rainy season during the week of San Lázaro, immediately before Holy Week, as the Indians were doing penitential flagellations in the settlement. One night, the *kurakas* assembled their *ayllu* and its animals around their tomb. They tearfully invoked Auqui Penchuca, their founding ancestor, asking health for themselves, their animals and crops, then offered camelid sacrifices (pp. 107–8). At this point, Alvarez recounts his search for and ultimate destruction of the tomb in question (pp. 108–10). Returning to the annual cycle, he mentions a celebration called *casi* that followed Easter and groundbreaking in fallow fields when the rains had stopped. In this celebration, people honored the *huacas* with a "solemn binge of drinking," after which they took in the harvest (pp. 110–11). Then a celebration called *chai* occurred around Corpus Christi. For Alvarez, it consisted of another binge with the additional detail that *kurakas* and other *ayllu* notables assembled in a large roundhouse to bless the children born that year. Mothers presented their children to these dignitaries, along with coca to burn in prognostications about the children's future, and camelids or their fetuses to be sacrificed for them. According to Alvarez, this ceremony ended like all others, in drunkenness and fornication under the Devil's influence (pp. 111–12).

This account of *ayllu* ritual and local organization is relatively schematic, but establishes all of the basic points developed in later accounts.[79] It portrays *ayllus* and their characteristic forms of political authority as based on ancestor worship that was in turn oriented toward the health and fertility of fields, flocks, and people. Alvarez shows how *ayllus* appointed priesthoods and set aside corporate holdings to provide offerings to maintain favorable relations with the ancestors through sacrificial and oracular rituals. Significantly, burial practices were the vehicle through which Alvarez "discovered" these dimensions of the *ayllu*. Since both Catholic parish and Andean *ayllu* constituted themselves through relations with the dead, their paths were bound to cross here. How participants perceived and acted upon this basic cultural similarity was another matter.

Alvarez portrayed Andean practices as a religious system opposed to Catholicism, one that needed to be understood, refuted, and eradicated. He describes his wavering commitment to this systematic inquiry into the nature of Indian idolatries, and how he abandoned it for some time in disgust with what he discovered, before deciding to persist (p. 107). Obviously this raises questions about his report and others in the same genre. Without adopting a facile antirealism that would reduce "idolatry" to a discursive fabrication and deny it any existence independent of the investigator's concerns,[80] we may nonetheless suspect that Alvarez projected his own commitments to codification and dogma onto the Andean ritual life he described. We may grant that *ayllus* existed and had the characteristics he identified, but still wonder whether the founding ancestor Auqui Penchuca actually was, as Alvarez claimed, the prophet of a doctrinal system that actively resisted Christianity (p. 108). Alvarez saw this dichotomy as inherent, but I would argue that it resulted from his deployment of the ideology of "purity of blood," which used codified religion as a racializing principle to impute clear boundaries and hereditary affiliations in a situation where neither actually existed.

Alvarez's own account shows that many Indians wanted church burial, even if they were not baptized or fully conversant with church doctrine. We should not let this important fact disappear in Alvarez's endless affirmations that Indians mocked the church and its sacraments and were as idolatrous as when the Spaniards first arrived. Exactly why these supposedly incorrigible pagans wanted his mortuary services is an open question. The most likely answer may be that they wished to maintain or reconstitute their ancestral community in the face of Alvarez's persecution, and were even willing to have it housed in the church provided he did not destroy the bodies of their dead. Whatever the case, many of Alvarez's parishioners did not adopt his polarized and exclusionary understanding of "conversion," and therefore asked for church burial despite maintaining some of their own practices. Even as Alvarez was constructing a pessimistic scenario of two tightly contained religious systems at loggerheads, leakages of people and ideas between the two were already well underway. Other parishioners, such as those who informed against the clandestine rites of their "pagan" neighbors, and those who held that the Spaniards had one origin and set of customs, and the Indians another, did accept the notion of opposed traditions, although not necessarily in the same way as Alvarez. The complexity of this situation and its politics are all too easily erased. At least three positions existed within this Andean community: one that accepted Christianity and understood it in exclusive terms; another that rejected it on similar grounds; and a third that partly accepted it but did not share its sense of boundaries or exclusivity. Undoubtedly diversity also existed within this latter camp, which deserves special attention not only because it refused the dichotomies of "conversion," but also because this was the perspective that eventually was to prevail among Andean people.

Checras, 1614: Baptizing the Ancestors

Several important documents regarding clandestine disinterment appeared immediately prior to and at the outset of the anti-idolatry campaign of 1609–22 in the archbishopric of Lima.[81] Of particular interest is one from the Checras region of Chancay, that dates to February 1614 and records the first anti-idolatry inspection of that area, which was also the first in the long career of the famous *visitador* Fernando de Avendaño.[82] Iwasaki published the first part of the document, which is a collective confession of the various "dogmatizers" in San Francisco de Musca.[83] It is a highly distilled account that contains none of the evidential conventions of a trial. Determinations of guilt and punishment must have taken place offstage, leaving Avendaño free to produce a quasi-ethnographic sketch of local pantheons, ritual, and cosmology. This sketch would prove not only his knowledge of such matters, but also that the natives had *doctrina*: a codified religion.[84] The pragmatic motive for producing such a document can be inferred from where it ultimately came to rest, in Avendaño's first curriculum vitae and request for promotion, for which it may well have been designed from the outset. One of the "errors" to which his convict-informants confessed was having

> preached and taught in this town to all of its Indians that the souls of Indians cannot go to heaven, and that they had converted to Christianity for nothing, since the law of Christ was not necessary for the

Indians to save themselves, and that the Spaniards have one law and the Indians another, and that the souls of Indians go to a place called Upaymarca where there is a bridge of hairs over which black dogs make the souls pass.[85]

Here we discover new fragments of Andean mortuary lore in combination with an avowal of religious separatism from below. While subsequent idolatry trials corroborate both points, and thus lend them plausibility, let us see whether the rest of the document actually confirms this separatist vision of the afterlife.

The second part of the document records various people in San Francisco de Musca, San Pablo de Ayaranga, and Santo Domingo de Apachi who were convinced to produce the bodies of relatives they had taken from the church. Duviols published the proceedings in the first two of these three villages.[86] In contrast to the first part of the document, which is interpretive in tone, the emphasis in the second part is essentially forensic: to produce and record the evidence. The rhetorical goal seems to have been to evoke the lurid factuality of native mortuary idolatries. Thus, various repentant ancestor worshipers "exhibited" the bodies of their dead relatives to Avendaño, and the names and relationships of the living and the dead were duly recorded. Once again, the judicial processes that led to these various "exhibitions" were not written down: the business of conviction and correction that was the usual stuff of these trials is curiously absent from the documentation.

In San Francisco de Musca, Avendaño recorded a long list of bodies taken from the church of Santo Domingo de Apachi. Not only did the living kin "exhibit" these bodies, they confessed to having taken them from the church "to the *huacas* where they were worshiped, offering them sacrifices." Although these bodies had been baptized and given Christian burial, Avendaño nonetheless had them burned in the plaza.[87] As we have seen above, the First Council of Lima mandated such treatment for the bodies of those who secretly requested interment outside churches, as Avendaño must have assumed them to have done.

Another list of bodies and kin was produced from the neighboring town of San Pablo de Ayaranga. The kin had taken these bodies from the church to the *huaca,* where they worshiped them, asking for life and health. Besides those bodies "stolen" from the church, the Indian parishioners also produced pagan corpses "for baptism." This is the single most remarkable piece of evidence from the trial. Apparently, they hoped to import their existing mortuary cult, including its "pagan" mummies, into that of the church. Of course, these unbaptized bodies were summarily burned in the plaza, along with those "stolen" from the church."[88]

For Avendaño, this request to baptize the pagan dead could only confirm that the Indians remained obstinately ignorant of the True Faith. Like the lists of exhibited cadavers, he probably offered this piece of information as raw evidence of religious error. Once we no longer presuppose the extirpators' sense of boundaries, however, we need not take the hope of baptizing the ancestors to indicate Andean ignorance or naivety. This wish also expresses an understanding, and not necessarily a superficial one, that Catholicism was also centrally concerned with the disposition and conservation of the dead, and might accept them as converts. After all, the church allowed emergency baptisms for the dying and Paul invoked baptism of the dead through living surrogates as a legitimate Christian practice (I Cor. 15:29), a point upon which Mormons later capitalized to justify baptizing the dead.[89] Andean people were neither the first nor the last participants in the Christian tradition to propose this practice. The parishioners of San Pablo de Ayaranga may not have fully grasped Catholic eschatology, but that was not necessarily because their own understandings of ancestors and the afterlife were irreconcilably foreign to Christianity. Andean people metaphorically represented their most sacred ancestral mummies as seeds (*malqui*), also the oldest Christian image for the resurrection of the body.[90] In a context of regular if imperfect doctrinal communication, the parishioners of San Pablo de Ayaranga must have understood enough about Catholicism to believe that their request would be granted; otherwise they would have hidden these bodies, as so many other Andean people did before and after them.

This incident completely undercuts the dichotomy between Indian and Christian afterlives that Avendaño had earlier attributed to the "dogmatizers" from this area. It suggests that as in Aullagas, the parishioners' main goal was to keep the dead together, preferably in the church. If the natives really subscribed to the religious separatism Avendaño was so busy enforcing, they would never have made this extraordinary request for Catholic inclusion. Perhaps the disagreement actually was, as the account suggests, between the "dogmatizers" who had a professional stake in separatism, and the rest of the population who did not.[91] Although Andean people sometimes accepted separatist ideas, the labor of differentiation fell primarily to churchmen like Avendaño at this early stage of the extirpation. If the parishioners of San Pablo de Ayaranga could ask for their ancestors to become baptized members of the church, they cannot have regarded Catholic and ancestral mortuary cults as mutually exclusive.

Finally, in the town of Santo Domingo de Apachi, site of the church from which the previously mentioned bodies had been taken, Avendaño produced another list of kin and cadavers. He burned these bodies, like all the others. Perhaps the most significant thing about all these lists is their generational shallowness. People produced no more than one or two lineal ancestors, who were the object of a restricted familial cult, albeit one that took place in the *huaca* (probably a place of interment shared by an entire *ayllu*). Missing in these accounts but present in others are the *malquis* or founding ancestors that all *ayllu* members worshiped.[92] Elaborate genealogies of mummified *kurakas* would have linked these founding ancestors to the shallow and much more ephemeral lineages of commoner mummies described in this document. As Doyle shows, *malquis* were vitally important to the religious life of their communities, whereas commoner mummies mattered only as long as their immediate families remembered them, later falling into neglect and decay.[93] Except for the mummies offered for baptism in San Pablo de Ayaranga, none of the bodies described in this document appears to have had *malqui* status. We may suspect that the parishioners held something important in reserve, and risked only what they would soon forget in any event.

CONCLUSION

The story of clandestine disinterment hardly ends here. Indeed, this chronological discussion stops short of what are commonly considered the two best sources on the topic, Arriaga's extirpation manual, and the extraordinary set of idolatry trials that Bernardo de Noboa staged in Cajatambo during the years 1656–1664.[94] By stopping at 1614, however, we can isolate an interesting historical moment, one in which the townspeople of San Pablo de Ayaranga were retrospectively trying to convert Andean ancestors to Christianity, as were native intellectuals like Santacruz Pachacuti and Guaman Poma in their contemporaneous writings. The convergence of purpose between such authors and the unlettered peasants accused of idolatry is remarkable. Although each approached the matter differently, their common goal was to secure a recognition of the ancestral past as part of the new Christian order. The attempt to convert ancestors in San Pablo de Ayaranga was not an isolated case. In later idolatry trials that otherwise seem to describe highly traditional rituals, Andean people describe their founding ancestors as bearded Spaniards, much as Guaman Poma had done.[95] In short, native chroniclers and idolaters of various levels of Andean society consistently tried to link Christian and Andean traditions in a strategy that persisted over time and prevailed over a wide geographical area, linking native chroniclers and idolaters at various levels of Andean society in previously unsuspected ways. Of course this dialogue still included *criollo* figures such as Ramos Gavilán and Calancha, who continued to convert Andean narratives of ancestral journeys into tales of wandering apostles even after

Andean people had begun doing so as well.[96] Their efforts sustained and validated indigenous attempts to posthumously convert the ancestors, which were neither as naive nor as original as one might suppose.

These recycled tales of wandering ancestor-apostles from the early missionaries clearly acquired a different meaning in the context of *reducción* and the extirpation of idolatry. They appear to propose a return to the status quo ante of indirect rule, in which the boundaries between cultural traditions were not as tightly drawn. The rhetoric of codified religious systems found in the "ethnographies" of Alvarez and Avendaño gave new oppositional significance to old conflations of ancestors and apostles. Yet the persistence of this early missionary device also shows that there was no tidy transition from a period of indirect rule featuring a Christian interpolation of the Andean past to a period of *reducción* featuring the extirpation of idolatry. While a long-term shift in boundary strategies from invasion and assimilation to differentiation and denigration has undoubtedly been part of the consolidation of power in many other colonial regimes, the teleological clarity of such a "model" is false and sterile. Aspects of *reducción* were implemented during the phase of indirect rule, just as many people, Andean and Spanish alike, continued to convert ancestors into apostles well into the seventeenth century. What changed was not so much the strategies available as where the center of gravity among them lay. A shift toward *reducción* certainly did occur, but it was not as abrupt, decisive, or early as the Toledo ordinances would suggest. Even under *reducción,* indirect rule remained an important if submerged reality, and in this light, Andean attempts to reconcile ancestor worship with Catholicism make sense. Parishes subsumed and moved *ayllus,* but hardly eliminated them. Andean people could reasonably expect the de facto coexistence of these two forms of local organization to be tolerated in ritual, as it was in economic, political, and administrative matters. Colonialism, and particularly the mining of precious metals that made it attractive to Spaniards, required a steady supply of indigenous labor that only *kurakas* could deliver. Their ability to make authoritative requests for their subjects' labor in turn depended on their role as privileged intermediaries in and sponsors of the mummy cults. For Andean people, mummy cults might therefore just as easily appear to be part of the colonial order as something outside of (or opposed to) it. Given that both parishes and *ayllus* defined themselves so extensively through relations with the dead, the only surprise is that extirpation sources do not reveal more attempts to baptize the ancestors. Perhaps such attempts did occur, and avoided the historical record by succeeding.

Despite the best efforts of men like Alvarez and Avendaño, there was considerable ambiguity about what counted as legitimate Catholic worship and what counted as idolatry. This was true not only for Andean people and their techniques of assimilating initially foreign deities, but also for Spaniards. To the extent that the Spanish project of conversion subsumed the Andes into a universalizing Christian history, it destabilized any geographically given boundaries between religious traditions and thereby partially undercut the requirement to shift allegiance from one to the other. As long as a retrospective alignment of traditions orchestrated the incorporation of the Andes into Christendom, indigenous people could justifiably claim that they were in some sense already practitioners of the True Faith. Although the extirpation of idolatry certainly curtailed and reorganized their ancestral practices, it did not extinguish them. Eventually, like so many intrusive outsiders before them, Spaniards and their deity revised and developed ancestral tradition as they incorporated them. Despite the many tensions between priests and parishioners, including periodic calls of extirpators and indigenous "dogmatizers" for purification, a modus vivendi emerged in which all parties could claim a modest victory, whether or not it counted as conversion.

NOTES

I wish to thank the History Department of Princeton University for the opportunity to write and deliver an earlier version of this paper as a Fellow at the Davis Center. Frances Slaney, Tony Grafton, Ken Mills, David Murray, and Susanna Elm offered particularly helpful comments.

1. K. Mills, *An Evil Lost to View? An Investigation of Post-Evangelization Andean Religion in Mid-Colonial Peru* (Liverpool, 1994); K. Mills, *Idolatry and its Enemies: Colonial Andean Religion and Extirpation, 1640–1750* (Princeton, N.J., 1997), chap. 8.

2. R. Levillier, *Organización de la iglesia y órdenes religiosas en el virreinato del Perú en el siglo XVI,* pt. 2 (Madrid, 1919), pp. 7–22.

3. See F. de Pizarro, "Encomenderos y encomiendas," *Revista del Archivo Nacional del Perú* 4, no. 1 (1926): 1–21.

4. S. Stern, *Peru's Indian Peoples and the Challenge of Spanish Conquest* (Madison, Wis., 1982), chap. 2.

5. P. Duviols, "Huari y llacuaz: Agricultores y pastores: Un dualismo prehispánico de oposición y complementaridad," *Revista del Museo Nacional* 39 (1973): 176–80; M. E. Doyle, "The Ancestor Cult and Burial Ritual in Seventeenth- and Eighteenth-Century Central Peru" (University of California, Los Angeles, 1988), pp. 151, 170.

6. B. de las Casas, *Obras completas,* vols. 6–8 (1550; Madrid, 1992).

7. On ancestral journeys see P. Duviols, "Un symbolisme andin du Double: La lithomorphose de l'ancêtre," *Actes du XLIIe Congrès International des Américanistes,* vol. 4 (Paris, 1978), pp. 359–64; Doyle, "Ancestor Cult," chap. 2; and P. Gose, "Segmentary State Formation and the Ritual Control of Water under the Incas," *Comparative Studies in Society and History* 35, no. 3 (1993): 480–514. On the plurality of Viracochas see J. de Betanzos, *Suma y naración de los Incas* (1551; Madrid, 1987); C. de Molina, *Relación de las fabulas y ritos de los Ingas . . .* (1573), pp. 47–134 in *Fábulas y mitos de los Incas,* ed. H. Urbano and P. Duviols, Historia 16 (Madrid, 1988), pp. 53–55; M. Polia, *La cosmovisión religiosa andina en documentos inéditos del Archivo Romano de la Compañía de Jesus 1581–1752* (Lima, 1999), p. 355; and F. Guaman Poma de Ayala, *Nueva corónica y buen gobierno* (1615; Paris, 1936), p. 49.

8. Las Casas, *Obras completas,* 7:874; P. de Cieza, *La Crónica del Perú,* pts. 1 and 2 (1553), in *Obras completas,* vol. 1. (Madrid, 1984), pp. 150–51; P. Sarmiento de Gamboa, *Historia de los Incas* (1572; Buenos Aires, 1942); Molina, *Relación de las fabulas y ritos,* pp. 51–55; and Miguel Cabello Valboa, *Miscelánea antártica: Una historia del Perú antiguo* (1586; Lima, 1951), p. 297, are among the chroniclers who depict Viracocha as the *hacedor* or creator along biblical lines. Molina, *Relación de las fabulas y ritos,* p. 51, and B. Cobo, *Historia del Nuevo Mundo* (1653), in *Biblioteca de autores Españoles,* vol. 92 (Madrid, 1956), p. 151, add that he created humanity out of clay; and Sarmiento, *Historia de los Incas,* p. 102, specifies that he made humanity "in his image."

9. P. Duviols, "Camaquen, Upani: Un concept animiste des anciens Peruviens," in *Estudios americanistas,* ed. R. Hartmann and U. Oberam, vol. 1., Collectanea Instituti Anthropos, vol. 20 (Bonn, 1978), pp. 132–44; G. Taylor, "Supay," *Amerindia* 5 (1980): 47–63; Gose, "Segmentary State Formation."

10. See Cabello Valboa, *Miscelánea antártica,* pp. 37–39; Polia, *La cosmovisión religiosa andina,* pp. 228–32; A. Ramos Gavilán, *Historia de Nuestra Señora de Copacabana* (1621; La Paz, 1976), pp. 27–35, 35–36, 39–41. Other sources that hint at this idea without explicitly proclaiming it are Betanzos, *Suma y naración de los Incas,* p. 14, and Sarmiento, *Historia de los Incas,* p. 108. Cieza, *Crónica del Perú,* p. 151, is probably the only early source to be overtly sceptical about this notion.

11. A. Arnoux, "De quelques représentations plastiques de Viracocha," in *Cultures et sociétés, Andes et Méso-Amerique: Mélanges en hommage á Pierre Duviols,* ed. R. Thiercelin, vol. 1 (Aix en Provence, 1991), pp. 67–77.

12. S. MacCormack, *Religion in the Andes: Vision and Imagination in Early Colonial Peru* (Princeton, N.J., 1991), p. 312; T. Bouysse-Cassagne, "De

Empédocles a Tunupa: Evangelización, hagiografía y mitos," in *Saberes y memorias en los Andes: In memoriam Thierry Saignes,* ed. T. Bouysse-Cassagne (Lima, 1997), pp. 157–202.

13. Cabello Valboa's underutilized *Miscelánea antártica* represents one of the most systematic attempts to integrate the Andes into this version of "universal history" by equating floods described in Andean origin narratives with the biblical Flood. J. Polo de Ondegardo, "Instrvcion contra las ceremonias y ritos que vsan los indios conforme al tiempo de su infielidad," in *Informaciones acerca de la religión y gobierno de los Incas* (1571), vol. I. (Lima, 1916), p. 52; M. de Murúa, *Historia general del Perú* (1613), Historia 16 (Madrid, 1987), p. 49; Cieza (*Crónica del Perú,* p. 149), Sarmiento (*Historia de los Incas,* pp. 102–4), and Molina (*Relación de las fabulas y ritos,* pp. 50–52, 55–57) achieve the same end.

14. Stern, *Peru's Indian Peoples,* chap. 3.

15. Ramos Gavilán, *Historia de Nuestra Señora de Copacabana,* pp. 49, 56–57; P. Duviols, *Cultura andina y represión: Procesos y visitas de idolatrías y hechicerías, siglo XVII* (Cuzco, 1986).

16. Garcilaso de la Vega, *Royal Commentaries of the Incas and General History of Peru* (1609; Austin, Tex., 1966), p. 40.

17. Ibid., pp. 70–72.

18. Ibid., pp. 75–76. Here, de la Vega blatantly contradicts his earlier discussion of the temple of Pachacamac (ibid, p. 71) to construct this immanent, dematerialized version of the deity.

19. Ibid., pp. 81–82.

20. Las Casas, *Obras completas,* 8:264–67.

21. J. de Santacruz Pachacuti Yamqui Salcamaygua, *Relacion de antiguedades deste Reyno del Piru* (1613; Lima/Cusco, 1993), p. 188.

22. Ibid., pp. 188–219.

23. Ibid., pp. 248–50, 213.

24. Guaman Poma, *Nueva corónica y buen gobierno,* p. 49.

25. Ibid., pp. 49–81.

26. Ibid., pp. 91–94.

27. A. Pagden, *The Fall of Natural Man: The American Indian and the Origins of Comparative Ethnology* (Cambridge, 1982), pp. 18 et passim.

28. *Reducir* and *reducción* have long been approximately cognate with "to reduce" and "reduction" in English, but their range of meaning in both languages was much broader in the sixteenth and seventeenth centuries than it is now. The oldest Spanish dictionary has the following entry: *"reducirse* is to become convinced. *Reducido,* convinced and returned to better order." S. Covarrubias, *Tesoro de la lengua castellana o española* (1611; Madrid, 1995), p. 854. Other uses of the term more specifically denote conversion

and incorporation into Catholicism, for example Pope Alexander VI's stipulation that "se procure la salvación de las almas y las naciones bárbaras sean reducidas a la fe cristiana" Levillier, *Organisación de la iglesia,* no. 7; cf. nos. 8, 12, 14. The sense of incorporation and order denoted by *reducción* was significantly (and sometimes primarily) religious or ideological, thus the policy was frequently discussed under the heading of ecclesiastical government. See, e.g., R. Levillier, *Gobernantes del Perú,* 14 vols. (Madrid, 1921–26), 4:397. Elsewhere, the term referred to an obedience that was both political and religious, as in Toledo's account of how armed men "rreduxeron estas prouincias a dios y a la corona real" (ibid., p. 72; cf. ibid., p. 352; ibid., 3:82, 309). It might also designate a purely political subjugation, as when a conquistador "los redujeron a la obedienzia y señorio y corona real de castilla" (ibid., 4:116; cf. ibid., pp. 127, 326; ibid., 3:98, 150, 270).

29. A. Málaga Medina, "Las reducciones en el Perú," *Historia y Cultura* 8 (1974): 141–72.

30. V. Fraser, *The Architecture of Conquest: Building in the Viceroyalty of Peru, 1535–1635* (Cambridge, 1990).

31. J. de Matienzo, *Gobierno del Perú* (1567; Lima, 1967).

32. F. de Toledo, *Francisco de Toledo: Disposiciones gubernativas para el Virreinato del Perú, 1569–1574* (Seville, 1986), p. 246.

33. Ibid., pp. 47, 95.

34. T. Abercrombie, *Pathways of Memory and Power: Ethnography and History among an Andean People* (Madison, Wis., 1998), p. 246.

35. Toledo, *Disposiciones gubernativas 1569–1574,* pp. 34–36.

36. Abercrombie, *Pathways of Memory and Power,* pp. 247–48.

37. E.g., Levillier, *Gobernantes del Perú,* 14:76.

38. T. Saignes, "Las etnías de Charcas frente al sistema colonial (siglo XVII): Ausentismo y fugas en el debate sobre mano de obra indígena, 1595–1665," *Jahrbuch für Geschichte von Staat, Wirtschaft und Gesellschaft Lateinamerikas* 21 (1984): 27–75.

39. See J. Cole, *The Potosí Mita, 1573–1700* (Stanford, Calif., 1985).

40. The following is a small sample of the material available: Levillier, *Gobernantes del Perú,* 14:76, 171); Lobo Guerrero to the king, 15 March 1610, 20 March 1610, 3 April 1617, 15 April 1619, in Archivo General de Indias (hereafter AGI), Audiencia de Lima, Legajo 301; Borja to the king, 24 April 1620, AGI, Lima 39; Guadalcazar to *corregidor* of Huamalies, 11 August 1625, copied to king 3 October 1625, AGI, Lima 302; Campo to the king, 15 October 1626, AGI, Lima 302; collated testimony with terminal date of 28 September 1626, AGI Lima 302.

41. The highlights of this documentation include M. de Monsalve, *Redvcion Vniversal de todo el Piru, y demas Indias, con otros muchos Auifos, para el*

bien de los naturales dellas, y en aumento de las Reales Rentas. Compuesto por el Padre Fray Miguel de Monfalue, de la Orden de Predicadores, morador del Reyno del Piru. Dirigido a la Catolica Magestad del Rey don Felipe, Tercero defte nombre nueftro Señor (Madrid, 1604), British Library; the position papers written for the great debate of 1633 in AGI, Lima 43; and that of the late 1650s in AGI, Lima 59.

42. Toledo, *Disposiciones gubernativas 1569–1574,* p. 33.

43. Ibid., p. 14.

44. Ibid., p. 135.

45. Ibid., p. 136.

46. Ibid., p. 137.

47. Levillier, *Gobernantes del Perú,* 6:53–54.

48. Toledo, *Disposiciones gubernativas 1569–1574,* pp. 245–49.

49. See L. Millones, *El retorno de las huacas* (Lima, 1990), pp. 209, 212, 220, 224, 231, 233, 235, 239, 244, 248, 250–51.

50. See Lobo Guerrero to the king, 3 April 1617, AGI, Lima 301; Campo to the king, 15 October 1626, AGI, Lima 302.

51. Toledo, *Disposiciones gubernativas 1569–1574,* pp. 281–82.

52. F. de Toledo, *Francisco de Toledo: Disposiciones Gubernativas para el Virreinato del Perù, 1575–1580* (Seville, 1989), pp. 229–231.

53. Ibid., pp. 413–14.

54. R. Vargas Ugarte, *Concilios Limensesu,* vol. 1 *(1551–1772)* (Lima, 1951), p. 21.

55. Polia, *La cosmovisión religiosa andina,* p. 409.

56. P. Brown, *The Cult of the Saints: Its Rise and Function in Latin Christianity* (Chicago, 1981), chap. 1.

57. B. Lobo Guerrero, *Lilbro* [sic] *primero de las Constituciones Sinodales de este Arzobispado de las Reyes del Perù* (1613), in B. Lobo Guerrero and F., Arias Ugarte, *Sinodas de Lima de 1613 y 1636* (Madrid, 1987), p. 138.

58. Duviols, *Cultura andina y represión,* p. 16.

59. A. Guiance, *Discursos sobre la muerte en la Castilla medieval (siglos VII–XV)* (Valladolid, 1998), pp. 60–77.

60. C. Eire, *From Madrid to Purgatory: The Art and Craft of Dying in Sixteenth-Century Spain* (Cambridge, 1995), p. 210.

61. See ibid., pp. 99–100.

62. Duviols, *Cultura andina y represión,* pp. 18, 14.

63. Eire, *From Madrid to Purgatory,* p. 91.

64. Ibid., pp. 85–86, 151–2; Guiance, *Discursos sobre la muerte,* p. 44.

65. See "Obras publicadas en el Concilio de Alcala de año 1481 presidido en nombre de don Alfonso Carrillo por don Vasco de Ribera Arcediano de Talavera," Biblioteca Nacional de Madrid, Ms. 13021, fols. 129–46.

66. See "Confirmacion del Cardenal Arzobispo de Toledo don Pedro Gonzalez de Mendoza de lo resuelto en la Congregacion que celebró en Alcala don Juan de Torres Arcediano de Medina y suspension de la censuras fulminados por algunas constituciones de don Alfonso Carrillo a 13 de noviembre de 1483," Biblioteca Nacional de Madrid, Ms. 13021, ff. 153–56. The Council of Granada effectively reinstated the decree of 1481 when in 1565 it ordered that both New and Old Christians be buried in churches. In 1591, Felipe II ordered "that all Moriscos be buried in churches, regardless of local customs" Eire, *From Madrid to Purgatory*, pp. 91–93, 94.

67. See A. Sicroff, *Les controverses des statuts de pureté de sang en Espagne du XVe au XVIIe siècle* (Paris, 1960); B. Netanyahu, *The Origins of the Inquisition in Fifteenth-Century Spain* (New York, 1995).

68. J. de Acosta, *De Procuranda Indorum Salute* (1576), vol. 2 (Madrid, 1984), p. 255. Acosta's views were authoritative. J. de Arriaga, *Extirpación de la idolatría en el Pirú* (1621), in *Biblioteca de Autores Españoles*, vol. 209 (Madrid, 1968), p. 195; J. de Solorzano de Pereyra, *Politica Indiana* (1648), vol. 1 (Madrid, 1972), pp. 443–45; and P. de Villagómez, *Carta pastoral de exhortación e instrucción contra las idolatrías de los indios del arzobispado de Lima* (1649), in *Colección de libros y documentos referentes a la historia del Perú*, vol. 12, ed. C. Romero and H. Urteaga (Lima, 1919), p. 38), were among the influential figures to reproduce them.

69. MacCormack, *Religion in the Andes*, pp. 85–94.

70. E. Lissón y Chaves, *La iglesia de España en el Perú*, 5 vols. (Seville, 1943–47), 1:143.

71. Vargas Ugarte, *Concilios Limenses*, 1:81–82.

72. Lissón y Chaves, *Iglesia de España en el Perú*, 2:305, 354–55.

73. Polo, "Instrvcion contra las ceremonias y ritos," p. 194.

74. Millones, *El retorno de las huacas*, p. 290,

75. B. Alvarez, *De las costumbres y conversión de los indios del Perú: Memorial a Felipe II (1588)* (1588; Madrid, 1998). All references in the text are to this work.

76. Note that this usage of *supay* differs from that described above, and seems cognate with the term *camaquen* in other regions of the Andes (Duviols, "Camaquen, Upani"; Taylor, "Supay").

77. Duviols, "Un symbolique andin du Double."

78. See L. Millones, "Los ganados del Señor: Mecanismos de poder en las comunidades andinas, Arequipa, siglos XIII–XIX." *Historia y Cultura* 11 (1978): 7–43; and L. Millones, "Religion and Power in the Andes: Idolatrous Curacas of the Central Sierra," *Ethnohistory* 26, no. 3 (1979): 243–63.

79. Arriaga, *Extirpación de la idolatría*; C. Romero, "Idolatrías de los Indios Huachos y Yauyos," *Revista Histórica* 6 (1918): 180–97; Duviols, *Cultura andina y represión*.

80. E.g., G. Ramos, "Política eclesiástica y extirpación de idolatrías: Discursos y silencios en torno al Taqui Onqoy," in *Catolicismo y Extirpación de Idolatrías: Siglos XVI–XVII,* ed. G. Ramos and H. Urbano (Cusco, 1993), pp. 137–68; H. Urbano, "Rituales andinos y discurso anti-idolátrico (s. XVI–XVII)," in *Estudios sobre el sincretismo en América Central y en los Andes,* ed. B. Schmelz and N. R. Crumrine (Bonn, 1996), pp. 137–52.

81. P. Gose, "Les momies, les saints et les politiques d'inhumation au Pérou, au XVIIe Siècle," *Recherches Amérindiennes au Québec* 25, no. 2 (1995): 35–51; Polia, *La cosmovisión religiosa andina.*

82. See Lissón y Chaves, *Iglesia de España en el Perú,* 5:225–26. The document is a notarized copy of the original inquest records from 1614, included in Avendaño's *relacion de servicios y méritos,* that dates to 27 March 1618, and can be found in AGI, Lima 327.

83. F. Iwasaki, "Idolatrías de los indios checras," *Historia y Cultura* 17 (1984): 75–90.

84. An account of 1613–14 by Pablo Prado takes this codifying tendency to a further extreme in its derivation of the idolatries of the Huachos and Yauyos region from a set of thirteen diabolical commandments. Romero, "Idolatrías de los Indios Huachos y Yauyos," pp. 187–89.

85. Iwasaki, "Idolatrías de los indios checras," p. 88).

86. P. Duviols, *La lutte contre les religions autochtones dans le Pérou coloniale (L'extirpation de l'idolatrie entre 1532 et 1660)* (Lima, 1971), pp. 355–56.

87. Ibid., p. 355.

88. Ibid., p. 356.

89. G. J. Adams, *A Lecture on the Doctrine of Baptism for the Dead* (1844; Bountiful, Utah, 1983).

90. C. W. Bynum, *The Resurrection of the Body in Western Christianity, 200–1336* (New York, 1995), p. 3.

91. Mills, *An Evil Lost to View?* chap. 6.

92. Duviols, *Cultura andina y represión.*

93. Doyle, *Ancestor Cult,* pp. 95–97.

94. Arriaga, *Extirpación de la idolatría;* Duviols, *Cultura andina y represión.*

95. Duviols, *Cultura andina y represión,* pp. 11, 55, 113, 119, 452.

96. Ramos Gavilán; *Historia de Nuestra Señora de Copacabana;* and Antonio de la Calancha, *Chronica moralizada del orden de San Augustin en el Peru, con Sucesos Egenplares en esta Monarquia* (1639), in *Cronicas agustinianas del Perú,* vol. 1. ed. M. Merino (Madrid, 1972).

7

CONVERSION AND IDENTITY

IROQUOIS CHRISTIANITY IN SEVENTEENTH-CENTURY NEW FRANCE

ALLAN GREER

"They live like angels," wrote a Jesuit missionary of the Iroquois converts of Sault St.-Louis (Kahnawake to the natives).[1] Heeding the Gospel message, they had abandoned their pagan homeland and torn themselves from idolatrous neighbors and kinfolk in order to travel north to the mission community on the banks of the St. Lawrence, opposite Montreal. There, according to Jesuit chroniclers of the 1670s and 1680s, they pursued an almost monastic existence comparable to the primitive church. Mass was at 5:30 in the morning—according to Father Claude Chauchetière, "they attend every day, without a single person being absent"—and public prayers were held every evening. "In addition to this," he continues, "the Indians come frequently during the day to visit the Blessed Sacrament, especially on their way to the fields and when they are returning home."[2] Some women went well beyond this pious routine, renouncing marriage, dedicating themselves to lifelong virginity, and pursuing experiments in heroic asceticism that left Chauchetière and his colleagues awestruck. Though Europeans may think of the original inhabitants of the Americas as irredeemable savages, observed the *Jesuit Relations,* there are more true Christians here than in "our civilized Europe."[3]

What are we to make of these accounts of what sounds like exceptionally intense Counter-Reformation devotional practices on the part of people who were, after all, heirs to a vibrant Iroquoian religious tradition stretching back over the centuries and who had been only recently introduced to Christianity? Over the years, historians interested in the history of the Iroquois,[4] and those whose research focuses on the French missions,[5] have examined, with great rigor and thoroughness, the political, economic, cultural, and military circumstances which led some natives to adhere to the French and accept Catholic baptism. Sustained by rich source materials

175

(mainly, but not exclusively, of Jesuit origin), an impressive historical literature has developed in this field; so far, however, there has been comparatively little interest, except insofar as it seems to indicate missionary success or failure, in the actual content of Iroquois Christianity.

Historians' discussions of conversion tend to be rooted to a surprising degree in the terms of a debate initiated centuries ago by rival religious colonizers. As the presiding clergy at the Sault and as the main missionary force in New France, the Jesuits were the source of enthusiastic reports such as the ones cited above. Their considerable rhetorical skills were dedicated to portraying this convert community—and others such as Lorette, the Huron village near Quebec—as the fulfillment of that perennial missionary fantasy, a sudden and fundamental transformation of individuals and societies. In some contexts, they might allow their writings to reveal just how uncertain, incomplete, and uncontrolled conversion had been, but the dominant theme for public consumption in Europe was one of the Holy Spirit working its magic upon natives assembled on the banks of the St. Lawrence. Jesuit propaganda did not go unchallenged, however. The order's many enemies within the Canadian church and in the secular administration were quick to denounce the whole Jesuit missionary enterprise as a fraud; natives baptized by the Jesuits, these critics maintained, remained pagan savages under a thin veneer of Catholicism.[6] "Real" conversion had not taken place.

The chimera of "true conversion" has enjoyed a long life. Even quite recent scholarly works on the Indian missions of New France tend to divide themselves into pro- and anti-Jesuit positions, affirming or denying that natives really did experience fundamental change. "Were Indian Conversions Bona Fide?" asks the symptomatic title of one article emanating from the pro-Jesuit camp. The author, James Axtell, answers his own question in the affirmative, while taking aim at a varied collection of anti-Jesuit writers who argue that Iroquois and other native converts either feigned conversion for strategic reasons, or did not understand Christian doctrine, or practiced a syncretic religion that the missionaries mistook for genuine Catholicism.[7] Current debates in mission history are frequently conducted in the secular language of "assimilation" and "resistance," but in fundamental respects the framework of discussion remains that inherited from the Jesuits and their seventeenth-century critics. That is to say, conversion is understood in bipolar terms—successful or unsuccessful, real or false, a sign of assimilation or evidence of covert resistance—with "syncretism" occasionally invoked to cover any intermediate result. The effect is to keep the focus upon the missionaries, their criteria and aspirations, rather than on the "missionized." When they come to the subject of the introduction of Christianity, some ethnohistorians have difficulty resisting the temptation to cast their narrative in an ironic form, with the contrast between missionary aspirations and missionary achievements structuring the story.[8]

This paper examines the adoption of Christianity as a phase in the religious history of the Iroquois. It aims, not so much to evaluate the success or failure of European missionaries, but to grasp the ways in which Iroquois people made use of imported myths and rituals, both in pursuit of familiar Iroquois purposes and in the service of novel ends. The starting premise is that conversion of the sort missionaries hoped for, a sudden rebirth that wipes out preexisting identities, was impossible. Also to be set aside is the modern notion that religious change can be understood as a decisive event in a zero-sum "contest of cultures."[9] A "totalizing concept" if ever there was one, the contest of cultures model tends to treat the complex and inconclusive religious encounter between natives and Europeans as one aspect of an all-embracing struggle for cultural supremacy. As I hope will be clear from what follows, military metaphors of victory and defeat are anything but helpful in understanding the process of Christianization among the Iroquois.

As we attempt to apprehend the encounter with Christianity in an Iroquois context, we are immediately confronted with problems of vocabulary and conceptual apparatus. How, for example, can we transcend the parochial connotations of the term "conversion"? The definition proposed in one recent article, "le passage d'une religion dans une autre,"[10] implicitly situates the discussion in a European universe of mutually exclusive creeds, but in Iroquoian traditions, the adoption of one form of prayer or view of creation does not imply the rejection of others. Ideas about the order of the cosmos could be quite tentative, with ample room for alternative visions; the "natural" and the "supernatural" constantly interpenetrated; and a wide and eclectic range of techniques were deployed by humans wishing to avoid harm or secure benefits from unseen forces. To speak in this context of a transition from one religion to another is to invoke a false sense of commensurability, as though Iroquois "religion" and European "religion" were the same sort of phenomenon and as though each were a neatly bounded package (a view, by the way, that is probably no more applicable to European Catholicism of the period than it is to native American religion).

Taking our cue from our Latin Americanist colleagues,[11] I suggest that we in the North American field begin to treat conversion not as a discrete, unidirectional event, but as a problem to be unraveled in all its ambiguity, instability, and local specificity. A helpful move in that direction, one also suggested by the Latin American literature, would be to decompose the category "religion" and stop treating "Christianity" and "Iroquois religion" as monolithic entities defined by belief. Creation myths, rituals of propitiation, theories of transubstantiation, and procedures for achieving mystical ecstasy do not necessarily form a seamless unitary package. We need to give separate attention to the heterogeneous assemblage of phenomena implied by the heading "religion" and try to examine them, as much as possible, within a specific social context, rather than as manifestations of a free-floating abstraction. In this connection, the term "local religion," originally proposed by a Europeanist,[12] and applied to studies of Latin American colonial religion, helpfully focuses attention on performance rather than belief, on specific settings among people with particular experiences and traditions rather than on theological systems with pretensions to universality.

To come to terms with Iroquois Catholicism as "local religion," this paper begins with a sketch of the natives involved and of their situation in the colonial society of New France. It then looks at the role of Christian and Iroquoian contributions to the construction of personal and collective identities. Next, attention shifts to the ways in which Iroquois converts drew upon the two traditions to promote their welfare in the world and, finally, the focus moves beyond the realm of mundane affairs to examine the ways in which some Iroquois synthesized techniques to help them probe sacred mysteries.

COMMUNITY FORMATION: THE INDIANS' MIDDLE GROUND

Over the course of the seventeenth century, the French settlements on the St. Lawrence River came to be ringed by Indian villages, all of them officially Catholic and under the supervision of Jesuits, Sulpicians, and other missionary orders.[13] More recently established than their European neighbors, the inhabitants of these missions were all, to one degree or another, the casualties of colonization. Though the French did not come to Canada as massacring conquistadors, their presence nevertheless set off waves of epidemics, bloody wars, and bewildering economic dislocation, with cumulatively devastating effects on the Algonquian and Iroquoian peoples of the region. On the whole, it was those most seriously and directly affected who adhered to the French. The Montagnais and Algonquin, battered by disease, hunger, and Iroquois raids, gathered mainly at Sillery, near Quebec, while refugee Hurons, survivors of the Iroquois onslaught that shattered their society in 1649, settled nearby at the Jesuit mission of Lorette. Later arrivals included bands of Abenaki, displaced from northern New England by the effects of King Philip's War; and, most significantly, a substantial number of Iroquois who settled at the Sulpician mission of Montreal (later moved to Oka) and at the Jesuit mission of Sault St.-Louis/Kahnawake, not far from Montreal.[14]

Indians made up a sizable—though not precisely measurable—percentage of the population of St. Lawrence Valley Canada, but in spite of their close proximity, they remained distinct from the French, with their own costumes, languages, bark houses (gradually replaced with timber structures only in the eighteenth century), and their traditional economic pursuits of hunting, gathering, and agriculture. Most mission communities were intimately involved in the French fur trade, but unlike the colonized natives of the Spanish empire, they were not integrated into the colonial labor system. There was no labor service requirement here, nor were Indians subjected to any form of tribute. Instead, they supported themselves independently through selling furs and handicrafts to pay for their purchases of imported goods. Politically, they guarded their autonomy jealously; accepting that the king was their father, they resolutely refused to subject themselves to his laws and his courts.[15] They manifested their loyalty to the French monarch by taking part in his wars against the English, doing so as allies not as subjects; they counted on rewards for their support and always reserved the right to withhold it.

Iroquois and other natives were a foreign element in the midst of French Canada. Adopting a Catholic identity and adjusting to European expectations in a variety of ways, they remained aloof from most aspects of the life of the European settlement. On the whole, the French had to be accommodating for they knew that, beyond a certain point, attempts to impose their cultural norms and political rule would simply induce the Indians to leave, an eventuality that would only damage the colony's fur economy and its defenses. From the late seventeenth century, Canada depended upon the military support of its resident natives.[16] In these circumstances, an Indian version of the "middle ground" took shape, one that mirrored the relations then developing in the Great Lakes region where a French-Canadian minority made its way in a predominantly native environment thanks to cultural compromises on both sides.[17] Here in the French-Canadian heartland, natives adjusted to the expectations of the ambient society, but without melting into it.

Relations between the Jesuit missionaries and the resident natives assigned to their tutelage were part and parcel of the larger pattern of the Laurentian middle ground. Early experiments with a disciplinary regime modeled on the *reducciones* of Latin America failed miserably as converts simply departed for the forest, but the Jesuits soon came to terms with the limits imposed by a colonial environment where natives were free to come and go and developed a loosely controlled system of mission governance.[18] By the time the Iroquois began arriving at Kahnawake, it was understood that convert communities would be largely self-governing.

The migration of Iroquois to the Montreal area in the years following the 1667 peace with the French has been thoroughly examined in the specialist literature.[19] After decades of bloody war against their Huron, Algonquian, and French neighbors to the north, the Five Nations finally opted for a rapprochement. Regional configurations of power had shifted, notably through the massive militarization of New France, and many Iroquois became convinced that closer alignment with the French was the best option, under adverse circumstances, for ensuring military security and economic prosperity. From the late 1660s to the early 1680s, large numbers from the pro-French factions within the Onondagas and Oneidas, but especially from among the Mohawks, migrated north to settle in the vicinity of Montreal. Jesuits were active evangelizing at both ends of this migratory trajectory, with the result that conversion to Catholicism sometimes preceded the change of residence and sometimes followed it. By the mid-1670s, a stable core of Christian settlers had rooted themselves at the Jesuit *seigneurie* of Sault St.-Louis in a village they called Kahnawake.

Migration to Canada and conversion to Christianity further divided already profoundly split Iroquois societies. The middle decades of the seventeenth century had seen smallpox and other epidemics wipe out a majority of the population; losses were largely compensated through the adoption of war captives, with the result that, while numerical strength remained high, social cohesion probably declined. Indications are that partially assimilated captives, some of whom may have been previously exposed to Catholic missionaries when they were Huron or Algonquin, predominated among the converts moving north. Other internal cleavages in Iroquoia played a part in conditioning the religious split between Catholics and non-Christians. Factionalism, long a feature of Iroquois political life, according to Daniel Richter, and one which frequently played itself out in relation to foreign policy options, became quite intense in the second half of the century as factions favoring a rapprochement with the French vied for ascendancy, in a context of rapidly shifting alignments of external power, with other factions wishing to align themselves with first the Dutch and then the English.[20] These cleavages coincided, to some degree, with the various lines of segmentation—clan, village, nation—within the Five Nations, with "pro-French" forces particularly strong in the easternmost Mohawk town of Gandaouagué, source of the largest contingent of migrants to Canada. Gandouagué happened to be the main home of the Mohawk Turtle clan and it also seems to have housed a large number of prisoners from the northern nations. Thus it becomes impossible to disentangle the lines of clan, village, political faction, and ethnic origin in creating a predisposition to conversion and migration.

It is clear that the mission community that grew up at Sault St.-Louis was composed of people from a wide range of backgrounds: Iroquois of the Mohawk, Oneida, and Onondaga nations were most numerous, but there was also a contingent of "Hurons" and other naturalized former captives of diverse origin.[21] Initially, there was considerable confusion and some conflict. It was never easy for this diverse assortment of humanity to live together in peace, but Jesuits and natives bent their efforts to forging a collective identity and building institutions of community. "Captains" were elected, though in a modification of Iroquois practice no doubt suggested by the missionaries, authority was divided between, not a civil captain and a war captain, but between a captain for secular affairs and one for religious affairs.[22] As will be seen below, Catholic Christianity was one of the binding agents that the Iroquois of Kahnawake used to consolidate their new community.

Relations between the Iroquois of the Sault and their compatriots who stayed in the old land of the Five Nations were highly problematic, particularly in the community's early decades. "Pagan" Iroquois tended to resent the converts for abandoning their nation, though there was some ambivalence in their attitude as they could also appreciate the diplomatic value of the new settlement as a listening post and a diplomatic intermediary in relations with the French. Goods, news, and people moved easily between the northern and the southern settlements and, in typical Iroquois fashion, loyalties could be complex and ambiguous.

For this breakaway group of Iroquois, issues of identity and affiliation were perennially challenging in the seventeenth century. More than simply reflecting these perplexities, religion formed a principal medium through which questions of identity were addressed.

CHRISTIAN IDENTITY AND AFFILIATION

Iroquois Catholicism of the seventeenth century has to be understood primarily as behavior rather than belief, if only because the converts of Sault St.-Louis had quite limited exposure to Christian theology. After all, they spoke only their native language(s) and, though the Jesuits did their best to master the Iroquois idioms, they were constantly frustrated in their efforts to convey fundamental points of doctrine. Father Jean de Brébeuf, in his "Huron Relation" of 1636, nicely illustrates some of the dilemmas inherent in any attempt to translate European religious ideas into a truly foreign Iroquoian tongue such as Huron.

> A relative noun for them always includes the meaning of one of the three persons of the possessive pronoun, so that they cannot say simply, father, son, master, servant, but are obliged to say one of these three: my father, your father, his or her father. To facilitate the task of translating prayers, I have designated one of their nouns to stand for the word "Father," but we nevertheless find it impossible to get them to say properly in their language, "In the name of the Father, and of the Son, and of the Holy Ghost."[23]

More fundamental than the absence of any general term for "father" was the fact that so much hinged on the peculiar European connotations of this kinship term: the immediate creator to whom offspring owe their life; the holder of family property; the main connecting link to lineage systems; the chastiser; and, above all, the legitimate fount of commanding authority. An Iroquois "father" was none of these things and so the domestic-celestial metaphor of "God the Father" was largely meaningless in Kahnawake. At almost every point, a Jesuit attempting to communicate doctrine to the Iroquois would have run into impenetrable linguistic roadblocks, symptomatic of the ultimately parochial nature of European religious philosophy.[24]

And yet the missionaries were undismayed, for they knew that theology was by no means the sum total of Christianity. So minor a part did it play in Indian missions, in fact, that the Jesuits only instituted formal catechism classes at Sault St.-Louis in 1682, when the mission was fifteen years old and had already produced its first native "saint"! They did give instruction in Christian lore through the use of pictures, especially depictions of the torments of hell, and through stories of saints and of the life of Jesus. For the most part, however, their days were filled with the rituals of Mass, confession, baptism, and the last rites—ministering as they did to nearby French settlers as well as to Indians—and with the mundane demands of mission management. Most of the educational work involved in inducting newcomers into the ways of the church and leading public prayers fell to natives elected as "prayer captains" or "dogiques." The latter were initially male, but in good Iroquois fashion, the office was soon taken over by the clan mothers who formed the stable core of any longhouse society.

The Sault St.-Louis community always sheltered a number of non-Christians, especially on the unstable fringe of comers and goers, yet it was understood on all sides that full membership in the community was reserved to baptized Catholics. The baptism ritual, which must have reminded Iroquois of the naming ceremony which conferred on individuals a particular social identity and thus connected them to the group, helped to cement a distinct local identity. So too did many other church rites and customs; the functional effect was to bind together in shared observances a community whose coherence always seemed problematic, given the internal stresses inherent in the life of any village, especially one with such a heterogeneous population.

The daily public prayers, which, much to Father Chauchetière's delight, everyone took part in, would have contributed to a sense of local solidarity, as would weekly services and the elaborately staged seasonal celebrations such as Christmas and Easter. These latter must have performed some of the same functions of reinforcing collective identities that formally similar calendrical feasts did in the Iroquois tradition. Obviously, there were fundamental differences between the Catholic rituals and their Iroquois counterparts, not least of which was the critical sacred role of the French clergy in most Christian observances, but the social function was comparable. Similarly, the material trappings of Catholicism could work as emblems of group identity in ways that were not unfamiliar to Iroquoians. Though they dressed very much like their pagan relatives in the old Five Nations lands, residents of Kahnawake were instantly recognizable by their Christian accessories such as crucifix pendants and rosary beads; the latter were either attached at the waist or, in a stylish aboriginal flourish, worn as hair ornaments. Items of apparel with sacred/magical associations were as familiar to Iroquois people as were seasonal festivals featuring prayers of thanksgiving for life and sustenance. These gestures and affectations, actively promoted by the Jesuits because they lent themselves, in a way that language-dependent matters of belief did not, to adaptation and cultural compromise, served as visible badges of identity uniting the disparate elements that made up the Christian village of Kahnawake.

Catholic identity looked outward as well as inward, defining relations with others even as it worked to give villagers a collective sense of themselves. Christian rituals and emblems served first of all to accentuate the division of the Iroquois and to assert the separateness of the breakaway settlement vis-à-vis the Five Nations rump. Looking in another direction, it embodied connection, most obviously with the French, but also with other converted native nations in the French orbit. Christianity, in some of its

most basic gestural and symbolic aspects, functioned as the religious component of the alliance relationship by which Iroquois bound themselves to
the French. More than simply an expression of affiliation, it was a vital
constituent of the affiliation between the groups. In the Iroquoian tradition,
a treaty of peace and alliance is not an arrangement agreed upon at a given
time and fixed for the future, it is a living relationship requiring the parties
actively to implicate themselves in the affairs of the other, constantly reaf-
firming and, when necessary, renegotiating the alliance.[25] For the Sault
Iroquois, it would have seemed natural to adopt Catholicism in order to
partake of what their allies presented as a central element of their identity.

Connected to the French partly through a shared Catholicism, the people
of Kahnawake remained separate from them, and quite deliberately so.
Accordingly, their array of socially integrating customs drew on Iroquois as
well as Christian traditions. Kinship structures, marital customs, and even
burial practices were only lightly affected by conversion. People continued
to define their families through female parentage (a situation that shaped
even the Jesuits' evangelizing strategies: they sought out families with
many daughters, refusing to waste their time on sons)[26] and they chose their
mates outside their own clan. The Jesuits did draw the line at polygamy—
not common among the Iroquois in any case—but they did not insist on
Catholic marriage. The result was that native marriage ceremonies prevailed
for many years, with church weddings only gradually gaining popularity.
Likewise, burial and condolence rites, of crucial importance in maintaining
social cohesion within an Iroquois village, continued largely unchanged for
many years.[27] At the Huron mission of Lorette, a year's crop of corpses was
disinterred every November on All Souls' Day and reburied in a common
grave; the Jesuits did their best to wrap the ceremony in Christian apparel,
but it was, to all intents and purposes, an Iroquoian Feast of the Dead.[28]

Clans remained central to social life; from them individuals received a
name and a personal identity that integrated them into a particular female
lineage, their main point of connection with the community. Everyone
received an Iroquois name through the women of their clan, as well as a
Christian name conferred by the church, with the result that residents of
the village carried double names: "Catherine Tekakwitha," "Anastasia Te-
gonhatsiongo," "Martin Skandegorhaksen." These names had the appearance of a European-style pairing of a personal name and a family name, but
they were something quite different, a badge of layered identity. A name in
this style proclaimed that an individual was simultaneously, for example,
Tekakwitha, the current embodiment of a resuscitated personage who had
belonged for generations to the Turtle clan, and a Christian baptized in
memory of Caterina da Siena.

SUPERNATURAL AID FOR HUMAN PURPOSES

The prayers of Iroquois converts cannot be seen purely as gestures of affiliation with the French. Along with their social function, the Catholic observances practiced so assiduously at Kahnawake were surely intended to affect relations between humans and the unseen forces that conditioned their lives. Commonly in colonial situations, the colonizers' gods and their modes of worship exercise great appeal over indigenous peoples who tend to see in them a means of partaking of the colonizer's power and prestige. Naturally, they were inclined to employ European procedures in the service of goals defined by their own indigenous traditions, but they also absorbed new, Christian, purposes, as well as styles of worship.

Catholicism as the Jesuits presented it was mainly a matter of resignation in the face of God's inscrutable will. One could ask, through the Virgin Mary or one of the saints, for luck in hunting or protection from smallpox, but there were no grounds for counting on the request being granted. The main thing was to embrace the divinely ordained outcome, even—especially—when it brought pain and suffering, and to remember that life after death was what really mattered. The *Relations* recount dozens of anecdotes highlighting the Job-like resignation of native converts faced with the death of a child or some similar "trial," but the language in which grieving mothers dedicate their sorrow to the Virgin tends to conform so closely to the formulas of conventional Catholic piety as to ring false.[29] No doubt Christian teachings did affect the way in which Kahnawake Iroquois reacted to affliction, and their assiduous prayers and observances probably betoken, among other things, a concern with ultimate salvation. But in their indigenous culture, transactions with the supernatural usually had a more immediate, practical purpose. Like the "popular" or "local" Catholicism of contemporary Europe—an aspect of Christianity not encouraged by the missionaries, quintessential representatives of the universal church—Iroquois religion was mainly about getting things done.

In the Iroquois tradition, supernatural or nonhuman beings exercised an influence over almost all aspects of life.[30] Accordingly, there was a wide range of procedures designed to prevent these forces from doing harm and to persuade them to assist an individual or a group. In addition to major public festivals, usually marked by music, dancing, and feasting, and generally intended to give thanks for blessings and to ensure the maintenance of a healthy balance in the society's relations with the cosmos, there were also more specifically focused rites. If someone was ill—and among the Iroquois "illness" had a broad sense encompassing physical, mental and emotional symptoms—then help would be sought in remedies that combined what outsiders might call "natural" and "supernatural" aspects. Relatives, a shaman, or a curing society might organize a lacrosse game; they might offer herbal medicines prepared according to ritual prescriptions; they might stage a feast with dancing as decreed by the patient's dreams. In the eclectic and experimental atmosphere of Iroquois medicine, the possibilities were limitless. Similarly, various magical procedures could be applied to such problems as gaining the love of another, protecting oneself from witchcraft, finding lost objects, or ensuring good fortune in war or hunting. Other-than-human beings were always part of the solution and the clear aim of each procedure was to respond directly to a human need.

The religion purveyed by the Jesuits proved utterly inadequate as a substitute for these practical and applied aspects of native religion. All through the Americas, in fact, Indian peoples had a basically similar reaction to the colonizer's faith: when famine threatened, when a child fell ill, or when a precious possession went missing, prayers addressed to the Virgin or to San Antonio seemed insufficient. Desperate people would turn then to the *huacas,* the shamans, and the diviners who had assisted their ancestors before the Europeans had come to denounce all these as evil. Sincere and devout Catholics in their public devotions, Maya of Yucatan, Quechua people of the Andes, or Nahuatl speakers of central Mexico thus maintained, usually in secret, some semblance of pre-Columbian religious traditions. In the absence of the oppressive—and therefore source-generating—campaigns to root out Indian "idolatry" from the Spanish empire, there are few documentary traces of such practices in New France.

And yet, it is possible to unearth evidence on this other side of Kahnawake religious life, thanks not to the repressive investigations of a fading Counter-Reformation, but to the curiosity of a nascent anthropology. Enter Father Joseph-François Lafitau. A Jesuit intellectual, the author of *Moeurs des sauvages américains comparées aux moeurs des premiers temps* (1724),[31] Lafitau is sometimes billed as a founding father of comparative ethnology. Though usually thought of as a theoretician, the denizen of Parisian libraries, and the formulator of an early version of the theory of cultural evolution, Lafitau actually got his start in the field as a missionary at Sault St.-Louis from 1712 to 1717. It was in Canada and at an early stage of his Jesuit career that he developed an interest in all things "savage," carefully observing the ways of the Christian Iroquois and interrogating senior colleagues about their experiences among the Hurons and other nations. This master of erudition was also a field researcher, rigorous and precociously modern in his methods according to William N. Fenton,[32] and it is in that capacity that his work interests us here.

Because his interest is in notionally primordial savage customs, Lafitau draws attention to quite different aspects of Kahnawake religion than those featured in the reports of his senior colleague Claude Chauchetière. "Among christianized Iroquois," Lafitau notes in passing, in a discussion of Indian curing rites, "it should be regarded as a heroic act when, in illnesses, one does not have recourse to shamans [*jongleurs*], especially if there is some indication or dream which causes a suspicion of sorcery." Sorcery, shamanism, dream divination are all signaled in this one brief sentence; all were considered flagrant contradictions of Christianity and none were ever mentioned in the earlier Jesuit reports from Kahnawake. Lafitau writes of Iroquois shamanism with the familiarity of the eyewitness: "The shamans have some innate quality which partakes still more of the divine. We see them go visibly into that state of ecstasy which binds all the senses and keeps them suspended . . ." For a Jesuit who spent his entire missionary career in this Catholic village, Lafitau knows a great deal about non-Christian Iroquois religion. On sacrifices to the sun, he writes: "Sometimes our Iroquois [*Our* Iroquois, please note, not *the* Iroquois] expose to the air on the top of their lodges strings and belts of wampum, braided strings of Indian maize and likewise animals which they consecrate to the Sun."[33]

"They are like angels," says one Jesuit in 1682; they worship the sun, follow the advice of dreams, and call on shamans to cure their ills, says another Jesuit in 1724. Two reporters, each with a particular agenda, focusing selectively on one portion of the broad range of techniques available to Iroquois converts attempting to gain the assistance of unseen forces. Was shamanism temporarily eclipsed in the early 1680s when Christian piety burned with an exceptional brightness, or did Father Chauchetière simply turn his gaze from unedifying scenes when he prepared his enthusiastic *Relations* for European readers? Either way, it is clear that traditional Iroquoian approaches to securing the favor of heavenly forces survived extended contact with Christianity. In colonial Kahnawake, there was no full triumph of one culture over another, nor was there the sort of mixing and merging suggested by the term "syncretism." Instead, two traditions remained basically intact and pursuing parallel tracks in the religious history of this convert community.[34]

REACHING TOWARD THE SACRED

There was far more to Iroquois Christianity in the seventeenth century than the establishment and affirmation of identity; more, too, than techniques for manipulating supernatural forces to maintain prosperity and avert danger. Catholicism also offered the people of Kahnawake procedures for slipping the bonds of mundane existence and crossing the threshold into the realms of the divine. The mystic-ascetic practices by means of which the spiritual elite of Catholic Europe sought to master the urgings of the flesh, atone for sin, and unite with God exercised a powerful appeal over native converts. In this as in other aspects of the religious encounter, there was the inevitable degree of misunderstanding as the two cultures attached somewhat different meanings to similar patterns of behavior. The point of contact with the Jesuits, however, was the common hunger, widespread across human cultures, for the liminal experience that can come through actions that purposely run counter to the natural impulse to seek comfort and ease.

Claude Chauchetière, himself a mystic in his own modest way, was amazed at the "mortification of the flesh" he saw and heard about at Sault St.-Louis.

You will be pleased to hear about the austerities practiced by certain Indian women. Although there may be some indiscretion in their behavior, it will show you their fervor. More than five years ago some of them learned, I know not how, of the pious practices followed by the nuns of the Montreal hospital. They heard of disciplines, of iron girdles, and of hair shirts. The religious life appealed to them and so three of them formed an association in order to set up some sort of convent, but we stopped them, because we did not think that the time had yet come for this. However, though they were not cloistered, they at least observed the rule of chastity, and one of them died with the reputation of sanctity, three years ago this spring. They, and some others who followed their example, would be admired in France if what they do were known there. The one who first initiated [these ascetic practices] began around Christmas of the year 1676, when she went to the foot of a large cross that stands beside our cemetery, took off her clothes and exposed herself to the air. This was during a snowstorm and she was pregnant at the time; and the snow falling on her back caused her so much suffering that she nearly died from it, along with her child, who was thoroughly chilled inside the mother's womb. It was her own idea to do this, and she said it was to do penance for her sins. She has since then acquired four companions who imitate her in her fervor. In the depth of winter, two of them made a hole in the ice and threw themselves into the water, where they remained during the time that it would take to say the rosary slowly and deliberately. One of the two, returning to her cabin and fearing that she would be found out, did not venture to warm herself at the fire, and so she lay down for the night with the ice still adhering to her shoulders. The men and women have invented several other such means of mortification by which to torment themselves as part of their habitual penance, but we have made them give up any excessive mortification.[35]

The Jesuits reported similar practices in the other missions of New France: Huron, Algonquin, and Iroquois converts lacerating themselves, exposing their bodies to ferocious cold, or simply refusing to have a decayed tooth removed in order to savor the pain.[36] Both sexes were involved, but among the Iroquoian peoples, ascetic self-punishment was primarily a women's phenomenon.

Some of the methods and instruments of self-torture mentioned here were clearly of European origin, likely modeled on French nuns' and priests' practices or inspired by stories and images of saints, but these mystics also followed established native techniques of punishing the flesh. Early Jesuit visitors to the Onondaga reported winter scenes of men cutting holes in the ice and plunging into frigid lake waters in response to dream visions. They also saw people running about naked at the beginning of the Midwinter Festival, noting that "they seemed insensible to the cold which is nearly unbearable even to those who are warmly clothed." Well before Catholicism had made any impact on the Iroquois, freezing baths and voluntary exposure to cold air appear to have formed part of their repertoire of gestures connected with the sacred.[37]

Some reports on the "penances" of the Iroquois of Kahnawake also mention burning, a form of "mortification of the flesh" that was virtually unknown in Counter-Reformation Europe.[38] Here too, there are ample precedents among the preconversion Iroquois. In curing rituals, Huron and Iroquois shamans frequently plunged their hands into a fire and came out grasping coals and hot ashes.[39] Sometimes, people burned themselves voluntarily when war threatened and they wanted to harden themselves against the possibility they would be captured and tortured by the enemy.[40]

For Michel Foucault, "mortification" is a quintessentially Christian "practice of the self," distinct from superficially similar Greek (and Iroquois, one might add) practices: "It is not a sacrifice for the city; Christian mortification is a kind of relation from oneself to oneself. It is a part, a constitutive part of the Christian self-identity."[41] Historians of Europe would probably prefer a more historically nuanced characterization of the relation between ascetic practices and the emergence of the self, but it would certainly be fair to situate Catholic asceticism of the seventeenth century in the context of an emergent modern self-identity. At Kahnawake, however, similar patterns of behavior intersected with a very different version of the self, one with much broader, more encompassing, boundaries.[42] These experiments in as-cetic ecstasy were not the work of isolated individuals, but of female couples and close-knit groups. Furthermore, they were performed, according to what the Jesuits were told, to expiate the sins of an entire people. One woman took her innocent six-year-old daughter with her on her penitential cold baths, clasping the child to her as she plunged into the frigid St. Lawrence.[43] Though the Jesuits could understand collective devotion, this extension of the self to include offspring seemed to them bizarre.

Besides beating and freezing and burning themselves, the mystics of Kahnawake also deprived themselves of the pleasures of food and sex. The combination of abstinence together with active mortification and visionary contemplation corresponded to patterns of ascetic devotion in the European Catholic tradition, but on every count there were also Iroquoian anteced-ents. Warriors preparing for campaigns avoided sex to enhance their phys-ical and spiritual strength, while hunters reduced their food intake in the belief that hunger would improve their eyesight and their luck; according to the Iroquois ethnologist, A. C. Parker, overeating was considered "a religious offence" that would also "destroy the capacity to withstand hun-ger."[44] The Jesuits frequently expressed their admiration for the way native peoples, and particularly the Iroquois, managed to restrain their physical appetites: eating simple, frugal meals and forgoing copulation, even within marriage under certain circumstances. Writing with an astonishment that speaks volumes about European marital norms, Father Paul Ragueneau re-ported on a woman who remained a virgin at age twenty-four after a suc-cession of marriages which never got past the trial stage of unconsummated intimacy. Women can with impunity refuse a mate his "husband's rights," he explained, "as it is not the custom of the Savages to violate one another, liberty being the greatest of all their blessings . . ."[45] At Kahnawake, some established married couples undertook to live without sex, cohabiting "like brother and sister."[46] This latter arrangement may have reminded the Jesu-its of the renunciation of sex within marriage as found in medieval Eu-rope,[47] but more likely it had its roots in a birth control strategy common among native North Americans.

According to the Jesuit chroniclers, the most devoted Iroquois Christians inflicted suffering upon their bodies in order to atone for sin. Should we then see their painful exercises as a sad case of natives internalizing the contempt of the colonizer? For the "sins" they reportedly atoned for were often the mere fact of being or having been pagan Iroquois. There was probably an element of an externally introduced sentiment of guilt at work here, but the mystic-ascetic women displayed rather more self-assertion than one would expect from people who had been cowed and demoralized

by the missionaries. In the passage quoted above, Claude Chauchetière referred to "excessive penances," and his ambivalent attitude is typical of
Jesuit remarks on the subject. From the missionaries' point of view, the
Iroquois converts tended to go too far; like many ascetic women of the
European Middle Ages, they wanted to push beyond established limits, not
only of bodily endurance, but also of clerical approval.[48] For the comparatively disempowered, this was a matter of critiquing and defying the authority of (European) male priests, an aspect of the complex Jesuit-native
relationship that sometimes drew explicit comment. In the early 1680s,
there was such extreme behavior that Claude Chauchetière became convinced that the devil had a hand in things: "He pushes them to excesses in
order to make Christianity seem repellent."[49] Most of these outlandish practices, he added, occurred in distant hunting camps, far from the supervising
influence of the missionaries. Another Jesuit quoted one of his penitents
who went to the woods with a hunting party expressly to escape his attempts to moderate her habit of diving through the winter ice of the river,
"disant en elle-même, au moins serais-je maîtresse de mon corps dans le
bois."[50] This is the response of a bold spiritual adventurer, not of a diminished personality paralyzed by guilt.

For almost every aspect of the mystic-ascetic movement that flourished at
Kahnawake in the years around 1680, one can find both Iroquoian and
European/Catholic antecedents. But along with the points of general correspondence, we must recognize the areas of divergence. The two cultures
started from different conceptions of the self; they drew very different boundaries between body and soul, mundane and sacred; and they differed on
crucial conceptions of guilt, spiritual debt, and moral responsibility. The
result was not a bland and shapeless mix of two widely divergent traditions,
but an intense, sharply defined spiritual experiment created through an
active engagement with elements of both. The Jesuit sources—all we have
to work with in this instance—may give a selective and distorted description of the ascetic devotions practiced at Kahnawake, but they cannot dis-
guise the powerfully original quality of a religious quest that resists reduction
to either of the cultural traditions on which it drew.

The local religion that developed among displaced Iroquois on the middle
ground of New France combined native and European elements in complex
ways. When we break down the abstraction "religion" into some of its
distinct facets, and when we emphasize performance over belief, we discover
an array of permutations and combinations: some synthesis, some unconsummated dialogue, some oil-and-water divergences. As constituents of group
identity, Iroquoian and Catholic rituals and emblems both did their work at

Kahnawake, though in separate ways that served different purposes. While both traditions contributed to internal solidarity and identity formation, the Christian strand formed a crucial link with French Canada. Local religion also responded to people's personal needs, desires, and fears and, in this area too, elements drawn from Europe and elements from Iroquoia tended to operate on separate planes. Christianity might have helped individuals cope with grief and distress, but aboriginal practices seemed more useful to those seeking practical help. Finally, there is the more "purely religious" phenomenon of mystical quests for sacred ecstasy. To all appearances, this dimension of local religion called forth a genuine synthesis, with Christian and Iroquois aspects interpenetrating to produce intense spiritual experiences. This version of conversion cannot be summed up by the familiar vocabulary of mission history with its simplifying tendency to reduce the religious encounter to "spiritual conquest," "assimilation," "covert resistance," or "syncretism." Instead we find different interactions operating at the various levels involved: parallel coexistence, selective borrowing, and localized syncretism.

NOTES

1. "Letter of Claude Chauchetière, respecting the Iroquois Mission of Sault St. François Xavier, near Montreal" (14 October 1682), in *The Jesuit Relations and Allied Documents,* ed. Reuben Thwaites, 73 vols. (Cleveland, 1896–1900) (hereafter *JR*), 62:189. Note that the name and precise location of this mission community changed over the years. From 1667 to 1676, native converts gathered, along with French-Canadian settlers, at the Jesuit *seigneurie* of La Prairie. Later they moved a few kilometers upriver to a spot the French called Sault St.-Louis. The Iroquois refer to this village as Kahnawake (sometimes spelled "Caughnawaga"). In the interests of simplicity, I shall refer to the community as "Kahnawake" or "Sault St.-Louis," even in circumstances where that designation is not strictly geographically correct.

2. Ibid., p. 171.

3. *JR* 58:85, Relation of 1672–73.

4. Highlights of the literature include: Anthony F. C. Wallace, *The Death and Rebirth of the Seneca* (New York, 1969); Francis Jennings, *The Ambiguous Iroquois Empire: The Covenant Chain Confederation of Indian Tribes with English Colonies from Its Beginnings to the Lancaster Treaty of 1744* (New York, 1984); Bruce G. Trigger, *Natives and Newcomers: Canada's "Heroic Age" Reconsidered* (Montreal, 1985); Daniel K. Richter, *The Ordeal of the Longhouse:*

The Peoples of the Iroquois League in the Era of European Colonization (Chapel Hill, N.C., 1992); Denys Delâge, *Bitter Feast: Amerindians and Europeans in Northeast North America, 1600–64* (Vancouver, 1993); Matthew Dennis, *Cultivating the Landscape of Peace: Iroquois-European Encounters in Seventeenth-Century America* (Ithaca, N.Y., 1993); Dean R. Snow, *The Iroquois* (Oxford, 1994); William N. Fenton, *The Great Law and the Longhouse: A Political History of the Iroquois Confederacy* (Norman, Okla., 1998).

5. Cornelius J. Jaenen, *Friend and Foe: Aspects of French-Amerindian Cultural Contact in the Sixteenth and Seventeenth Centuries* (Toronto, 1976); John Webster Grant, *Moon of Wintertime: Missionaries and the Indians of Canada in Encounter Since 1534* (Toronto, 1984); James Axtell, *The Invasion Within: The Contest of Cultures in Colonial North America* (New York, 1985); Dominique Deslandres, "Le modèle français d'intégration socio-religieuse, 1600–1650: Missions intérieures et premières missions canadiennes," (Ph.D. diss., University of Montreal, 1990); Peter A. Dorsey, "Going to School with Savages: Authorship and Authority among the Jesuits of New France," *William and Mary Quarterly,* 3d ser., 55 (July 1998): 399–420; David Murray, "Spreading the Word: Missionaries, Conversion, and Circulation in the Northeast," in *Spiritual Encounters: Interactions Between Christianity and Native Religions in Colonial America,* ed. Nicholas Griffiths and Fernando Cervantes (Lincoln, Neb., 1999), pp. 43–64.

6. The rival Recollet order, a reformed branch of the Franciscans, was the source of some pointedly anti-Jesuit publicatioons. See Louis Hennepin, *A New Discovery of a Vast Country in America,* ed. R. G. Thwaites (1698; Chicago, 1903), p. 587; Chrestien Le Clercq, *First Establishment of the Faith in New France,* trans. J. G. Shea, 2 vols. (New York, 1881), 2:24–25.

7. James Axtell, "Were Indian Conversions Bona Fide?" in *After Columbus: Essays in the Ethnohistory of Colonial North America* (New York, 1988), pp. 100–121. The contrary position, the one against which Axtell's polemics are directed, is best represented by the following works: David Blanchard, ". . . To the Other Side of the Sky: Catholicism at Kahnawake, 1667–1700," *Anthropologica* 24 (1982): 77–102; Jaenen, *Friend and Foe;* Trigger, *Natives and Newcomers.* For the "pro-Jesuit" interpretation, see also Axtell, *Invasion Within.* Of course my brief summary of this debate can hardly do justice to the arguments that have come forward in all their complexity. The thrust of the present essay is to propose a reframing of questions about conversion and its aftermath; like any revisionist scholarship, it builds upon previous work in the field even as it critiques certain widely held presuppositions.

8. See Catherine Desbarats's analysis of Bruce Trigger's narrative strategies: "Essai sur quelques éléments de l'écriture de l'histoire amérindienne," *Revue d'histoire de l'Amérique française* 53 (Spring 2000): 491–520.

9. Axtell, *Invasion Within*. See especially that work's "Prologue" (pp. 3–6) where militaristic images of "cultural offensives" and "cultural warfare" predominate. Of course, war and other forms of violence characteristic of colonialism formed a crucially important backdrop to Christian evangelization in New France, but the thrust of Axtell's Hegelian rhetoric is to obscure the critical distinction between episodes of physical fighting on the one hand, and the long-term encounter of two abstractions, "French culture" and "Indian culture," on the other hand.

10. Pierre-Antoine Fabre, "Présentation," *Annales: Histoire, sciences sociales* 54, special issue on religious conversions (July–August 1999): 807.

11. "Issues in Local Religion," an introductory essay in William B. Taylor's *Magistrates of the Sacred: Priests and Parishioners in Eighteenth-Century Mexico* (Stanford, Calif., 1996), pp. 47–66, does a superb job of surveying the literature and examining the methodological challenges inherent in the study of colonial religious change. Sharing Taylor's substantive focus on Mexico are several other important works: Serge Gruzinski, *La colonisation de l'imaginaire: Sociétés indigènes et occidentalisation dans le Mexique espagnol, XVIe–XVIIIe siècle* (Paris, 1988); Nancy M. Farriss, *Maya Society under Colonial Rule: The Collective Enterprise of Survival* (Princeton, N.J., 1984); Inga Clendinnen, "Ways to the Sacred: Reconstructing 'Religion' in Sixteenth-Century Mexico," *History and Anthropology* 5 (1990): 105–41. Equally significant work, with a similar basic thrust, has also been done on South America: Sabine McCormack, *Religion in the Andes: Vision and Imagination in Early Colonial Peru* (Princeton, N.J., 1991); Kenneth Mills, *Idolatry and Its Enemies: Colonial Andean Religion and Extirpation, 1640–1750* (Princeton, N.J., 1997).

12. William A. Christian Jr., *Local Religion in Sixteenth-Century Spain* (Princeton, N.J., 1981).

13. Cole Harris, ed., *Historical Atlas of Canada*, vol. 1: *From the Beginning to 1800* (Toronto, 1987), plate 47; Marc Jetten, *Enclaves amérindiennes: Les 'réductions' du Canada 1637–1701* (Quebec, 1994); Axtell, *The Invasion Within*, pp. 43–70; James P. Ronda, "The Sillery Experiment: A Jesuit-Indian Village in New France, 1637–1663," *American Indian Culture and Research Journal* 3 (1979): 1–18; Daniel K. Richter, "Iroquois versus Iroquois: Jesuit Mission and Christianity in Village Politics, 1642–1686," *Ethnohistory* 32 (1985): 1–16; Louise Tremblay, "La politique missionaire des Sulpiciens au XVIIe et début XVIIIe siècle, 1668–1735" (M.A. thesis, University of Montreal, 1981).

14. On the history of Kahnawake/Sault St.-Louis, see Edward James Devine, *Historic Caughnawaga* (Montreal, 1922); Henri Béchard, *The Original Caughnawaga Indians* (Montreal, 1976); Gretchen Green, "A New People in

an Age of War: The Kahnawake Iroquois, 1667–1760" (Ph.D. diss., College of William and Mary, 1991); Denys Delâge, "Les Iroquois chrétiens des 'réductions,' 1667–1770: I—Migration et rapports avec les Français," *Recherches amérindiennes au Québec* 21, no. 1–2 (1991): 59–70; Denys Delâge, "Les Iroquois chrétiens des 'réductions,' 1667–1770: II—Rapports avec la Ligue iroquoise, les Britanniques et les autres nations autochtones," ibid., no. 3 (1991): 39–50.

15. Jan Grabowski, "The Common Ground: Settled Natives and French in Montréal, 1667–1760" (Ph.D. diss., University of Montreal, 1993).

16. "Nous les [the Iroquois of Sault St. Louis] regardons comme le soutien de la Nouvelle-France. . . . La foi seule les engage de rester parmi nous . . . " Bacqueville de la Potherie, *Histoire de l'Amérique septentrionale,* 4 vols. (Paris, 1753), 1:363.

17. Richard White, *The Middle Ground: Indians, Empires, and Republics in the Great Lakes Region, 1650–1815* (Cambridge, 1991).

18. On these early experiments in authoritarianism, see Ronda, "The Sillery Experiment"; Jetten, *Enclaves amérindiennes,* pp. 30–56.

19. See, in particular, Richter, "Iroquois versus Iroquois."

20. Richter, *Ordeal of the Longhouse,* pp. 105–32.

21. The tendency for established communities to split, with people of diverse backgrounds migrating to distant locations and forming new settlements with distinctive identities, was not unique to the Iroquois. Some scholars suggest that this process of "ethnogenesis" occurred across the Americas as a characteristic product of colonization. See Jonathan D. Hill, ed., *History, Power, and Identity: Ethnogenesis in the Americas, 1492–1992* (Iowa City, 1996).

22. *JR* 58:77, Relation of 1672–74; Claude Chauchetière, *Narration de la mission du Sault depuis sa fondation jusqu'en 1686,* ed. Hélène Avisseau (1686; Bordeaux, 1984), p. 27.

23. Jean de Brébeuf, "Relation of 1636," in *The Jesuit Relations: Natives and Missionaries in Seventeenth-Century North America,* ed. Allan Greer (Boston, 2000), p. 39. Brébeuf's observations on Huron would apply to the closely related Iroquois languages. Cf. Jaenen, *Friend and Foe,* pp. 52–53.

24. The linguist John Steckley has examined the texts of Jesuit sermons delivered in the Huron language and demonstrates just how drastically Christian stories and precepts had to be modified in translation. Jesus, for example, emerges as an Iroquoian war captain. John Steckley, "The Warrior and the Lineage: Jesuit Use of Iroquoian Images to Communicate Christianity," *Ethnohistory* 39 (Fall 1992): 478–509.

25. Iroquoian approaches to alliance are examined in Bruce Trigger, *The Children of Aataentsic: A History of the Huron People to 1660* (Montreal, 1976),

passim. See also White, *The Middle Ground,* on the similar diplomatic customs of the Algonquians of the Great Lakes.

26. Chauchetière, *Narration,* p. 32.

27. *JR* 59:265, Relation of 1675; Chauchetière, *Narration,* pp. 34–35.

28. *JR* 60:31–41, Relation of 1675.

29. See William B. Hart, "'The Kindness of the Blessed Virgin': Faith, Succour, and the Cult of Mary among Christian Hurons and Iroquois in Seventeenth-Century New France," in Griffiths and Cervantes, *Spiritual Encounters,* pp. 65–90. I am not convinced by Hart's suggestion that Marian devotion was particularly strong among Iroquoian converts. This author relies too heavily, in my opinion, on the most dubious passages of the *Jesuit Relations,* those in which the writers place implausibly conventional speeches, brimming with Counter-Reformation clichés, into the mouths of pious natives. And even if these orations are taken as exact translations of sentiments originally expressed in a native tongue, the frequency of references to the Virgin Mary does not seem to exceed the "base level" of Marian piety found throughout the seventeenth-century Catholic world. Certainly Iroquoian Catholicism was not as Mary-centered as, for example, native Mexican Christianity was.

30. In addition to the works cited in note 4 above, see Elisabeth Tooker, ed., *Native North American Spirituality of the Eastern Woodlands: Sacred Myths, Dreams, Visions, Speeches, Healing Formulas, Rituals, and Ceremonials* (New York, 1979), pp. 33–68, 268–81; Horatio Hale, ed., *The Iroquois Book of Rites* (1883), reprinted with an introduction by W. N. Fenton (Toronto, 1963); Christopher Vecsey, "The Story and Structure of the Iroquois Confederacy," *Journal of the American Academy of Religion* 54 (1986): 79–106; James W. Herrick, *Iroquois Medical Botany,* ed. Dean Snow (Syracuse, N.Y., 1995).

31. Joseph-François Lafitau, *Customs of the American Indians Compared with the Customs of Primitive Times,* ed. and trans. William N. Fenton and Elizabeth L. Moore, 2 vols. (Toronto, 1974). William Fenton's ample introduction to this edition provides exhaustive background on the author and the text.

32. William N. Fenton, "Introduction," ibid., 1:lxxx.

33. Ibid., 1:246, 243, 133.

34. Lafitau relates a revealing anecdote, in this case a second-hand report on Abenaki divination by fire, which sheds light on what may have been a widespread native attitude towards religious pluralism. Taken to task by a missionary for practicing pyromancy, a baptized Abenaki woman replied, "I have never understood what harm there is in it and I still have great difficulty in seeing any. Listen, God has given men different gifts. To the

Frenchmen, he has given the Scriptures by which you learn the things which take place far from you as if they were in front of you; to us he has given the art of knowing, by fire, things remote in time or place. Suppose then that this fire is our book, our Scriptures, thou willst [sic] not see that there is any difference or more harm in the one than in the other." Lafitau, Customs, 1:245–46. Recognizing that official Catholicism considered such "diabolical practices" a sin, the Abenaki made routine use of confession and absolution to mediate the conflict between the two realms of spirituality. Quite likely, the Christian sun worshippers of Sault St.-Louis followed a similar strategy to maintain their different openings to the supernatural.

35. Letter of Father Claude Chauchetière, 14 October 1682, in Greer, Jesuit Relations, pp. 150–51. For similar reports, see Chauchetière, Narration, pp. 41–42; JR 58:74–89, Relation of 1672–73.

36. Jetten, Enclaves amérindiennes, pp. 103–7; JR 49:74–87, Relation of 1663–64, Lorette; ibid., 61:34–55, Huron Relation of 1677–78; ibid., 62:43–45, letter of Jacques Bigot, Sillery, 24 June 1681.

37. JR 42:152–53, 156–57, Relation of 1655–56.

38. Claude Chauchetière, "The Life of the Good Katharine Tekakwitha, Now Known as the Holy Savage," in The Positio of the Historical Section of the Sacred Congregation of Rites on the Cause for Canonization and Beatification and on the Virtues of the Servant of God, Katharine Tekakwitha, the Lily of the Mohawks, Being Original Documents First Published and Presented for the Edification of the Faithful, ed. Robert Holland (New York, 1940), p. 182.

39. JR 42:171, Relation of 1655–56; William N. Fenton, The False Faces of the Iroquois (Norman, Okla., 1987), p. 73.

40. "The Indians . . . seem to prepare for this event from the tenderest age. People have seen children press their two bare arms against each other, putting burning coals between them, challenging each other as to who would hold out with most firmness and win the contest in endurance." Lafitau, Customs of the American Indians, 2:160–61. See also JR 42:170–71, Relation of 1655–56.

41. Michel Foucault, "Politics and Reason," in Politics, Philosophy, Culture: Interviews and Other Writings, 1977–1984, ed. Lawrence D. Kritzman (New York, 1990), p. 70.

42. This observation is inspired by the suggestive work of J. Jorge Klor de Alva on colonial religion among the people of central Mexico. "'Telling Lives': Confessional Autobiography and the Reconstruction of the Nahua Self," in Griffiths and Cervantes, Spiritual Encounters, pp. 136–62.

43. Chauchetière, Narration, p. 47.

44. A. C. Parker, "Iroquois Uses of Maize and Other Plant Foods," in Parker on the Iroquois, ed. William Fenton (Syracuse, N.Y., 1968), p. 64. See

also Snow, *The Iroquois,* p. 127; *JR* 10:206–7, Relation of 1636; ibid., 12:65, Relation of 1637; Lafitau, *Customs of the American Indians,* 2:113.

45. *JR* 37:152–57, Relation of 1651–52. Ragueneau does not specify the nation of this married virgin; the marital customs sound Iroquoian, though the Jesuit was writing from Sillery, a mission populated mainly by Algonquins and Montagnais.

46. Chauchetière, *Narration,* p. 51.

47. Dyan Elliott, *Spiritual Marriage: Sexual Abstinence in Medieval Wedlock* (Princeton, N.J., 1993).

48. Caroline Walker Bynum, *Holy Feast and Holy Fast: The Religious Significance of Food to Medieval Women* (Berkeley, Calif., 1987), pp. 84–85.

49. Chauchetière, *Narration,* p. 47.

50. Pierre Cholenec, "Vie de Catherine Tegakouita, première vièrge Iroquoise," p. 47, Archives de la société de Jésus, Canada français (St.-Jérôme, Quebec), no. 345.

8

OBJECT LESSONS

FETISHISM AND THE HIERARCHIES OF RACE AND RELIGION

DAVID MURRAY

This essay will look at some instances of the deployment of the terms "fetish" and "fetishism," particularly in relation to North America. I want to show how the concept of fetishism emerges as a product of multiple cultural and linguistic conversions of value, rather than as a description of any actual system of indigenous primitive practice or belief, and then becomes a crucial instrument in the development of ideas about primitive religion. After outlining the concept's origins in the eighteenth century, and moving through its employment in the discourses of anthropology and religion in the nineteenth, I focus on its use in the characterization of North American Indians. Although associated from the beginning with African manifestations of fetishism, Indian beliefs were nevertheless progressively distanced in the later discussions from what was seen as the base materiality of African practices. I argue that the particular "spirituality" which became associated with Indians, and is still evident in New Age versions, needs to be seen in relation both to a persistent hierarchy of religious beliefs and to assumptions about the differential mental and spiritual capacities of Indians and African Americans. These combined forces were enough to place African American folk practices, like "conjure," below what came to be presented as Indian religion.

The word "fetish" developed out of a term used on the Guinea coast by Portuguese traders and Africans, and was applied to a range of objects of economic as well as religious value or importance before becoming elevated into the concept of fetish*ism* by Charles de Brosses in the eighteenth century. It was then employed through the nineteenth century as a key concept in formulating ideas of a primitive or original form of religious belief in contrast to that of the West. Earlier discussions of beliefs and practices which involved the ascription of magical or religious power to objects had taken place round the idea of "idolatry," but "fetishism" reflected a new configuration, which was about civilization and progress as well as Christianity. Enlightenment interests in primitive beliefs began to focus not on questions of true or false worship but on the progression from polytheism to monotheism, and the idea of fetishism played an important role in focusing attention on states of mind rather than religious validity, as was always implicit in the use of the term "idolatry."

Though it was later superseded or rejected as a term in anthropology, the idea of fetishism has continued to have a curious half-life. Its general use to describe a false ascription of special value to some undeserving material thing has made it a useful term in the skeptical questioning of all sorts of objects and systems of value, and it is in this role that it was taken up in the discourses of Marxism and psychoanalysis where, as well as in the area of art criticism, it is mainly found today.[1] In the context of religion it represents the importance of a stubborn materiality, and that materiality's relation to the spiritual or transcendent categories claimed by the "higher" religions. Fetishism was to be found in folk belief as well as in the beliefs of those groups who were the target of conversion, but as it became systematized in the eighteenth and nineteenth centuries, it took its place as the lowest level in a hierarchy of beliefs which was, of course, racialized. Contemporary primitive people of certain races were lumped with "our" ancestors as examples of a mentality which was mired in materiality, and was without the capacity for abstraction and spiritual awareness to be found in advanced peoples.

What this account leaves out, though, and what William Pietz's genuinely groundbreaking work on the development of the term itself draws attention to, is the way that the fetish and fetishism are products of a situation of cross-cultural economic, cultural, and religious exchange. It is an idea about materiality which has its own material base, and to understand its persistent role as a point of misrecognition and disavowal, we need therefore to see its full historical dimensions. Pietz insists on the etiology of the term as itself a product of exchange and hybridity.[2] The term crosses over from the use of *feitico,* used by Portuguese sailors to describe their own culture's witchcraft or magic (stemming from the Latin *facticius*) to a pidgin form, *fetisso,* which seems to have become used by Africans and Portuguese to describe something of value, both religious and commercial. The term was then reused, first by the Portuguese and later by everyone else, to apply to what was seen as the particular form of worship of objects found on the Guinea coast, as if it were an African word.

Pietz argues that it is in the space where several different systems of value meet—in this case Christian feudal, African lineage, and merchant capitalist—that the fetish emerges to point to "the capacity of the material object to embody—simultaneously and sequentially—religious, commercial, aesthetic, and sexual values."³

Pietz's detailed treatment of the West African origins is invaluable, as are his later accounts of the operation of the term in other colonial contexts, and in later Marxist discourse. Nevertheless his account of the development of the term in the theorizing of the primitive gives little sense of the more complex racial categories, which involved America as well as Africa, and I want here to open up the question of the differential and comparative use of races and cultures, and to show how this affects the use of the idea of fetishism in America. This involves distinctions between Indians and African Americans and their religious practices, which operate within a set of oppositions which include purity versus pollution or mixedness, and the spiritual versus the material.

When Charles de Brosses published his *Du Culte des dieux fétiches, ou parallèle de l'ancienne Religion de l'Egypte avec la Religion actuelle de Nigritie* in Paris in 1760, he drew upon a wide range of scholarly and travel writings. As the title suggests, his book was part of a larger comparativist impulse of the time,⁴ but what was new was the creation of a whole new category, and its application across time and across cultures.

The word "fetish" in different forms had been present in travel accounts and descriptions since the sixteenth century, used as a description of a number of different objects and practices developing, like the pidgin *fetisso,* out of the interchanges between Portuguese traders and Africans on the coast of West Africa. The Dutch traveler William Bosman, for instance, describes the Africans, when about to "make offerings to their Idols," crying out "Let us make *Fetiche*; by which they express as much, as let us perform our Religious Worship."⁵ Offerings are made to these "idols" to bring good fortune for oneself, or inflict evil fortune on others. Bosman and other commentators actually acknowledge in their accounts a range of practices and beliefs among the Africans, including a belief in more abstract or overarching deities, but the assumption of limited mental capacities for the Africans means that the more abstract ideas are often put down to Christian influence, and the Africans are taken as representing just the early stages of mental development. John Atkins, in 1734, anticipating de Brosses, describes the first stage, in which, unable to reach above a "material God," people worshiped the equivalent of "the *Fetishes* of the *Negroes,*" namely "*Stocks, Stones, Serpents, Calves, Onions, Garlick, &c.*" This sense of the randomness and worthless nature of what is worshiped is also found in William Bosman's reference to "all sorts of Excrementitious and filthy Trash," used in the Africans' worship.⁶

De Brosses extends this idea of the fetish as the most basic form of belief to other places and peoples and thereby creates the category of fetish*ism*. As de Brosses uses it, the term is at first sight not so different from the traditional usage of "idolatry" to describe the polytheistic worship of false gods. In David Hume's *Natural History of Religion* of 1757, for instance—a work from which De Brosses borrowed extensively—Hume rejects the standard Christian view of idolatry as a falling away from an original revelation. In this view humanity degenerated from an original monotheist belief in the true God to polytheism and worship of heathen gods, animals, and idols. In accounting for this degeneration, Christians saw polytheism, in Frank Manuel's words, as "a bad habit which had slowly crept up on mankind."[7] Hume, on the other hand, begins with the idea of the primitive man as locked in the physical and immediate, and rejects the idea that we regressed from an original monotheism or original knowledge of the true God. This would be to believe of ancient people that

> while they were ignorant and barbarous, they discovered truth, but fell into error as soon as they acquired learning and politeness. . . . We may as reasonably imagine, that men inhabited palaces before huts and cottages, or studied geometry before agriculture; as assert that the Deity appeared to them as a pure spirit, omniscient, omnipotent and omnipresent, before he was apprehended to be a powerful, though limited being.[8]

Underlying this is the idea that even when mankind has progressed to monotheism it is driven by the same needs and fears rather than by reason. So Hume sees a fluctuation between concrete and abstract, or idolatry and monotheism, rather than a steady progression—what he calls the "flux and reflux of polytheism and theism."[9]

Hume's cool treatment of religious sentiment not as a primary and fundamental part of humanity but as a stage in humanity's fitful struggle to overcome fear and aspire to something more rational is ultimately corrosive of religion's claim to centrality. The fundamental concern with origins during this period carries through into the nineteenth century formulations of what comes to be constituted as the primitive mind. The nature of Christian belief could be interrogated under the cover of an exploration of pagan or primitive belief, and the relation of that conception of religion itself to Christianity could be left deliberately unarticulated.

But if de Brosses's new formulation of fetishism is just an extension of Hume, what is the added dimension that the term offered, which enabled it to be taken up so widely in the next century, and to have led such a strange half-life thereafter? William Pietz points to "the untranscended materiality of the fetish."[10] Building on this, my argument is that fetishism, as a theory *about* misrecognition and the false ascription of value or divinity to worthless things, itself embodies a process of misrecognition and disavowal. In the discourse of fetishism in the nineteenth century and even into the twentieth, there is first an insistence that there can be a way of worshiping things in themselves. Then, as soon as it is asserted, this idea of material power without spirit is seen as problematic, and is replaced by the idea of a spirit behind or within matter, and a consequent denial that pure fetishism could ever have existed. Yet the term and idea persist, only to be denied. This pattern of disavowal is similar to the mechanism of the fetish in the psychoanalytic tradition, which goes "I know it isn't (the woman's body, the phallus, etc.) but even so . . . " More relevantly here, perhaps, it is also similar to the operation of religious symbols, which, as Krips puts it, "signal the presence of the divine by the paradoxical device of admitting their own poverty of representation."[11] In other words it transposes the tensions about representation and materiality previously played out within the idea of idolatry.

With the creation of fetishism, what was previously contained within the accusation of idolatry became separated off as the ultimate contrast to monotheism, and idolatry became more of a middle position, in that it was not entirely mired in the concrete, and suggested a capacity for representation and therefore figuration, if not abstraction. Fetishism gave the possibility of moving attention from the true or false gods to the mentality and psychology of the worshiper or fetishist, to consciousness rather than behavior. To this end de Brosses isolates a rudimentary human behavior which can be found in the ancient world as well as in present-day primitive people. The evidence is clear, he says, that "What is now the religion of black African and other savage tribes was formerly the religion of ancient peoples; and down through the ages and whichever part of the world you choose you will find established there this direct worship, rendered, without figures, to animal and vegetable objects."[12] Here we have the central element which is to distinguish the idea of fetishism from that of idolatry, the lack of any mediation or representation ("without figures"). There is no attempt on de Brosses' part to explain the logic of this. In fact, "common sense makes it difficult to claim any plausible reasons for such a senseless doctrine."[13] People worship "the first material thing which it pleases each nation or individual to choose"; and he produces a list which goes from mountains and trees to a lion's tail, a pebble, a scallop shell, or salt. This idea of random fixing on the first object they happen upon is recycled with great frequency by de Brosses and later commentators, and underlines the sheer contingency and materiality which forms the contrast with proper religion, but de Brosses also points to an operation of mind, a sort of mechanical connection or associationism. "Man is so constituted that, left in his raw and savage natural state, not yet shaped by any reflexive idea or by any imitation, he is the same in his primitive customs and his way of doing things in Egypt as in the West Indies, in Persia as in Gaul; everywhere it is the same mechanism of ideas from which their actions spring."[14]

One of the key elements in the book is the parallel of ancients and primitives as animal worshipers, but the really significant factor is de Brosses's identification of a category of people who operate in this way because of their mental limitations rather than, as with idolatry, because they have slipped backwards because of sloth or evil. Thus the idea of fetishism became useful partly as a baseline position from which a series of different arguments about progress and ways of thinking could be developed. By positing a materialist conception of the world, it allowed philosophers and rationalists to sidestep the terms of idolatry versus true faith, as well as the other materialism of magic. In the many accounts of fetishism which followed de Brosses there was a constant recourse to a narrative of origin and development, in line with the developmental and later evolutionary climate. This narrative functioned as a way of both explaining and dismissing fetishism, as it was seen to be transcended by later forms. In this sense fetishism has always been regarded as the lowest or most basic form of consciousness, from which abstract thinking, whether in the form of religion or philosophy, could be distinguished.

De Brosses drew heavily on a wide range of travel accounts, as well as classical texts, to show the widespread nature of fetishism. For the Americas, he referred to Oviedo, Le Clercq, Lafitau, Lery, Harriott, and Marquette among others, and it is instructive to follow up one particular source to see his relation to these accounts. Father Joseph Francois Lafitau's *Moeurs des Sauvages Ameriquains, Comparees aux Moeurs des Premiers Temps* of 1724 drew on firsthand observations from his work as a missionary to the Mohawk Indians in New France, but as the title indicates, his book has a larger sweep, which in some ways anticipates de Brosses. Where he differs, though, is in his concern not just to show the similarities between ancient and contemporary American beliefs and customs, but to demonstrate that they are all a falling away from an initial unity of revelation. There is a tension in Lafitau as a Jesuit, between condemnation of Indian practices as evil and an interest in them as ethnography, which reveals his affinity with some Enlightenment ideas. We see this in a telling vignette, in which Lafitau examines some of the objects surrendered by the Indians when they renounced their religion for Christianity.

Father Garnier had in his hands several of these charms which the
Indians whom he had converted had given him. One day I begged him
to examine them with me, arousing his curiosity for the first time.
There was a great quantity of them; they were little bundles of twisted
hair, bones of serpents or extraordinary animals, pieces of iron or bronze,
figures of dough or corn husks and other similar objects which could
not, in themselves, have any connection with what they were supposed
to effect but could operate only by supernatural power in consequence
of some formal or tacit agreement.[15]

He refers to bags in which the shaman (*jongleur*) carries, together with
tobacco and pipe, "what I have called his *Oiaron* and his *Manitou* which may
be regarded as his talismans in which all his virtue resides."[16] And elsewhere he comments that "each has his own personal God which they call
their *Manitou*. It is a serpent, bird, stone, or other similar thing, of which
they have dreamed while sleeping, and in which they put all their confidence for the success of their war, hunting, or fishing."[17]

Lafitau uses the word "Manitou" here to describe a specific or familiar
god or spirit rather than the overgeneralized concept of a Great Spirit—
which is how "Manitou" often later gets translated—and it is in this context that Lafitau makes a brief comparison of American Indian and African
religion. In a footnote to a quotation about African women, where the word
fetisso appears, Lafitau explains that "The fetish is a kind of talisman or
something which corresponds to the *Manitou* of the American [Indians].
These idolatrous negroes of Africa have, especially in things pertaining to
religion, customs very like those which are seen widespread in America."[18]
This is the single use of the term by Lafitau in the French original[19]—as a
synonym for "idol. But what he is content to leave merely as a passing
comparison, de Brosses elevates into a fundamental approach, and it is this
shift which reflects the shift from Lafitau's Christian view to a more Enlightenment comparativism. "[A]lthough, in its specific meaning it particularly relates to the African Negro's beliefs, I inform you from the outset
that I also intend to use it in speaking about any other nation whatsoever
where animals or inanimate entities are deified as cult objects."[20]

In spite of this general application of the term, though, what is significant for my later argument is that the term "fetishism" tends to stick to
Africa as if it were the name of an actual religion there, even though, to
return to Pietz's main point, the term is not a native one and does not refer
to anything specifically African at all. In the nineteenth century it is used
to characterize Africa as uniquely primitive, as in Hegel's sweeping dismissal of it as outside the realm of history. His view of Africans as fetishists,

worshiping "the first thing that comes their way," allows him to see them as lacking "the principle which naturally accompanies all *our* ideas—the category of Universality."[21] The reduction of people to this conceptual level has clear relevance in justifying the economic and political actions which were enslaving them, and this will also be relevant in the context of African American slavery and its aftermath. What I am particularly interested in, though, are some of the ways this differentiation of races and capacities is reflected in theorizing about the primitive mind and religion. "Fetishism" becomes incorporated (if that is the right word) into "animism," but to some degree at the expense of its emphasis on materiality, and I want to look briefly at some of the most prominent expositions of these ideas, before moving to specifically American adaptations.

The anthropologists of the nineteenth century, who tried to formulate a concept of primitive thought and religion within their presentation of a linear progression to monotheism, constantly came up against the problem of conceptualizing the supposed base materiality of fetishism, and its relation to religion and to magic. Perhaps the most important formulation was Tylor's animism. The two large volumes of his *Primitive Culture* are prefaced by a quotation from de Brosses about the need to see mankind for what it is rather than what it might become, and Tylor begins by trying to establish a lowest common denominator for religion, namely "the belief in Spiritual Beings"[22] which he calls "animism." One of its most fundamental elements is reverence for natural objects, and belief that a spiritual power resides in them. This, as he says, has been identified by de Brosses and later by August Comte as "fetishism," but he wants to confine this latter term to "that subordinate department which it properly belongs to, namely, the doctrine of spirits embodied in, or attached to, or conveying influence through, certain material objects. Fetishism will be taken as including the worship of 'stocks and stones,' and thence it passes by an imperceptible gradation into Idolatry."[23] Once Tylor has established fetishism as the lowest condition, idolatry's place is seen as "intermediate" between it and the higher spiritual activities found in advanced civilizations. As soon as the stone, or other natural object, is made to resemble something else it can be seen as an idol. "A few chips or scratches or daubs of paint suffice to convert the rude post or stone into an idol."[24] This can also point towards a change in the mental process. Instead of seeing the object as powerful in itself the worshiper sees it as a material representation of a spiritual power. This change from what is effectively a metonymic to a metaphoric approach is, though, a slippery one as Protestant critics of Roman Catholic "idolatry" have always pointed out. One of Tylor's larger problems in wanting to expand religious belief into a large area of belief in spirit and nature is that there are some areas he cannot include as religion. One of these is magic, or occult science, which "belongs to a lower level of civilization" but has persisted as a "survival." As "one of the most persistent delusions that ever vexed mankind" it is contrasted not with religion but with science.[25] Magic is the point of resistance, and represents the fault lines of the religion/ science distinction. In this respect, though Tylor has apparently included the fetish within the history of religion, he has only done so by stressing its kinship with forms of belief in an underlying spirit beneath the material, and by downplaying its materiality, as well as its claims to material efficacy, which would take it into the realm of magic.[26] As Peter Pels puts it, fetishism is "animism with a vengeance. Its matter strikes back." For Pels, if animism was spirit *in* matter, fetishism was the spirit *of* matter.[27]

Animism attempts to solve the problem by an overarching idea of spiritual presence, but this presence is not one which acts specifically and materially, and so Tylor is left with the problem of magic. In discussing the inhabiting of objects by the souls of the dead he quotes an instance from Charles Darwin's journal of two Malay women "who held a wooden spoon dressed in clothes like a doll; this spoon had been carried to the grave of a dead man, and becoming inspired at full moon, in fact lunatic, it danced about convulsively like a table or a hat at a modern spirit-séance."[28] The reference to nineteenth-century spiritualism here is in fact very relevant. Tylor did say that if the word had not already been in use for the modern movement, "spiritualism" would have been his preferred term for what he calls "animism," and he himself had firsthand, if extremely skeptical, experience of seances.[29] Most relevantly, spiritualism was grappling with precisely the problems which animism was failing to address in magic, for while spiritualism stressed the realm of the spirit it was precisely by the most crude material effects that it was judged. Thus it presented a curious and often bathetic scenario of the clash of the highest idealism and the lowest material trickery—as another student of religion's relation to the material world, Karl Marx, was also keenly aware.

In his famous passage about commodity-fetishism, Marx, too, uses the idea of the animated table: "as soon as it steps forth as a commodity, it is changed into something transcendent. It not only stands with its feet on the ground, but, in relation to all other commodities, it stands on its head and evolves out of its wooden brain grotesque ideas, far more wonderful than 'table-turning' ever was."

To find an analogy with the "mystical character" of commodities, Marx directs us to "the mist-enveloped regions of the religious world" where "the productions of the human brain appear as independent beings endowed with life. So it is in the world of commodities with the products of men's hands. This I call the Fetishism which attaches itself to the products of labour, so soon as they are produced as commodities."[30] Marx's use of the idea of the fetish here, based on his reading of a German translation of de Brosses, is designed both to show the "magical" nature of the ascription of inherent value to commodities, and of course to demystify the process, so he is using "fetishism" in Enlightenment fashion to critique modern society's retention of the primitive or irrational practices that it prides itself on having outgrown.

In the United States the anthropological and religious debates played themselves out in slightly different ways and were inflected by America's particular configuration of races. The different status of Indians and African Americans was reflected or paralleled in the assertion of a clear distinction between the mental and spiritual capacities of the two races. This distinction was not always explicit, but operated differentially, and I want to argue that much of the theorization of the primitive which concentrates on Indians in the later nineteenth and early twentieth centuries needs to be seen in relation to African Americans even when—and perhaps especially when—they are absent from the discussion.

At the 1893 World's Parliament of Religions held in Chicago as a counterpart to the inclusive and celebratory impulses of the World's Columbian Exposition, the representation of different races was revealing. Though it proclaimed its worldwide scope and inclusiveness, the Parliament's idea of what constituted a religion effectively limited the participants to representatives of the "higher" religions, and there was a pervasive assumption that human evolution was about what Julia Howe called "an evolving of a God out of the material man."[31] Judaism, Islam, Buddhism, and Hinduism had their own representatives, while African religions were completely ignored, and those African Americans who were there were representing Christian churches. Native Americans did not apparently merit a full presence, but there was an account of Indian religion in a presentation by the ethnographer Alice Fletcher, which perhaps suggests their intermediate status in the scale of religions.

This differential racism combined with two different strands in ethnographic methodology to exacerbate the divisions between the two racial groups. First of all, the scientific racism of the later nineteenth century encouraged a hierarchy of races—and not only a separate treatment of them but an assumption that the products of the mixing of races, both human and cultural, were undesirable and degenerate. Secondly, though the rise of Boasian anthropology, with its stress on culture rather than biology, meant a rejection of such racial categories as definitive, its own methodological assumptions also often meant a marginalizing of mixtures of cultures in the concern to find, salvage or reconstruct whole cultures—even though Boas himself always recognized the need to take into account the dynamic and mixed nature of cultures. Any sign of academic interest in the mixing of races is more likely to be found in places like the *Journal of Negro History* or in folklore studies, than in anthropological work on Indians.[32] Even so, the statement of intent in the founding issue of the *Journal of American Folklore* in 1888 sounds less comfortable with its African American than with its Indian materials. Whereas American Indian lore is to be "the most promising and important part of the work," that of the American Negroes is important because "for good or ill," they are to form an indissoluble part of the body politic.[33]

American contributions to the theorizing over the development of religion follow Tylor in finding a fundamental belief in spirit animating matter, rather than the brute worship of objects, and when American Indian materials are used, it is to support this idea of animism and nature worship. Daniel Brinton's wide-ranging *Religions of Primitive Peoples* of 1899 insists that what is called "fetishism, polytheism and idolatry, the worship of stocks and stones" is not in fact a worship of objects. "Every fetish, be it a rag-baby or a pebble from the roadside, is adored, not as itself, but as possessing some mysterious transcendental power, by which it can influence the future."[34] He relates this directly to the role of totemic animals of North American tribes, which, far from being the fearful animal worship of de Brosses, is a worship of higher forces. "The totemic animals or 'eponymous ancestors' of the clans or gentes among the American Indian, are not to be taken literally. They were not understood as animals of the sort we see today, but as mythical, ancient beings, of supernatural attributes, who clothed themselves in those forms for their own purposes."[35]

This is a characteristic movement from materiality to a mythical or ideal level. Whereas de Brosses, for instance, noted that the Manitou of Algonquian tribes could refer to material objects, which he identified as fetishes, as well as to a wider, spiritual entity, the word increasingly gets used to describe the wider more abstract concept only. Accordingly, while the possession of charms and medicine bundles was regularly described, these were not usually described as fetishes, and increasingly by the end of the nineteenth century what was being stressed was the harmony of Indians with a nature which was immanent in these objects. We find a late example of this in the work of Hartley Burr Alexander. Using the developmental model, and illustrating it through a range of Indian tribes, he does find fetishism and a development towards monotheism, but for him all of these stages involve a spiritual awareness of nature. The fundamental mode is animism, and he describes fetishism as "merely highly localized animism."[36] Even the presence in one of his books of a bizarre illustration titled "Fetish Necklace of Human Fingers" (Cheyenne) is neither commented on, nor allowed to spoil the generally celebratory style. The title, *The Religious Spirit of the American Indian: As Shown in the Development of His Religious Rites and Customs,* tells us all. This is to be about religion and spirit, and looks forward to the plethora of New Age books invoking or aping what they call Native American "spirituality." What Alexander calls "the primitive inability to think an abstraction other than concretely" played into the Indians' role as exemplars of Romantic pantheistic belief, where the concrete and material tends to be natural and aesthetically pleasing because it is seen as a fragment of a larger, less material whole.[37]

As I have already suggested, though, this stress on nature and natural religion, while having its own logic within the development of anthropological thought and inquiry, was also linked to a larger agenda about the spiritualization of Indians as opposed to Africans and African Americans. Indians could be elevated to spirituality by downplaying the material specificity of their fetish practices and objects, or their mixedness. African religion, on the other hand, as presented in a steady stream of accounts produced as a result of increased commercial and missionary activities, retained its character as fetishist, even if only in the title, which was then disowned, in a typical act of assertion and disavowal, during the course of the book.[38] Even if it was recognized that African religion had a spiritual system beyond its material practices, there could be no question of extending this to African American religion. What seemed to have traveled to America was not a religion so much as a set of superstitious practices, which in their use of whatever was at hand, seemed to exemplify the concern for the impure and the low, which needed to be transcended. The only time Negroes were "spiritual" was when associated with Christianity as in the "Negro spirituals."[39] What was categorically not spiritual or acceptable was the folk practices of conjure and hoodoo.[40]

But if the terms of difference which marked off black people and their beliefs revolved around an unredeemed materiality, it is, of course, also true that around their physical material bodies revolved the whole edifice of slavery, and the way that the black body remained as a fetishized site of white desire and denial has recently been much discussed. As Rachel Harding argues, it was the American experience that made the African body a contested site, and to that extent slaves could be said to stress the material as the only thing they had.[41] This approach puts the emphasis not on yearning and transcendence, which is the comforting image created by hearing the spiritual only as an expression of black subjectivity, but on the physical which was the ultimate resource for slaves to help themselves. Frederick Douglass recounts in the various versions of his autobiography how, at the crucial moment when he was able to summon up the power and sense of self to confront the slave-breaker Covey, he had a root, given to him by another slave for protection. He is ambivalent about its power, but in a book notably short on expressions of Christian sentiment its inclusion is telling. It can be related to other evidence of the use of magical power as a slave resource, as in the role in the Denmark Vesey conspiracy of Gullah Jack, identified in contemporary reports as a conjurer. Such use of magic or superstition as a site of possible resistance to white authority was the antithesis of the elevated and unthreatening spirituality of African American Christianity, expressed in spirituals, but it was also distinguished from Indian religious practices, even though the actual use and meaning of material objects like medicine bundles may have been little different from that of conjure bags.

Not only may the differences between the actual use of objects as charms or fetishes have been much less clear than the racially inflected theoretical distinctions built on them, but there were also, in any case, cultural exchanges and mixing between the races. These were often undocumented and hard to locate, but we do have an unusual glimpse into this world of intermingled races and beliefs in the writings of Mary Alicia Owens, based on her experience of her mixed-blood neighbors in Missouri. She presents folk tales told by a group of old women, whose mixed racial origins, ranging from full Indian to full African, she records in detail. One of them, of Indian and French blood, has a faith "of as many hues as Joseph's coat, as was evinced by her keeping her medicine-pipe and eagle-bone whistle along with her missal and 'Key to Heaven'; by carrying a rabbit's-foot and rosary in the same pocket, by wearing a saint's toe dangling on her bosom and the fetich known as a 'luck-ball' under her right arm."[42] Other characters are part Indian and part African American and the tales are similarly mixed. In his introduction to the book, the folklorist Charles Leland acknowledges that "we find the African Voodoo ideas very strangely mixed with the Indian," but he nervously separates out the Indian beliefs, which he associates with Aryan ones, from the African. Whereas the former are based on fasting, contemplation, and prayer, the African cures are "fouler and far more revolting" than the Indian "medicine."[43] The form of the book, with a white child being told stories by old women, is reminiscent of Joel Chandler Harris's Uncle Remus stories, itself only recently seen as a product of Indian as well as African trickster traditions.[44] In a later novel, though, Owens made more traditional distinctions, and the Indian-white heroine, when offered the chance to use magical charms by an African-white woman, draws the conventional lines. "I am not a Voodoo. I have no belief in your tricken-bags, your luck-balls, your mysterious revelation from the snake, and spells from conjure-stones. Frighten the poor Negroes out of all they can earn and steal, but let me alone."[45]

Objects used in this (black) magical way are supposed to be the province of Negroes, not Indians, and I suggest that this represents a more general perception about the different orientations of the races. The changing representation over the centuries of a famous sorcerer may also reflect this. Described consistently as an Indian by her Puritan contemporaries, Tituba, the servant at the center of the Salem witch trials, is gradually transformed into an African in later commentaries, so that by the time Arthur Miller, in *The Crucible,* portrays her as a credulous black slave she is fulfilling a larger assumption about the role of magic in African as opposed to Indian religions. This was not necessarily present in earlier centuries, when, for the Puritans and Jesuits, Indians were as much associated with magic as Africans.[46] There is a general agreement that Tituba came from Barbados and may have learned these beliefs in the mixture of cultures there, but the resistance to leaving her an Indian in later representations reflects the desire to separate out the appropriate racial religious propensities.[47]

My argument has been twofold: firstly that the way that the fetish persists as a place of denial and misrecognition is related to the urge to transcend or disown aspects of materiality in religious and anthropological theorizing in the nineteenth century; secondly that in America this took a quite specific form, which reflected and played into the differing characterizations of races—itself related to the very different economic and material role of Indians and African Americans, so that while African Americans were restricted to magic the Indians were elevated above it into the realms of spirituality.

Evidence of continuing investment in such Indian spirituality can be found in an odd survival of the term "fetish,": which might seem to run counter to my argument about the distancing of Indians from fetishism. The small stone sculptures of the Zuni Indians of New Mexico are today regularly called "fetishes," and this stems from Frank Hamilton Cushing's "Zuni Fetiches," which appeared in the *2nd Annual Report of the Bureau of Ethnology* of 1880–81.[48] Cushing, following Tylor's formulations, gives an account of the animistic beliefs of the Zuni, and stresses that the term for these fetishes is actually the term for the prey gods, and is associated with hunting. Strangely, the term has stuck for this single group of objects, which, together with Indian products from the Southwest in general, have become "collectable." Recent books reveal what is being collected. Hal Zina

Bennett's *Zuni Fetishes: Using American Objects for Meditation, Reflection, and Insight* offers a generalized pantheistic view of nature, which he believes is the Indian one. He uses fetishes as "guidance toward enjoying a more loving relationship with nature, with this beautiful blue planet that is our Mother."[49] Accordingly he feeds the fetishes in the traditional way and treats them as animated. In a New Age mixture of executive and religious language he tells us of having a "conference" with his fetishes to get guidance. Other glossy catalogues, complete with price guides, reveal more of the commodity aspect. Thus, although the term fetish is preserved in this one instance, it has lost any of the danger of magic or materiality. What we have left is not just commodity fetishism but a commodification of the fetish. This account of the present would be incomplete, though, without a final reminder of the ways in which these limiting and reductive definitions have been reworked by Indian and African American writers and artists like Leslie Silko, Gerald Vizenor, Jimmie Durham, Ishmael Reed, and Renee Stouts even if their influence seems to be swamped by the mass popularity of the New Age commodifications.

NOTES

1. For an indication of such uses, which are beyond the scope of this paper, see Roy Ellis, "Fetishism," *Man,* n.s. 23, no. 2 (1988): 213–15; William Pietz, "Fetish," in *Critical Terms for Art History,* ed. Robert S. Nelson and Richard Schiff (Chicago, 1996), pp. 197–207; Laura Mulvey, "Some Thoughts on Theories of Fetishism in the Context of Contemporary Culture," *October* 65 (1993): 3–20; Steven F. Kruger, "Fetishism, 1927, 1461," in *The Postcolonial Middle Ages,* ed. Jeffrey Jerome Cohen (New York, 2000), pp. 193–208.

2. His work consists of a string of essays. See especially William Pietz, "The Problem of the Fetish," pts. 1, 2, and 3, *Res* 9 (Spring 1985): 5–17, 13 (Spring 1987): 23–25, and 16 (Autumn 1988): 105–23; "The Fetish of Civilisation: Sacrificial Blood and Monetary Debt," in *Colonial Subjects: Essays on the Practical History of Anthropology,* ed. Peter Pels and Oscar Salemink (Ann Arbor, Mich., 1999), pp. 53–81; "Death of the Deodand: Accursed Objects and the Money Value of Human Life," *Res* 27 (1993): 97–108.

3. "The Problem of the Fetish, Part 1," p. 7.

4. See Margaret T. Hodgen, *Early Anthropology in the Sixteenth and Seventeenth Centuries* (Philadelphia, 1964).

5. William Bosman, *A New and Accurate Description of the Court of Guinea* (London, 1705), p. 148.

6. Ibid., p. 150.

7. Frank E. Manuel, *The Eighteenth Century Confronts the Gods* (Cambridge, Mass., 1959), p. 130. See also Francis Schmidt, "Polytheisms: Degeneration or Progress?" *History and Anthropology* 3 (1987).

8. David Hume, *The Natural History of Religion, Philosophical Works of David Hume* (Edinburgh, 1826), pp. 437–38.

9. Ibid., p. 471.

10. "The Problem of the Fetish, Part 3," p. 23.

11. Henry Krips, *Fetish: An Erotics of Culture* (Ithaca, N.Y., 1999), p. 58.

12. Charles de Brosses, *Du Culte des dieux fétiches, ou parallèle de l' ancienne Religion de l'Egypte avec la Religion actuelle de Nigritie* (Paris, 1760), p. 182.

13. Ibid., p. 183.

14. Ibid., pp. 18, 83–84.

15. Joseph Francois Lafitau, *Customs of the American Indians Compared with the Customs of Primitive Times* (1724), ed. and tr. William Fenton and Elizabeth Moore, 2 vols. (Toronto, 1974), 1:243.

16. Ibid., 2:210.

17. Ibid., 2:178.

18. Ibid., 1:179.

19. Fenton and Moore in their English edition insert the subheading "Fetishes or Charms" to the section quoted above in which Garnier and Lafitau examine the Indian objects, without indicating, as they customarily do, that this is their own insertion—presumably as a result of the influence of de Brosses, whom they discuss in their introduction.

20. De Brosses, *Du Culte*, p. 10.

21. G. W. F. Hegel, *The Philosophy of History* (1837), tr. J. Sibree (New York, 1956), p. 93. For an account of relevant aspects of the European representation of Africa, see Christopher L. Miller, *Blank Darkness: Africanist Discourse in French* (Chicago, 1985). Miller is illuminating on de Brosses, but as with Pietz, there is no sense that de Brosses refers to anywhere but Africa.

22. Edward Burnet Tylor, *Primitive Culture: Researches into the Development of Mythology, Philosophy, Religion, Language, Art and Custom*, 2 vols. (1871; New York, 1889), 1:424. For a broader context, see George W. Stocking, *Victorian Anthropology* (New York, 1987).

23. Ibid., 2:144.

24. Ibid., p. 168.

25. Ibid., 1:113, 112. Frazer was later to systematize these relations, in his tripartite distinction of magic, religion, and science, and the category of sympathetic magic. Wouter J. Hanegraaff's "The Emergence of the Academic Science of Magic: The Occult Philosophy in Tylor and Frazer," in

Religion in the Making: The Emergence of the Sciences of Religion, ed. Arie L. Molendijk and Peter Pels (Leiden, 1998), pp. 253–75, has some excellent insights into the status of magic and religion in the period.

26. See Tomoko Masuzawa, "Troubles with Materiality: The Ghost of Fetishism in the Nineteenth Century," *Comparative Studies in Society and History* 42, no. 2 (2000): 242–67, which takes a similar approach to mine here.

27. Peter Pels, "The Spirit of Matter: On Fetish, Rarity, Fact and Fancy," in *Border Fetishisms: Material Objects in Unstable Places* (New York, 1998), p. 91.

28. *Primitive Culture,* 2:152.

29. Ibid., 1:426. For Tylor's skeptical encounter with spiritualism see George W. Stocking Jr., "Animism in Theory and Practice: E. B. Tylor's Unpublished 'Notes on "Spiritualism,"'" *Man,* n.s. 6 (1971): 88–104.

30. Karl Marx, *Capital: A Critique of Political Economy,* trans. S. Moore and E. Aveling, 3 vols. (London: Lawrence and Wishart, 1970), 1:70–72. For discussion of Marx's use of "fetishism" see Maurice Godelier, *Perspectives in Marxist Anthropology* (Cambridge, 1977); William Pietz, "Fetishism and Materialism: The Limit of Theory in Marx," in *Fetishism as Cultural Discourse,* ed. Emily Apter and William Pietz (Ithaca, N.Y., 1993), pp. 119–51; Jean Baudrillard, *For a Critique of the Political Economy of the Sign* (St. Louis, 1981), pp. 8–101. See also Jacques Derrida, *Spectres of Marx: The State of the Debt, the Work of Mourning, and the New International* (New York, 1994) for a further discussion of questions of materiality and Marx's legacy. Perhaps the most interesting anthropological development of these ideas, focusing on the extent to which native beliefs in a magically animated world of objects might actually offer a conceptual tool for the understanding of capitalist exploitation, has been in the work of Michael T. Taussig. See, for example, *The Devil and Commodity Fetishism in South America* (Chapel Hill, N.C., 1980). For an appraisal and rather different application of these ideas, see Peter Gose, "Sacrifice and the Commodity Form in the Andes," *Man,* n.s. 21, no. 2 (1986).

31. Eric J. Ziolkowski, *A Museum of Faiths: Histories and Legacies of the 1893 World's Parliament of Religions* (Atlanta, Ga., 1993), p. 321. See also Richard Hughes Seager, ed., *The Dawn of Religious Pluralism: Voices from the World's Parliament of Religions, 1893* (LaSalle, Ill., 1993).

32. More recently this has changed. See, for instance, Jack D. Forbes's groundbreaking *Black Africans and Native Americans: Color, Race and Caste in the Evolution of Red-Black Peoples* (Oxford, 1988), and Karen I. Blu, *The Lumbee Problem: The Making of an American Indian People* (New York, 1980).

33. *Journal of American Folklore* 1 (1888): 5. The differences between the more inclusive and less critical approach of the folklorists and the more

hierarchical concern of the religionists with more spiritualized expressions of belief are clear in Andrew Lang's sharp critiques of Max Muller and his concern for "higher" religions. See Andrew Lang, *Custom and Myth* (1884; London, 1910).

34. Daniel G. Brinton, *Religions of Primitive Peoples* (New York, 1899), p. 131.

35. Ibid., p. 161. The role of "totemism," which was added to the battery of systematizing and categorizing terms for primitive thought and belief by McLennan in 1869, as "fetishism plus certain peculiarities," offers a parallel story to "fetishism," in its wide general use, despite its rejection by specialists. This was given a series of quite extensive critiques within American anthropology some time before Claude Lévi-Strauss's definitive demolition in *Totemism* (Boston, 1963). For an account of the American critiques, see Warren Shapiro, "Claude Lévi-Strauss Meets Alexander Goldenweiser: Boasian Anthropology and the Study of Totemism," *American Anthropologist* 93, no. 3 (1991): 599–610. For a far-ranging analysis of the ideological underpinnings of debates over totemism, see Patrick Wolfe, *Settler Colonialism and the Transformation of Anthropology: The Politics and Poetics of an Ethnographic Event* (London, 1999), esp. pp. 106–28.

36. *The Religious Spirit of the American Indian: As Shown in the Development of His Religious Rites and Customs* (Chicago, 1910), p. 6.

37. Ibid., p. 49. See also Alexander's later book, *The World's Rim: Great Mysteries of the North American Indians* (Lincoln, Neb., 1953). On the development of these views, see Christopher Vecsey, "American Indian Environmental Religions," in *American Indian Environments: Ecological Issues in Native American History,* ed. Christopher Vecsey and Robert W. Venables (Syracuse, N.Y., 1980), pp. 1–37. For negative Native reactions, see Bron Taylor, "Earthen Spirituality, or Cultural Genocide? Radical Environmentalism's Appropriation of Native American Spirituality," *Religion* 27 (1997).

38. See, for instance, Robert Hamill Nassau, *Fetichism in West Africa: Forty Years' Observation of Native Customs and Superstitions* (New York, 1904), where Nassau is at pains to rebut the allegations of simple object worship. A. B. Ellis's "The Indwelling Spirits of Men," *Popular Science Monthly* 36 (April 1890): 794–801, was one of the few instances of comparisons between African and Indian beliefs.

39. See Jon Cruz, *Culture on the Margins: The Black Spiritual and the Rise of American Cultural Interpretation* (Princeton, N.J., 1999), and Ronald Radano, "Denoting Difference; The Writing of the Slave Spirituals," *Critical Inquiry* 22 (Spring 1996): 506–44.

40. On charms and conjure see Albert J. Raboteau, *Slave Religion: The "Invisible Institution" in the Antebellum South* (Oxford, 1978), pp. 75–87,

275–88; Philip D. Morgan, *Slave Counterpoint: Black Culture in the Eighteenth-Century Chesapeake and Low Country* (Chapel Hill, N.C., 1998), pp. 620–27; Michael A. Gomez, *Exchanging Our Country Marks: The Transformation of African Identities in the Colonial and Antebellum South* (Chapel Hill, N.C., 1998), pp. 49–50, 283–90: William D. Pierson, *Black Yankees: The Development of an Afro-American Subculture in Eighteenth-Century New England* (Amherst, Mass., 1988). pp. 74–86; Lawrence Levine, *Black Culture and Black Consciousness: Afro-American Folk Thought from Slavery to Freedom* (Oxford, 1977), pp. 55–83.

41. See Rachel E. Harding, *A Refuge in Thunder: Candomble and Alternative Spaces of Blackness* (Bloomington, Ind., 2000). pp. 27–33, 147–56. In her use of Pietz's stress on the materiality of the fetish to apply to the objects and general orientation of candomble, as well as her stress on the material bodies of the slaves, she offers a fruitful approach to conjure.

42. *Old Rabbit, the Voodoo and Other Sorcerers: Voodoo Tales As Told among the Negroes of the Southwest,* collected from original sources by Mary Alicia Owens (New York, 1893), p. 8. See also Mary Alicia Owen, *Folklore of the Musquakie Indians of North America and Catalogue of Musquakie Beadwork and Other Objects in the Collection of the Folk-Lore Society* (London, 1904).

43. Owen, *Folklore,* p. vi.

44. See Jay Hansford C. Vest, "From Bobtail to Brer Rabbit," *American Indian Quarterly* 24, no. 1 (2000): 19–43.

45. *The Daughter of Alouette* (London, 1902), p. 163.

46. Peter Benes, ed., *Wonders of the Invisible World, 1600–1900* (Boston, 1995), pp. 17–52.

47. Chadwick Hansen, "The Metamorphosis of Tituba, or Why American Intellectuals Can't Tell an Indian Witch from a Negro," *New England Quarterly* (March 1974); and Elaine G. Breslaw, *Tituba, Reluctant Witch of Salem: Devilish Indians and Puritan Fantasies* (New York, 1996).

48. (Washington, D.C., 1883).

49. (New York, 1993), p. 14.

9

"To see inside of an Indian"

Missionaries and Dakotas in the Minnesota Borderlands

ANDREW C. ISENBERG

By 1838, the Presbyterian missionary Gideon Pond had spent two years at Lac qui Parle, an Eastern Sioux village on the Upper Minnesota River. He had become fluent in the Indians' language, but still he despaired that he did not understand the Indians' worldview. In an effort to gain that understanding, Pond accompanied a group of Indians on an extended duck-hunting excursion. A fellow missionary at Lac qui Parle, Stephen Riggs, wrote, "Mr. Pond had been yearning to see inside of an Indian. He had been wanting to be an Indian, if only for half an hour, so that he might know how an Indian felt, and by what motives they could be moved." From the perspective of the Indians, the hunting expedition proved to be a spectacular failure. A cold spell discouraged the return of ducks to the north. Other game was similarly scarce. The hunting party, including Pond, went hungry most of the time. "But Mr. Pond was seeing inside of Indians," Riggs wrote, "and was quite willing to starve a good deal in the process."[1]

Riggs and the other missionaries at Lac qui Parle shared Pond's eagerness to experience the Indians' world, including its privations, as the Indians did. The missionaries steeped themselves in Indian language and culture in part because the success of their mission to convert the Indians demanded it: in western Minnesota in the 1830s, the Eastern Sioux, or Dakotas, controlled the pace and timbre of acculturation. Yet the missionaries' willingness to suffer alongside the Dakotas sprang as well from an even deeper religious source; it was a manifestation of the asceticism that had originally brought them to Lac qui Parle. After a few years in the Minnesota borderlands, the missionaries expressed and understood that asceticism in terms of the culture and environment of the Dakotas.

Few ethnohistorians have portrayed missionaries as motivated to understand, much less share, the suffering of American Indians. Indeed, among ethnohistorians, the irreconcilability of Christian missionaries and native cultures is nearly an article of faith. Since the publication of Robert F. Berkhofer's *Salvation and the Savage* in 1962, most ethnohistorians have portrayed the interaction between Indians and missionaries as a contest between native cultural persistence and Euroamerican cultural imperialism.[2]

On the surface, the Lac qui Parle missionaries resemble Berkhofer's type: ethnocentric agents of assimilation. Like Marcus Whitman, a Presbyterian evangelist so odious to the Cayuse Indians of Oregon that they massacred him and his household in 1847, the Lac qui Parle evangelists were devout Presbyterians. Like him, they established their mission in the mid-1830s as Euroamerican settlers began to surge into the trans-Mississippi West. Like the Cayuse, who rebelled in 1847, the Dakotas rose up against Euroamerican settlers in 1862. Since the 1960s, historians of encounters between Dakotas and Euroamericans have categorized the Lac qui Parle missionaries together with Whitman, seeing them as threats to the Dakotas' precontact cultural integrity. Roy W. Meyer and Gary C. Anderson, the leading historians to study the nineteenth-century Dakota, have argued that the Lac qui Parle missionaries were, at best, culturally insensitive to the Dakotas and, at worst, bent on the eradication of Dakota culture.[3]

Curiously, when reconstructing nineteenth-century Dakota culture on its own terms—one of the central goals of ethnohistory—these scholars relied heavily on the writings of the missionaries they excoriated. Particularly helpful were Samuel Pond's detailed study, *The Dakota or Sioux of Minnesota As They Were in 1834,* a model of ethnographic description; and Stephen Riggs's *Dakota Grammar, Texts, and Ethnography,* a work so authoritative that John Wesley Powell published it in a Bureau of American Ethnology series.[4] The Lac qui Parle missionaries were capable of misinterpretations of Indians, but unlike Whitman, they were sensitive and scholarly observers of the Dakotas.

A close look at Lac qui Parle reveals that the missionaries fit poorly into the role of cultural imperialists, while the Dakotas are miscast as exemplars of precontact culture. With a few exceptions, notably their insistence that male converts cut their hair and don Euroamerican clothing, the missionaries did not insist upon acculturation to Euroamerican norms. Rather, the missionaries were alienated from many aspects of secular Euroamerican culture. The Dakota community was not in pristine cultural isolation when the missionaries arrived but had been transformed by nearly two centuries of cultural and economic change resulting from the European presence in the western Great Lakes and eastern grasslands.

Accordingly, Lac qui Parle in the 1830s and 1840s was not the scene of a simple conflict between monolithic cultures, but was a culturally eclectic community where missionaries accommodated to some aspects of Dakota culture and some segments of the Dakota community adjusted to the presence of the missionaries. The Dakotas and the missionaries compromised in order to achieve a common goal: both groups sought to preserve Lac qui Parle's relative autonomy from Euroamerican society. The Indians wanted to maintain what remained of their economic and political independence. The missionaries sought to isolate themselves and their converts from a Euroamerican society they regarded as thoroughly sinful. Accommodation was by no means perfectly harmonious. Rather, as in the tense, contested, French-Algonquian "middle ground" that Richard White described in the eighteenth-century Great Lakes region, Dakotas and missionaries periodically struggled with cultural differences, misinterpreted each other, become frustrated, and vowed to quit their endeavor. Rather than being simply evidence of an irreconcilable conflict, however, those struggles were part of the creation of their common mission.[5]

The missionaries who traveled to Lac qui Parle had two objectives. Their first purpose, of course, was to convert the Dakotas to evangelical Protestantism. Their second goal, however, was to remove themselves from secular Euroamerican society, which they considered to be thoroughly corrupted by sin. Much like the members of utopian or cooperative communities, the Lac qui Parle missionaries sought to find in the Lac qui Parle community a rarefied moral atmosphere.

The missionaries—Thomas and Margaret Williamson, Alexander and Lydia Huggins, Stephen and Mary Riggs, and Samuel, Gideon, and Sarah Pond—were exactly the sort of antebellum Euroamericans that social historians have identified as acutely liable to religious revivalism.[6] Before their emigration to Minnesota, they inhabited the most fertile soil for revivalism in the United States: western New England and the northern tier of the trans-Appalachian West. The combination of the market revolution and westward migration had unsettled these regions. The commercialization of agriculture prompted the migration of thousands from the overcrowded New England countryside to the "Yankee West." The rise of commercial agriculture buoyed the fortunes of the father of Margaret Williamson and Sarah Pond; he owned a thriving farm in Brown County, Ohio. It buffeted the opportunities of the Pond brothers, who in the early 1830s found themselves, like many young men in antebellum New England, working as hired farmhands.[7] Whether they profited from the market revolution or not, many members of the Yankee diaspora felt themselves to be spiritually rootless in a commercialized and mobile society. In this environment, religious revivalism thrived.

The prevailing interpretation of early nineteenth-century missions to American Indians is that they stemmed from the Second Great Awakening, the evangelical movement for revival and reform that inflamed the Yankee diaspora, particularly in western New York, in the 1820s and 1830s.[8] Gideon and Samuel Pond were so affected by the revival that swept through Washington, Connecticut, in 1833 that they left New England for Minnesota the next year. "I want to be God's servant," Gideon explained to his sister in 1838 in an explicitly religious rejection of the mores of the market. "I strive not to desire a treasure in this world but I want to be 'rich in faith'—an heir to the kingdom of Heaven."[9] Yet the Second Great Awakening provides little guide to the nature of nineteenth-century missions, because it was a disparate movement in time, space, and faith. Because millennialism and the idea of human "perfectibility" propped up the emerging Whig ideology of hard work, sobriety, and social mobility, historians have paid considerable attention to these features of the movement.[10] Yet not all evangelical Protestants joined the temperance movement and the Whig Party.[11] Some, such as the Lac qui Parle missionaries, preferred to retreat from American society rather than try to reform it. The Lac qui Parle missionaries were what Max Weber called "otherworldly" ascetics. Instead of concentrating on the improvement of society, the focus of the "worldly" ascetics who dominated the Second Great Awakening reform movements, the Lac qui Parle missionaries sought spiritual solace in a withdrawal from earthly entanglements.[12]

The impetus for withdrawal was rooted in the missionaries' dour emphasis on sin. Rather than the spiritual perfection toward which social reformers strove, the Lac qui Parle missionaries were obsessed with their moral shortcomings. After Samuel Pond attended a series of evangelical meetings in 1831, he did not experience the heady enthusiasm typical of some Second Great Awakening revivals. Rather, he felt the moral despair reminiscent of early Calvinism. "Soon after I joined the church I lost all hope that I was, or ever could be a Christian, and for many months my mental sufferings were intense."[13] Two years later he confessed that "my salvation never appeared more difficult. . . . If I am ever saved it will be an astonishing act of free grace & sovereign mercy."[14] The feeling of moral inadequacy continued to plague the missionaries after they had migrated to Minnesota. Gideon Pond recorded in his diary in 1837 that he was "entangled in the snare of the devil," and that "my heart is filth and pollution and my life but corruption." On his twenty-eighth birthday he remarked on the swift passage of the last year and regretted that "I find myself the same vile and hateful sinner I was when it commenced."[15] Similarly, Thomas Williamson confessed to Gideon Pond in 1840 that "The Wicked One" had "assailed" him during the last winter. "I have not for twenty years been so much tempted to anger and fretfulness."[16]

Obsessed with their own moral frailties, the missionaries were similarly sensitive to the moral culpabilities of others. Traveling to Minnesota in 1833, Samuel Pond described Galena, Illinois, as "one of the strongholds of the prince of darkness," because Sabbath-breaking, drunkenness, gambling, profanity, Catholicism ("that religion is worse than no religion"), and poor church attendance prevailed.[17] On their way to Lac qui Parle in 1837, Stephen and Mary Riggs stopped to observe the Sabbath in Davenport, Iowa. Mary Riggs was horrified by the "frequent volleys of dreadful oaths" that emanated from a grocery near her hotel, "a devil's den indeed." The young couple found the environment so unbearable that their consciences "did not chide for removing, even on the Sabbath," to more Christian accommodations.[18] After their brief sojourns in these frontier towns—which appear in their descriptions as Sodom and Gomorra on the Mississippi—the missionaries moved on to Minnesota, out of reach of the corruption of civilized society. The Riggs's decision to retreat from Davenport was indicative of their spiritual character; to remain in Euroamerican society, even as advocates of temperance and sabbatarianism, might have distracted them from the contemplation of their own sins, and might indeed have imperiled their salvation by tempting them into moral compromise and complacency.[19]

Convinced of their own proclivity toward wickedness, the Lac qui Parle missionaries had no confidence in their ability to resist the vices that surrounded them in the United States. Accordingly, even before their emigration to Minnesota, they associated only with other Protestant religious radicals, ministers, seminary students, and their families. They found spouses within this clique; after a few years most of the Lac qui Parle missionaries were related by blood or marriage. To further remove themselves from the reaches of temptation, these like-minded Protestants, who had isolated themselves within Euroamerican society, emigrated to Lac qui Parle, a place which, according to one of the missionaries, was "farther from civilization than any . . . village of Indians south of Alaska."[20] The missionaries' urge to withdraw from Euroamerican society was not uncommon among religious or intellectual radicals in the early nineteenth century. Many groups established religious, cooperative, or utopian communities in antebellum America, most of them short-lived. Altogether, one hundred utopian communities were founded in the United States between the Revolution and the Civil War.[21] The Lac qui Parle missionaries welcomed the isolation afforded them by their mission to the Dakotas. They were not so much apostles of nineteenth-century Euroamerican culture as apostates from it.

Westward migration, the missionaries believed, would take them closer to primitive purity and away from commerce and corruption. Alexander Huggins, Thomas Williamson, Margaret Williamson, and Sarah Pond followed the examples of their fathers who had migrated to Ohio from the Carolinas and Kentucky to escape "the wrong of slavery."[22] The missionaries' ideological rejection of secular society became actual when they exiled themselves to Lac qui Parle. "A resurrection to new life had just taken place," Stephen Riggs later recalled about his arrival in Minnesota in 1837.[23] Once established, the missionaries considered the relative isolation of Lac qui Parle from American society an advantage. They idealized the Dakotas as noble savages: heathens, to be sure, but as yet unsullied by secular Euroamerican culture. In 1834, Samuel Pond urged that every effort be made to convert the Dakotas before "white men and whiskey are among them."[24] By 1840, only three years after he had come to Lac qui Parle, Stephen Riggs was already considering moving farther west. After a visit to the Teton Sioux near Fort Pierre on the Missouri River, he wrote, "those Indians seem more favorably disposed to receive the gospel than most of the tribe in the vicinity of Lac-qui-Parle and especially Fort Snelling. As yet they have not formed a prejudice against it."[25] In 1840, Thomas Williamson likewise warned Gideon Pond that the Dakotas would be irredeemable once they had been fully exposed to the vices of Euroamerican secular culture.[26] Williamson's warning reflected the central tenet of the missionaries' religion: the denial of worldly pleasures as an ascetic rejection of sin and temptation. He imposed his loathing of secular Euroamerican culture onto his perception of the Dakotas.

As they isolated themselves from Euroamerican society, the missionaries integrated themselves into the community of four hundred Dakotas at Lac qui Parle. While Lac qui Parle seemed isolated to the missionaries, the region around the Dakota village had been the scene of complex cultural interactions since the mid-seventeenth century. The Minnesota borderlands—the Upper Minnesota River and Red River valleys—were for two centuries a zone of cultural and economic mediation and accommodation. The region was a borderland in the classical sense as the historian Herbert Bolton first defined it: one of the contested places where imperial rivals and Indian groups met.[27] Ecologically, the region was a border zone between the grasslands to the west and the woodlands to the east.[28] Economically, the Dakotas were intermediaries in intertribal trade between woodland groups to the east and the Teton Sioux in the plains.[29] Beginning in the seventeenth century, Euroamerican fur traders widened the scope of trade, creating a highly fluid hybridization of native and Euroamerican cultures. By the early nineteenth century, the region was a mélange of Siouan, Algonquian, French, British, and American cultures. By the late 1820s, the Great Lakes region—which included the Minnesota borderlands on its western periphery—had a métis population of ten to fifteen thousand.[30]

Lac qui Parle was the hub of cultural interaction among Indians and between Indians and Euroamericans in the Minnesota borderlands. Situated on the Minnesota River and close to the headwaters of the Red River, the village served for decades as an important post in the fur trade. Since the seventeenth century, French fur traders had resided among the Dakotas, often acquiring Dakota spouses and fathering children in the process. The offspring of one such union, Joseph Renville, born in 1779, exemplified the multicultural character of the Minnesota borderlands. Renville served as a scout for Zebulon Pike's Upper Mississippi exploration in 1805, but fought with the British against Pike and the United States in the War of 1812. He became an influential fur trader after the war, centering his trade at his post near Lac qui Parle. There, according to Samuel Pond, he "lived in barbaric splendor quite like an African king," maintaining a retinue of thirty to forty young men "formed into a sort of society, which he often feasted and harangued. . . . Their adherence to him and devotion to his interests added greatly for a time to his importance."[31]

Pond interpreted Renville's largesse toward the Dakotas as the vanity and indulgence of a half-breed. He failed to appreciate the importance of reciprocal giving among biological or fictive kin in the Dakota community, a cultural tradition that cushioned the impact of change in the borderlands. Since the seventeenth century, in response to the influx of strangers such as Renville's father, the Dakotas had incorporated important visitors into their network of "social kinship," enveloping the strangers in bonds of reciprocal obligation. Marriage between a fur trader and an Indian woman, for instance, helped to solidify the outsider's social obligations to the community. Renville's generosity certainly added to his prestige in Lac qui Parle, but as one of the wealthiest persons in the Lac qui Parle community, any other course of action would have been an egregious social breach. As a métis culturally fluent in Dakota and Euroamerican mores, Renville used his prestige to mediate change.[32]

While the Dakotas could integrate the commercialism of the fur trade into the culture of reciprocal obligations and social kinship, they could not mitigate the fur trade's demands for game. As befitted a borderland society, the Lac qui Parle Dakotas combined the subsistence patterns of two environments, gathering, hunting, and planting in the forests for most of the year and traveling to the plains in the late summer to hunt bison.[33] The Dakota role in the fur trade placed this subsistence strategy in jeopardy, however. As it had elsewhere in North America, the fur trade contributed to the rapid depopulation of game in the area around Lac qui Parle. In 1823, the fur trader Charles H. Keating commented on the almost complete absence of game of any kind on the Minnesota River.[34] When beavers, whose pelts were most valuable, had been nearly eliminated, the Dakotas began to hunt less valuable but more populous animals, particularly muskrats. By the late 1820s, game was so scarce that the trade in furs had shifted away from the Minnesota borderlands. Few furs passed through Lac qui Parle to Canada, but rather the trade went to St. Louis via the Missouri River.[35] In the 1820s and 1830s, faced with a waning fur trade and depleted populations of game near Lac qui Parle, many Dakotas confronted a crisis of subsistence. Some died each year in dangerous winter hunting expeditions. An Indian agent reported that a severe winter in 1829 caused the Lac qui Parle Dakotas to resort to cannibalism.[36] Shortly after his arrival in Lac qui Parle, Alexander Huggins noted, "Some days ago one woman came to the Dr.'s, said they were starving; one man, she said, was past sitting up; the Dr. gave the woman some turnips and potatoes and went to see the man; he was far gone."[37] Gideon Pond recorded that the Dakotas were "poor and needy—many of them absolutely suffering from want, naked and hungry."[38] While Renville was wealthy by Lac qui Parle standards, as the trade declined in the 1830s he slipped steadily into a sort of genteel poverty. By 1843, he owed forty-two hundred dollars to his corporate superiors, the American Fur Company.[39] By that time, his fur-trading operation had become a means to support his social obligations to the Dakota community.

The labor of the Dakotas was strictly divided by gender: men were responsible for hunting; women for planting and gathering. As hunters were increasingly unable to find game, the contributions of women to the subsistence of the Dakota community assumed critical importance. In 1814, to help alleviate the community's crisis, Renville had persuaded Dakota women to intensify their cultivation of corn.[40] It was he who invited the missionaries to Lac qui Parle in the hope that they could help to make the Dakota community agriculturally self-sufficient. Beginning in 1834, the missionaries brought, along with their religious message, livestock, seeds, implements, and methods of intensive agriculture. Indeed, Huggins and the Pond brothers initially came to the Dakota mission not as ministers but as farmers. "From the beginning," wrote Stephen Riggs, "it had been part of our work to make more than two stalks of corn grow where one grew before."[41] By 1837 the Lac qui Parle missionaries had a small horse-powered grinding mill, and they farmed five acres of corn, potatoes, wheat, peas, and turnips. The Dakota women, who tilled their corn fields with digging sticks, envied the missionaries' plot. "Plowing," Samuel W. Pond, Jr., noted, "was one of the arts of civilization which Indians, and especially Indian women, could appreciate."[42] By 1839, Huggins plowed fifty acres each spring for the Indian women to plant their corn. In the late 1830s, owing to the missionaries' advice and assistance to Dakota women, forty Lac qui Parle families could store enough corn each winter to forgo the dangerous winter hunts.[43]

The missionaries' agricultural prowess helped them to convert Dakotas, especially women. One of the obstacles to conversion was the mobility of the Dakotas; expeditions to hunt and gather food interrupted the missionaries' lessons. Greater yields of corn, however, contributed to the number of Dakotas who remained in Lac qui Parle during the year. The missionaries' advice and assistance on agricultural matters facilitated contact between them and Dakota women, and helped to raise the missionaries' prestige. For their part, the missionaries were favorably disposed toward Dakota women, praising them for their chastity and industry. For these reasons, forty of the fifty Dakota converts between 1835 and 1842 were women. Many appear to have been former wives of Euroamerican fur traders, left without a hunter in the household to provide for them when their Euroamerican husbands abandoned Lac qui Parle.[44]

Like their strict division of labor, many Dakota rituals assigned specific roles based on gender. The missionaries' success in converting women caused a number of Dakotas to regard the mission church as "an assembly of women." The first Dakota man to join the church, Simon Anawanymane, in 1841, was accused by his peers of having "made himself a woman." In a ritual sense, this is exactly what Anawanymane had done: for a Dakota man, gender identity was bound up in religious rituals; according to Stephen Riggs, he "had been inducted into manhood through the ceremonies of his religion."[45] Moreover, the missionaries insisted that male converts cut their hair and adopt Euroamerican dress. If Riggs was insensitive to Dakota notions of masculinity, at least he was no hypocrite; he sometimes attended to certain household chores, such as milking, that were quintessential women's work in nineteenth-century rural America.[46] The stiffest resistance to the mission church came from the all-male warrior societies which were periodically empowered to police community behavior. In the village, the societies sometimes took it upon themselves to keep children from attending the mission school and women from the church.[47] When particularly frustrated, some Dakota men surreptitiously killed the missionaries' cattle—a direct assault on the Euroamericans' intensive agricultural regime to which Dakota women had increasingly adapted.[48]

Yet these spasms of resistance were relatively rare. Even the most irreconcilable Dakota men understood that the missionaries contributed to the subsistence and independence of the community. As long as the Dakotas remained autonomous, they were able to accept or reject the missionaries' message. Ethnohistorians call this pattern of acculturation "permissive," or "non-directed," and generally associate it not with missionaries but with explorers and fur traders who were among the first Euroamericans to encounter Indians.[49] Because of the missionaries' assistance, the Lac qui Parle Dakotas were in enviable circumstances when compared to the Dakotas in eastern Minnesota, the Mdewakantons, who continued to rely primarily on diminishing supplies of game. By the 1830s, the Mdewakantons were dependent on stipends from the federal government. In an 1837 treaty, the United States capitalized on that dependence to force the Mdewakantons to cede their land east of the Mississippi River.

Rather than acting as advance agents of Euroamerican expansion, the missionaries contributed to the autonomy of the Lac qui Parle community. While Marcus Whitman saw his facilitation of Euroamerican expansion in Oregon as his "greatest work," the Lac qui Parle missionaries more resembled the Presbyterian missionaries to the Cherokees and Choctaws in the 1820s and 1830s who galvanized Indian resistance to removal. Some of these missionaries helped the Cherokees draw up a constitution and claim sovereignty in the effort to avoid removal from Georgia. Likewise, in the 1850s, when many of the Dakotas had been relegated to a reservation at Hazelwood, Minnesota, Stephen Riggs established the "Hazelwood Republic," in the hope of achieving a measure of Dakota political autonomy on the reservation.[50]

Recognizing the missionaries' contribution to the community, some Dakotas incorporated the missionaries into Lac qui Parle's social kinship network. One of the Indians' first steps was to give the missionaries names in the Dakota language. When Stephen and Mary Riggs's son, Alfred, was born in 1837, the Dakotas named him *Zitkadan Washtay,* or Good Bird. "In those days," Riggs wrote, "it was a habit with them to give names to the white people who came among them."[51] Riggs apparently viewed the Dakotas' naming as no more than a colorful custom. Among the Dakotas, however, naming was an act of ritual importance that implied social kinship. More than mere formality, it represented incorporation into the community and the Dakota network of reciprocal obligations. Other aspects of the Dakota religion likewise emphasized social integration. Pledges of comradeship and membership in various dancing societies, for instance, were mediated by and expressed in religious terms. These ceremonies and others bound the Dakotas together: elder relatives with children, comrades with one another, society members toward their common purpose. By tightening the social ligaments that connected individuals and small groups within Lac qui Parle, these religious institutions aimed toward preserving the autonomy and strengthening the cohesion of Dakota society.[52]

Whether or not they understood the social importance of naming, the missionaries certainly were drawn into the Indians' social network. Mary Riggs was unable to breastfeed Alfred/Zitkadan Washtay, and relied on Dakota women both to nurse her son and to attend to her health.[53] On Alfred/Zitkadan Washtay's first birthday, his only present was "a very small bow and arrow, from an Indian man who is a frequent visitor," according to his father.[54] Older male relatives among the Dakotas were responsible for instructing and disciplining boys. As Alfred grew, the Dakota man might be expected to provide him with larger weapons, and teach him something of their manufacture and use. The missionaries reciprocated: Stephen and Mary Riggs adopted a ten-year-old Dakota girl, *An-paye-too-o-kee-tan In-win,* or Appearing Day, in 1839. By 1851, three métis children had joined their household.[55]

The missionaries' study of the Dakota language further integrated them into the Lac qui Parle community. Thomas Williamson believed that Indians "can only be instructed in religion in a language in which they think." He criticized other missions to Native Americans where "the money and labor have been chiefly expended in trying to instruct them in the English language, instead of preaching the gospel to them in their own language."[56] The missionaries, therefore, struggled to learn the Dakota language and used it to conduct their lessons and services. A settler who visited Lac qui Parle in 1837 was struck by the novelty of the bicultural mission church: "Nothing could be more interesting than to see the Savage of the wilderness assemble with the sons and daughters of the Lord in the place appointed for prayer; to hear the wild and rude sons of the forest sing the praises of their Maker and Savior, in their own uncultivated and barbarous tongue."[57] The use of the Dakota language at the mission was more than a novelty, however. Language is an important part—perhaps the most important part—of cultural identity. By translating their message into the Dakota language the missionaries invited Indians to convert without abandoning this crucial aspect of Dakota culture.

Because the success of their mission depended on their mastery of the Indians' language, the missionaries were eager to learn Dakota. Upon his arrival in Minnesota in 1834, Samuel Pond learned from a fur trader how to ask the name of a thing in Dakota. "He told me and I wrote it down, and then, approaching a Dakota who was standing by a pile of iron, I asked its name. He promptly replied *maza* and then dipped a little water in his hand from the river and said *mini*—then took up a handful of sand and said *wiyaka.*" No other discovery, Pond wrote, "ever afforded me so much pleasure as it did to be able to say in Dakota 'What do you call this?' . . . We began the study of the language there on the banks of the Mississippi." From that moment on, the Pond brothers "were ever on the alert to catch some new word or phrase from the mouths of the Indians."[58] In order to further his knowledge of the Dakota language, Samuel Pond, like his brother Gideon, accompanied some Dakotas on a hunting trip. "The language was the game I went to hunt, and I was as eager in pursuit of that as the Indians were in pursuit of deer."[59] Stephen Riggs and Alexander Huggins did likewise, accompanying a group of Dakotas on a bison-hunting expedition to the Missouri River in the fall of 1840.[60] Riggs and the Pond brothers were able to hold conversations with the Dakotas within a year of their arrival in Minnesota.

Mastering the Dakota language became the chief intellectual activity of Thomas Williamson, Stephen and Mary Riggs, and the Pond brothers. With the assistance of Renville, the missionaries busied themselves translating portions of the Bible into Dakota. They peppered their correspondence with Dakota terms, and competed in the effort to compile the most complete lexicon. In 1836, Samuel Pond issued a Dakota spelling book, and in 1839 the Pond brothers published a Dakota translation of the *History of Joseph*, from Genesis 37–47. Also in 1839, Gideon Pond and Riggs collaborated on a *Dakota First Reading Book*. Samuel Pond wrote to his sister in 1840 that "I spend most of my time in writing Sioux. I have lately finished a Dictionary containing about three thousand words. I have written a small Grammar."[61] In 1842, Samuel Pond wrote a *Second Dakota Reading Book,* which consisted of stories from the Hebrew Scriptures, and in 1844 he published a Dakota *Catechism.* When Stephen Riggs went to Boston in 1842 to publish the portions of the Bible that the missionaries had translated to Dakota, he found it difficult to remember some English words. "We had been forgetting our mother tongue somewhat in the effort made to learn Dakota."[62] The Dakota language had become, by the early 1840s, the medium of the missionaries' isolation from Euroamerican society.

It was also the medium of evangelization. To preach, the missionaries had to render ideas and metaphors into symbols that were meaningful to the Dakotas. Like all clerics, the missionaries chose to preach from scriptural stories that they hoped would resonate with their listeners. It was not happenstance that one of the first stories that the missionaries translated was of Joseph, which told of people saved from famine by divine guidance. The missionaries also seized on Dakota idioms. To translate the term "to pray," the missionaries adopted the Dakota term *chakiya,* "to cry to," a term otherwise used to describe a young man's "vision quest": *hanblekiya,* "to cry for a vision."[63] Riggs wrote that when one Dakota woman was "troubled to know how prayer could reach God[,] I told her in this we were all little children. . . . He made the ear, and shall He not hear? He made, in a large sense, all languages, and shall he not be able to understand Dakota words? . . . Prayer was now, as through all ages it had been, the child's cry in the ear of the great Father."[64]

Religious practice at Lac qui Parle was an ongoing negotiation between doctrine and popular understanding, between Euroamerican clergy and Dakota laity. Particularly, the Dakotas pressed the missionaries to emphasize Christian practices that resembled Dakota traditions of reciprocal social obligations. In August 1837, Gideon Pond recorded in his diary that the principal chief at Lac qui Parle reproached the missionaries "because we teach that we should love others as ourselves and do not share with them what we ourselves possess."[65] In 1838, Joseph Renville, whose family was among the first of the Dakotas to join the mission church, successfully encouraged the Dakota converts to boycott a service at the church. Renville called for the boycott because the missionaries refused to lend their spinning wheel to Renville's daughters. "If you can do without me I can do without you," Renville told the missionaries.[66] An apology from Riggs settled the matter, but the Dakota converts continued to press the missionaries to share their resources, particularly the corn, potatoes, and turnips from their gardens. The significant aspect of these exchanges was not, as the missionaries sometimes lamented, that the Dakotas were improvident and inveterate beggars, but that they perceived the similarity between the Dakota obligation to share and the missionaries' assertion of Christian charity.

Dakota listeners interpreted the Christian message, such as the parable of the prodigal son (Luke 15:11–32), according to their traditions of social kinship and reciprocity. In the parable, a father splits his inheritance between his two sons. The elder son abides by his father but the younger leaves home and squanders his wealth. Utterly impoverished and hungry— a condition with which many Dakotas could identify—the son returns to his father, who welcomes him by clothing him and slaughtering a fatted calf for a feast. The reunion between forgiving father and repentant son, the killing of the calf, and the celebration that follows reflect the core of the Christian message. The prodigal son represents all sinners, and his father the forgiving God. The slaughtered calf, in this sense, is the crucified Christ. The feast represents the prodigal son's redemption. In recognition of the importance of this part of the parable, the missionaries plainly tried to render it in Dakota idioms. The father clothes his repentant son not in a robe and shoes but in a *sina* (blanket) and *hanpa* (moccasins). The elder son, who in the Old World version of the parable complains that despite his steadfastness his father had never sacrificed even a kid for him, complains in

the New World version that his father has not given him even a *tacincadan*
(fawn). A still more compelling challenge for the missionaries was translating "calf" in a way that both maintained the narrative integrity of the
parable and the symbolic importance of the calf as representative of the
crucified Savior. In Dakota, *pte* referred to both bison and domesticated
cows. The term for "calf" that the missionaries employed in the parable,
ptezicadan, could mean either a bison calf or a domesticated calf.[67] This story
of hunger and feast, of the sacrifice of a calf to celebrate a reunion of kin,
must have resonated among the Dakotas. The bison was an important material and social resource. During the course of the summer hunts, the
Indians consumed bison meat in communal feasts that, while contributing
to subsistence, more importantly reaffirmed kinship and social solidarity.[68]
In short, the missionaries told a story of faithlessness, repentance, and forgiveness; a parable of otherworldly salvation. The Dakotas heard a story of
faithlessness, repentance, and forgiveness; a tale of the obligations of kinship and community.

The missionaries struggled to maintain their interpretation of doctrine
against the Dakotas' efforts to interpret it to their liking. When Renville's
son journeyed from Traverse des Sioux to Lac qui Parle on a Sunday, Williamson asked him, "you did not intend to travel on the Sabbath when you
left Traverse des Sioux,' but he replied, 'Yes, I did intend to travel . . . but
I expected to repent of it when I got home." Like the Dakotas' appeal to the
Christian ideal of charity, this plea for forgiveness sought to make Christian
doctrine conform to Dakota custom. The missionaries, however, saw it as
laxity. They attributed such moral lapses to the influence of Renville, "whose
ideas of religion were derived chiefly from Catholics," according to Samuel
Pond (for whom "Catholic" had only a pejorative meaning). In 1838, Pond
refused to admit to the church several members of Renville's retinue on the
grounds of their inadequate knowledge of the Gospel. Renville threatened,
"I have prepared these persons for admission to the church and if you do not
admit them they will never attend your meeting again." A compromise was
reached: the men were admitted after a period of catechizing.[69] Renville did
not desist in his efforts to loosen the strictures for conversion; in the spring
of 1839, he attempted to replace the Presbyterians with a Catholic mission,
which he hoped would be less doctrinaire. Unable to bring a priest to Lac
qui Parle, he and his family returned to services after a few months' nonat-
tendance.[70]

The missionaries tuned their message to the ears of the Dakotas, but
accepted the conversions only of those Dakotas and métis who met their
stringent requirements. The missionaries' brand of Christianity was not
open to all. Just as the missionaries formerly had chosen to associate only

with a small number of like-minded ascetics, they selected for church membership only the most committed converts from the ranks of the Dakotas: three people in 1836, four in 1837, nine in 1838, ten in 1839, five in 1840, and nine in 1841.[71] At Lac qui Parle, unprepared applicants were rejected. In 1838, Gideon Pond wrote, "five or six women have offered themselves as candidates for admission but were not received on account of their ignorance of the doctrines of the gospel."[72] Perhaps because of the missionaries' efforts to instruct converts, backsliding was rare in Lac qui Parle. Of the fifty Dakotas who converted to Christianity between 1835 and 1842, only two were later expelled from the church. The missionaries were interested in the quality, not the quantity, of their converts.[73]

Members of the Dakota community apparently regarded the mission church as a new ceremonial society. Like other Dakota ceremonial societies, such as the one that oversaw the *Wakan wacipi,* or Sacred Dance, the mission church was open only to those who had undergone a rigorous initiation. In some ways, the rituals of the mission church were familiar. The *Wakan wacipi,* for instance, was a life renewal ceremony in which dancers symbolically died and were resurrected during a day-long ceremony. Perhaps because both the Sacred Dance and the mission church made the celebration of a resurrection to new life central, one of the leading members of the society, Toteedootawin, or Scarlet House, moved quickly from membership in the society to the leadership of the mission church. While Stephen Riggs was repulsed by the heathenism that the Sacred Dance represented, he praised Toteedootawin (whom the missionaries renamed "Catherine"—they, like the Dakotas, welcomed converts into their new fellowship through a naming ceremony) as giving "as good evidence of being a christian as any that have been received" at the time of her admission to the mission church.[74]

As with most of the religious, utopian, and cooperative communities in the antebellum United States, the isolation at Lac qui Parle was short-lived. The decline of the community had two causes. First, a late frost in the spring of 1842 caused the Lac qui Parle corn crop to fail. Many of the Indian women who had converted to Christianity migrated elsewhere, either to the plains to join the bison hunters, or east to receive federal stipends like the Mdewakantons. Some never returned.[75] Second, and more importantly, the enormous influx of Euroamericans to Minnesota in the 1840s and 1850s destroyed the relative isolation that both the missionaries and the Indians coveted. In 1835, the missionaries had been, except for a few fur traders, nearly the only Euroamericans in Minnesota west of the Mississippi River. By 1850, Minnesota Territory had a Euroamerican population of 20,000. Between 1855 and 1856 the population rose from 40,000 to 100,000. In 1857, one year before Minnesota was admitted to the Union, the territory had a Euroamerican population of over 150,000.[76] Although the missionaries continued their efforts to convert the Dakotas until the 1870s, the borderlands, characterized by cultural accommodation, had become a frontier, characterized by the progressive marginalization of the Indians. The autonomy and isolation of the Lac qui Parle community had been lost.

As the Dakotas steadily lost territory to Euroamerican settlement, Dakota holy men rallied cultural resistance to Euroamerican encroachment. In the summer of 1862, a large number of Dakotas—primarily Mdewakantons and Wahpekutes rather than the Wahpetons of Lac qui Parle—rose up, killing seven hundred Euroamericans and forcing thousands to flee. In the reprisals that followed, the leaders or suspected leaders of the uprising were executed; hundreds of Dakota men were imprisoned, and virtually all of the Dakotas were exiled to reservations in Nebraska or the Dakota Territory to the west.

The uprising permanently altered the character of the Dakota mission. The violence shattered Dakota communities, making it impossible to reestablish a mission among an existing Dakota village. Those Dakotas remaining in Minnesota were imprisoned. Stephen Riggs, Thomas Williamson, and Gideon Pond devoted three years to ministering to the hundreds of Dakota men imprisoned first at Fort Snelling and later at Davenport, Iowa (where the profanity had offended Riggs fifteen years earlier). Judged by the number of converts, the missionaries experienced their greatest success during these years, converting 450 Dakotas, mostly men, in the prisons.[77] The prison mission, however, marked the end of the "permissive" acculturation of Lac qui Parle, where the Indians had been at liberty to accept or reject the missionaries' message, and the onset of "directed" acculturation. The transition was completed by John Williamson and Alfred Riggs, who succeeded their parents in mission work among the Dakotas. As boys, they had been playmates of Dakota children at Lac qui Parle. From those children, they learned to speak Dakota with native fluency. As adults, however, John Williamson and Alfred Riggs administered reservation boarding schools for the Dakota and Yancton Sioux in Nebraska and South Dakota—institutions notorious for their efforts to repress native cultures. Also absent from the next generation's religious sensibility was an estrangement from Euroamerican culture. When John Williamson decided, in 1860, to exchange his pulpit in Indiana for the Dakota mission, he rued the loss of civilized comforts.[78]

The differences between Thomas Williamson and his son John, like the differences between the Lac qui Parle missionaries and their contemporary

Marcus Whitman, showed that all missionaries were not cut from the same cloth. The Lac qui Parle missionaries' religious rejection of mainstream Euroamerican culture and their appetite for ascetic deprivation impelled them to go to Minnesota. There, their religious asceticism acquired the character of the borderlands. "In order to prosecute their work successfully," Samuel Pond's son later wrote, the missionaries "deemed it essential that they should fully understand the language, habits, customs, hopes, and fears of an Indian; that they should be able to talk like a native, and, as far as might be, live like one—on Indian fare, in an Indian tent, with Indians if need be."[79] In effect, the missionaries' ascetic zeal for the rejection of Euroamerican society became an ascetic zeal to share the culture and the deprivations of the Dakota community.

Accordingly, the Lac qui Parle mission station was far from being an outpost of acculturation to Euroamerican mores. The missionaries' essentialist interpretation of Christianity—the belief that the true nature of the faith transcended all human cultures—made possible this estrangement from Euroamerican culture. Their essentialism also permitted them to view Dakota culture with an anthropological detachment. For the Lac qui Parle missionaries, the idea of replicating all aspects of secular Euroamerican culture among the Dakotas was unthinkable. The salvation that the Lac qui Parle missionaries offered the Dakotas did not depend on their assimilation. Just as the missionaries' faith had taken them outside of their own society, they delivered to the Dakotas the message that Christianity superseded secular culture, whether Euroamerican or Dakota. They won a few adherents—mostly métis and women whose marriages to fur traders had partly estranged them from the Dakota community. For these outliers of Dakota society, the mission church offered the comfort of social integration.

Whether they recognized it or not, the Lac qui Parle missionaries joined in the ongoing negotiation between cultures in the borderlands. Like the fur traders before them, the missionaries found themselves enveloped in obligations to the Dakota community. It was an envelopment that the missionaries—seeking refuge from the temptations of secular Euroamerican culture—welcomed. For a few years, the Dakotas and the missionaries found a common mission: maintaining the autonomy of Lac qui Parle. It was by no means a perfect arrangement but both Indians and missionaries knew it to be better than incorporation into Euroamerican society. After 1850, however, the trickle of Euroamerican settlers turned into a torrent, overwhelming the delicate balance that had sustained these cultural negotiations between missionaries and Dakotas.

NOTES

1. Stephen R. Riggs, *Mary and I: Forty Years with the Sioux* (Chicago, 1880), p. 15.

2. See Robert F. Berkhofer, *Salvation and the Savage: An Analysis of Protestant Missions and American Indian Response, 1787–1862* (Louisville, Ky., 1962); Virgil J. Vogel, "The Missionary as Acculturation Agent: Peter Dougherty and the Indians of Grand Traverse," *Michigan History* 51 (Fall 1967): 185–201. Berkhofer drew heavily on G. Gordon Brown, "Missions and Cultural Diffusion," *American Journal of Sociology* 50 (November 1944): 214–19. See also Henry Warner Bowden, *American Indians and Christian Missions: Studies in Cultural Conflict* (Chicago, 1981); Robert H. Jackson and Edward Castillo, *Indians, Franciscans, and Colonization: The Impact of the Mission System on California Indians* (Albuquerque, N.Mex., 1995). There is a small counterinterpretation emphasizing Indian cultural adaptability and the open-mindedness of certain missionary groups, particularly Jesuits and Pietists, who are depicted as exceptions to the rule. These studies are typified by James Ronda, "Generations of Faith: The Christian Indians of Martha's Vineyard," *William and Mary Quarterly,* 3d ser., 38 (1981): 369–94; Jane T. Merritt, "Dreaming of the Savior's Blood: Moravians and the Indian Great Awakening in Pennsylvania," ibid., 54 (October 1997): 723–46; William G. McLoughlin, *Champions of the Cherokees: Evan and John B. Jones* (Princeton, N.J., 1990); James Axtell, "Were Indian Conversions *Bona Fide?*" in *After Columbus: Essays in the Ethnohistory of Colonial North America* (New York, 1989).

3. Roy W. Meyer, *History of the Santee Sioux: United States Indian Policy on Trial* (Lincoln, Neb., 1967), p. 53; Gary C. Anderson, *Kinsmen of Another Kind: Dakota-White Relations in the Upper Mississippi Valley, 1650–1862* (Lincoln, Neb., 1984). See also Bruce Forbes, "Evangelization and Acculturation among the Santee Dakota Indians, 1834–1864" (Ph.D. diss., Princeton University, 1977), p. 1.

4. Samuel W. Pond, *The Dakota or Sioux in Minnesota as They Were in 1834* (St. Paul, 1986). Pond wrote this study between 1865 and 1875; it was originally published in *Collections of the Minnesota Historical Society,* 12 (1908): 319–501. Riggs, *Dakota Grammar, Texts, and Ethnography,* ed. James Owen Dorsey, Contributions to North American Ethnology, vol. 9 (Washington, D.C., 1893). Riggs completed a draft of the study before his death in 1883. For a definition of ethnohistory, see James Axtell, *The European and the Indian: Essays in the Ethnohistory of Colonial North America* (New York, 1981), pp. 3–15.

5. Richard White, *The Middle Ground: Indians, Empires, and Republics in the Great Lakes Region, 1650–1815* (New York, 1991), pp. 51–93. Gideon Pond was ready to quit in 1838. See Gideon Pond to Rebecca Hines, 27 September 1838, and to Ruth Pond, 21 October 1838, Pond Brothers Papers, Minnesota Historical Society, St. Paul, Minnesota (hereafter MHS). For an overview of the Lac qui Parle community, see Charles M. Gates, "The Lac qui Parle Indian Mission," *Minnesota History* 16 (June 1935): 133–51; Jon Willand, *Lac qui Parle and the Dakota Mission* (Madison, Minn., 1964); Donald Dean Parker, *Lac qui Parle: Its Missionaries, Traders, and Indians* (Brookings, S.Dak., 1964); Theodore C. Blegen, "The Pond Brothers," *Minnesota History* 15 (September 1934): 273–81; Gertrude Ackermann, "Joseph Renville of Lac qui Parle," ibid., 12 (1931): 231–46.

6. Paul E. Johnson, *A Shopkeeper's Millenium: Society and Revivals in Rochester, New York, 1815–1837* (New York, 1978), p. 9. For migration from New England, see Alan Taylor, *William Cooper's Town: Power and Persuasion in the Early Republic* (New York, 1995); Susan E. Gray, *The Yankee West: Community Life on the Michigan Frontier* (Chapel Hill, N.C., 1996), pp. 119–38.

7. Eli Lundy Huggins, "Boyhood Reminiscences of General Huggins," Alexander G. Huggins Papers, MHS. Maida Leonard Riggs, ed., *A Small Bit of Bread and Butter: Letters from the Dakota Territory, 1832–1869* (South Deerfield, Mass., 1996), pp. iii–v. Stephen Riggs, *Mary and I,* p. 4; Samuel W. Pond Jr., *Two Volunteer Missionaries among the Dakotas* (Boston, 1893), p. 13.

8. Berkhofer, *Salvation and the Savage,* p. 1; Michael Coleman, *Presbyterian Missionary Attitudes toward American Indians* (Jackson, Miss., 1985), pp. 9–11; Ronald G. Walters, *American Reformers, 1815–1860* (New York, 1978), p. 31.

9. Gideon Pond to Ruth Pond, 21 October 1838, Pond Brothers Papers, MHS.

10. See, for instance, Johnson, *A Shopkeeper's Millenium.*

11. For the attempt to reestablish a form of the patriarchal social norms of the eighteenth century in a religious response to the market revolution, see Paul Johnson and Sean Wilentz, *The Kingdom of Matthias* (New York, 1994), pp. 3–11.

12. Weber defined otherworldly asceticism as "a radical ethico-religious critique of the relationship to society. . . . Not only do the simple, 'natural' virtues within the world not guarantee salvation, but they actually place salvation in hazard. . . . The 'world' in a religious sense . . . is a realm of temptations. . . . Concentration upon the actual pursuit of salvation may entail a formal withdrawal from the 'world': from social and psychological

ties with family, from the possession of worldly goods, and from political, social, and erotic activities." Max Weber, *Economy and Society: An Outline of Interpretive Sociology,* vol. 2 (New York, 1968), p. 528.

13. Samuel Pond's Narrative, vol. 1, Pond Brothers Papers, MHS.

14. Samuel Pond, Galena, Illinois, to Gideon Pond, Washington, Connecticut, 6 October 1833, Pond Brothers Papers, MHS.

15. Gideon Pond Diary, 1 July 1837, 18 July 1837, and 30 June 1838, Pond Brothers Papers, MHS.

16. Thomas S. Williamson to Gideon Pond, 24 February 1840, Pond Brothers Papers, MHS.

17. Samuel Pond to Gideon Pond, 6 October 1833, Pond Brothers Papers, MHS.

18. Stephen Riggs, *Mary and I,* pp. 12–13. Mary Riggs likewise called St. Louis a "depot of iniquity." Mary Riggs to Martha Longley, 10 May 1837), in Maida Leonard Riggs, *A Small Bit of Bread and Butter,* pp. 27–28.

19. Weber, *Economy and Society,* 2:528.

20. Williamson, "Planting the Gospel in Minnesota among the Dakotas," Thomas Smith Williamson and Family Papers, MHS.

21. Walters, *American Reformers,* p. 40.

22. Stephen Riggs, "In Memory of Rev. Thomas S. Williamson, M.D.," New York *Evangelist,* 17 July 1879.

23. Stephen Riggs, *Mary and I,* p. 15.

24. Samuel Pond to Dr. Fowler, May 1834, Pond Brothers Papers, MHS.

25. Stephen Riggs, "Journal of a Tour from Lac-qui-Parle to the Missouri River," *Missionary Herald,* April 1841.

26. Williamson to Samuel Pond, 23 September 1840, Pond Brothers Papers, MHS. See also Williamson, "The Indian Tribes, and the Duty of the Government to Them," *American Presbyterian and Theological Review* 13 (1864): 593.

27. Herbert E. Bolton, "Defensive Spanish Expansion and the Significance of the Borderlands," in *Bolton and the Spanish Borderlands,* ed. John Francis Bannon (Norman, Okla., 1964), pp. 32–64. Jeremy Adelman and Stephen Aron, "From Borderlands to Borders: Empires, Nation-States, and the Peoples in Between in North American History," *American Historical Review* 104 (June 1999): 814–41.

28. Janet Spector and Eldern Johnson, eds., *Archeology, Ecology, and Ethnohistory of the Prairie-Forest Border Zone of Minnesota and Manitoba* (Lincoln, Neb., 1985).

29. W. Raymond Wood, "Plains Trade in Prehistoric and Protohistoric Intertribal Relations," in *Anthropology on the Great Plains,* ed. W. Raymond Wood and Margot Liberty (Lincoln, Neb., 1980), pp. 98–109.

30. Jacqueline Peterson, "Many Roads to Red River: Métis Genesis in the Great Lakes Region, 1680–1815," in *The New Peoples: Being and Becoming Métis in North America,* ed. Jacqueline Peterson and Jennifer H. Brown (Lincoln, Neb., 1985), p. 63.

31. Samuel Pond, *The Dakota,* pp. 17–18.

32. Renville was what cultural historians have termed a "cultural broker," an individual who bridged gaps between cultures. See Daniel K. Richter, "Cultural Brokers and Intercultural Politics: New York–Iroquois Relations, 1664–1701," *Journal of American History* 75 (1988): 40–67. For the woodland fur trade and "social kinship," see Anderson, *Kinsmen of Another Kind,* pp. x–xii, 51, 58–76, 95. For "social kinship," see Ella C. Deloria, *Speaking of Indians* (New York, 1944), pp. 24–26. For women in the fur trade, see Sylvia Van Kirk, "The Role of Native Women in the Creation of Fur Trade Society in Western Canada, 1670–1830," in *The Women's West,* ed. Susan Armitage and Elizabeth Jameson (Norman, Okla., 1987), pp. 53–62.

33. Samuel Pond, *The Dakota,* pp. 26–31; Meyer, *History of the Santee Sioux,* pp. 20–23; Anderson, *Kinsmen of Another Kind,* pp. 2–7.

34. Charles H. Keating, *Narrative of an Expedition to the Sources of the St. Peter's River* (Minneapolis, 1959), pp. 302–3.

35. Richard White, "The Winning of the West: The Expansion of the Western Sioux in the Eighteenth and Nineteenth Centuries," *Journal of American History* 65 (September 1978): 319–43.

36. Amos J. Bruce, *Report of the Commissioner for Indian Affairs* (St. Peter's Agency, S. doc. 1, 27th Cong., 3d Sess., Serial 413, pp. 427–31).

37. Alexander Huggins, 18 January 1838), Huggins Papers, MHS.

38. Gideon Pond to Ruth Pond, 21 October 1838, Pond Brothers Papers, MHS.

39. Ackermann, "Joseph Renville of Lac qui Parle," p. 238.

40. Bruce, *Report of the Commissioner for Indian Affairs,* Serial 413, pp. 427–31.

41. Stephen Riggs, "The Dakota Mission," *Collections of the Minnesota Historical Society* 3 (1870–80): 119.

42. Samuel Pond Jr., *Two Volunteer Missionaries,* p. 37. For a discussion of the missionaries and agriculture, see Gates, "Lac qui Parle Indian Mission," p. 138.

43. Bruce, *Report of the Commissioner for Indian Affairs,* Serial 413, pp. 427–31.

44. Samuel Pond, *The Dakota,* pp. 140–53.

45. Stephen Riggs, *Tah-koo Wah-kan, or, The Gospel Among the Dakotas* (Boston, 1869), pp. 176–77.

46. For Stephen Riggs's domestic labors, see Mary Riggs to Martha Longley, 31 July 1837, in Maida Leonard Riggs, *A Small Bit of Bread and Butter*, p. 43. According to John Mack Faragher, a man who milked a cow in nineteenth-century rural America was held in "supreme contempt." See Faragher, *Women and Men on the Overland Trail* (New Haven, Conn., 1979), p. 51.

47. Riggs, "The Dakota Mission," pp. 118–22.

48. Williamson to Gideon Pond, 24 February 1840, Pond Brothers Papers, MHS.

49. See Berkhofer, "Protestants, Pagans, and Sequences among North American Indians, 1760–1860," *Ethnohistory* 10 (Summer 1963): 201. Richard White recycled the idea of permissive acculturation as his dominant motif in *Middle Ground*.

50. For Whitman, see Patricia Limerick, *Legacy of Conquest: The Unbroken Past of the American West* (New York, 1987), p. 40. For the Cherokee mission, see McLoughlin, *Champions of the Cherokees*; for the Choctaws, see W. David Baird, "Cyrus Byington and the Presbyterian Choctaw Mission," in *Churchmen and the Western Indians, 1820–1920,* ed. Clyde Milner and Floyd O'Neil (Norman, Okla., 1985), pp. 19–40.

51. Stephen Riggs, *Mary and I,* p. 51.

52. See Deloria, *Speaking of Indians.*

53. Mary Riggs to Thomas and Martha Longley, 15 December 1837, in Maida Leonard Riggs, *A Small Bit of Bread and Butter*, p. 58.

54. Stephen Riggs, *Mary and I,* p. 51.

55. Mary Riggs to Thomas and Martha Longley, 22 March 1839, and to Moses Longley, 10 July 1851, in Maida Leonard Riggs, *A Small Bit of Bread and Butter*, pp. 92, 205.

56. Williamson, "The Indian Question," *Presbyterian Quarterly and Princeton Review*, n.s. 5 (October 1876): 613, 619. In this respect, the Lac qui Parle mission resembled Evan and John Jones's work among the Cherokee; they, too, labored to translate their message into the Indians' native language. See McLoughlin, *Champions of the Cherokees,* pp. 35–40.

57. Peter Garrioch Journal, 1837–41, MHS.

58. Samuel Pond's Narrative, vol. 1, Pond Brothers Papers, MHS.

59. Samuel Pond, "Two Missionaries in the Sioux Country," ed. Theodore Blegen, *Minnesota History* 21 (1940): 28.

60. Stephen Riggs, "Journal of a Tour from Lac-qui-Parle to the Missouri River," p. 330.

61. Samuel Pond to Ruth Pond, 7 January 1840, Pond Brothers Papers, MHS. For the missionaries' efforts to learn Dakota, see Williamson to Samuel Pond, 28 May 1840, Pond Brothers Papers, MHS.

62. Stephen Riggs, *Mary and I*, p. 75.

63. See William K. Powers, *Oglala Religion* (Lincoln, Neb., 1975), p. 91.

64. Stephen Riggs, *Mary and I*, pp. 50–51.

65. Gideon Pond Diary, 14 August 1837, Pond Brothers Papers, MHS.

66. Samuel Pond's Narrative, vol. 1, Pond Brothers Papers, MHS.

67. Stephen Riggs, *Dakota Grammar, Texts, and Ethnography*, pp. 150–51.

68. Andrew C. Isenberg, *The Destruction of the Bison: An Environmental History, 1750–1920* (New York, 2000), pp. 85–86.

69. Samuel Pond Memoirs, vol. 1, Pond Brothers Papers, MHS.

70. See Mary Riggs to Thomas and Martha Longley, 22 March 1839, and to Martha Longley, 22 April 1839, in Maida Leonard Riggs, *A Small Bit of Bread and Butter*, pp. 92, 97.

71. Stephen Riggs, *Tah-koo Wah-kan*, pp. 143–44.

72. Gideon Pond to Rebecca Hines, 27 September 1838, Huggins Papers, MHS.

73. Williamson, "Planting the Gospel in Minnesota," Williamson Papers, MHS.

74. For Riggs's endorsement of Toteedootawin's faith, see Stephen Riggs to Samuel and Gideon Pond, 28 December 1838, Pond Brothers Papers, MHS. See also Stephen Riggs, "Dakota Portraits," *Minnesota History* 2 (1918): 481–568. For a description of the Sacred Dance, see Samuel Pond, *The Dakota*, pp. 93–96; Gideon Pond, "Dakota Superstitions," *Collections of the Minnesota Historical Society* 2 (1860–67): 222–28; Stephen Riggs, *Dakota Grammar, Texts, and Ethnology*, pp. 227–29.

75. Williamson, "Planting the Gospel in Minnesota," Williamson Papers, MHS.

76. Theodore Blegen, *Minnesota: A History of the State* (St. Paul, Minn., 1975), p. 173.

77. Williamson, "Planting the Gospel in Minnesota," Williamson Papers, MHS.

78. Winifred W. Barton, *John P. Williamson: A Brother to the Sioux* (New York, 1919), pp. 44–45.

79. Samuel Pond Jr., *Two Volunteer Missionaries*, p. 58.

10

TICKETS, CONCERTS AND SCHOOL FEES
MONEY AND NEW CHRISTIAN COMMUNITIES IN
COLONIAL ZIMBABWE, 1900–1940

CAROL SUMMERS

Today, Zimbabwe can be referred to as a Christian country. This does not mean that every individual is a committed believer. Instead, it implies a change in dominant cultural connections and their ideological significance from the complex and varied patterns of precolonial, pre-Christian Zimbabwe, to a new and equally complex mosaic of personal belief and institutional practice in which Christianity, in one form or another, is normative. This change—a sort of communal conversion—happened during the first half of the twentieth century, especially during the period from 1908 to 1945. During these years, the African majority of Zimbabwe increasingly accepted, and began to rely on, Christian institutions, models of leadership, charisma, and spiritual authority, and on a mission- and education-centered vision of a progressive future.

Along the path to this communal transformation, some individuals experienced personal spiritual transformations, and some worked in creative ways to connect Christianity to older forms of religion, incorporating mediums, ancestors, and rain.[1] Yet despite the existence of individuals with deeply spiritual personal conversions and others who pursued inculturation strategies, the early twentieth century was characterized principally by the power of very conventional, institution-building, mission-centered models of Christianity. At least in the early years, it was the conventional Christianity that grew, sometimes pulled into new villages and regions by African activists even faster than the European missionary leadership could push their preachers, schools, and institutional leadership. Missionaries were daunted by the demands African activists put on the missions as community spokesmen requested schools, evangelist/teachers, and mission affiliation.

It is worth exploring how this new identity emerged. In standard mission history narratives, European missionaries emphasized their own role and that of God, appealing for more funds from Europe and America within a heroic evangelical narrative which characterized missionaries as pioneers harvesting African people, like ripe grain, for Jesus. This theme has been echoed by African church historians who have tended to focus on church leadership and the ways officials overcame challenges and built institutions.[2] More recently, anthropologists and historians have emphasized how communities under pressure from colonial contact, conquest, and institutionalization found in Christianity a way of shaping the trajectory and consequences of the forces pushing for change.[3] But instead of following or simply critiquing these standard narratives, I offer here another, potentially more polyvalent, somewhat more impressionistic, image of how people and their communities became Christians. In this essay, I explore the symbolic and sacramental ways missionaries, preachers, believers, and officials in colonial Zimbabwe marked out a new Christian world through cash payments.

To explore the connections between money and Christian identity and meaning, I narrow my focus to the British Wesleyan mission and its adherents. This mission and the churches it sponsored have left behind accessible records not merely in Britain, but also in Zimbabwe, two bodies of mission records which differ in significant ways but, together, provide glimpses of not merely the planning and planting of mission activity, but also the processes and prospects of grassroots growth and the weeds of dissent. And the Wesleyans were neither the most nor the least successful of the missions active in Southern Rhodesia during the difficult years of the 1920s and 1930s. Instead, they were entirely ordinary and mainstream.[4]

By looking closely at money in this mission, it is possible to begin to sort out what happened during the critical years of mission institutionalization, community transformation, and the construction of a new relationship between Christians and the state. Money—getting it, spending it and auditing it—was central to Zimbabweans' construction of this new world. I do not propose a strict materialistic functionalism. Instead, I suggest that in the boom and bust (and mostly bust) economy of interwar Southern Rhodesia, where segregation intensified Africans' understandings of what they did not have and were increasingly barred from getting, money was critically important not merely as a way of surviving, but as a way of defining individual identity and status and pursuing community values. James Ferguson has suggested that cultures, particularly cultures in the midst of change, are complex, and may be best understood not by general questions regarding belief or assumptions, but by the concrete signs and objects that congeal these changes, at least momentarily. "Publicly exhibited signs," he emphasizes, provide possibilities of insight into processes otherwise "fundamentally unstatable."[5] Hats, coats, shoes, and books have marked out change—in highly ambiguous ways—for observers from early African and European witnesses to present-day historians and anthropologists.[6] Money—the cash that could buy these commodities, pay tribute or taxes, or go in a variety of other directions combining either selectively or promiscuously with funds from other sources—marked off change by its existence as congealed value, and through its transfer as tithing money, enthusiastic concert contributions, and dedicated payments for future schooling. It provides an important beginning point in our analysis of new Christian identities not simply because of what it did or what people did with it, but because it was central to a wide variety of debates, and points us toward significant meanings and images. In a discussion of the historical anthropology of money, Maurice Bloch and Jonathan Parry have suggested that historians and anthropologists have often viewed money as an impersonal form of value which, as it comes into circulation, draws a distinction between the earlier personal economic interactions of a traditional world, and the abstract and impersonal transfers of a newly modern world.[7] But in colonial Zimbabwe, money was scarce, and far from impersonal. Instead, in earning it, spending it, and donating it, Zimbabweans attached money to people (e.g. her bridewealth, his tax money, their school fees) and marked out new types of relationships and identities. Thus, by following discussions and fights over money in the Wesleyan Methodist churches of interwar Southern Rhodesia, we can track a changing community, and begin to sort out the mechanisms and meanings of its transformations.

HISTORICAL CONTEXT

Around 1908, after the conquest, the Ndebele and Chimurenga wars, and the South African War, the British South Africa Company—and its mission allies and critics—launched the expensive work of systematic administration in what was then Southern Rhodesia. For missions, one of the most significant markers of the new system of governance was the Order D of 1908, providing for administrative funding of mission schools based on school type and enrollment. Missions combined this source of money with land grants and resources contributed both from abroad and locally. These funds provided an incentive and the monetary means for missions' institutional and evangelical activities to spread rapidly. Even in 1923, when a new settler government established "responsible government"—local self-rule based on a very limited electorate of literate property holders—the administration continued to fund missions as principal providers of education, health, and social services to Africans, and missions grew. Many Africans flocked to missions, sought education, and embraced Christianity as they tried to establish themselves in the new society as something more than simple downtrodden workers. These new Christians considered themselves civilized men who might eventually benefit from Cecil Rhodes's widely publicized slogan "equal rights for all civilized men south of the Zambezi." Mission institutions—-simultaneously churches and schools—-were the centers of new Christians' identities. These men succeeded so well in differentiating themselves from the masses and claiming a new status that by 1930, as the Depression shattered the Southern Rhodesian economy, white leaders reacted to Africans' successes by shifting state policies from tacitly racist (assuming that Africans could not challenge white power) to aggressively segregationist (knowing and fearing Africans did challenge white dominance, and trying to obstruct Africans' initiatives). Worried settlers increasingly deployed the state to limit Africans' economic and social opportunities through the Land Apportionment Act, restrictions in education and social funding, job reservation, etc. This context, increasingly polarized, racialized and tense, supported active, sometimes frenetic, church-building efforts not simply by missionaries, but by Africans who saw Christianity, or at least mission resources, as providing ways to shape these restrictions into something survivable.[8]

Missions in Southern Rhodesia operated in a competitive and crowded environment. Climate and government support, in an atmosphere of hopes (not always fulfilled) for rapid economic development, helped create a region full of rival missionary organizations. Though the government regulated this competition to a limited degree, requiring that mission schools in rural areas be at least three miles apart, it facilitated missions' growth and competition by providing limited funding and land leases for schools and education. By the 1930s, missions in Southern Rhodesia included those of the Catholic Jesuits, Dominican Sisters, and Trappist Fathers, and of Protestants ranging from the congregationalist and low church American Board and London Missionary Society, through the Church of England, with theologically more marginal groups such as the Salvation Army, Seventh Day Adventists, Dutch Reformed Church, and Pentecostalist Apostolics sharing in the mission boom. Even the Methodists were split between the British-sponsored Wesleyan Methodists, the American-sponsored Methodist Episcopals, the schismatic Primitive Methodists, and a variety of African Methodist Episcopal new churches.

Most mission centers were on mission farms where the missions leased land to tenant farmers, often insisted on mandatory school attendance, and could enforce a church-dominated disciplinary system outside the state.

Central stations anchored "circuits" of schools and churches staffed by African teachers and evagelists. Wesleyan Methodist missions which fit this model included Tegwani (on the railway line in Matebeleland), Nengubo/Waddilove (near Marandellas, in a prime High Veldt settler farming area), and Epworth (outside the rapidly growing regional capital of Salisbury). Each of these circuits was in an area of intensive economic change. Other circuits, such as Wedza (more closely tied to peasant agriculture) and Selukwe and Gatooma (near mining development) were not as prosperous, and did not receive as much investment in educational and physical development as the three main circuits. Wesleyan Methodism began and remained closely tied to urban and industrial development. South African Mfengu leaders pushed its early growth, and both at Waddilove and Tegwani, institutes classified by the government as "first class schools" trained local young men as workers for the new settler-dominated economy. From the earliest years of the mission, schools and stations expanded specifically into areas with African patrons able to pay for teachers and construction costs. And schools and churches closed when communities failed to make their pledges, whether because parents disapproved of a specific teacher, or because economic downturns had destroyed cash reserves.[9] Truly poor or distant areas were left out of the mission boom until much later.[10]

MISSIONS AND MONEY

Missions and mission churches often had problematic relationships with money. Missionaries almost invariably perceived themselves as self-sacrificing and starved of the funds essential to their lives and work. They portrayed themselves as spiritually rich, but materially poor, and encouraged their followers to be likewise. Abel Muzorewa, for example, born into a devout Methodist family, remembered growing up singing hymns asserting "I don't want much money" and calling for believers to "Take the name of Jesus in all your poverty."[11] New mission adherents, on the other hand, frequently looked not at what missionaries said about the need for new funds, but at the resources missionaries seemed to command not just spiritually, but in the intensely materialistic sense of cloth, sweets, and cash. This unequal relationship was a fundamental root of much mission success, as it provided inquirers with sensible, concrete reasons to pay attention to missionaries' more spiritually based appeals. Cynics, indeed, may argue that materialism and monetary advantage have been basic to Christianity's appeal to generations of Africans seeking to make survival, profits, and selves out of a challenging colonial and postcolonial context. Muzorewa himself, despite his years of hymn singing, rejected what he saw as the missionaries' "pie in the sky by and by" emphasis on self-sacrifice. Instead, he noted that he and the other men he trained with found more appealing those programs aimed at producing material results. "The crops which our parents sold to buy clothes and bicycles and to pay our school fees—were these not also blessings from God?" Muzorewa asked rhetorically, going on to emphasize a "whole gospel for the whole man that would speak to what was going on in the day-to-day life of our people."[12]

As a type of Christianity which emphasized Bible reading, Wesleyan Methodism would have exposed neophyte Christians not merely to the material civilization of settler life, as lived by British missionaries and observed by young men employed in homes, townships, and mines as they earned their tuition and tax money, but also to the more radical observations and prescriptions of Scripture, such as:

> Lay not up for yourselves treasures upon earth . . . but lay up for yourselves treasures in heaven. . . . For where your treasure is, there will your heart be also. . . . I say unto you, take no thought for your life, what ye shall eat or what ye shall drink, nor yet for your body, what ye shall put on. . . . Behold the fowls of the air; neither do they sow nor reap nor gather. . . . Consider the lilies of the field. . . . they toil not neither do they spin. . . . seek ye first the kingdom of God and his righteousness, and all these things shall be added unto you. (Matthew 6:19–33)[13]

Yet while white missionaries might understand themselves as providing, through lives of sacrificial service to Zimbabweans, a literal reading of this admonition, local Christians appear to have extracted an entirely different meaning. "Treasures," earthly and spiritual, were too closely entwined to disentangle in the local institutions and spiritual manifestations of faith. Thus, local Christians wore jackets, paid for hymnals, took jobs with regular salaries that supported both their secular and church obligations, and celebrated enthusiastically with song and contributions when God provided the necessary funds to the people and church. They sought to lay up treasure in heaven through individually and communally collecting money on earth. In becoming Christians, Africans in Southern Rhodesia converted not just to a faith, but to a pattern of monetized materialism, in which they marked out the new community of the present in the coins of ticket money and concert contributions, and prayed for a new future through their children's school fees.

Though the mission church sponsored this monetized transformation, and pushed it on when individual preachers or believers sought different ideas of faith, this monetized Christianity, again as Scripture suggested, carried its own drawbacks: "'Verily I say unto you, that a rich man shall hardly enter the kingdom of heaven. And again I say unto you, It is easier for a camel to go through the eye of a needle than for a rich man to enter into the kingdom of God.' When the disciples heard this they were exceedingly amazed, saying 'Who then can be saved?'"(Matthew 19:3–25). While new Christians were hardly rich, they certainly sought wealth. And the school system, with its hope of civilized status and higher wages, was the key to this much-wanted transformation. As the school system was increasingly funded and regulated by the administration, its intimate tie with the Christian community was undermined. As parents and students pursued Christian-style prosperity by investing in education, schools desperate for funds accepted increased levels of government control, and parents and students increasingly lost control over mission schools. By the 1940s, schools, funded but twisted under segregationist regulations, could no longer provide a straightforward entry into the hoped-for future on earth or heaven.[14]

Money and wealth determined where in a region Methodists evangelized, and three central issues in Wesleyan mission Christianity during the 1920s and 1930s—tickets, that is, receipts for payment of church membership fees, concerts, and school fees—provide points of entry illuminating various aspects of Wesleyan Methodists' Christianity and communities. Through these three issues, we can explore the meanings of money to Christian belief and institutional affiliation in the 1920s and 1930s in Southern Rhodesia. Tickets, mandatory for church members, conveying membership in a participatory form of church governance and producing an audited, regulated pool of locally raised money, were central to the institutionalization of Wesleyan churches in the region. Concerts, enthusiastic fund-raisers planned and coordinated by ambitious and organized African evangelists, producing inspirational moments, were part of the charismatic and unaudited authority of individual African church leaders. And school fees constituted the mission and the people's payments for a future, negotiated with the government, within the rules of a segregationist administration.

MISSION ORGANIZATIONAL BACKGROUND

Like the other government-recognized missions of Southern Rhodesia, the Wesleyans worked within a set of administrative regulations that demanded white oversight. Fearful of the political and military implications of independent African churches, the government demanded such oversight and authority at each level of mission and school. White missionaries accepted this requirement that they maintain the last word in the new churches, schools, and institutions they worked to build. They met separately from African ministers and lay leaders, and elected white missionary representatives to the interdenominational Southern Rhodesian Missionary Conference, which both cooperated with and lobbied the administration on African social policy issues. More parochially, white missionaries were automatically part of the interracial synods that constituted the official governing body of the local church. Unofficially, they dominated these meetings. Below the level of the synod, Wesleyan activity was divided into circuits, each under the supervision of a minister. Since these circuits were circuits of schools, as well as churches, and the government demanded that a white missionary be in charge of inspecting schools and auditing attendance records, each was headed by a white missionary. From the perspective of white missionaries and the government, the Wesleyan Methodist church in Southern Rhodesia was a formal structure directed by missionaries, paternalistically working for the benefit of Africans. When the Southern Rhodesian Missionary Conference defended Africans against egregious tax increases or objected to the Land Apportionment Act, missionaries spoke as white paternalists, not as delegates of their discontented African population. Missionaries' salaries, and ultimately their loyalties, were seen by them, and by the administration, as coming from Britain and the British church.

But to understand the Wesleyan church in Southern Rhodesia, it is essential to look below the level of missionary councils, synods, and circuits to the centers of local Christian life, the churches that were also schools. This double status was not an accident: the evangelists and local preachers who coordinated Sunday activities were teachers during the week, and the Sunday church sanctuary was used as the weekday schoolroom. Preachers were even admonished to make sure they held active Sunday school meetings as well as praise and worship services, and student attendance at Sunday worship services was generally mandatory.[15] Practices within the space—attendance taking, singing, catechism, and Bible reading—also characterized both church and school. Those interested in Christianity, but not yet church members, were given labels with clear indications of the connections between school and religious practice: individuals began as "listeners," and moved up to become "readers," before being eligible for baptism and confirmation. They then became "members on trial," organized into "classes," each of which met for examinations of conscience and spiritual growth, as well as playing a role in church maintenance and governance. The structure paralleled the monitor structure used in nineteenth-century schools in England, which persisted in Southern Rhodesia, as more advanced pupils and Christians were employed to lead newer pupils and converts to higher levels. Without the school, there could be no church, as missionaries generally required literacy for baptism, confirmation, and church membership. In the Southern Rhodesian context, however, the most important characteristic of this grassroots Christianity was that it constructed and institutionalized an African community of believers that white missionaries visited, but where they did not belong. Each of the various forms of membership in this local African Christian community was marked out by the regular and public payment of money.

During the week, the local teacher/preacher would supervise a schoolroom of 20 to 150 students probably in First Year, substandards A and B, and maybe also Standard I. (Standard I was approximately equal to U.S. third grade, and introduced English-language teaching.) Large schools frequently supported an assistant teacher as well as the teacher in charge. The teacher and his wife could legally cultivate up to five acres around the school, with part of that designated as the "school garden," worked on by students and their parents by the students as part of their industrial education, and by the parents as a form of tuition payment. And students were responsible for school fees. At least four times a year, the school would be visited by the white missionary school superintendent, who would check to ensure that the attendance register had been kept, audit school accounts, examine students, and listen to their singing.[16]

On Sundays, the school building would be transformed into a church. Evangelists and Local Preachers, licensed and with paid-up tickets from the Methodist mission, would preach and lead the congregation in a worship service which could go on for hours, with several sermons. Women's groups would have a separate women's association meeting, and women both purchased the physical markers of their association—the red blouses of respectable women, for example—and paid a regular membership fee. Women, men, youths, and girls would have separate "class" meetings at which they would study the Bible, talk about their spiritual lives, and collect and record church contributions, whether "ticket money" or "free will offerings." Individual evangelists and church activists also founded additional societies that evangelized, and helped with the day-to-day maintenance of church facilities.[17] And each quarter, probably combining church visits with school inspections, an ordained minister would come by, meet with members and delegates in a quarterly meeting, check members' tickets, and administer sacraments, such as communion, baptism, and confirmation, to those who qualified.

In practice, therefore, rather than accepting the top-down vision of the African church as a white-led paternalistic institution given from on high, local Wesleyan Christians were expected to see schools, churches, class meetings, local preachers, class leaders who monitored ticket money, delegates elected to synods, and an intricate social web of women's groups and student choirs as their own community's church. This vision was somewhat convincing even in the face of white power and a segregationist administration because members, holding their tickets and taking pride in their voting rights in synods and meetings, linked money, voice, and control.

TICKETS

Tickets were the central concrete objects that provided a focus for the participatory and democratic features of this African church. The word "ticket" has a variety of meanings in Southern African English. In the most common usage, a "ticket" was a work-related document. Men would accept or be forced into a contract to work for six tickets of, for example, thirty days. Sometimes referred to as a six-month work contract, this was nothing of the kind. An employer only marked an employee's ticket when the day's task was done to his satisfaction. Sickness, rest days, broken tools, inefficient work, or temperamental and stingy employers, all could lead to a worker's not getting his ticket signed for the day. The ticket was seen as a means for employers to exercise control and quality assurance over a difficult work force.[18] This, however, was not what the church meant by the word. A secondary meaning of the word ticket implies the token of payment for transport or admission to entertainment. But church members would probably have rejected this interpretation of the church tickets as well.

Instead, Wesleyan tickets marked off regular payment of the quarterly "class money" that provided the basis of a self-supporting and self-governing African church. In Rhodesia, however, the ticket system was also the mechanism through which membership in not merely a bureaucratic church structure, but God's community itself, was defined. Membership was not a function of belief alone; even the sacrament of communion became contingent on the believer's ability to pay, and pay on schedule, in money rather than cattle or work.[19]

From at least 1913 onward, membership in a Wesleyan church had implied the regular payment of quarterly fees. These were generally collected at big, celebratory services when a minister, either European or African, visited the service to check tickets, audit accounts, administer sacraments, and chair the quarterly meeting. This linked money, sacrament, and community not just conceptually, but temporally and in a very concrete way as a congregation effectively paid for communion. In 1913, payments were set at sixpence per member per quarter. By the 1920s, Epworth charged one shilling a quarter for rural members and two shillings a quarter for those in towns.[20] By the 1930s, as the government cut back on its funding for teachers' salaries, some African ministers pushed for ticket money to be raised to two shillings per quarter regardless of location.[21] This money covered the basics. Additional sacraments, baptisms, and Christian marriage were subject to additional fees. In 1913, fees for baptism were only one shilling, and for Christian marriage, ten shillings, paid by the groom, but by 1941, Epworth charged six shillings for baptism.[22] Members were also pushed to pay contributions to the Annual Missionary Collection and other special collections.[23] Membership in the active church women's organization had a separate additional set of costs.[24] Under normal circumstances, the cost of tickets was relatively trivial, especially for wage earners who were generally making at least one to two pounds per month. But class money applied to all church members, men, women, and adolescents. The church did not offer remittances in times of hardship, falling commodity prices, or ongoing unemployment. Instead, during the financial crises of the 1920s and 1930s, the mission pushed for more systematic payment of ticket money.[25] Administrative decisions involving ticket money were guided explicitly by the needs of the church, not by believers' poverty or ability to pay.

Repeatedly, missionaries and ministers admonished local evangelists to collect ticket money systematically. African ministers and evangelists found that their mission superiors, the white missionaries who controlled staffing, salaries, and placements, judged them according to how effectively they managed to collect the ticket money.[26] Ministers' visits were closely associated with payment of money. In situations where this payment was seen as necessary rather than onerous, circuit quarterly meetings might even request more visits by European ministers to spur giving, or at least provide the ministers with a firsthand understanding of how congregations were sacrificing to pay.[27]

European missionaries emphasized ticket money not merely for its own sake, but as a sign that the congregations were committed to Christian lives and identities. The money was the key symbol of Africans' commitments and priorities, rather than primarily a resource for white missionary use and control. It was the basis for Wesleyan hopes of a self-supporting African church, as opposed to a church supported out of charitable contributions from abroad.[28] Missionary salaries, however, came from Britain, with government copayments for those who performed educational duties. The bulk of the money to operate and expand the Wesleyan churches/schools of the 1920s and 1930s came from the government, which effectively subcontracted almost all education for Africans out to missions that received government grants-in-aid in return for meeting certain minimal educational standards.

Ticket money was explicitly earmarked for African agency, and translated directly into salaries and resources for African ministers, evangelists, and local preachers. At sixpence per church member per quarter, an evangelist needed at least 120 paying members to fund a minimal salary of one pound per month. Few if any congregations were this large. And better-qualified evangelists and ministers asked for notably higher salaries, or found employment as teachers with other missions prepared to pay better wages.[29] Initially, the concept of a self-supporting, self-reliant, self-governing African church was something that European missionaries simply approved of on general principles. But during the late 1920s and throughout the 1930s, remittances from England decreased and government funding also became uncertain. As a result European missionaries did increasingly emphasize local fund-raising and the ideal of a self-supporting African church, and their own successes in maintaining and expanding the network of Wesleyan evangelism became increasingly contingent on Africans' payments. In 1929, for example, Reverend Hardaker "appealed for support from all evangelists and other workers in raising circuit funds . . . so that the work of God can proceed. . . . money *must* be raised by the people themselves—it is their work to help themselves . . . "[30] By the 1930s, rural circuits in need of money were engaging in complex maneuvers to transform local believers' agricultural efforts into the cash the system required. By 1931, the missionaries of the Nengubo circuit were acting as marketing agents for local maize so that growers could turn produce into cash.[31]

For European missionaries, who prized conversions and evangelical expansion above notions of quality and elite class formation, ticket money was an important symbol. But for African ministers and evangelists who were being judged according to how effectively they extracted and managed it, and whose salaries were being paid through ticket funds, tickets were an even more serious matter. One of the earliest and most dynamic African ministers of the region, Moses Mfazi, was dismissed primarily for his political views, but the excuse the missionaries gave was that his account books were unclear.[32] Reverend Esau Nemapare left the Methodists under similar circumstances.[33] And the same charge was used against Thompson Samkange, another early African minister.[34] For these men, ticket money became a form of tribute. Missionaries expected it, and when it was diverted to local congregational needs, or collected in an irregular fashion, it signaled the dangers and disloyalty of African church leaders acting outside mission guidelines.[35]

At lower levels within the church, mission employees resented missionaries' understanding of ticket money as a symbol of church loyalty and affiliation, rather than a sacrificial payment. Ministers who administered and guided circuits, but were not local church members, had the ticket requirement waived or received "free tickets" for their full time devotion to Christian activity. Missionaries insisted, however, that local preachers pay their ticket money and show their tickets at meetings and sacraments, setting a good example for the congregations, of which they were members, not superiors. These lower-level employees, however, local preachers who drew little or no salary and experienced serious financial difficulties during the Depression, argued that if European ministers did not pay ticket money, they, too, should be exempt as church leaders. Both European and African ministers tended to interpret this activism as disloyalty, a failure to deliver on a token payment which constituted a basic form of tribute and membership.[36] During the 1930s, quarterly meetings repeatedly forwarded resolutions for the reinstatement of salaries which missionaries had unilaterally cut under the financial strain of the Depression. By 1935, local preachers were refusing to take tickets, rejecting the most basic symbol of adherence to the church, and in some places calling for increased African authority within church governance, effectively suggesting that through unilateral salary reductions the mission had undermined their connection to the missionary leadership.[37]

Under pressure to collect money despite depression, crop failure, and lack of markets for agricultural commodities, classes began to use creative methods of collecting ticket funds. In areas where local traders had begun to refuse to pay cash for crops, offering only store credit, local churches became marketing agencies. Members were allowed to pay ticket money in grain and requested to do so at the beginning of the harvest in order to yield the best prices.[38] The synod even considered altering the Wesleyan rulebook to allow harvest payments to substitute for the four-times-yearly quarterly ticket money.[39] Other churches pushed members to either work on church market gardens, or set aside specific gardening plots of their own to grow produce to sell for church fees.[40] These, however, were local African initiatives at odds with the Wesleyan image of the church as a community of people who understood how to manage money and resources. White missionaries blocked local efforts to collect ticket money only once a year with the payment of all four quarters' contribution at harvest time. Though a logical move for people whose incomes were agrarian and annual, such a system would undermine the ongoing, ritually periodic nature of quarterly class money.

The most controversial aspect of this aggressive effort to collect ticket fees even in difficult times, though, was that tickets were enforced not merely by moral suasion or persuasive pleas, but by denial of the benefits of church membership. During the 1920s and 1930s, the mission increasingly purged the membership rolls of one-time members who failed to keep up their ticket money, as well as those who got caught with second wives, beer-brewing operations, or nonmarital affairs. Missionaries also used their veto over quarterly meeting resolutions to exclude church members who had failed to take tickets, whether through poverty or as acts of protest, from participation in the quarterly meetings, just as they ruled out of order efforts to rewrite mission attitudes toward marriage and alcohol. Missionaries and ministers were intransigent toward issues of both membership and sacraments. In 1933, Nengubo Circuit ruled that no one could take communion without showing their paid-up ticket to the minister officiating. Similar policies were apparently followed in other circuits as well. This restriction of the sacraments to those with money happened despite missionaries' and ministers' acknowledgment that under the poverty conditions of the Depression, ticket money was more than many people could afford.

In denying both the quarterly meeting vote and communion, the principal symbols of community and personal connection with God, the mission was making explicit the connection between money, the Christian community, and God. Those who paid gained access, and those who could not or would not pay were put out of the community and kept from approaching God. The connection between fees and God was particularly clear since in the parallel case of nonpayment of school fees, the mission ordered teachers to keep children in school all the same: it needed the government grant that was earned by attendance of a given number of students. Since God did not pay directly for those taking communion, however, nonpayers were turned away in a judgment parallel to the morally based turning away of adulterers, polygynists, beer brewers, and others who violated church rules.

CONCERTS

Tickets, though, and the organized, institutional apparatus that they supported, were not the only way to approach God, or to connect God and finance. By the 1920s, hard-pressed teacher-evangelists were experimenting with new fund-raisers that were under their own control, unaudited by unsympathetic European ministers. Concerts proved the most successful fund-raisers and community builders for the more energetic teachers of the

Wesleyan church.[41] From early in the mission encounter, music had been a major constituent of evangelization and school. Government inspectors, indeed, sometimes complained that even reading classes were a form of chanting. And these inspectors regularly made fun of the amount of time devoted to singing not merely in Shona or Sindebele, but also in some unintelligible version of English. Church services, too, were long, and involved not merely preaching, but also singing and general celebrations which could easily last five hours. Concerts of mission music as fund-raisers for specific churches and circuits, though, appear to have become prominent only in the 1920s, and grown essential to circuit finances in the 1930s.

The earliest records of fund-raising concerts I have found date to 1908, when someone coordinated an apparently successful occasion of this kind in Bulawayo.[42] Less systematic and controlled than other aspects of church life, concerts were not well recorded in mission records, and African teacher/evangelists may have actively concealed the scope of their activities as impresarios.[43] By the 1920s, though, evangelists were regularly holding concerts as fund-raisers. And as evangelists became increasingly organized, attending school, training sessions, and conventions together, they had increased opportunities to organize joint concerts. From Bulawayo, concerts spread to Epworth (just outside Salisbury), Nengubo, and beyond. Concerts were most effective when held near a labor center, where wage laborers would have actual cash to contribute to the choir they considered the best or to pay the concert coordinator to have their chosen choir sing for longer than the other groups.[44] Whatever side payments or embezzlement occurred, concerts made substantive contributions to circuit funds that became subject to auditing and accounting rules. Nengubo Circuit balanced its budget in the 1930s through concerts. In 1935, for example, desperate to stop a string of deficits, Nengubo Circuit had at least six concerts between 31 April and 6 July.[45]

Concerts raised substantial amounts of money, and missionaries therefore accepted them reluctantly. But they also had consequences. The evangelist-teachers who scheduled and coordinated the concerts sought to maximize revenue by holding them on Saturday night, when most workers could come. They also allowed the concerts, which were not merely performances but competitive events, to go on and on. Mission and government injunctions that concerts should end by 11:00 P.M. were routinely ignored.[46] Not only did concerts not end by dark (which would have been around six o'clock, making it impossible for workers to attend) they frequently did not end by midnight. Sometimes they only broke up at dawn.[47] This created some interesting problems for the missions. Technically, concerts were alcohol-free. The Wesleyan mission was supposed to be dry. Not all concertgoers, though, would be church members, and it might be difficult, after dark, to monitor who was drinking what, especially as the atmosphere sometimes paralleled that of a traditional beer-drink, with singing, dancing, and socializing.[48] Choirs competed with each other as popular entertainment, and might include in their performances elements that evoked the dance and music of traditional religions, or the sexually suggestive maneuvers of European dance.[49] Missionaries also complained about smoking (presumably tobacco) which was also off limits to church members, at least at religious events.[50] Worse yet were community perceptions of the event. Youth traveled to the concert site, sang, listened, and spent the night.[51] Elders skeptical of mission activities found it easy to complain about the moral implications of such events, even if they were chaperoned.

The money raised, though, was so important to evangelists that they repeatedly ignored mission rules intended to bring concerts more closely in line with notions of decorous entertainment. Evangelists flatly rejected efforts to move concerts from Saturday nights to Fridays. Saturday night concerts effectively destroyed any hope of energetic church services on Sunday mornings. Most people went home to sleep, and some people slept through church. Missionaries therefore repeatedly pushed regulations through the Synod demanding that concerts be held on Fridays, and end at a reasonable hour. These regulations were ignored in practice, and in 1937, evangelists actually confronted the Synod, explaining that all of them had held concerts on Saturdays despite repeated admonitions to stick to Fridays.[52] Nengubo and Epworth, in particular, were known for concerts which were effectively illegal, as youth traveled too far, concerts were held too late at night, and the atmosphere was distinctly different from that of a controlled, disciplined, school classroom or church service.

If ticket money became a form of tribute and a symbolic linkage of African Christians to the institutional structure of the church as a way to God, concerts represented a different form of Christianity, one coordinated by African evangelists rather than white missionaries, and relying on enthusiasm and sensory appeal rather than reason, schoolbooks, and bureaucratic order. No other mission's evangelists appear to have pursued the concert strategy as diligently as the Wesleyan Methodists did, but the Wesleyan movement parallels closely in time the emergence of other more charismatic approaches to Christianity under African leadership. Dutch Reformed evangelists became leaders of independent African churches. American Methodists started having camp meeting revivals. Even Anglicans pursued a revitalization movement. The American Board imported an American evangelist to hold spiritual awakening meetings.

The concert movement, however, complemented rather than rejecting hierarchical structures within the Wesleyan church. For all the defiance of Synod regulations, concerts were coordinated by African evangelists and local preachers and teachers not as an independent movement but as an entrepreneurial version of Wesleyan Christianity in which mediation between God and the community took place not through the European-controlled formal mission structure, but in the inspirational moments arranged by African evangelists and impresarios.[53] The ticket money, with its systematic structure and association with methods of labor control, constructed money as a link between a disciplined people and an institutionalized God. The concert movement spurred entertainment and enthusiasm, unsystematic gifts to those who provided the entertainment, and moments of inspiration.

School Fees

If ticket money was about institutions, and concerts about the enthusiasm and inspiration of the moment, school fees were about the construction of a future. From the beginning of the twentieth century, the Wesleyan mission supplied teachers to communities in response to communities' requests, gifts, and payments. If communities paid more, they got more highly qualified teachers. If payments fell short, and parents failed to volunteer work on school gardens, the mission withdrew its teachers, and sometimes closed the schools.[54] In Wesleyan areas, close to wage work opportunities in Bulawayo and Salisbury, parents were generally willing to pay for even preliminary education in very basic schools. Furthermore, the Wesleyan central institutions, particularly Nengubo/Waddilove, rapidly gained status, to the point that parents paid quite hefty tuitions of several pounds a term to send their sons to this elite school.[55]

The mission received money for schools not merely from students and parents, but also from the government, under a system of administration which paid a capitation fee for each student. By the mid-1920s, therefore, Wesleyan school financing rested on local sources: parent and student payments; government capitation grants; and the sale of school garden products. The British mission society provided only capital improvement grants, and the salaries of some missionaries and a very few African agents.

In some ways, the school became even more central than the church as the fundamental institution of Rhodesian Wesleyan Christianity. The evangelists and local preachers who staffed the preaching circuits on Sundays worked five days a week running a variety of out-schools. The government helped fund the mission's training program for evangelists only when that training program increased the qualifications of teachers. By the mid-1920s, financial arrangements reflected this lack of distinction between school and church activities by amalgamating school fees and ticket money[56] and rejecting would-be evangelists and local preachers if they lacked government-recognized academic qualifications as suitable teachers. Evangelists and ministers were key participants in the formation of the teachers' unions; though some ministers and evangelists wished for a more spiritual church, the school was the place where African Christianity in Southern Rhodesia happened.[57]

Under the tight financial constraints of the Depression, the mission made even stronger efforts to extract school fees than it did to secure ticket money or funds from concerts. It experimented with a variety of approaches. First, attempting to maximize government grants even when parents became unwilling or unable to pay school fees, it ordered that students be pressured to pay, but allowed to attend school even without payment, in order to secure the government capitation grant.[58] This strategy proved problematic, though, given a reduction in government grants and parents' difficulty in paying for their children's education. Parents and students also rejected unpaid work on mission gardens and in mission construction projects.[59] By 1936, this strategy was proving untenable. In Wedza Circuit, the mission threatened to close schools, and began demanding that students without books and slates be expelled. This was particularly the case when the government began demanding that all students have these items, and that those without them be supplied with equipment from the teachers' own salaries. The idea was to make teachers enforce the regulations. In practice, however, teachers were squeezed as the amounts of money coming in decreased, while demands from missions continued. In this context, the popularity of the concerts among teachers desperate to raise cash becomes understandable, as do parents' allegations in some areas that teachers were embezzling money from concert receipts.[60]

In the schools, the linkage between payments and control became brutally clear, however, as the schools moved from the parent-funded institutions of the 1910s to the government-regulated institutions of the 1930s. In the process, the mission, which initially built schools as churches and continued to view schools as primarily evangelical institutions, watched without having the funds to intervene as its Native Agents redefined themselves from the evangelists of the early years, into teacher-evangelists, and then into the increasingly professional teachers of the 1930s who formed teaching associations and identified themselves according to education.

ISSUES

The Wesleyan Methodists in Southern Rhodesia were one of the most progressive, even radical, missions in the country. Early on, missionaries such as John White and Frank Noble had exposed British South African Company abuses and fought government forced labor, high taxes for Africans, and segregationist land policies. Heads of their mission, especially John White, were among the most prominent local spokesmen for African rights in the region. At Waddilove they provided some of the best education for Africans available in Southern Rhodesia. Yet the mission paralleled the conservative Dutch Reformed Mission in its aggressive efforts to assess and regularly collect "donations"; the innovative efforts of its teachers to raise funds from the African community independently of mission audits; and its increasingly harsh efforts to collect school fees from all scholars, from the elite at the central schools to the first-year students learning the alphabet and catechism.

The close structural parallels between the Wesleyans and the Dutch Reformed Church suggest that the mission's obsessive focus on money was a function not of some racist or exploitative attitude toward the African population, but of a deeper, less malleable sense accepted by both white missionaries and local Christian communities that money and Christianity were intimately and inextricably connected.[61]

Mission rules regarding tickets implied that, for the Wesleyans, no African without money was worth being included in the Christian community. This was more than just an implication: Christians required ticket money, tax money, funds for clothes, soap, and children's school fees. They had to forswear revenues from their daughters' bridewealths, and find some way other than beer parties to collect the labor necessary for harvesting and land clearance. Being wealthy in the traditional sense, with plenty of family, wives, children, and cattle, with sufficient funds to throw the occasional beer party, was not a Christian characteristic. Instead, Christians required monetary wealth, and they expected God to provide it. Often, God did, as "mission boys" frequently had skills in English, crafts, arithmetic, and literacy which facilitated monetized life. Money, therefore, became the key link between Christian status and the Christian God.

The ticket and class monies linked church members to an audited church community, carefully structured with a responsible hierarchy. Money was so important as a part of the Christian message, though, that it did not vanish even when teachers and evangelists sought to move outside of the disciplined structure, and into the world of concerts and charisma. Money and the maximum return on investment, rather than church regulations or the needs of the Sunday church services, dominated this spiritual interaction as well. The linkage was, indeed, not merely a function of teachers' efforts, but so deeply embedded in the consciousness of those who attended that a revival meeting without an offering left Christians complaining of a lost opportunity to thank God.[62] The close tie between money and God, however, meant that when the money came from government, as it increasingly did in mission schools fallen on hard times, the schools became increasingly secular no matter how many pronouncements the government made regarding the need for a Christian message in the schools.

Mission efforts during the early years of the century taught a solid connection between God and money, a connection which proved one of the most enduring facts of the mission legacy, a connection that persisted even when it failed to serve missionary purposes. Initially, ticket money was a form of tribute, a linkage to God, and a way of providing for commoners' connections to the institutions of Christianity. Ticket money indeed provided the basis for more participatory and intense organization in the Methodist Church than was common in other denominations. Building on this conceptual linkage, evangelist-teachers had, by the 1920s and 1930s begun to promote money as a form of prayer. The concerts, with the enthusiasm and donations they promoted, provided for a less institutional, more spontaneous connection between the individual believer and God, but they remained fund-raising concerts, and that connection was mediated by cash. In this context, where both institutionalized belief and spontaneous prayer were intimately tied to money, missionary efforts proved untenable when missions tried, in the face of decreased missionary funds and increased reliance on government grants, to convince evangelists that they could be faithful to God and serve as Christian leaders without reasonable amounts of money. These Christian leaders had absorbed the conceptual linkage between money and God. For them, increasingly secular efforts to pursue better training, more respect, and higher wages were necessary parts of their faith. Modeling themselves on the missionaries who had consistently judged loyalty, taught faith, and pursued evangelism through audits and fund-raising, they, too, followed money.

Teachers' increasing secularization, organization, and pursuit of money rather than evangelization during the 1930s and 1940s were not contradictions of their mission role as evangelists and local preachers. Instead, this pursuit of money grew directly from long-standing mission traditions. It was the European missionaries, rather than the African believers, who suddenly switched their policies when earlier practices began to fail them. But in the segregated, white-dominated context of Southern Rhodesia, it was hard for missionaries, however self-sacrificing they perceived themselves to be, to be convincing when they informed African agents that they must pursue faith, not money, while living on salaries five to ten times that of the highest-paid Africans, with housing and school benefits denied to even elite African ministers. African agents tended to retain a belief in pursuing their faith by making money, and saw a moral and religious connection between money and God.[63]

Southern Rhodesian mission Christianity was an immensely worldly phenomenon, embedded in a specific colonial context, a local pattern of racism, and the economic realities of Rhodesia's monetization, boom and bust. In this context, the explicit linkage between money and faith mostly served the missions well. Though congregations rarely proved affluent enough to achieve full self-support without mission subventions and government schooling grants, the ideal of responsible government by church members with paid-up tickets was a remarkably democratic, though frequently overruled, method of assuring that members cultivate their church and circuit rather than seeing these as gifts, sources of plunder, or otherworldly patrons. The concerts and similar revival meetings allowed people to experience the more ecstatic aspects of faith, while nevertheless keeping afloat the institutions that provided a context and support for these momentary inspirations. Even school fees, which became a flashpoint for controversy as families found them difficult to pay, forced families to take education seriously as investments for their children's future.

Yet the emphasis on money which gave church members, evangelists, and parents such a strong stake in and sense of ownership of church resources proved fundamentally problematic for missions over the longer term. Terence Ranger, in his book *Are We Not Also Men?* has emphasized how the Wesleyan mission provided a basis for an African nationalism, growing out of Africans' resentment of white missionaries, a resentment which grew as privileged missionaries cut African salaries, proved reluctant to actually hand authority and resources to Africans, and blocked African teachers' efforts to innovate and develop the churches. J. Keith Rennie emphasized similar points in his study of the relatively liberal American Board mission, and M. I. Daneel's examinations of the roots of breakaway Shona churches point to parallel tensions.[64]

Mission emphasis on money and control, though, was more than just a general phenomenon producing general resentments. It, like much of the display of white power and African deference in the region, was most explicit in its use of specific, concrete objects. The communion ticket, without which a believer had no right to the sacrament, paralleled the poll tax and pass, without which an African man could not move around the country.

Concert funds provided a concrete way to judge religious enthusiasm in pounds, shillings, and pence, analogous to the way European observers noted workers' more worldly enthusiasm by their store purchases, put away in boxes and paid for on time. And the school fees, in a region which provided free education for white children, expressed both marginalization and aspiration, as Africans faced the reality of denial of resources and the hope that in the future they would be able to get more.

Christianity, morality, and money were inextricably linked in the Southern Rhodesia of the early twentieth century, to the point where violations of the material code, such as a preacher talking without his jacket on a warm summer day, or an evangelist unable to afford his own hymnbook and Gospels, counted as a violation of the faith. When poverty made it difficult for some congregation members and evangelists to adhere to Christian material codes, their failures were judged not as poverty, but as moral failings.[65]

Becoming Christian in Southern Rhodesia in the interwar years was a clear, formal process for both individuals and communities. From the individual's perspective, it meant going to school long enough to become literate, finding some way to earn the money necessary for not just taxes, but also school fees, church contributions, and the material necessities of Christian life, ranging from key books to Westernized clothes and soap. From a community's perspective, becoming Christian meant assembling the money necessary to sponsor and maintain a school, with teacher-evangelist and school farm. Individuals and groups celebrated and subsidized this institutional conversion through the concerts that peaked during difficult times. And conversion transformed the way Christians raised their children as they sent them to others for schooling, rather than raising them at home, in a material and substantive declaration of how the future would be one of change rather than continuity. Money did not simply sponsor missionization, it was woven into the many meanings of what Christianity could bring, not in a mere quantitative sense, but in the qualitative reconstruction and recreation of community it brought as individuals, families and congregations, getting and spending money in new ways, for new wants and needs, remade their society.

NOTES

1. For example, see David Maxwell, *Christians and Chiefs: A Social History of the Hwesa People* (Westport, Conn., 1999), which focuses on the 1950s

and 1960s in a remote part of Rhodesia, but describes the processes of conversion admirably.

2. See, for example, C. J. M. Zvobgo, *The Wesleyan Methodist Missions in Zimbabwe 1891–1945* (Harare, 1991); John Wesley Kurewa, *The Church in Mission: A Short History of the United Methodist Church in Zimbabwe, 1897–1997* (Nashville, Tenn., 1997).

3. Important works employing variants of this theme include T. O. Beidelman, *Colonial Evangelism* (Bloomington, Ind., 1982; Jean Comaroff and John Comaroff, *Of Revelation and Revolution,* 2 vols. (Chicago, 1991–97); and, perhaps most powerfully, Paul S. Landau, *Realm of the Word* (Portsmouth, N.H., 1995). In addition to these book-length studies, a conference "Africans Meeting Missionaries" at the University of Minnesota, Minneapolis, 1997, assembled a variety of work in progress on similar themes.

4. For many other well-documented missions, either locally held records (as in the case of the American Board mission at Mount Selinda, on the Mozambican border) or home records (as in the case of the Jesuits) have been inaccessible.

5. James Ferguson, *Expectations of Modernity: Myths and Meanings of Urban Life on the Zambian Copperbelt* (Berkeley, Calif., 1999) pp. 104–5.

6. For example, a quarterly meeting which was sufficiently liberal that it endorsed Mrs. Efa Mavu as a local preacher nevertheless exclaimed in horror that "A preacher had appeared in a pulpit without a coat" and reminded all local preachers of the need for suitable dress. Quarterly Meeting Minutes (hereafter QM), Epworth, 20 March 1937, Methodist House, Harare (hereafter MHH; note that MHH materials are not indexed or boxed in a standardized form).

7. M. Block and J. Parry, *Money and the Morality of Exchange* (Cambridge, 1989) pp. 6–7.

8. This is treated in more detail in Carol Summers, *Colonial Lessons: Africans' Education in Southern Rhodesia 1918–1940* (Portsmouth, N.H., 2002). See also Carol Summers, *From Civilization to Segregation* (Athens, Ohio, 1994).

9. For an early example of this pattern, consider the case of a teacher recruited and initially paid for by the parents of students at Bembesi school, Bulawayo Circuit, in 1908. According to plan, thirty homes would contribute fifteen shillings a year (or individual students sixpence a month) in school fees to provide the teacher (probably Robert Njokweni) with an annual salary of twenty pounds. But parents stopped paying his salary. By 1911, the school was "very unsatisfactory" and the teacher had resigned. The missionary, however, offered to send John Faku, a highly qualified Mfengu teacher, if the people would pay at least half his salary. The com-

munity agreed, but then failed to keep their agreement. So the mission substituted Thomas Mniki, a less qualified man, at a lower salary, threatening that if the community did not pay at least enough to support Mniki, the mission would close school and church, since "the people were in a position to pay for the education of their children," and the region suffered from an acute teacher shortage. At other locations, such as Sipongweni, the mission carried through on its threatened closures. QM Native Church, Bulawayo, 16 July 1907, 17 October 1907, 16 July 1908, 4 July 1911, 13 September 1911, 27 December 1910, 9 September 1913, 19 March 1914, 23 December 1914.

10. See Maxwell, *Christians and Chiefs*, p. 1, who discusses the Hwesa as Cinderella people, only brought into the mission movement in the 1950s.

11. Abel Muzorewa, *Rise Up and Walk* (Nashville, Tenn., 1978), p. 33.

12. Ibid., p. 33.

13. All scriptural quotations are from the King James Version.

14. See Summers, *Colonial Lessons*. For a Methodist example, however, consider the wave of school strikes and student activism which hit Tegwani and other institutions in the late 1930s and early 1940s. See for example, principal's interim report to assistant commissioner of Tegwani, 21 March 1939, MHH, which reported eight students implicated in a break-in and burglary of the school safe and a strike by all students except prefects and evangelists. Epworth, meanwhile, reported a fire which might have been arson during a period where government inspectors complained of the school's inefficiency and wastefulness. Minute Book of the Epworth Committee, July 1941, MHH.

15. John White, Chair, QM, Nengubo, 26 September 1924.

16. Records were not always well kept. For example, one of the most frequent injunctions in the minutes of the Quarterly Meeting, Bulawayo, was for teachers to keep records more systematically. See QM, Native Church, Bulawayo, 5 April 1911, 4 July 1911, 26 March 1912, 7 August 1915, 24 May 16.

17. The Wedza Circuit was particularly vocal on the subject of congregations which failed to maintain churches and cultivate for the school. QM, Wedza, 1935–40. Minutes of the synod held 11–17 January 1922, MHH, report discussion (and approval) of the formation of local societies.

18. For a classic discussion of this system, see Charles van Oneself, *Chibaro* (London, 1976).

19. Discussions of how to collect ticket money came up regularly in quarterly meeting minutes. The Nengubo Quarterly Meeting of 2 December 1933 resolved unanimously that church members must show their paid-up tickets before communion; QM Nengubo. Other circuits followed the

same rules, and, when they became lax, remembered with nostalgia earlier times of checking tickets before communion. QM Epworth, 29 March 1941.

20. QM Epworth, 28 December 1924.

21. The African minister who proposed this received a free ticket by virtue of his status in the church. QM Nengubo, 2 December 1922.

22. Rhodesia District Synod Minutes for 1913, MHH; QM Epworth, 29 March 1941.

23. See Zvobgo, *Wesleyan Methodist Missions,* p. 113.

24. QM Nengubo, 2 December 1933. Women paid a shilling a year in Ruwadzano membership in 1928, in addition to paying for the extra commodities demanded by Christian life—utensils for cooking, clothes, soap, etc.

25. Moss argues that prior to 1931, ticket money was sometimes waived for widows living on mission farms but that after that, it was systematically required for all. Moss, "Holding Body and Soul Together," p. 115. Quarterly meeting and synod minutes from the 1930s recorded an increased demand for systematic collections of ticket money, as well as an increase in ticket fees. For examples, see the minutes of quarterly meetings at Epworth, Nengubo, and Wedza, where the meeting announced: "Christians must show faith with gifts." QM Wedza, 27 February 1937.

26. For examples, see QM Bulawayo, 5 January 1924; Discipline Cases Notebook for Kwenda (Historical Record, 1927), MHH; and QM Epworth, 6 June 1925 and 21 September 1925.

27. Report of the Chimanza Circuit and report of the Bulawayo Circuit, Minutes of the Synod of the Rhodesia District, 4–12 January, 1921. University of London, School of Oriental and African Studies, Wesleyan Methodist Missionary Society Archive, Box 349. From Chimanza, the minister complained that because he only visited most congregations when they were collecting ticket money, his visits were associated with payment. And in the Bulawayo Circuit the minister reported: "The native ministers of the circuit are of mind that more frequent visits by the European minister are necessary [and would produce more ticket money]." Compare the way that Anglican congregations came to associate proper services with money: Olive Lloyd to her family and friends, 17 September 1933, National Archives of Zimbabwe, Historical Manuscripts Collection, ANG 16/11/1.

28. The Wesleyan attitude on this, and I believe the attitude of most of the missions, was different from the practices of the Dutch Reformed Church or the Jesuits. In the Dutch Reformed Church, individual missionaries became personally wealthy as a result of African contributions; see Summers, *Colonial Lessons.* The Jesuit mission apparently used student labor in

its quarry to finance mission expansion beyond Chishawasha; see L. Vambe, *Ill-Fated People* (Pittsburgh, 1972).

29. Calculations are complicated because most evangelical workers also taught, and thus their salaries were underwritten to some degree by the government. A school, however, was supposed to have a teacher for every forty to fifty pupils. Thus a congregation with 120 members might be sending two hundred children to school, and need to pay four teacher/evangelists rather than just one. Such schools were rarely fully staffed. Schools tried to make up the funding gap through freewill offerings, concerts, and, significantly, school gardens, at which parents and students were required to work. Complex revenue and expenditure patterns make even honest mission bookkeeping hard to follow. Account Books, MHH. In 1938, the Quarterly Meeting at Nengubo/Waddilove joined the regular refrain from other missions complaining about "the growing tendency for . . . trained teachers to accept appointments in other Missions in preference to those available in their own church." Minute Book, Nengubo Quarterly Meeting, 20 September 1938, MHH. I discuss teachers' decisions in Summers, *Colonial Lessons*.

30. QM Epworth, 6 April 1929.

31. See, for example, QM Nengubo, 8 September 1931, where the principal agrees to take mealies for class money at the rate of four shillings per bag. Produce from school gardens was also widely seen as a way of earning basic revenue. For example, QM Nengubo, 12 April 1932, 4 September 1932, 5 December 1932, 4 April 1944. By the late 1930s, the practice was sufficiently standardized that quarterly meetings merely reiterated that church contributions in maize should be given at the beginning, not the end, of the harvest period so that the mission would be able to sell the grain for the best prices. QM Nengubo, 2 April 1938, 2 July 1938.

32. Note that Mfazi was hardly the only minister with unclear accounts. Many of the European ministers were acknowledged by their peers as hopeless from an economic point of view. Missionaries Burman and Howarth lacked enough education and were merely craftsmen. And the mission chairman in Southern Rhodesia complained of James Stewart, D. W. Evans, and Frank Ockenden that "Indeed a great amount of my time is taken up in going to Circuits and trying to extricate these raw lads out of financial and administrative tangles from which a little common sense would have saved them." Frank Noble to Secretary of Works Thompson, 27 November 1933, University of London, School of Oriental and African Studies, Wesleyan Methodist Missionary Society Archive, Box 834.

33. Terence Ranger, *Are We Not Also Men: The Samkange Family and African Politics in Zimbabwe, 1920–1964* (Portsmouth, N.H., 1995), pp. 83–84.

34. Minutes of synod held 8–16 January 1919, MHH.

35. In his examination of the Samkange family, one of the most prominent early Methodist families in Rhodesia, Terence Ranger argues that accusations of financial improprieties were not based on real misappropriations,
but on a failure to acknowledge local autonomy and local uses for church
funds. See the discussion of how Thompson and Grace Samkange raised
both their own and foster children, promoted education, and built local
institutions with ties to nationalism, rather than mere patronage ties with
the mission. Ranger, *Are We Not Also Men,* pp. 32–123.

36. See the discussions at the Epworth Quarterly Meeting, 1935.

37. The mission needed local preachers, but viewed their level of commitment with suspicion. In 1921, for example, when LPs petitioned Epworth Circuit for the mission to issue them with hymn books, so that they
would not need to buy them, the missionary chair responded that "the
question re hymn books and testaments should never have arisen. A man
who did not possess them was not equipped to serve as a local preacher."
Stanlake, QM Epworth, 14 June 1921. By 1925, local preachers were coming to quarterly meetings without tickets, as a way of putting pressure on
the missionary in charge, who responded by issuing more stern warnings.
QM Epworth, 6 June 1921, 5 April 1930, 20 June 1931. Local preachers
and other delegates responded to their critics by arguing that church leaders
with free tickets should give some offering at the time of issue of their
tickets, showing Christian duty and love for God, lest they be accused of
receiving the gifts of God all year without giving back, a hypocrisy which
would indicate that love was dead. Leaders' Meeting, 21 September 1925,
Epworth, MHH.

38. See, e.g., QM Nengubo, 1938.

39. See QM Selukwe and Wedza, 1936. This idea had been unsuccess-
fully suggested earlier by J. Butler who worried that "Whether our system
of quarterly tickets is the best one for a community which grows and sells
its crops once a year is, I think, open to question and it would be worth
while considering whether it would not be better to have one yearly ticket
and one annual payment." Chimanza Circuit Report, 1921, in "Minutes of
the Synod of the Rhodesia District 4 to 12 January 1921," WMMS, Box
349.

40. See, e.g., QM Kwenda 1935, QM Nengubo 1930.

41. Other missions pursued other alternatives. The work parties of the
Dutch Reformed Church are discussed in Summers, *Colonial Lessons,* and the
Jesuit lime quarries are discussed in Vambe, *An Ill-Fated People.* The London
Missionary Society apparently relied on market gardening. Barbara Moss
suggests that the American Methodist (as opposed to Wesleyan Methodist)

turn toward revivals and concerts was closely linked to the enthusiasms for fertility, motherhood, and spirituality generated within the Ruwadzano movement. "Holding Body and Soul Together: Women, Autonomy and Christianity in Colonial Zimbabwe" (Ph.D. diss., Indiana University, 1991), p. 136.

42. QM Bulawayo, 8 October 1908.

43. Indeed, the best available institutional history of the Wesleyan Mission, Zvobgo, *Wesleyan Methodist Missions,* does not discuss them at all. In a novel set around this time, however, concerts (along with football) are described as one of the major communal activities of young men in Bulawayo. Ndabaningi Sithole, *The Polygamist* (New York, 1972), p. 112.

44. See, for hints of how the system worked, the discussion at an Epworth staff meeting, 10 November 1938, MHH, where Mr. M'Kombacato said that choirs collected money to give to the concert chairman for them to sing, but the parents (who were requested to provide this seed money) generally thought that the teachers collecting it "have a chance of robbing a good deal of the money." Other speakers asserted that money paid to the chairman to enable choirs to sing "is their own choice." As a reform measure, the meeting concluded that all children should individually pay for admittance, whether singing or not, and that "The man in the audience should be given the chance to offer for whichever choir he likes to listen to." This attempt to bypass the teachers' role in collecting money and sponsoring choirs was evidently very controversial. Though accounting is sparse (and would include only money paid for entry or honestly declared by the concert chair, not paid to teachers), one concert at Epworth in 1925 collected receipts of £10 5s. 9d., as against expenses of £2 19s. 10d. QM Epworth, 1925.

45. QM Nengubo, 1935–36.

46. QM Epworth, 21 October 1933.

47. See Mather's complaint and Samkange's response regarding all-night concerts in Ranger, *Are We Not Also Men,* pp. 79–80.

48. Beer—less for concerts than for work teams at harvest time—was a serious point of tension between the mission and the local churches. Not just ordinary church members, but local preachers and even evangelists routinely violated the mission's prohibition on brewing and consumption of beer. See, for example, QM Wedza, 6 October 1936 and 21 June 1947.

49. At Nengubo in 1931, for example, meeting participants objected to "some of the features of the big school-children's gathering at Samriwo. Opinion was divided as to the character of some of the action songs." QM Nengubo, 2 December 1931. European dancing was generally seen by Africans in Southern Rhodesia as lewd, since men and women danced together rather than separately.

50. Ironically, Europeans attending these concerts were the worst offenders regarding smoking. QM Epworth, 29 March 1941.

51. See, for example, QM Epworth, 26 March 1938.

52. QM Epworth, 16 March 1933, 20 November 1937, 26 March 1938; QM Nengubo, 25 September 1937.

53. Ranger's study of the Samkanges does suggest linkages between concerts, schools, and nationalism. And the controversy over Pakame definitely brought all these together. On the other hand, the Samkanges remained within the church. Their actions in this generation fit a model of entrepreneurial action better than one of breakaway nationalism, though clearly, by the 1940s, nationalist institutions were beginning to become a viable and attractive option. For a more generational model of African intellectual movements, see Flora Veit-Wild, *Teachers, Preachers and Non-Believers: A Social History of Zimbabwean Literature* (Harare, 1993).

54. See, the controversy over schools described in Summers, *Colonial Lessons.*

55. Even non-Methodists recognized Waddilove's prestige value: J. D. Rubatika remembered that his father. despite being a fervent Anglican, had sent him to Waddilove as the best available schooling. Interview with John Daniel Rubatika by Dawson Munjeri, 3 July 1979, National Archives of Zimbabwe, African Oral History 57.

56. For example, QM Bulawayo, 1924.

57. Thompson Samkange, for example, complained about this, wishing that things could have been more spiritual. Ranger, *Are We Not Also Men,* p. 81.

58. This was not a purely humanitarian gesture for the children. The financial motive was explicit in the directive. QMM Nengubo 1932, 1934.

59. Note that education for European children was free, paid for from general tax revenues, to which African taxpayers contributed.

60. QM Epworth, 1938.

61. Colleen McDannell, *Material Christianity: Religion and Popular Culture in America* (New Haven, Conn., 1995), pp. 4–16, evokes the connections between the spiritual and the material in the comprehension and practice of religion. She suggests that we explore material connections not as a means of denigrating popular faith, but as a means of reassessing a misleading dichotomy between spiritual and material. Her suggestions are directly relevant in the Rhodesian context.

62. Olive Lloyd to family and friends, 17 September 1933, NAZ ANG 16/11/1.

63. This comes through clearly in Ranger's discussion of the Samkange family, *Are We Not Also Men.* It can also be detected in the writings of elite

Africans who evoked their status through their material possessions. See, for example, Walter Chipwayo's inventory of what he lost in a house fire, or George Mhlanga's discussion of the basics necessary for civilized life in his complaints about working for the Dutch Reformed Church.

64. See, for example, J. Keith Rennie, "Christianity, Colonialism and the Origins of Nationalism among the Ndau of Southern Rhodesia, 1890–1935" (Ph.D. diss., Northwestern University, 1973) and M. Daneel, *Old and New in Southern Shona Independent Churches,* vol. 3 (Gweru, 1988).

65. These judgments were made by African Christians as well as by missionaries. See, for fictional examples, Tsitsi Dangarembga, *Nervous Conditions* (London, 1988). pp. 122–48, where her narrator Tambudzai and the educated school superintendent see close connections between poverty and dubious marriages; or the teacher's horrified anticipation of his mission-educated fiancée's reaction to the failure of his father to buy clothes and goods and goods in the Christian style, in Sithole, *The Polygamist,* pp. 122–27.

11

LITERACY IN THE EYE OF INDIA'S CONVERSION STORM

GAURI VISWANATHAN

In an otherwise cheerless and desultory year, euphoria seized India as it celebrated the award of the 1998 Nobel Prize to Amartya Sen for his work on welfare economics. The distinctiveness of this work lay in Sen's commitment to a concept of human development aimed at realizing social and political processes for the betterment of human life. In insisting that all forms of human deprivation such as hunger, malnutrition, and illiteracy should be brought within the purview of public policy, Sen transformed economics into a moral science, challenging the direction of a discipline focused primarily on those social aspects that are only instrumentally useful for human life. Among the deprivations he targets as most ignored by public policy is the citizenry's right to education, full access to which is still an unrealized goal in postcolonial India, despite the professed commitments to universal literacy. On hearing the news that Sen had won the Nobel Prize, even those on both the left and the right in India who had long questioned the pragmatic usefulness of his work suspended their skepticism and joined the rest of the country in lauding his achievement.

There was, however, a lone voice of dissent and disapproval, and it came from the Vishwa Hindu Parishad (VHP), the right-wing Hindu religious organization currently backing the ruling BJP government. VHP president Ashok Singhal gave a sinister turn to Sen's economic program, darkly interpreting his Nobel award as a Western conspiracy to promote literacy in developing societies in order to bring them within the ultimate pale of a global Christian order, and thus "wipe out Hinduism from this country."[1] "Despite the accuracy of Prof. Amartya Sen's conclusions," he charged, "the same could prove harmful to Hindu society as Christians would be bringing in more money ostensibly for promoting education, but actually proselytization would increase and everything in India would be undermined."[2]

Incidentally, Ashok Singhal had earlier launched a scathing attack on Mother Teresa's Nobel Prize as well. Then too he accused the Nobel committee of rewarding only those who promoted the work of Christian charity. Skeptical of Mother Teresa's work as properly deserving to be called social service, he insisted that the driving aim behind all the activities of the Missionaries of Charity was to convert poor and ignorant Hindus to Christianity. At that time, unlike on the occasion of Sen's prize, Singhal's voice was joined by others, though admittedly not in huge numbers. Publicly at least, few cared to endorse his views on Sen, as a result of which he was isolated from other hard-liners in his own party. Even the prime minister of the BJP-led government, Atal Behari Vajpayee, denounced such provocations as churlish, intemperate, and irresponsible.[3]

Yet, even as he refused to participate in Singhal's denunciation of Sen's award, the prime minister simultaneously urged that there be a "national debate on conversion" following the attacks on Christians and their places of worship since December 1998. As if in repetition of the horrendous anti-Muslim violence of 6 December 1992, which resulted in the destruction of the Babri Masjid mosque in Ayodhya by Hindu extremists, Christian churches were razed to the ground. In a series of particularly gruesome events, a Christian missionary and his sons were burned alive and, most recently, in September 1999, a nun was stripped and forced to drink the urine of her would-be rapists.[4] Ostensibly a response to Christian proselytization, the violence began in the western state of Gujarat, but spread to other states as well, including the eastern state of Orissa, which witnessed not only the burning alive of the Australian missionary Graham Staines but also the murder of a Roman Catholic priest, Arul Das, in September 1999. To a country that had come to expect communal clashes as involving Hindus and Muslims primarily, the sudden surge of hostility toward Christians took many Indians by surprise, accustomed as they had become to the central role of Christian mission schools and hospitals in Indian life. In this context, Vajpayee's appeal sounds innocuous enough, outwardly a sincere attempt to engage in serious dialogue and discussion about the motive force behind the violence.

THE CONSTITUTION AND CONVERSION

However, the call for a debate was clearly intended to reopen the discussions that took place at the time of Indian independence, when the Constitution was framed. In the Constituent Assembly discussions that were held between 1946 and 1950, there was a strong move by powerful Hindu lobbies to ban conversions altogether. The call for constitutional provisions against conversion was made in response to the widespread fear that Hinduism, typically described as a nonproselytizing religion, would be under threat and its numerical strength diminished if conversions to other religions were allowed. While all religious groups may theoretically disseminate their beliefs, it has been a long-standing belief among Hindus that only Christians and Muslims actively proselytize, placing Hinduism at a disadvantage. This conviction lay behind the attempt by the Hindu lobby to bar conversions altogether and achieve a level playing field among the various religions. Furthermore, Gandhi's famous distrust of Christian missionaries and Christian conversions offered a screen behind which the anti-Christian lobby could conveniently hide.[5] The fear of conversion produced a strange marriage between Gandhi and the Hindu nationalists, who in all other instances denounced him for making concessions to Muslims but nonetheless heralded him as the voice of reason when he opposed Christian proselytism. In his deep skepticism about the work of missionization, Gandhi imbued Indian nationalism with a Hindu ethos that laid the groundwork for an identitarian notion of Indianness. His resistance to Christian conversions simultaneously affirmed a Hindu past which had the power to assimilate different communities and produce a sense of oneness. Of course, the vital difference between Gandhi's position and that of Hindu nationalists was that while he believed Christian conversions were the instrument of British colonialism and therefore must be resisted as vigorously as British rule, Hindu groups had no such larger aim and remained trapped within their own self-interest.

The final draft of the Indian Constitution effectively resisted all such attempts to outlaw conversions, and instead made the propagation of religion permissible under the law. Article 25 (1) of the Constitution gives everyone the fundamental right to "profess, practice, or propagate religion," a right that is only circumscribed by considerations of "public order, morality, and health."[6] Whereas the constitutional freedom of conscience is described as a mental process, the right to propagate religion externalizes the mental freedom of conscience, rendering active propagation a field of open and lawful endeavor.[7] Freedom of conscience was thus broadly interpreted to mean the right not only to *choose* one's religious views but also to *disseminate* them. Not until 1977 was this provision modified in an Indian Supreme Court ruling which specified that the right to propagate religion did not necessarily extend to the right to convert. The ruling further allowed states to legislate "Freedom of Religion" bills forbidding the conversion of minors, as well as requiring Hindus converting to Christianity to provide magistrates with an affidavit. Such forms of legislation brought civil officials directly into the administration of spiritual affairs, a move that seriously qualified the secular conception of the modern state and challenged the tacitly accepted division between religious faith and law.

The impetus for the Supreme Court judgment came from a series of rulings set in motion by the findings and recommendations of a pivotal commission chaired by Justice Bhavani Shankar Niyogi. Set up in 1954 to investigate the role of foreign missionaries in the state of Madhya Pradesh, located in the geographical center of India, the Niyogi Commission produced a report that, in the eyes of many missionaries, was intended to regulate Christian conversions and drive foreign missions out of the country.[8] Noting that the term "propagation" was originally intended to refer to freedom of expression and conscience, Niyogi's report implied that conversion militates against such freedom and therefore cannot be regarded as a disinterested dissemination of religious knowledge. By calling for a constitutional amendment reserving the right to propagate religion to Indian citizens, the report was clearly generated in a climate of chauvinism and ultranationalism. But the report went further than merely reopening the constitutional debates on conversion, just as Prime Minister Vajpayee, in calling for a national debate on conversion, had more than an academic exchange in mind. The Niyogi Report introduced a new argument by highlighting loss of control over free will through weakness, ignorance, and poverty as a reason for outlawing conversion altogether, since it left the economically deprived sectors of Indian society particularly vulnerable to the inducements of converting to another religion. Such a view was possible only by representing India's economically weaker sections as essentially disabled, incapable of distinguishing motives, and inexperienced in the exercise of their own judgment. The report painted a picture of conversion as a form of exploitation threatening the integrity of the Indian state, an assault so heinous that it justified the state's curbing of missionary activities on the grounds that they posed a danger to national unity. Conversion is construed as a form of mental violence, no less severe than bodily assault. The Niyogi Commission's landmark report set the lines of an argument that have continued to the present day, blurring the lines between force and consent and giving very little credence to the possibility that converts change over to another religion because they choose to. Interestingly, in charging that Christian missionaries take advantage of the weakened will of the poor and the disenfranchised, the report confirmed an elitist view of free will and autonomy as a privilege of the economically advantaged classes. As in the fiery age-of-consent debates over prepubertal marriages of females, "consent" is not allowed as an option among the poor, and the missionaries' promise of new religious possibilities is construed entirely as a violation akin to the rape of women.

Over the years the ambiguity in the semantic distinctions between "propagation" and "conversion" went a long way in creating a charged environment culminating in such incidents as the fractious ones in Gujarat in December 1998, when scores of Christians and Christian places of worship were attacked. Indeed, the mounting violence against Christians since late 1998 replays an ongoing battle between Christian missionization and Hindu nationalism which was often fought in the houses of the Indian Parliament to introduce legislation banning conversion. So-called "Freedom of Religion" bills were routinely proposed seeking extension of state protection to those being wooed away from their religion. "Freedom of religion" came to be a euphemism for freedom *from* religion. Ostensibly secular in motivation, the bills to ensure freedom of religious conscience were primarily intended to protect Hinduism against the incursions of other proselytizing religions, revealing the collusion of the state in the preservation of Hinduism. "Conversion" implies force, a radical takeover of people's will, whereas "propagation" acquires a more intransitive connotation, a middle term between force and instruction. Slipping from one meaning to another in the recent debate on conversion, the VHP general secretary Praveen Togadia invoked comparative history in order to argue that no other society gave a free rein to conversion, which has never been able to escape the connotations of force and disruption. Seeking a universalist point of reference, he linked economic well-being with free will to argue that "if these are the views of even the developed countries, how can we allow conversion in India where a large section of the society is poor and illiterate?"[9] Here again is the evocation of poverty as mental disability, leaving the masses peculiarly vulnerable to religious manipulation. In rehearsing the earlier constitutional debates on conversion, Togadia failed to mention that the constitutional framers invoked Western precedent, particularly that of American freedom of conscience, when they decided to include provisions to permit propagation of religion. Selectively calling up the West as a reference point to argue against conversion, Togadia's comparative perspective evidently breaks down in its inability to deal with the multiple genealogies of religious freedom comprising the constitutional debates. These genealogies make room for the notion of conversion as a matter of individual choice and conscience, which the constitution is obliged to protect.

CONVERSION AND THE HISTORICAL LEGACY
OF CONQUEST

Yet, despite such constitutional protection of religious conscience, nationalist discourse has turned conversion into a threat, a challenge to the cohesiveness of tightly woven communities. This is not difficult to understand, given that nationalism's recourse to concepts of ethnicity, race, religion, and language is precisely what conversion contests. Conversion's interest for a postnationalist culture is its resistance to positivist ways of conceptualizing difference through such essentializing markers as race, religion, color, ethnicity, and nationality. When identity is destabilized by boundaries that are so porous that movement from one worldview to another can take place with the regularity of actual border crossings, a challenge is posed to the fixed categories that act as an empirical grid to interpret human behavior and actions.

While terms like "hybridity" are offered as an alternative to essentializing identities, "hybridity" does not capture the dynamism of movement signified by conversion, which regards crossovers of identity not merely as items of exchange or even fusion but as a remaking of the categories that define identity. Nor is "syncretism" a satisfactory term to describe the overlapping of identities, since, as its etymology and historical usage indicate, it constitutes a blurring rather than a negotiation of differences.[10] Moreover, "syncretism" is as much a construct as are terms like "tradition" and "modernity." In destabilizing the determinants of race, religion, gender, and so on, conversion unsettles the understanding of difference through purely essentialist categories. It shifts the focus away from visible markers of difference (such as race or gender) to the distance in viewpoints emerging from the pragmatics of communication. Such gaps in communication are the starting point for conversion's reconstructive role in initiating movement between opposing viewpoints. The fact that neither origin nor destination is finite and determinate allows the convert to be critical of the religion to which she converts, even as she seeks to reform the religion she has repudiated. This sense of critical distance and fluidity gives conversion its peculiar power—the power to destabilize which belongs to the individual who moves incessantly between disparate viewpoints.

I am therefore suggesting that conversion performs the epistemological function of negotiating differences in viewpoints. Yet historically the term "conversion" has been associated with violence and erasure rather than mobility and communication. To those who patrol the barriers around religion, conversion rudely shuts down communication and is forcible by definition; it is "a colonization of consciousness."[11] Violence is at its core, as it tears away the secure lineaments of identity and orders the extinction of an individual's most innate beliefs and understandings. Even when conversion works by persuasion, it is no less coercive in that it leaves the individual vulnerable to alluring promises. This is violence of the most hateful kind, because it induces assent by planting the seeds of hope for a better life. The legacy of historical conquest has made this notion of conversion a palpable and uncontestable one, even though violence does not inhere in conversion but rather in the historical moment in which conversion occurs. Indeed, when examined as a form of intersubjective communication, conversion can be understood as the outcome of a process whose alternative end point is violence, especially when the differences between parties remain unresolved.[12]

Coercion, erasure of identity, and forced assimilation are embedded in colonial desire, which has assigned conversion a set of meanings rooted in violence. Yet the fact remains that conversion becomes violent only when shifts to another worldview turn into a desire to make it prevail. This, of course, is Matthew Arnold's classic definition of culture, which is deeply rooted in the logic of conversion by virtue of its ambition to be expansive and all-embracing. Translating the spread of culture into the terms of religious expansion, Robert Hefner describes conversion as a "great transformation" that assimilates local cults into world religions. This description, however, can be parsed further to reveal an inherent tension in conversion between being a break in the continuity of knowledge and representing a prelude to the institutionalization of new knowledge systems. What appears as a violent erasure of identity—"epistemic violence," to use Gayatri Spivak's term—is more precisely an effect of discontinuous knowledge. But while, on the one hand, discontinuity of knowledge makes universalist propositions more difficult to sustain, on the other hand the very presence of competing systems creates a different set of compulsions leading towards violence. In the first instance, discontinuity prevents false universalisms, but in the second the desire to make the new system prevail reintroduces universalism. Violence is contingent upon the latter, but it also signifies the implacable opposition of claims. Not only does violence symbolize the disruptive power of difference but it also preserves and reproduces it. The history of religious transformations cannot be written outside the framework of these dual impulses: of knowledge interrupted and then transformed from *dissent* into *assent*.[13]

Discontinuity and radical pluralism make culture vulnerable to what Habermas terms "legitimation crises." Such crises reveal the need for a theory of religious communication that moves beyond relativism, even as it repudiates universalism in values. Some critics prefer to look toward notions of faith as the "establishment of a ground or foundation immune to the relativizing powers of Enlightenment and providing, thereby, a basis for the legitimation of belief."[14] Conversion's proactive nature, combined with its maneuvering between discrepant belief systems, makes it a powerful epistemological tool to face the broad challenges of a pluralistic society. If pluralism is not to be reduced to a slogan of "live and let live" but imagined as the groundwork of community, communication between disparate groups on lines other than the assertion of their separate identities is the first step toward that goal. Conversion highlights the crisis of pluralism as the absence of a point of reference for religious groups to negotiate their differences and conflicting needs. Religious absolutism sets up a single center of values as the ultimate arbiter in conflicts, overriding individual self-definitions.

On the other hand, while constitutional provisions for freedom of religion relativize religious difference and thus repudiate the exclusionary force of doctrine, they leave nothing in its place to enable religious communication between groups. To a large extent, this is the dilemma of secularizing societies. The failure of relativism enables the return of conversion in post-emancipation society, not as forcible assimilation but as intersubjective communication.[15] In its challenge to thwart the violence that results when groups interact as equal but competing members of civil society, pluralism's real test is to find new philosophical ways of conceiving relationality, particularly to heal the wounds inflicted by restrictive laws on communities in the colonial past of societies. Kept out of full civic participation in the past, communities are robbed of the conditions to relate effectively with one another, especially when consensus in civil decision making is thwarted by the historical baggage of colonialism, which includes the perception that colonial rule was intended to obliterate indigenous religions. However, other than to sanction freedom of religious conscience, the constitutional protection of the right to propagate religions does nothing to establish new conditions for communication or promote the proactive exercise of tolerance, even though civil pluralism forces communities to rethink their relations with each other on principles other than that of religious difference.

THE ROLE OF THE MISSION SCHOOLS

The perceived threat posed by conversion reminds one that, for formerly colonized societies, the history of colonial education is also the founding moment of violence. This conviction underwrites Indian prime minister Vajpayee's call for a national debate on conversion. In so doing, he insists on revisiting the role of missionary institutions in India: to ask, in other words, whether their aim was to propagate religion—which could also broadly include morality, civic virtue, and character—or to convert people to Christianity. Without attacking the Constitution itself, Vajpayee asserted that, while the right of religious propagation was constitutionally guaranteed, "the country must ensure that it is not misused."[16] This statement is no less than a dire warning to those who would use constitutional provisions as a license to apply force. "Poverty cannot be a reason for conversion," warned Vajpayee, firmly dissociating economic circumstances from the imperatives of religious change. Regardless of his own disapproval of Singhal's attack on Amartya Sen, Vajpayee kept the two issues of Christianization and welfare economics squarely within the same frame of reference, however much he may have denied that there was any connection between the two. It is thus no coincidence that Amartya Sen is denounced for advocating basic education—-and religious conversion by extension—-at the same time that Christianity is under siege in south Gujarat for promoting tribal conversions. In being forcibly linked with conversion, literacy is disengaged from development issues and relocated as an exclusively religious issue. In an effort to reclaim literacy from Christian uses, Sen's critics pointed to what is now a consistent thematics of antimissionary resistance: literacy has legitimacy only when it is a marker of indigenous cultural identity. Either way, the development issue drops out of the picture.

The public repudiation of Singhal's viewpoint, however, does not mean that his is an aberrant one, the voice of a lunatic fringe unable to make a dent on mainstream opinion. On the contrary, India's history of colonial education provided a real context for the deep suspicion cast upon the Nobel Prize committee's recommendations. That this context was exploited to detach literacy from issues of social reform is perhaps one of the dimensions of the conversion controversy that needs more analysis and clarification than it has received. Views such as those held by Ashok Singhal have been sustained over time and buttressed by references to India's colonial history. The deep distrust of missionary institutions has a colonial past providing Hindu nationalists with a much-needed moral stance to defend Indian religion and culture. (The collapsing of "Hinduism" and "India" is not the least of the rhetorical slippages.) It is well known that Christian missionaries were attacked long before the BJP and the VHP came on the scene. Hinduism put up a stiff resistance to Christianity on both an organizational and a theological level.[17] Richard Fox Young has meticulously documented the development of a whole tradition of anti-Christian polemics in nineteenth-century India focused on a refutation of Christian doctrine, point by point.[18]

There is nothing new in the Hindu antagonism to missionary schools as hotbeds of conversion activity ("wolves in sheep's clothing," as they were often called in an ironic use of a Christian metaphor).[19] Opposition to literacy reform has long been motivated by fear that its ultimate intent is religious change. On the other hand, why Sen's research would benefit Christians more than any other group is never clear in the VHP attacks on him. But it is telling that one of their chief complaints is that the Nobel

Prize was never awarded to social activists like Gandhi or Baba Amte who had both worked tirelessly for the uplift of the poor and other marginalized sections of society.[20] Yet social activism in India, even that practiced by a Gandhi or an Amte, has never been totally removed from a related compulsive desire to contest the reach of Christian missionaries, particularly in tribal and outlying areas. In regions where lower castes and outcastes were denied the educational facilities open to higher caste groups, missionaries often stepped in to fill a social vacuum.[21] In the light of caste tensions, it is easy to see why social reform has been as strongly contested as conversion itself. Neither can be separated from a colonial history that continues to inform attitudes to an ethics of improvement, the content of which, to many today, is still indistinguishable from the *mission civilisatrice*. This is by no means to justify the crudest premises of cultural nationalism, but we are obliged to acknowledge the complex historical formations driving nationalists to the depths of paranoia and suspicion.

Historically, missionary schools opened their doors to socially excluded groups, while the schools run by the colonial government had as their main clientele students from the upper castes. Yet this division so heavily reinforced the caste structure that it appeared as if the very form and spirit of colonial education were driven by caste feeling. There was more complacency than truth in colonial administrators' belief that English studies altered attitudes to caste. The Serampore missionary John Marshman wryly observed that "I am not certain that a man's being able to read Milton and Shakespeare, or understand Dr. Johnson, would make him less susceptible of the honour of being a Brahmin."[22] The association of missionary schools with vernacular education and of government schools with English education marked the differential development of languages and literary instruction.[23] Yet precisely because missionary schools were so closely identified with lower-caste education, missionaries found their aims compromised by their desire to lure the upper castes to their schools, if only to extend the range of Christian influence. Partly this was motivated by their fear that, by attracting only "the most despised and least numerous of society," they were creating a new virulent strain in Indian society, "a new class superior to the rest in useful knowledge, but hated and despised by the castes to whom their new attainments would always induce us to prefer them."[24] Caste lines being as implacable as they were, missionaries dreaded that the huge efforts they expended on the education of the lower castes would remain confined to these groups and not spread farther. Recognizing that the reform of Hindu society was impossible without involving all castes, they modified their instructional objectives, expanding their curricular offerings to include English literature alongside the vernaculars. In time, the lines between missionary and government schools blurred as both types of institutions competed for students from the upper castes.

Interestingly, the work of vernacular education started by missionaries was taken up by Hindu reformist organizations, such as the Ramakrishna Mission and the Arya Samaj. The linguistic stratification was so rigid that the vernacular schools produced a militant brand of youth who pledged themselves to the preservation of Hindu culture, religion, and language against the encroachments of an English-educated, Westernized elite. So it is somewhat ironic that this form of cultural nationalism developed as a consequence of the vernacular missionary schools and the government schools switching their linguistic orientation, with the former increasingly moving toward English instruction primarily and the latter now having virtually become vernacular-medium schools. The development has also inspired the defenders of Hinduism to view the English-language press, which has extensively covered the atrocities against Christians in the past year, as a key player in the drama of linguistic, religious, and caste stratification, its corps of writers having themselves often been educated in Christian mission schools. Therefore, while the English-language newspapers have gone a long way in bringing the violence against Christians to public attention, they have also been attacked by Hindu nationalists as complicit with the work of Christian missionaries in propagating an alien culture.

Historically, in seeking to break out of narrow caste identification, the missionary schools set in motion a number of significant developments. The original objectives of imparting basic literacy skills were considerably qualified by the new infusion of literary content. If missionary schools initially sought to remedy the exclusionary effects of caste prejudice by offering educational opportunities denied to lower castes, their turn to an English course of studies took them in a markedly different direction. That conversion rather than caste or poverty relief more often engaged their interest is evident from the perfection of certain pedagogical techniques to produce belief. Catechism and hermeneutics are prominent among these. The Word offered access to the world, but it also opened up access to faith through the power of imagination. Education in imagery supplemented, and in time surpassed, instruction in the fundamentals of literacy. In all its clarity and brilliance, imagery pointed the way to the Bible, to the power of arguments, reasons, and demonstrations vividly impressing themselves on the mind, to an experience of truth that could only be known when seen and felt. To missionaries aware of the hostility that direct Christian instruction might produce, there was no better way to convey the deep swell of religious feeling than through the rich tapestry of images, sensations, and impressions found in the best of English Romantic writers like Wordsworth, Cowper, and Young.

These alternating instructional objectives in missionary institutions kept the pendulum swinging between poverty and caste relief, on the one hand, and conversion, on the other. Let us recall Vajpayee's admonition that "poverty cannot be a reason for conversion." He was far closer to the course of colonial history than he may have realized, for institutional developments suggest a complex evolution of conversion motives not always directly related to economic circumstances. The violence against Christians in Gujarat and elsewhere since late 1998 was caused by the perception that missionaries were targeting poor tribals to convert them to Christianity, often by imparting literacy skills to them. Radical Hindu groups interpret Christian conversion as an inducement, an enticing avenue of escape from grinding poverty. But conversion is just as importantly involved in the constructions of new selves, and it is this shift from the ground of economics to that of culture that continues to alarm Hindu opponents, perhaps even more than the threat of religious change. Their will is steeled, therefore, to reclaim culture as the ultimate goal of all future attempts at literacy reform.

Religions assign different functions to reading and writing. In religions of revelation the word is the Word. Hinduism's self-description as a non-proselytizing religion has also meant that it conceives of reading and writing in different ways. One point of difference is the creation and affirmation of community. This does not necessarily mean an interpretive community, however, but a community marked by systems of inclusion and exclusion, which are in turn determined by criteria of purity and pollution. Verbal acts are modes of community affirmation as much as they are forms of communication. But where the use of language signals the expression of faith in a supreme being, religions that employ such language open up the new possibility that language can cause changes in one's conceptions of divinity. Are these then proselytizing religions? It can be argued that Hinduism establishes a relation between literacy and faith different from that of Christianity and Islam. If, as is maintained about Hinduism, faith does not lie in words, then a Hindu can have access to the world without the mediation of language. Language, however, is threatening when it is tied to faith. Literacy arouses suspicion because it can alter faith by providing a different form of access to the world. Access to language is essential for economic betterment, yet it also contains the potential to introduce worldviews at variance with those affirmed by the community. The conflicting perspectives on literacy throw open the divide between economics and culture, which further translates into artificial distinctions between religions on the basis of whether they proselytize or not.

Ironically, the VHP leaders who attacked the Christian conversions of illiterate tribals do not accept that literacy can also be a defense against forcible conversions of any kind, Christian, Hindu, Muslim, or of any other religion. Their unquestioned assumption is that illiteracy is gullibility. But if its opposite is also true—-that literacy is skepticism and critical judgment—-then the threat posed by the lure of other faiths should be diminished. The Word may be the source of faith, but it is also the maker of selfhood and independent judgment. However, the rhetoric of the VHP suppresses this fundamental understanding of literacy's role, which, in offering the tools of knowledge, discrimination, and evaluation, shapes the modern self. We are led to inquire whether literacy as self-making, independence, and private judgment poses the real threat—an unnamed one perhaps, acknowledged only as a tool of Christianization but not of Hindu modernity.

LITERACY, ECONOMICS, AND THE CULTURE OF CONVERSION

At this point I want to return to Amartya Sen and his Nobel Prize for Economics. We may now place Ashok Singhal's diatribe in the framework of a perceived shift in literacy's address from economics to culture. That is why no matter how much of a non sequitur his comments may appear, his view that Sen's mass literacy would benefit only Christians reflects how definitively culture, not economics, has become the contested ground for discussions of development issues. In part, this shift has strategic uses for a government seeking to deflect attention from the dismal failure of *swadeshi* (self-sufficient) economics, despite the BJP's campaigning for power on this issue. And as its economic policies have met with one disaster after another, the BJP has needed to keep economics out of public discussion. Religion has always been its surrogate theme, and it is not surprising that turning even literacy into a conversion issue offsets the government's dismal showing on the economic front. But apart from turning the focus away from a string of economic failures, the perception that mass literacy is a tool of cultural imperialism undermines the developmental rhetoric of secular progress that literacy reform, on the other hand, also tends to generate. Singhal's denunciation of Amartya Sen reflects attitudes toward literacy that are part of an ongoing tension between development priorities and cultural purity.

By objecting to literacy as a missionary-inspired practice, do Hindus really want to say they object to the introduction of social benefits to the people? Most would probably say no, but the ethics of social reform has been challenged in the mounting anti-Christian rhetoric since the BJP assumed power in early 1998. It can and should be argued that if missionaries give people services they would otherwise not have had, no one has a right to restrict their activities, particularly when there are no other state-supported or private initiatives. After all, missionaries do not have a monopoly on the opening of new schools and hospitals, and there is nothing to stop Hindus or any other group from doing likewise. But the cumulative effect of the attack on Christianity has been a fierce questioning of whether social benefits can ensue at the cost of religious and cultural integrity. This is nothing less than an anti-Orientalist response to a condition sewn into Indian history through the reformist ideology of British colonialism. But its corollary is that social reform has, and always will be, politicized in postcolonial India. The view that social service has a national or a religious identity suggests that no act of reform or service can take place in postcolonial India without its being measured against a corresponding degradation of Hindu customs and rituals in the process.

But I think there is something fundamentally more worrying in the antiliteracy, anticonversion posture of the VHP. The numbers of Hindus who actually converted to Christianity are far less than the numbers of those who detached themselves from Hinduism over time and affiliated themselves to more secular conceptions of modernity. Today we call the latter group "secular Indians," though that term has its own problems. The main difference between these two groups of Hindus is that the former have converted to Christianity and the latter to modernity. The mechanism is the same, even though the characterization may be different. Critics will argue this was the effect of mission-school education on the middle classes. But there are deeper issues involved. Hinduism is once again at the crossroads of change. Instead of attending to the problems of overwhelming illiteracy, caste and gender discrimination, and poverty, the most extreme among the Hindu nationalists have narrowed their agenda to attack other groups—notably Muslims and Christians—for the erosion of cultural traditions. India's struggle to keep pace with a changing world is most pronounced in a stagnant educational system which, while professing secularism, is still caught up in the forms and practices of a religious culture. Is the desire to interrogate mass literacy ultimately a desire to renounce the modern world altogether? Is the quest for cultural integrity so supreme that it creates a longing in Hindus to supplant modernity with a more reassuring past in which their traditions are uncorrupted? These are difficult questions, but they go to the heart of the resistance to literacy as a development issue and the antagonism to conversion in general.

Significantly, even as some Hindus recoil from the demands of modernity, at another level they are reclaiming literacy as a hallmark of Hinduism's cultural past. Indeed, when literacy performs the work of culture in Hinduism, it is assigned an economic role denied in the work of missionary schools. In the context of an ancient past, literacy extends beyond reading and writing to encompass a range of technical and vocational skills. This is illustrated in the comments of Vajpayee and other government figures on indigenous technical education. On a trip to the southern city of Mysore, Vajpayee lauded the work of Basaveshwara, a social reformer who made significant efforts in educating the masses while also promoting women's education. Vajpayee pointed to the Veerashaiva *mutts* (religious centers run by a Hindu sect that also impart education) as ideal service institutions providing training for literacy—-training that the government ought to provide but did not. The Veerashaiva *mutts,* he further added, were the only institutions serving society for a long period of time with the same missionary zeal as that of Christian educational institutions.[25] As if on cue in a musical duet, the state chief minister who hosted him glorified the work of institutions like the J.S.S. Mahavidhyapeetha, saying they were providing opportunities for the disabled and the disenfranchised to become useful citizens. (The J.S.S. Mahavidhyapeeta, founded in 1954 by a Hindu pontiff, Jagadguru Shivarathri Rajendra, promotes techncial education with a view to creating a self-sufficient society.) Significantly, both political figures consider the indigenous schools important because they are first and foremost technical training institutes. The vocational training offered in these indigenous institutions becomes the site of difference turning basic literacy, on the other hand, into a colonized space, a zone of foreign domination.

Conflicting approaches to developmentalism underscore a deep ambivalence about literacy that has remained unresolved since the framing of the Indian Constitution. Amartya Sen reopened the old debates about rights versus directives when he released the Public Report on Basic Education (PROBE) on 1 January 1999. The PROBE report is described as "a people's report" on school education. Prepared by a team of independent academics and social activists, it set out to counter the prevalent official myths about Indian schooling. The report claims to be the first attempt of its kind to examine the condition of India's elementary education from the standpoint of the underprivileged. It demolishes a set of ruling myths that have guided Indian education since the country's independence. Among these are, first, that poor parents are not interested in sending their children to school, as is conventionally believed; second, that child labor is the main obstacle to school attendance and therefore to universal literacy; and third, that elementary education is free. Most important, the report attempted to clarify the links between child labor and schooling by showing that, far from being unable to go to school because they have to work, full-time child laborers often work because they have dropped out of school, typically for family reasons.[26] Amartya Sen had argued against this form of educational deprivation for a long time, noting with chagrin that "child labour is considered perfectly acceptable for the boys and girls of poor families, while the privileged classes enjoy a massively subsidized system of higher education."[27]

Encouraged by the report's conclusion that, contrary to popular perception, education remains sought after even by the most economically disadvantaged sections of society, Sen declared that the time for demanding elementary education as a fundamental right had arrived. Simultaneously, he unveiled his plans to set up a charity trust with the Nobel money for development of education and health in India and Bangladesh.[28] Stressing the West's economic progress as a function of its planned development of human resources, Sen persuasively spoke of how the general availability of elementary education would enhance a sense of citizens' participation in India's overall economic expansion. He sounded a theme that placed the economic imperatives of educational growth in the perspective of social choice theory. Economic advantages, he appeared to suggest, were the fruit of participatory democracy whose foundations rested on basic literacy.[29]

EDUCATION AS A RIGHT

If, then, literacy is the chief basis of economic development and social change, education as a fundamental right has still remained largely undefined in the Indian Constitution. On the other hand, articles 25 and 26 of the constitution, comprising the section on fundamental rights, were careful to give "every religious denomination" the right to propagate religion and maintain religious institutions. Constituent Assembly discussions struggled to untangle the contradiction between the secular goals of Indian democracy and the permission granted to religious groups to practice (and preach) their religious philosophies in their own institutions. Article 30 addresses educational rights, but it is less interested in universalizing education than in providing for the rights of minorities to maintain their own educational institutions and have full control over curricular content. The right-to-education needs of citizens still remain largely undefined. Vajpayee acknowledged the continued failure of his own government to address educational needs, uttering in a moment of utter candor, "We pray to Saraswati (the Hindu goddess of learning) but make no arrangements to educate our children."[30] Hence his admiration for the efforts of nongovernmental institutions like the Veerashaiva *mutts* or the Mahavidhyapeeta for doing what the government was obliged, but had failed to do. Unable to invest adequately in education, the Indian government has appeared to be resigned to the possibility of nongovernmental organizations taking the initiative. Yet social strife results when religious groups (operating as parallel NGOs) undertake the work of education—often work that is considered disruptive of another religious tradition. And in order to resolve conflicts of such a nature, the state is required to intervene, even though it prefers to leave educational initiatives to nongovernmental organizations. This contradiction remains at the core of the state's fraught relation with the education of its citizens.

By proposing universal education as a fundamental right, Amartya Sen has called for alternative ways to rethink "inconsistencies of means and ends," by which he means the present arbitrary distribution of resources and the uncertain division of labor between government and nongovernmental (minority) agencies.[31] To be sure, he is less forthcoming about the sources of investment in education, for it is never entirely clear whether he would be willing to settle for an education funded by nongovernmental agencies to supplement government funding. To some extent, this uncertainty has augmented the deep anxiety of his opponents that groups seeking to propagate their own beliefs—such as Christian missionaries—would seize the momentum for educational change. But Sen's most important intervention is in shifting freedom away from a concept that denotes a community's right to practice and propagate its beliefs. Rather, freedom for him is the creation of conditions for the wholesome participation of citizens in the democratic process. Universal literacy is the key to this process. As the instrument for securing the representation of people belonging to the unorganized sector, universal primary education is more than an entrée into people's participation in their economic advancement. By enacting democracy, it confers a reality on participatory processes that Indian democracy still lacks, despite its adult suffrage.

At the same time Amartya Sen has been careful not to make freedom an all-encompassing category overriding goals of equality, such that one person's freedom becomes another's unfreedom. His suspicion of freedom as an unqualified term leads him to argue that the freedom accruing from a market economy is attended by far too many dangers of inequality and poverty stemming from the market.[32] Instead, he proposes five kinds of freedom: (1) enabling freedom, which signifies that each individual is able to participate in social and economic activities, and that the quality of life is improved through education and health facilities; (2) political freedom, which invariably involves democracy and civil rights; (3) economic freedom, which involves transactions and the market, and could thus promote efficiency and equity; (4) transparency freedom, which encompasses a person's right to know that he or she was not being cheated in a transaction; and

(5) protective freedom, which is freedom from the effects of droughts, floods, and famine. These freedoms are important insofar as they constitute the legitimate end of development.[33]

Thus, for Sen literacy is not exclusively an economic issue, as some commentators believe. His notion of freedom encompasses culture—-the kind of life we would like to lead—as an essential goal of development.[34] What his critic Ashok Singhal evidently feared was that culture would be made synonymous with social choice, and to that extent Amartya Sen's notion of freedom uncannily confirmed Singhal's anxiety that development had a Christian trajectory. Singhal obviously got the story wrong in most of the particulars. But on the subject of choice Sen offered a new set of questions that could potentially have more bearing on how individuals construe selfhood, as opposed to being affirmed by their community, and it is this move that set alarm bells ringing for Singhal. Instead of asking the old question, "Is it possible to have socially rational decisions based on the interests and preferences of the members of the society?" Sen proposed asking, "Which of the various ways of equity and justice are most relevant to the pursuit of freedom?" The choice, he suggests, is between different ways of evaluation whose ultimate validity is that they draw upon foundational notions of justice and fairness. Even the apparently scientific subject of choosing a suitable measure of poverty for a nation or a state can be approached in terms of the competing values reflected in different ways by distinct statistical measures. Because welfare economics and social choice theory link knowledge with practice, their operative premise is that self-construction is national construction. So even though economic development has merged into an issue of culture in the rhetoric of the postcolonial state, driven by its own sense of cultural nationalism, the question of choice is deliberately suspended. Where it does appear, it is turned into proof of forcible conversion.

NOTES

1. "Sangh Parivar Comes under Fire," *The Hindu* (Madras), 29 December 1998, p. 13.

2. "Singhal Statement on Amartya Sen Misquoted," ibid., 3 January 1999, p. 7.

3. "Vajpayee Criticises VHP Remarks on Christians," ibid., 31 December 1998, p. 1.

4. The nun claimed, in her police report, that her assailants queried her about the number of conversions her convent brought about, while also

warning her that the killings, rapes, and kidnappings would continue as long as the Christian missions engaged in proselytization. "Nun's Assailants Untraced," ibid., 25 September 1999, p. 1.

5. See M. K. Gandhi, *My Experiments with Truth* (1929; Boston, 1957), pp. 122–25.

6. Ministry of Law, Justice and Company Affairs, Government of India, *The Constitution of India (as Modified up to the 1st August, 1977)* (New Delhi, 1978), p. 14.

7. M. M. Singh, *The Constitution of India: Studies in Perspective* (Calcutta, 1975), p. 480.

8. Andrew Wingate, *The Church and Conversion* (Delhi, 1997), p. 35.

9. "VHP Charge against Sonia Gandhi," *The Hindu,* 9 January 1999, p. 13.

10. Gauri Viswanathan, "Beyond Orientalism: Syncretism and the Politics of Knowledge," *Stanford Humanities Review* 5, no. 1 (1995): 18–32.

11. Robert W. Hefner, "World Building and the Rationality of Conversion," in *Conversion to Christianity: Historical and Anthropological Perspectives on a Great Transformation,* ed. Robert W. Hefner (Berkeley, Calif., 1993), p. 5.

12. David J. Krieger, "Conversion: On the Possibility of Global Thinking in an Age of Particularism," *Journal of the American Academy of Religion* 63, no. 2 (1990): 238.

13. It was John Henry Newman's special contribution to reverse the institutionalization of assent and produce a grammar of dissent. His major philosophical treatise, *A Grammar of Assent,* bears an ironic title in that, in order to arrive at an affirmation of faith, the knowing believer must proceed through successive stages of dissent from accepted premises. See Gauri Viswanathan, *Outside the Fold: Conversion, Modernity, and Belief* (Princeton, N.J., 1998), pp. 44–72.

14. Alan Olson, "Postmodernity and Faith," *Journal of the American Academy of Religion* 58, no. 1 (Spring 1990): 44.

15. By "emancipation," I refer to the series of bills passed in early nineteenth-century England enfranchising Jews, Catholics, Dissenters, and other non-Anglican groups and bringing them within the national fold. The price of such emancipation was, as I argue in *Outside the Fold,* that religious groups were often asked to forgo the specificity of their religious beliefs in order to become citizens of the state.

16. "PM Calls for National Debate on Conversion," *The Hindu,* 11 January 1999, p. 1.

17. See Antony Copley, *Religions in Conflict: Ideology, Cultural Contact, and Conversion in Late Colonial India* (Delhi, 1997).

18. Richard Fox Young, *Resistant Hinduism: Sanskrit Sources on Anti-Christian Apologetics in Early Nineteenth-Century India* (Vienna, 1981).

19. See Copley, *Religions in Conflict,* for a compelling account of Hindu attitudes to Christian mission schools, particularly fears about conversion. See also my *Outside the Fold,* particularly chapter 3, "Rights of Passage," for a discussion of the antagonism felt by Hindu parents toward Christian missionaries, whom they blamed for the Christian conversions of their young children. Deprived of their rights to inheritance on conversion, converts were often assisted by missionaries in bringing their cases to court so that their rights would be restored.

20. "Singhal Statement on Amartya Sen Misquoted," *The Hindu,* 3 January 1999, p. 7.

21. Sathianathan Clarke, *Dalits and Christianity: Subaltern Religion and Liberation Theology in India* (Delhi, 1998).

22. Great Britain, House of Lords, "Second Report from the Select Committee of the House of Lords, Together with the Minutes of Evidence," *Parliamentary Papers,* 1852–53, evidence of J. C. Marshman, 32:119.

23. See Gauri Viswanathan, *Masks of Conquest: Literary Study and British Rule in India* (New York, 1989), pp. 151–52.

24. Great Britain, *Parliamentary Papers,* 1831–32, minute by M. Elphinstone, December 13, 1823, 9:519.

25. "Poverty Hindering Spread of Literacy: PM," *The Hindu,* 4 January 1999, p. 10.

26. The Probe Team, *Public Report on Basic Education in India* (Delhi, 1999), pp. 14–17. On child labor, the report is not entirely convincing, as it tries to distinguish between family and hired labor and in so doing vacillates between empathy for family needs and condemnation of capitalist exploitation.

27. Amartya Sen, "Basic Education as a Political Issue," in *The Amartya Sen and Jean Dreze Omnibus* (Delhi, 1999), p. 120.

28. "Sen to Set up Charity with Prize Money," *The Hindu,* 28 December 1998, p. 14.

29. Sen's research in Indian villages consistently pointed to the special value of basic education as a tool of social affirmation. As the *Probe Report* later confirmed, even among the most socially and economically disadvantaged groups, education was strongly valued for enabling upward mobility. Sen punctures the myth propagated by upper castes that the lower castes do not place much importance in literacy because they view education as an instrument of upper-caste domination. On the contrary, as the *Probe Report* also affirms, education remains highly desirable to low-caste groups.

30. "Poverty Hindering Spread of Literacy: PM," *The Hindu,* 4 January 1999, p. 6.

31. Sen, "Basic Education as a Political Issue," p. 117.

32. See Amartya Sen, *Inequality Examined* (Delhi, 1992), in which Sen trenchantly shifts the question economists typically ask (should there be equality?) to the more important one: equality of what? Sen forces the discussion to concentrate on the diversity of human populations, which inevitably involves different standards of equality; in other words, what is equal to one group of people might be deemed inequality to another. The heterogeneity of social groups requires one constantly to rethink how a range of human capabilities might be harnessed to achieve specific goals, from which standpoint questions of rights and equality can be raised more profitably.

33. See Amartya Sen, "Well beyond Liberalization," in *The Amartya Sen and Jean Dreze Omnibus,* for an exploration of these themes, as well as an assessment of India's recent economic reforms. His conclusion that the "un-caging of the tiger has not—-at least not yet—-led to any dynamic animal springing out and sprinting ahead" (p. 180) draws attention to the still unfulfilled promises of participatory growth, evident in the alarming illit-eracy rates and social deprivations.

34. See particularly Sen's essay "Freedom, Agency and Well-Being," in *Inequality Reexamined,* which describes freedom as our right to set goals for ourselves and our ability to get what we value and want; in short, to lead a life we would *choose* to live (pp. 60–61).

Notes on Contributors

Valerie I. J. Flint is G. F. Grant Professor of History at the University of Hull, U.K. Among her recent books are *The Rise of Magic in Early Medieval Europe* (1991), *The Medieval Landscape of Christopher Columbus* (1992), and *Honorius Augustodunensis of Regensburg* (1995).

Peter Gose is Professor of Anthropology at the University of Regina, Canada. He is the author of *Deathly Waters and Hungry Mountains: Agrarian Ritual and Class Formation in an Andean Town* (1994) and many articles in leading anthropological journals.

Anthony Grafton teaches European history at Princeton University. His books include *Joseph Scaliger* (1983–93), *The Footnote: A Curious History* (1997), and *Bring Out Your Dead* (2001).

Allan Greer is Professor of History at the University of Toronto. He is the author of *The People of New France* (1997), *The Patriots and the People: The Rebellion of 1837 in Rural Lower Canada* (1993), and *Peasant, Lord, and Merchant: Rural Society in Three Quebec Parishes, 1740–1840* (1985). He is currently completing a volume entitled "Mohawk Saint: Catherine Tekakwitha and the Jesuits."

Brad S. Gregory is Associate Professor of History at Stanford University. His first book, *Salvation at Stake: Christian Martyrdom in Early Modern Europe* (1999) has received six book awards.

R. Po-chia Hsia is Edwin Erle Sparks Professor of European and Asian History at Pennsylvania State University. He is the author and editor of many books, most recently, *The World of Catholic Renewal 1540–1770* (1998) and *Calvinism and Religious Toleration in the Dutch Golden Age* (2002).

Andrew C. Isenberg teaches environmental history, Native American history, and the history of the American West at Princeton University. He is the author of *The Destruction of the Bison: An Environmental History, 1750–1920* (2000).

Kenneth Mills is a historian of colonial Latin America and the early modern Spanish world at Princeton University, where he is the Director of the Program in Latin American Studies. His recent work includes *Idolatry and Its Enemies: Colonial Andean Religion and Extirpation, 1640–1750* (1997) and, with William B. Taylor and Sandra Lauderdale Graham, *Colonial Latin America: A Documentary History* (2002).

David Murray is Professor of American Literature and Culture in the School of American and Canadian Studies, University of Nottingham, England. He is the author of *Forked Tongues: Speech, Writing and Representation in North American Indian Texts* (1992) and *Indian Giving: Economies of Power in Early Indian-White Exchanges* (2000).

Carol Summers is Associate Professor of History at the University of Richmond. She is the author of *Colonial Lessons: Africans' Education in Southern Rhodesia, 1918–1940* (2002), *From Civilization to Segregation: Social Ideals and Social Control in Southern Rhodesia 1890–1934* (1994), and articles on the history of social policy in colonial Zimbabwe and Uganda.

John Van Engen is Andrew V. Tackes Professor of Medieval History at the University of Notre Dame. He is the author of *Rupert of Deutz* (1983), *Devotio Moderna* (1988), and most recently co-editor of the volume of essays, *Jews and Christians in Twelfth-Century Europe* (2001).

Gauri Viswanathan is Class of 1933 Professor in the Humanities at Columbia University. She is the author of *Masks of Conquest: Literary Study and British Rule in India* (1989) and *Outside the Fold: Conversion, Modernity, and Belief* (1998), which won the MLA's James Russell Lowell Award, among other awards.

Ines G. Županov is a Research Fellow at the Centre Nationale de la Recherche Scientifique and a member of the Centre d'Etudes de L'Inde et de L'Asie du Sud in Paris. She is the author of *Disputed Mission: Jesuit Experiments and Brahmanical Knowledge in Seventeenth-Century India* (1999), and of articles on the Portuguese and missionary presence in early modern India.

INDEX